INTERPRETING
MAIMONIDES

CHICAGO STUDIES
IN THE
HISTORY OF JUDAISM

EDITED BY

William Scott Green and Calvin Goldscheider

INTERPRETING
MAIMONIDES

STUDIES IN
Methodology, Metaphysics, and Moral Philosophy

Marvin Fox

The University of Chicago Press

Chicago and London

Marvin Fox is the Philip W. Lown Professor of Jewish Philosophy at
Brandeis University. He is the author of *Modern Jewish Ethics: Theory
and Practice* (1975).

Published with the assistance of the Lucius N. Littauer Foundation.

The University of Chicago Press, Chicago 60637
The University of Chicago Press, Ltd., London

Library of Congress Cataloging-in-Publication Data
Fox, Marvin.
  Interpreting Maimonides : studies in methodology, metaphysics, and
moral philosophy / Marvin Fox.
    p.   cm. — (Chicago studies in the history of Judaism)
  Includes bibliographical references.
  ISBN 0-226-25941-2 (alk. paper)
    1. Maimonides, Moses, 1135–1204.   2. Maimonides, Moses, 1135–1204
—Ethics.   3. Philosophy, Jewish.   4. Philosophy, Medieval.
5. Ethics, Jewish.   I. Title.   II. Series.
B759.M34F68   1990
181'.06—dc20   89-29190
                                                            CIP

⊗ The paper used in this publication meets the minimum requirements of the
American National Standard for Information Sciences—Permanence of Paper
for Printed Library Materials, ANSI Z39.48—1984.

For June

ומד׳ אשה משכלת

Contents

Preface

Moses Maimonides has been the subject of uninterrupted interest and study since the appearance of his earliest works. Living in Egypt in the twelfth century, Maimonides was already in his own lifetime recognized throughout the Jewish world as a scholar and teacher of supreme stature. No other figure in post-talmudic Jewish intellectual history seems to have exercised the same kind of fascination for each succeeding generation. His legal writings in particular have been examined by generations of scholars with the most meticulous care. Every word, indeed every nuance, has been studied and interpreted. Yet the well does not run dry, and students of the Law and of the entire rabbinic literature continue to uncover new insights and new dimensions in the works of the great master.

There has not been the same kind of continuous involvement with Maimonides the philosopher-theologian, however, or the same kind of painstaking care in the study of his philosophic writings as has been accorded to his halakhic works. In some generations his *Guide to the Perplexed* and his smaller philosophical essays were treated with the same regard that the legal writings evoked. Scholars invested immense intellectual effort and energy in the process of understanding and explicating that inordinately complex and difficult book. The results are present in some of the great medieval commentaries that are indispensable to this day for every serious reader of the *Guide*. In other periods, however, the philosophic work of Maimonides has been ignored or, in the worst circumstances, treated as outright heresy. The sad history of the anti-Maimonidean polemic is well known. In recent centuries the study of Maimonides the philosopher was almost suppressed in the yeshivot of Eastern Europe, at the very time that he was being viewed in those very same yeshivot as ever more important for sophisticated talmudic studies.

With the general growth of interest in Judaic scholarship since the nineteenth century, and the unparalleled burgeoning of the field in recent decades, there has been a remarkable renewal of interest in the philosophic work of Maimonides. This interest has been especially stimulated by the development of the academic field of Jewish philosophy in universities throughout the world. One can hardly pick up any journal dealing with Jewish thought without finding an article or two on Maimonides. Books are being published in various languages, and diverse schools of interpretation have emerged, each with its own understanding of how to read Maimonides and its own account of his doctrines. The level of Maimonidean studies has also been enhanced by those who have labored to provide us with excellent critical texts of his various works. When one adds to this the growing philosophical sophistication of the last few generations, it may well be that we are in a better position than most of our predecessors to provide a sound account of his thought.

My own studies of Maimonides began in my early youth, and he has never ceased to occupy my thought and my attention. I have benefited immeasurably from the medieval and modern literature on Maimonides in ways that I hope will be evident to readers of this book, even where I have not spelled out my debt. To add to the existing literature takes a certain boldness. One wonders whether there can be anything new to say, and whether it is still possible to find improved ways of setting forth insights and ideas long established in the Maimonidean literature. Over the years I have become convinced that there are, in fact, dimensions of Maimonides' work that have not been grasped or explicated as correctly or as fully as possible. I share the results of my studies with my readers in the hope that they may find in them some useful ideas and even some illumination.

I consider Maimonides to be the greatest and most creative Jewish thinker since the close of the Talmud. There may have been other Jews of comparable stature in other fields of learning, but I believe no one has made contributions to Jewish learning, Jewish law, and Jewish thought equal in depth or in originality to the heritage of Maimonides. That is why study and restudy of his works never fails to be a rewarding experience.

My first objective in this book is to make some contributions to the method with which we should approach the arduous task of reading Maimonides, particularly in the case of his philosophic works. This is the burden of Part I, whose chapters deal primarily with questions of methodology. Because the important work of Leo Strauss and his followers has for the last five decades dominated modern scholarly thinking about how to read Maimonides, I devote considerable space to engaging the Straussian school. I have tried to show that, with all its well-deserved influence, their method contains certain serious flaws, and I have offered what I consider to be a needed corrective.

Methodology by itself does not solve substantive problems, nor does it generate specific doctrines. Only when we apply our method to specific texts and particular issues can we see its significance and effectiveness. I have done this in Parts II and III, where I deal with issues in Maimonides' moral philosophy, metaphysics, and religion.

My concern with ethical theory first led me to question standard interpretations of Maimonides' views, which seemed to me to ignore his explicit philosophical analyses, deriving instead from preconceived notions about what he must have meant. Indeed some critics of my earlier work were particularly distressed because I did not find any evidence that Maimonides' supposedly strict rationalism includes the theory that moral principles are established by reason. On the contrary, I tried to show that he denies in principle that there can be moral rules that are derived from and validated by reason alone. I have not seen any reason to change my views on this important question. In fact, I argue in Part II that Maimonides' recognition that moral claims are noncognitive is one more piece of evidence showing how excellent and perceptive a philosopher he was. In discussing these questions I was also concerned with showing how much creative skill he used in interpreting the relevant scriptural and rabbinic sources.

In similar fashion I show in Part III how my way of reading Maimonides causes us to revise our views about his position on certain fundamental metaphysical and religious issues. In the Epilogue, I spell out some of the general lessons we can learn from Maimonides that are of value in contemporary Judaism's struggle to define itself.

Some themes and key quotations occur in more than one place in the book because they are critical for more than one topic and in more than one context, and in most cases are of major importance in themselves. It is my judgment that in these instances repetition is a virtue rather than a vice. A number of chapters are based on papers published earlier in various forums. These papers have been revised and integrated into the structure of the book. The details of original publication are recorded along with the acknowledgments. I express here my thanks to the original publishers for agreeing to my use of these materials.

There is no limit to my debt and gratitude to my teachers, who taught me how to read a text and how to approach philosophical issues with critical judgment. Many years have passed since I was a student, but what I learned from all my teachers has never left me. It is not possible to note here every teacher, colleague, and friend with whom I have had fruitful exchanges over the years. In particular, however, I want to recall the most important and gracious of all my teachers in philosophy, the late Professor Fritz Kaufmann, who trained me when I was an undergraduate student at Northwestern University. He was a rare figure both as a scholar and as a human being. I have never forgotten or ceased to be astounded by his immense learning and his methodological rigor, and I cherish the memory of his human warmth and unfailing kindness.

My work has also been deepened and sharpened by the challenges of the many students whom I have tried to introduce to the subtleties and complexities of Maimonides' philosophy. As I look back on more than forty years of university teaching, I have fond memories of classes and seminars where the sharp questions and critical responses of my students caused me to rethink my position and to refine the way in which I formulated my own account of Maimonides. My students at Ohio State University, the Hebrew University, Bar-Ilan University, and Brandeis University have contributed much to my thinking, and I am grateful for the privilege of teaching them and learning from them.

My friend, Nahum M. Sarna, has been especially important to me, both personally and for the development of my work. He and I have lived in a close intellectual relationship since the day I arrived at Brandeis University. He has helped me to understand countless biblical passages that were important to my thinking. I have, however, been the beneficiary of far more than his deep and comprehensive biblical scholarship. Despite his regular protestations that he is not a specialist in philosophy, our frequent conversations have stimulated my thought and have often given me valuable insights into problems on which I was working. I am grateful for the privilege of his friendship.

I also owe a special debt of gratitude to the staff of the Judaica Division of the Brandeis University Library, who have always extended themselves to help me. In particular, I thank James Rosenbloom who has been available over the years to offer me his high level of professional help and to provide those services that can come only from a first-rate librarian.

My work on Maimonides has extended over many years and has been supported from time to time by various foundations. I offer my special appreciation to the American Council of Learned Societies for awarding me the fellowship that enabled me to begin my serious research on Maimonides. More recently I received a fellowship from the National Endowment for the Humanities which made it possible for me to advance my work considerably, and I record here my gratitude for their support.

This book is dedicated to my wife, June T. Fox. She has been my treasured life companion, a never-ending source of encouragement, and my most friendly and rigorous critic. As the dedication indicates, she is the most precious gift that the Almighty has granted me, an unearned blessing for which there can be no sufficient expression of gratitude.

Acknowledgments

A number of the chapters in this book are revised versions of studies published earlier in various places. The author wishes to thank the following editors and publishers for their kind permission to make use of this material in this book.

Bar-Ilan University Press for "A New View of Maimonides' Method of Contradictions," *Annual of Bar-Ilan University,* XXII–XXIII, Moshe Schwarcz Memorial Volume, 1987.

Institute for Judaism and Contemporary Thought for "Ha-Tefillah be-Mahashavto shel ha-Rambam," *Ha-Tefillah ha-Yehudit: Hemshekh ve-Hiddush,* 1978.

Journal of the History of Philosophy for Review of Moses Maimonides, *The Guide of the Perplexed,* translated with an Introduction and notes by Shlomo Pines, with an Introductory Essay by Leo Strauss, vol. 3, no. 2, October, 1965.

KTAV Publishing House, Inc. for Prolegomenon to A. Cohen, *The Teachings of Maimonides,* 1968.

The Library of Jewish Law for "Law and Morality in the Thought of Maimonides," *Maimonides as Codifier of Jewish Law,* 1988.

Tel Aviv University Faculty of Law for "Maimonides and Aquinas on Natural Law," *Dine Israel,* vol. 3, 1972.

University of Alabama Press for "The Doctrine of the Mean in Aristotle and Maimonides: A Comparative Study," *Studies in Jewish Religious and Intellectual History Presented to Alexander Altmann,* 1979.

University of Chicago Press for permission to quote selected passages from Moses Maimonides, *The Guide of the Perplexed,* trans. S. Pines, © 1963 by The University of Chicago. All rights reserved.

PART I
ON READING
MAIMONIDES

1

The Many-Sided Maimonides

It is remarkable that despite the vast literature on many aspects of the work of Moses Maimonides, we do not have even one comprehensive study of his thought that compares in quality and scope to the great works that have been written on almost every important Western philosopher. If we think of such major works as I. M. Crombie's *An Examination of Plato's Doctrines*, W. D. Ross's *Aristotle*, Norman Kemp Smith's *The Philosophy of David Hume*, Harry A. Wolfson's *The Philosophy of Spinoza*, and similar works that abound in the literature of philosophy, we realize that nothing similar exists for Maimonides in any language, not even Hebrew. Consider also that we have for other philosophers great books of commentary and exposition that are direct studies of their major philosophical writings. I have in mind such classic books as *What Plato Said* by Paul Shorey, the three volumes of Paul Friedländer's *Plato*, *Kant's Metaphysics of Experience* by H. J. Paton, Norman Kemp Smith's *A Commentary to Kant's Critique of Pure Reason*, and others of this type. We have nothing comparable for Maimonides.

We do have works of commentary and exposition for Maimonides' legal writings, primarily the *Mishneh Torah*, which is his codification of the law, but no commentaries on a similar scale for his philosophical writings. While we are deeply indebted to the medieval commentators, whose glosses constitute an indispensable resource for the student of the *Guide of the Perplexed*, their work is not of the range and scope of the commentaries of Shorey, Friedländer, Paton, and Kemp Smith. The literature on the philosophy of Maimonides consists mostly of articles on specific topics, an occasional monograph on a specialized subject, and a few books that deal with aspects of Maimonides' thought but do not even claim to be comprehensive studies on the model of those mentioned above.[1]

---

1. The single outstanding exception is the superb book by Isadore Twersky, *Introduction to the Code of Maimonides (Mishneh Torah)* (New Haven, 1980). In this book he devotes much attention to philosophical issues, but he does not intend it to be a treatise on the philosophy of Maimonides. In fact, this book makes the point we have been arguing. It is a model of what such a study can and should be, but nothing written on the philosophy of Maimonides can compare in scope, depth, and comprehensiveness of treatment with this work which is focused on the *Mishneh Torah*.

How shall we understand this phenomenon? It is certainly not the result of inattention or lack of interest. In the eight hundred years since the *Guide of the Perplexed* first appeared, there has never been a time when interest in the *Guide* or Maimonides' other philosophic works was absent. At times it may have been more the interest of antagonism and heresy hunting than of study for the purpose of understanding. But Maimonides has never disappeared from the Jewish scholarly agenda. In our century, in particular, he has been the object of intense philosophical study in various parts of the world, generating an immense literature in a variety of languages. Yet out of all this study no single, thorough, and comprehensive account of his philosophy has emerged.

The most likely explanation arises from the situation in which students of Maimonides find themselves. The effort to provide a unified account of his thought, fully integrated and having a single focus, almost always comes to grief—a phenomenon that I believe derives initially from the deliberately esoteric character of Maimonides' philosophical writing, particularly in the *Guide*. It is intensified by the fact that Maimonides is a name of such overarching stature and authority that almost every interpreter seeks support for a personal point of view by claiming to find it in Maimonides. As a result, the many different modes of understanding and explaining Maimonides have yielded directly contradictory results.[2] We still cannot say with certainty just what could be considered a thoroughly reliable account of Maimonides' doctrines, whether in the form of an interpretation of his views about some particular philosophical or theological issue, or of a systematic exposition of his entire philosophy.

A major development in the study of Maimonides in this century has been the work of Leo Strauss, whose studies have forced us to reject the easy certainties about Maimonides that were long accepted. No one has done more to make us aware of the complexity, the subtlety, and the inherent difficulty in understanding any of Maimonides' works, and above all the *Guide*. In his provocative and challenging studies Strauss has renewed some neglected ways and opened new ones for the serious study of Maimonides.[3] He

2. Other major philosophers have also inspired diverse modes of interpretation, so that we have various conceptions of Plato, Aristotle, or Kant. Yet the commentators on the major Western philosophers do not seem to have the same personal investment in their studies as has historically been the case with Jewish students of Maimonides. The Jewish scholars seem to look to Maimonides to validate and authenticate their individual understanding of Judaism in a way that is not paralleled by even the most devoted interpreters of other major philosophers. Whether the present book has succeeded in freeing itself from this regrettable tendency to recreate Maimonides in the image of the author will have to be judged by its readers.

3. See Leo Strauss, "The Literary Character of the *Guide of the Perplexed*," in *Essays on Maimonides*, ed. Salo W. Baron (New York, 1941); reprinted in Leo Strauss, *Persecution and*

repeatedly emphasizes the fact that the *Guide* is an esoteric book, that is, a book whose surface doctrine hides another, very different set of teachings. In doing so Strauss has forcefully reminded us of what Maimonides himself made explicit to his readers.

For example, in his introduction to the *Guide* Maimonides speaks repeatedly of the "secret" doctrine that must be set forth in a way appropriate to its secret character. Rabbinic law, to which Maimonides as a loyal Jew is committed, prohibits any direct, public teaching of the secrets of the Torah. One is permitted to teach these only in private to selected students of proven competence; even to such students it is only permissible to teach the "chapter headings."[4] Thus, anyone who proposes to write a book dealing with the natural philosophy and metaphysics of the Torah faces a problem. Because a book, by its nature, is available to an unrestricted readership, there is no way to guarantee that it will fall only into the hands of those whom we may expose to this subject matter. Furthermore, if the author sets forth his teachings openly so as to make them readily available to his readers, he violates the rule against teaching more than "chapter headings."

It would seem that there is no way to write such a book without violating rabbinic law. For a faithful Jew this is not acceptable. Yet, at times it is urgent to teach a body of sound doctrine to those who require it. Indeed, in a generation in which worthy and qualified students are spread throughout the Diaspora and there are few fully qualified teachers, it would seem that there is no choice but to write a book that conveys the true teaching. It can be distributed widely, thus transcending the geographical limitations that hamper the live teacher. The problem is to find a method for writing such a book in a way that does not violate Jewish law while conveying its message successfully to those who are properly qualified.

Centuries earlier, in classical Greece, Plato had formulated the problem with his characteristic incisiveness. Although not constrained by rabbinic law, Plato nevertheless recognized the hazards of publishing:

> You know, Phaedrus, that's the strange thing about writing, which makes it truly analogous to painting. The painter's products stand before us as though they were alive, but if you question them, they

the Art of Writing (Glencoe, Ill., 1952). See also Leo Strauss, "How to Begin to Study the *Guide of the Perplexed*," in Moses Maimonides, *The Guide of the Perplexed*, trans. Shlomo Pines (Chicago, 1963), xi–lvi. We now have available in English also Leo Strauss, *Philosophy and Law* (Philadelphia, 1987). See also Leo Strauss, "Notes on Maimonides' Book of Knowledge," in *Studies in Mysticism and Religion Presented to Gershom G. Scholem* (Jerusalem, 1967).

4. See *M. Ḥagigah,* 2:1, and the talmudic discussion thereon.

maintain a most majestic silence. It is the same with written words; they seem to talk to you as though they were intelligent, but if you ask them anything about what they say, from a desire to be instructed, they go on telling you just the same thing forever, and once a thing is put in writing, the composition, whatever it maybe, drifts all over the place, getting into the hands of those who understand it, but equally of those who have no business with it; it doesn't know how to address the right people, and not address the wrong. And when it is ill-treated and unfairly abused it always needs its parent to come to its help, being unable to defend or help itself.[5]

Maimonides was intensely aware of these hazards, particularly when dealing with subjects that the law forbids the author to discuss in public. His problem then is clear. How does one fulfill the obligation to convey the message to those who need to know while remaining in full compliance with the restrictions that are imposed by the law?

He decided that to abide by the rabbinic ruling, he would have to write his book in such a way that it would offer no more than "chapter headings." The presentation would have to be so artful that none but the most highly qualified students would be able to follow his explanations and come to know his teachings. For this reason, as he tells us, even the chapter headings "are not set down in order or arranged in coherent fashion in this Treatise, but rather are scattered and entangled with other subjects that are to be clarified. For my purpose is that the truths be glimpsed and then again be concealed, so as not to oppose that divine purpose which one cannot possibly oppose and which has concealed from the vulgar among the people those truths especially requisite for His apprehension."[6] Such an exposition must be carefully constructed so as to protect people without a sound scientific and philosophical education from doctrines that they cannot understand and that would only harm them, while making the truth available to students with the proper personal and intellectual preparation.

Maimonides describes one of the methods he uses. "In speaking about very obscure matters it is necessary to conceal some parts and to disclose others. Sometimes in the case of certain dicta this necessity requires that the discussion proceed on the basis of a certain premise, whereas in another

---

5. Plato, *Phaedrus*, 275de, R. Hackforth, trans., in *The Collected Dialogues of Plato*, ed. E. Hamilton and H. Cairns (New York, 1961).

6. Maimonides, *Guide of the Perplexed*, Introduction to the First Part, in the translation by Shlomo Pines (Chicago: University of Chicago Press, 1963), 6–7. All quotations from the *Guide* and references to it in this book will be from this edition, unless otherwise noted. The citations, hereafter noted in the text, are by part, chapter, and page.

place necessity requires that the discussion proceed on the basis of another premise contradicting the first one. In such cases the vulgar must in no way be aware of the contradiction; the author accordingly uses some device to conceal it by all means" (I, Introduction, p. 18).[7]

Despite the inherent hazards in producing such a book, Maimonides felt it was his absolute duty to find an acceptable way of preserving his insights and understanding of the highest truths in a form accessible to others. He says that "if I had omitted setting down something of that which has appeared to me as clear, so that that knowledge would perish when I perish, as is inevitable, I should have considered that conduct as extremely cowardly with regard to you and everyone who is perplexed" (III, Introduction, pp. 415–16). It is one of the mysteries of our intellectual history that these explicit statements of Maimonides, together with his other extensive instructions on how to read his book, have been so widely ignored. No author could have been more open in informing his readers that they were confronting no ordinary book. Comparatively few readers and commentators over the centuries, however, have undertaken the hard work necessary to read the *Guide* as its author requires. Attempting an account of the reasons for this strange phenomenon would involve us in studies in social and intellectual history which are not germane to this book. For us it is enough to recall that the contemporary generation of readers has been fully alerted by Leo Strauss, so there is no excuse for us if we fail to exercise appropriate caution and to avoid some of the mistakes our predecessors made in studying Maimonides.

Once we begin to read Maimonides in the way he requires, we can no longer be comfortable about the confidence with which straightforward accounts of his general philosophy have been written, nor can we always trust the writers' statements about Maimonides' views and doctrines. Only the most painstaking study makes it possible for us even to hazard an opinion concerning the views of Maimonides, and such an opinion is reliable only if it emerges from a sensitive confrontation with the obstacles and subtleties of the texts. When we consider the variety of opinions that recognized scholars hold concerning major problems in the interpretation of Maimonides, we can see that reading Maimonides as if he were an ordinary writer leaves us with no control whatsoever over the teachings embedded in his philosophic writings. The *Guide of the Perplexed* provides the classic example of what concerned Plato in his reflections on the hazards of writing books and learning from them.

We begin with the question whether Maimonides should be viewed as a

7. In chapter 4, we shall have occasion to discuss in detail the so-called method of contradictions which Maimonides employs.

model of traditional piety or, as some assert, as a veiled heretic. That the latter charge is not utterly fantastic can best be understood if we remember the great controversy that arose shortly after his death and tore apart Jewish communities in Europe and the East. In some places his philosophic writings were banned, and it was a serious violation for anyone to study them. Intense feelings built up to a tragic climax when copies of the *Guide* were burned in a public ceremony in France some thirty years after its author's death.[8] In a variety of ways the controversy continued for centuries. Only a generation ago there were yeshivot in eastern Europe where the study of Maimonides' *Guide* was considered prima facie evidence of severe heretical tendencies. That attitude can, no doubt, still be found in some circles today.

Even when Maimonides was not being accused of personal impiety, there were always those who attacked one or another of his doctrines as contrary to the fundamentals of the Jewish faith. Every student of the *Mishneh Torah* is familiar with the often bitter criticisms of R. Abraham ben David of Posquieres (Rabad), some of which are on theological points. Rabad suggests, for example, that the views of Maimonides on resurrection and the world to come are contrary to the established teachings.[9] He even expresses doubt concerning the legitimacy of Maimonides' views on the incorporeality of God.[10] In the same standard editions of the *Mishneh Torah* containing the glosses of Rabad, we also find such commentaries as *Leḥem Mishneh, Migdal 'Oz,* and above all the *Kesef Mishneh* of Rabbi Joseph Karo, the sixteenth-century author of the *Shulḥan 'Arukh.* These commentaries often defend Maimonides against the attacks of Rabad, not only with respect to issues in law and jurisprudence, but also in regard to controversies concerning matters of theology and the fundamentals of faith.

This pattern continues through the ages. To one group Maimonides is a heretic, or at least propounds heretical views; to another his teachings are a model of conventional orthodoxy. Naḥmanides, in his commentary on the Pentateuch, attacks Maimonides almost without restraint at some points. In a familiar passage, he goes so far as to say that certain views expressed in the

---

8. For the anti-Maimonidean controversy and the literature thereon see, among others, Joseph Sarachek, *Faith and Reason: The Conflict over the Rationalism of Maimonides* (New York, 1935), and Daniel Jeremy Silver, *Maimonidean Criticism and the Maimonidean Controversy, 1180–1240* (Leiden, 1965).

9. See Rabad's glosses to *H. Teshuvah,* 8:2, 8:8. In the former he accuses Maimonides of bordering on the heresy of denying the resurrection of the body and insists in very strong language that he has deviated from the teachings of the Sages. For the classic study of Rabad as a thinker, his relationship to Maimonides, and the way in which we should understand his acerbic language, see Isadore Twersky, *Rabad of Posquieres* (Cambridge, Mass., 1962).

10. See gloss to *H. Teshuvah,* 3:7.

Guide "directly contradict the teachings of Scripture so that it is forbidden to listen to them and certainly forbidden to believe them."[11]

We know, of course, that the same Nahmanides was often a defender of Maimonides against similar attacks by others. What is perhaps less known is that Maimonides found another vigorous defender against these attacks in R. Yom Tov ben Abraham of Seville. This great fourteenth-century talmudist composed a small book, the *Sefer ha-Zikkaron,* specifically to explain and defend the teachings of Maimonides that Nahmanides had criticized.[12] These few examples are only a minute part of the literature around Maimonides, a literature that is often polarized between bitter attack on the legitimacy of his doctrines and equally intense defense of him as the most fully authentic of Jewish teachers. My purpose here is only to point out that already in his own time and throughout the subsequent centuries the pendulum swung back and forth between the portraits of Maimonides as near-heretic or actual heretic and as a model not only of Jewish learning but of classical piety.

Even among recent and contemporary writers the battle continues. Ahad Ha-ʿAm represented Maimonides as a pure rationalist who imposed reason on faith and, when necessary, adjusted the norms of rabbinic law in order to force them into conformity with the demands of reason. His famous essay on Maimonides is entitled "Shilton ha-Sekhel" ("The Supremacy of Reason"). This picture of Maimonides is strenuously opposed by Aaron Kaminka, who claims that for Maimonides reason, philosophy, and science were all subordinated "to the absolute supremacy of his strongly held faith in the truth and eternity of the Torah of Moses and the talmudic tradition which derives from it. That faith welled up from the depths of his heart . . . and it alone can explain the integrity of all the remarkable achievements of his life."[13]

Kaminka presents peculiar evidence for the complete orthodoxy of Maimonides and for the assertion that, although he assimilated philosophy into the tradition, philosophy as such never dominated his thinking or his teachings. He expresses complete certainty that deviation by Maimonides in any slight degree from the norms of rabbinic doctrine would have been detected at once and the Jewish world would not have accepted him as an unexcelled authority in matters of law and faith. It is characteristic of the

---

11. See Nahmanides, gloss to Gen. 18:2.

12. Yom Tov ben Abraham, *Sefer ha-Zikkaron,* ed. M. Y. Blau (New York, 1957).

13. See "The Supremacy of Reason," in *Ahad Ha-ʿAm: Essays, Letters, Memoirs,* ed. and trans. Leon Simon (Oxford, 1946), 139–82, and A. Kaminka, "Ha-ʾEmunah ve-ha-Bikoret ha-Sikhlit be-Mifʿalo shel ha-Rambam," *Ha-ʾAretz,* no. 4788 (5695), 17–18.

blindness or tendentiousness of such Maimonidean scholarship that Ka-minka was able to ignore the mass of familiar animadversions on Maimonides, since to recognize them would have forced him to abandon his own thesis. Chaim Tschernowitz, on the other hand, casts serious doubts on the orthodoxy of Maimonides. He asserts that Maimonides was so commit-ted to the primacy of worldly learning that not only did he make philosophy the judge of what should be an article of faith, but also "with respect to every matter of law with which he dealt, if there was any contradiction between scientific knowledge and the traditional view he almost always decided in favor of science. . . . Maimonides, the philosopher, is clearly visible be-hind the walls of his own structure of traditional Jewish law."[14] Finally, any study of the writings on Maimonides of Leo Strauss or Shlomo Pines reveals, at least between the lines, the conviction that the true doctrines of Maimonides were far from conventional orthodoxies. According to this view, the main purpose of his esoteric style in the *Guide* is to make it pos-sible to express heretical or near-heretical ideas without injuring either the social structure or the naive and useful faith of simple unphilosophical believers.[15]

An extension of the controversy over the orthodoxy of Maimonides emerges in differing views concerning his relationship to Aristotle and Aris-totelian philosophy. It is a textbook commonplace that Maimonides deeply admired the philosophy of Aristotle and adopted much of it as a basis for his own work. The only generally recognized exception is his stand on the cre-ation of the world *ex nihilo* against the Aristotelian doctrine of the eternity of matter, and opinions differ even about this.[16] In an early study, Harry Aus-tryn Wolfson, one of the greatest historians of medieval philosophy, argues that Maimonides can only be understood as an Aristotelian. He "is a true convert to Aristotelian philosophy. To him the thorough understanding of Aristotle is the highest achievement to which men can attain." Wolfson holds that Maimonides' primary purpose was to show that scriptural and rab-binic teachings are in harmony with the philosophy of Aristotle. "Maimonides was not a rabbi employing Greek logic and categories of thought in order to interpret Jewish religion; he was rather a true medieval

14. C. Tschernowitz (Rav Tza'ir), "Lu lo' Kam ke-Moshe," *Me'oznayim*, III, no. 4–5, 396–97.

15. See the Strauss essays referred to in note 3, and Shlomo Pines, "Translator's Introduc-tion: The Philosophic Sources of the *Guide of the Perplexed*," in Maimonides, *Guide*, trans. Pines.

16. See the discussion of this subject in chapter 10.

Aristotelian, using Jewish religion as an illustration of the Stagirite's meta-physical supremacy."[17] Wolfson concludes that Maimonides' personal piety should not be questioned. He was without doubt a meticulously observant Jew, but his personal piety was in no way derived from or connected to his Aristotelian philosophic system. Isaac Husik goes even further, stating that although the doctrines of Aristotle radically oppose the teachings of the Hebrew Bible, Maimonides was a devoted Aristotelian who tried to achieve a harmony between Greek philosophy and the doctrines of the Torah.[18]

Similar debates occur with respect to Maimonides' ethics. Because he subscribed to the doctrine of the mean, his ethical theory is often taken to be essentially Aristotelian in origin and content. M. Lazarus in his *Ethics of Judaism* and David Rosin in *Die Ethik des Maimonides* affirm without question the almost pure Aristotelianism of Maimonides' ethics. Their understanding of Maimonides is by far the most common. Yet no less a philosopher than Hermann Cohen differs sharply. Cohen's famous and controversial essay, "Charakteristik der Ethik Maimunis," is a major attempt to demonstrate that Maimonides' ethics are completely independent of Aristotle's and that he is, in fact, fundamentally opposed to Aristotle. Cohen holds that if Maimonides' ethics were not independent of Aristotle his doctrine would be self-contradictory and unphilosophical and could, as a result, have no place in his own system. One of the main burdens of Maimonides' thought, according to Cohen, is his battle against materialism. His great achievement is the victory of idealism over materialism and, for this reason, he must not be construed as supporting the essentially materialist views of Aristotle. Even Maimonides' doctrine of the mean is thought by Cohen to differ radically from the Aristotelian doctrine.[19] Because Maimonides often uses Aristotelian terminology, people have been misled into thinking that he was a follower of Aristotle's philosophy. Cohen claims that this is only a strategem employed by Maimonides to gain a favorable hearing. Given the dominance of Aristotle over medieval thought it would have been intellectual suicide to oppose Aristotle openly. The trick, which Maimonides

17. Harry A. Wolfson, "Maimonides and Halevi: A Study in Typical Jewish Attitudes Toward Greek Philosophy in the Middle Ages," *Jewish Quarterly Review*, n. s. 2 (1912), 306, 314; reprinted in Wolfson, *Studies in the History and Philosophy of Religion*, vol. 2 (Cambridge, Mass., 1977).

18. Isaac Husik, *A History of Medieval Jewish Philosophy* (Philadelphia, 1944), 299–300.

19. This subject, including some comments on Cohen's views, is discussed extensively in chapter 5.

mastered superbly, was to sound like an Aristotelian while undermining all the foundations of the Peripatetic philosophy.[20]

These differences concerning the interpretation of Maimonides are not necessarily related to the private commitments of the scholars holding these views. We find that Zvi Diesendruck, who was a professor at the Hebrew Union College, a Reform rabbinical seminary in Cincinnati, and R. Ya'akov Moshe Harlap, a model of old Orthodox piety in the religious quarter of Jerusalem, both agree with Hermann Cohen that Maimonides was no Aristotelian. They not only take this position with respect to Maimonides' ethics but include practically the whole of his philosophy. Diesendruck argues that "the entire philosophy of Maimonides is one continuous endeavor to overcome Aristotle in the most essential points. . . . Maimonides differs from him in all matters of importance in metaphysics as well as ethics; in these fields he regards the Aristotelian teachings as erroneous and even dangerous."[21] Though there is no reason to believe that Harlap knew the work of Diesendruck, he follows a remarkably similar line of argument. Granting that Maimonides incorporated some elements of Greek philosophy into his works, Harlap proclaims that beyond all doubt these elements were totally transformed and Judaized by Maimonides before he gave them a place in his writings. The terms Harlap uses for this process of intellectual transformation are those normally used for the process of religious conversion into the Jewish faith.[22]

As the pendulum swings again to the opposite extreme, we find one more contemporary writer affirming Maimonides' Aristotelianism and, with it, his complete heresy. Yaakov Becker's picture of Maimonides seems in certain respects strikingly reflective of the work of Leo Strauss, although he gives no direct indication that he has been influenced by Strauss. His Maimonides is an esoteric writer who has made a conscious decision to set forth in a single book two opposed systems of thought. One is a system of traditional Jewish beliefs intended for the consumption and protection of the untutored masses. The other is an Aristotelian philosophy that is the truth, representing Maimonides' actual views and contradicting the religious tradition at almost every crucial point. We have here a special version of a "double truth" theory, with Maimonides hiding his true doctrines from the eyes of the vulgar.

20. Hermann Cohen, "Charakteristik der Ethik Maimunis," *Moses ben Maimon*, vol. 1 (Leipzig, 1908); reprinted in Cohen, *Jüdische Schriften*, vol. 3 (Berlin, 1924), and in Hebrew translation in Cohen, *'Iyyunim be-Yahadut uve-Be'ayot ha-Dor* (Jerusalem, 1977).

21. Zvi Diesendruck, "The Philosophy of Maimonides," *CCAR Yearbook*, 45 (1935), 358.

22. Y. M. Harlap, *Mei Marom: Misaviv le-Shemonah Perakim* (Jerusalem, 1946), 13, 85–86.

In Becker's opinion, "Maimonides never resolves the contradictions between the Torah of Moses and the philosophy of Aristotle. On the contrary, he expands and deepens them. His war against Aristotle was only apparent. At the profoundest levels of the *Guide of the Perplexed* he continually deepens the abyss between these two world views. He makes absolute distinctions between them, while justifying each as appropriate for different spheres of human life."[23] Becker goes on to show, at least to his own satisfaction, that for Maimonides the true philosophy was that of Aristotle. His God, like Aristotle's, is in no significant respect the God of the Torah. He is not the creator of the world; He is not the power that sustains the world; there is no providence; and God has no relationship whatsoever to the world. Maimonides' God has none of the characteristics attributed to Him in Scripture, nor does He in any way reflect the more or less established teachings of the rabbinic tradition. In short, Becker's Maimonides is a complete heretic who chooses, for political reasons, to masquerade as a pious believing Jew.

What shall we make of such a welter of contradictory opinions about Maimonides? Our first conclusion must be that we can no longer rest easy with the comfortable certainties that characterize the work of many writers on Maimonides' philosophy. The problem of interpretation is, of course, not peculiar to Maimonidean scholarship. Many major philosophers have evoked similarly contradictory interpretations. As examples, we need only think of the range of opinions regarding the relationship of Aristotle to Plato, or of the diverse interpretations of Plato's theory of Forms. Yet if Maimonides does not differ in kind from other philosophers, he surely differs in degree. It can be argued (and, I believe, demonstrated) that rarely has there been such deep disagreement, over so many issues and for so many centuries, about the views of a single philosopher. The reasons are not difficult to isolate. One is the effect of Maimonides' literary style. Esoteric writers deliberately lay themselves open to wider ranges of interpretation and misinterpretation than do straightforward writers. In the case of Maimonides we must always make a special effort to find out not only what he seems to say, but also whether it is identical with what he is actually saying. We must depend on subtle clues, obscure hints, and our own capacity to construct an ordered system out of texts in which there appears to be only disorder. If any serious text requires meticulous attention to every detail on the part of the reader, this requirement is multiplied many times over in the case of Maimonides.

Let us have Maimonides speak for himself. In his Introduction to the

---

23. Yaakov Becker, *Mishnato ha-Pilosofit shel ha-Rambam* (Tel-Aviv, 1955), 19–20.

Guide, under the heading, "Instruction with Respect to This Treatise," he states:

> If you wish to grasp the totality of what this Treatise contains, so that nothing of it will escape you, then you must connect its chapters one with another; and when reading a given chapter, your intention must be not only to understand the totality of that chapter, but also to grasp each word that occurs in it in the course of the speech, even if that word does not belong to the intention of that chapter. For the diction of this Treatise has not been chosen at haphazard, but with great exactness and exceeding precision, and with care to avoid failing to explain any obscure point. And nothing has been mentioned out of its place, save with a view to explaining some matter in its proper place. You therefore should not let your fantasies elaborate on what is said here, for that would hurt me and be of no use to yourself (I, Introduction, p. 15).

When an author puts such difficulties in the way of his readers and makes such inordinately high demands, it is hardly surprising that there is no commonly accepted unified interpretation of his work.

The problem of interpreting Maimonides is compounded by the range of his subject matter, the varying purposes for which he wrote, the diverse styles that he employed, the number of years that separate his earliest and latest works, and the question of the interrelationships of his various works. Consider as an example the attempt to arrive at a coherent and integrated understanding of any one central issue in Maimonides' thought, while keeping in mind all the relevant passages in his various works. A single case can make the point clear. It is well known that in Maimonides' organization of the commandments of the Torah the number fourteen plays a very significant role. His *Sefer ha-Mitzvot (Book of the Commandments)* sets forth a series of fourteen "roots," general principles for identifying, enumerating, and classifying the commandments. His great legal compilation, the *Mishneh Torah,* is a codification of the commandments divided into fourteen books. Finally, in the *Guide* he informs us that he has "divided all the commandments into fourteen classes" (III, 35, p. 535).

Because we know how careful a writer Maimonides was, it would be reasonable to assume that these three separate classifications of the commandments into fourteen divisions are closely and meaningfully related, if not identical. Yet a first reading shows the classifications to be quite different from each other; if there is a relationship it is by no means obvious. In any case, we might expect that scholars would have dealt with the problem and solved it. Instead we find in the literature casual discussions and contradictory opinions with little careful attention to the texts. What is most disturbing is that these discussions and opinions are found in the works of the most distinguished scholars. Isidore Epstein, for example, the dean of Jewish scholars in England in the middle of this century, says that the division of the commandments in the *Guide* is a classification and summary of the fourteen books of the *Mishneh Torah*.[24] Yet, as we shall see shortly, the differences between the classifications in these two works are so great and so obvious that no one, least of all a responsible scholar, should be guilty of identifying the two as alternate versions of the same scheme.

Other scholars, however they may differ in background and method, also tend to treat the three "fourteens" in a very casual way, although this approach hardly seems faithful to what we know of Maimonides and his literary method. Isaac Herzog, the late Chief Rabbi of Israel, says of the three fourteens: "This is, of course, sheer coincidence. There is no sort of logical correspondence between the respective divisions."[25] The same view is expressed by Irving Levey, a well-known scholar in the Reform movement, when he asserts that "mere coincidence has thrown the number 'fourteen' into great prominence in the works of Maimonides."[26] S. Rawidowicz, one of the outstanding contemporary scholars in the field of Jewish philosophy, shares this opinion. He writes that the only thing these three classifications of the commandments have in common is the number fourteen; there is no other significant connection among them, either in their theoretical foundations or in their practical consequences.[27]

In contrast to these views we have the analysis of Leo Strauss. He takes with utmost seriousness Maimonides' account of his method and is thus never willing to believe that anything is purely coincidental in Maimonides' writings. In Strauss's view we certainly should not casually dismiss as coincidental something as obviously connected as the threefold classification of the same set of commandments into fourteen groups. He argues that it is Maimonides' deliberate plan to give the impression that the three fourteens are essentially the same in order to mislead the casual student. (It appears that he succeeded even with diligent students, given the example of Ep-

---

24. Isidore Epstein, "Maimonides' Conception of the Law and the Ethical Trend of His Halachah," in *Moses Maimonides: Anglo-Jewish Papers in Connection with the Eighth Centenary of His Birth*, ed. I. Epstein (London, 1935), 64.

25. Isaac Herzog, "Maimonides as Halachist," in *Moses Maimonines: Anglo-Jewish Papers*, ed. Epstein, 143. Rabbi Herzog repeated this opinion in several other places.

26. Irving Levey, "Maimonides as Codifier," *CCAR Yearbook*, 45 (1935), 368–96.

27. S. Rawidowicz, "Sefer ha-Petiḥah le-Mishneh Torah," *Metzudah*, 7 (1954), 137; reprinted in Rawidowicz, *'Iyyunim be-Maḥashevet Yisrael* (Jerusalem, 1969), 381–464.

stein.) Strauss would have us study these three cases carefully, note the precise differences, and from these differences and other relevant evidence determine just what Maimonides has hidden under the outer surface of the fourteens.[28] Unhappily, Strauss does not carry his analysis further, so we do not know his solution to the problem.

It is fruitful for our purposes to examine the texts more closely in this case, so we can see a classic example of just how complex and subtle the problem is, and can gain added insight into the challenge of reading Maimonides well. In III, 35 of the *Guide,* Maimonides sets forth his division of the commandments into fourteen classes. Because he seems to relate this division explicitly to the fourteen books of the *Mishneh Torah,* it is natural to assume that the connection exists. However, when we study his text carefully, we are struck by a series of remarkable incongruities and inconsistencies. Of the fourteen books in the *Mishneh Torah,* only nine are specifically mentioned in the classification in the *Guide.* A discerning student will, of course, ask why five of the books are omitted and what principle determines which are omitted and which included. In addition, and remarkably enough, the first book of the *Mishneh Torah,* the "Book of Knowledge," is not mentioned at all, although Maimonides views it as the philosophical-theological foundation for all that follows in his code. On the other hand, each of the first three classes of commandments in the *Guide* is associated directly with a particular section of the "Book of Knowledge," and each of these sections is identified by name. If the structures of the classifications were parallel, each class of commandments set forth in the *Guide* would be the counterpart of one book in the *Mishneh Torah.* Here, however, we find three classes, each associated with one section of one book of the *Mishneh Torah.* Sometimes Maimonides refers to an individual section by its full name, such as *Hilkhot Yesodei ha-Torah (Laws of the Foundations of the Torah).* Other times he refers to the contents of a section, but not to its full name. For example, he tells us that included in the first class, in addition to the commandments that are listed in *Hilkhot Yesodei ha-Torah,* are *Teshuva (Repentance)* and *Ta'aniot (Fasts).* Why does he not refer specifically to the full names of the sections of the code that bear these titles: *Hilkhot Teshuvah* and *Hilkhot Ta'aniot?* Is he suggesting in the *Guide* that he now wants to include only certain portions of those sections, but not all of them? Or is there some other less compromising explanation?

Again we note that two sections of the same book in the *Mishneh Torah* are assigned to two different classes in the *Guide* and, conversely, that sections from different books in the former are assigned to a single class in the

28. Strauss, *Persecution and the Art of Writing,* 63.

latter. Thus, the Laws Concerning Forbidden Foods are in the thirteenth class in the *Guide* and the Laws Concerning Prohibited Sexual Relations are in the fourteenth class, although they are both contained in a single book, *Sefer Kedushah,* in the *Mishneh Torah.* (It is worth noting that this book is among those whose names are omitted by Maimonides in this part of the *Guide.*) In turn we find, for example, that the fourth class in the *Guide* includes commandments from at least four different books of the *Mishneh Torah.*

It is important for a serious student to be aware of the complexity that we must cope with in almost every Maimonidean text. The complexity is multiplied if we try to view the various works of Maimonides and their parts in any kind of intelligible and coherent interrelationship. To ascribe such a problem as the three fourteens to mere coincidence, as some have done, is far too simple and crude a solution. To assure us, as Strauss has, that the repetition of the fourteens is deliberate, is a necessary first step in taking the texts seriously. The real achievement, however, is to discern and lay out with care the similarities and differences among the three versions of the four-teens, and then go forward to solve the puzzle. We need to explain just what Maimonides had in mind and what he was trying to teach us. We must ac-count for the similarities, differences, inconsistencies, and obscurities that have turned this seemingly simple scheme of classification into a dark and impenetrable mystery.[29] We have here one striking example of the heavy demands that are made on every generation of students of Maimonides, and we can see why we cannot hope to achieve easy certainties in the interpreta-tion of his thought.

Our grasp of the difficulties confronting us in the effort to understand Maimonides' teachings will be even firmer if we consider some additional problems of interpretation. A question central to the thought of Maimonides is that of our knowledge of God. Everything we know of Maimonides' thought suggests that he considered the true knowledge of God to be a neces-sary condition for attaining the highest human perfection. The first obligation of a Jew that he records in the first section of the first chapter of the first book of the *Mishneh Torah* is that we are commanded to know that God exists, that He is the necessary source of all else that exists, the source and the foundation of all being. Similarly, the first commandment listed in

---

29. Although I first wrote about this matter of the three fourteens in 1968, and the present discussion reproduces, in part, some of that paper, I confess with regret that I have not worked out a solution to the problem. I hope that in this book I have managed to solve some other diffi-cult problems in the works of Maimonides, and that I shall have succeeded in laying down methodological canons that point the way to a solution of this problem as well.

his *Sefer ha-Mitzvot* is the commandment to believe in the existence of God. Rabbi Chaim Heller, in his critical edition of the Hebrew version of that work, suggests that according to the reading in the Arabic text it would be appropriate to render this commandment as requiring us to *know,* not just to believe, that God exists. This same theme permeates much of the *Guide* and reaches its climax in the last chapters, where the true knowledge of God is presented as the ultimate end of man. Philosophers and prophets agree on this, according to Maimonides.

Yet there are some troubling questions that no student can afford to ignore. How can we be commanded to know anything, especially something as arcane and inaccessible as the ultimate truth about the world? If we truly have knowledge of God (and *knowledge* here clearly means intellectual apprehension), then we have penetrated the secret of the very ground of all being. To strive for this goal may be everyone's duty, but it is strange to insist that we are all commanded to reach the goal. It is a standard principle of ethics that 'ought' implies 'can', that whatever a person is truly obligated to do, he or she is able to do. Conversely, we cannot be obligated to do something that we are incapable of doing. How puzzling then that Maimonides, who often asserts that only a small, intellectual elite is capable of achieving true knowledge of the highest matters, makes this highest knowledge obligatory for all Jews.

The confusion grows greater if we consider further aspects of the question. In I,15 of the *Guide* Maimonides seems to be saying that whoever makes the effort to know God succeeds; thus we can properly be commanded to make such an effort. Moreover, in II,1–2, Maimonides claims to have presented rational demonstrations of the existence, unity, and incorporeality of God. If these are, in fact, valid demonstrations, as he apparently believed them to be, then anyone should be able to grasp them. To assert that every human being, *qua* human, is endowed with rational powers means among other things that all human beings have the power to follow a rational argument. That human beings, by their very nature, are endowed with such intellectual powers is established in I,1 of the *Guide,* where Maimonides interprets the biblical statement that man was created in the image of God to refer to man's intellectual capacity.

So far, then, it appears reasonable to command man to know God. As we continue to study the texts, however, a typical set cf Maimonidean puzzles emerges, and our earlier certainties are no longer so easily tenable. In the same first chapter of the *Mishneh Torah* where we are commanded to know God, we are surprised to discover that Maimonides also says that the genuine truth about God's nature is beyond all human knowledge. "The truth of the matter is that the human intellect does not understand God and is

18

incapable of grasping Him or penetrating His reality." Even Moses, who stood above all other persons in his prophetic and intellectual capacity to apprehend God, was "incapable of truly knowing Him."[30] This point is repeated and elaborated in the *Guide,* with a specific reference to the earlier passage in the *Mishneh Torah.* Speaking of Moses' expressed desire to know God fully, Maimonides points out that Scripture tells us that his plea was denied by God, who hid this ultimate knowledge from him. "When I say He hid from him, I intend to signify that this apprehension is hidden and inaccessible in its very nature" (I, 21, p. 49).[31] If Moses could not know God truly, then surely no other human being can achieve such knowledge. In fact, Maimonides goes on in the following sentences to warn that once man has reached his intellectual limits, any effort to go beyond is only destructive. So it now appears that we cannot really know God, and we are mystified by the commandment which says that we must.

When we consider what Maimonides says we can know about God, our situation seems even less promising. We are told explicitly that we can gain no positive knowledge whatsoever of God. We know Him only through negative attributes. This means that we can know only what He is not, but never what He is. Even when we speak of God as having certain positive qualities we must interpret them negatively. Thus to say that God is living is only to say that He is not dead. "Of this thing [i.e., God] we say that it exists, the meaning being that its nonexistence is impossible" (I, 58, p. 135). It is a strange kind of knowledge, indeed, that is purely negative. Maimonides seems to say that no one is able to fulfill the commandment to know God, making us wonder whether there is any meaningful sense in which it can be a commandment at all. Yet there is no doubt that Maimonides explicitly and repeatedly records and codifies such a commandment.

We know that Maimonides considers knowledge of the negative attributes a significant way of having some knowledge of God. He explicitly says, in various places, that it is significant knowledge. As he develops his theory of negative attributes, however, Maimonides seems to present the paradoxical doctrine that the less we know about God, the more we know about Him; thus our ideal should be to negate everything that is predicated of Him in order to know everything about Him.

> Accordingly the negative attributes make you come nearer . . . to
> the cognition and apprehension of God. . . . Desire then whole-

30. *H. Yesodei ha-Torah,* 1:9, 1:10.

31. God hid from Moses "the apprehension called that *of the face* and made him pass over to something different . . ." (I, 21, p. 49).

heartedly that you should know by demonstration some additional thing to be negated, but do not desire to negate merely in words. For on every occasion on which it becomes clear to you by means of a demonstration that a thing whose existence is thought to pertain to Him should rather be negated with reference to Him, you undoubtedly come nearer to Him by one degree. . . . On the other hand, the predication of affirmative attributes of Him, is very dangerous (I, 60, p. 144).

What can we claim to know about God, whom we are commanded to know, if all we can do is state what He is not? If we deny only some of the positive qualities, then we leave open the possibility that the innumerable remaining positive qualities may properly be predicated of God. If, on the other hand, we deny, in principle, every positive quality without undertaking the impossible task of identifying and enumerating them, then we would appear to be in danger of the blasphemous heresy that God is nothing. It helps little if we call Him by such mystical names as the Holy Nothingness.

Although there is every reason to think that Maimonides did not want to fall into this trap, it is extremely difficult to find a way out of it. Conventional commentators, if they recognize the dilemma at all, try to resolve it by appealing to Maimonides' doctrine that we predicate positive terms of God analogically, rather than literally, and that what we can affirm of Him are the so-called attributes of His actions that we are able to infer from our own experience of the world. Although Maimonides explicitly introduces the notion of the analogical use of terms with respect to God, it is not helpful, as he himself seems to recognize in other places. The key to the problem is that a term used as a common predicate for two subjects must be either univocal or equivocal, that is, it must either have the same meaning in both cases or a different meaning. If I say that God is wise and compassionate and that Ms. Smith is also wise and compassionate, I must determine whether the predicates mean the same thing in each case. If they do, then I can rightly claim that I understand God's wisdom and compassion on the model of Ms. Smith's wisdom and compassion. Of human wisdom and compassion I have some direct experience, and I can, therefore, justly claim to know something about God—namely, that He is wise and compassionate in a way similar to human beings.

However, this alternative has been explicitly closed to us by Maimonides' doctrine which denies that I can ever have such positive knowledge of God. For this reason, I must say that I use these terms equivocally, that is, with different meanings in the case of God and of human beings. With respect to God they have meanings whose content I cannot specify. It follows that when I speak of God as wise and compassionate, I am not saying anything intelligible, since I have no idea of what these predicates mean and can put no content into them. Thus, analogical predicates are not much help, and we return to the negative attributes with which we began. This is acknowledged by Maimonides himself, despite the fact that he has earlier introduced the idea of analogical terms. He says that "it has already been demonstrated that anything that we think of as a perfection—even if it existed as pertaining to Him—in accordance with the opinion of those who believe in the attributes, nevertheless would not belong to the species of perfection that we think of, *save only by equivocation,* just as we have made clear. Accordingly you must of necessity go over to the notion of negation" (I, 60, p. 144; emphasis added).

The familiar Maimonidean solution to all this is usually taken to be the notion that, although we do not know any positive attributes of God, we can know His actions or the consequences of His actions in the world. We speak of these as if they had been done by God just as a person would have done them. So when there is a great natural catastrophe that harms people and property we speak of God as being angry because only great anger would move a person to behave in this way. At best, this is only a way of speaking; it adds no illumination and no knowledge. However convenient we may find it to speak this way, even the attributes of action provide us with no true knowledge of God, since in principle this knowledge is beyond us. It is doubtful whether on Maimonides' own grounds we can properly speak of God's actions. To speak of His actions leads ultimately to affirming positive attributes and thus to the same compromises of His absolute unity that Maimonides has taken the greatest pains to avoid.

Here again we see how difficult it is to gain a clear understanding of the teachings of Maimonides. He records the duty to know God as the very first commandment. He speaks in many places about knowledge of God as the true perfection of man. He treats it as an ideal toward which every man should direct his supreme efforts and identifies the realization of that ideal with the summit of human self-fulfillment. Even the most casual reader could cite numerous passages from Maimonides' various books to show that this is his teaching. Yet when we examine it in the total context and full development of his own analysis, we seemingly must conclude that this ideal is not only impossible, but empty of content and meaning.

There are great hazards here. First is the serious danger of misunderstanding and misinterpreting Maimonides. For those who are predisposed to remove Maimonides from the traditional religious community, it is not difficult to read him in such a way that he turns out to be a crypto-heretic. Considering all that we know of the man and his life, his piety, and his meticulous commitment to the Law, this hardly seems to be a tenable position. With some ingenuity, however, this interpretation can certainly be worked out and made plausible. It is just as easy to read the texts in such a way that the author emerges as a man of unquestioned and conventional orthodoxy. It must be stressed that no responsible scholarly reading of Maimonides may be so tendentious as to ignore what does not fit into the reader's preconceived scheme. Maimonides must be read as he asked us to read him, with great effort and with penetrating intellect. Only then can we hope for a reliable and sound understanding. The second danger is one that deeply concerned Maimonides: namely, that casual readers might misunderstand him and be corrupted by their misunderstanding. He tried strenuously to avert this danger by composing his books, especially the *Guide,* in the way he did. Nevertheless, casual students may well reach destructive conclusions on the basis of their limited and confused understanding of this great thinker.

The subjects raised briefly in this chapter will be discussed more fully in what follows. It is important, however, to set forth now the basic methodological line that I follow in interpreting Maimonides. It seems clear to me that Maimonides was exquisitely sensitive to his own problems. He was fully conscious of all the issues raised explicitly and implicitly in his works, and equally conscious of the intrinsic difficulties in his efforts to give a philosophical account of Judaism. Most interpreters have inclined to the view that Maimonides can be made consistent with himself only by reducing his views to a single monochromatic position. He must be either an Aristotelian or a non-Aristotelian. He must be either a model of naive piety or a heretic or crypto-heretic. He must affirm either that we have the capacity to know God fully or that we are incapable of knowing anything whatsoever about God. I hope to show that this is a superficial way of understanding Maimonides, and an approach that distorts and misconstrues his views.

In my judgment, Maimonides should be understood as a thinker who seeks to exploit every possibility of true knowledge but is at the same time thoroughly cognizant of the limits on our knowledge. He is a thinker who considers it our duty to use our intellect to its ultimate capacity, but he knows there is a limit to that capacity. He understands that, even within the operations of the intellect itself, we often are unable to justify a choice between opposed positions. His approach to this more or less paradoxical situation is to eschew the way of 'either/or' and to adopt instead the way of 'both/and'. Maimonides regularly takes seemingly opposed positions on certain issues, not because he is intellectually muddled or dishonest, or has a program for the elite that differs from his program for the untutored masses. No one who knows his work could accuse him of being intellectually muddled. Cer-

22

tainly, no one who follows him closely through his struggles with the most difficult and challenging questions would accuse him of being intellectually dishonest. It is certainly true that he often sets forth a program for the philosophically naive that is different from that designed for highly trained, educated, and sophisticated minds.

In my opinion, however, this stance, with its social-political overtones, does not provide us with a proper account of Maimonides' method and goals. On many issues, he deliberately takes the position that opposed views may each have so much to recommend them that we must commit ourselves to both and hold them in a balanced dialectical tension. This makes inordinately heavy intellectual as well as emotional demands, but in Maimonides we have the classic model of how to meet those demands with the deepest insight and most rigorous intellectual care, and with elegance and grace. For him the choice is never between philosophy and science on the one side and Judaism and Torah on the other. His triumphant affirmation is that both sides legitimately claim our personal and intellectual loyalty and that both sides must reign simultaneously in our life and our thought. This solution is not, as the conventional accounts suggest, some sort of artificial synthesis of faith and reason. It is no such synthesis at all. Rather it is the affirmation of 'both/and' with the elements interpenetrating each other as far as legitimately possible and being held in balanced tension when that becomes necessary.

Let us consider one final question in this preliminary discussion of basic issues in the study of Maimonides. Granted that Maimonides is a difficult and puzzling writer who demands inordinate efforts of his readers, we certainly must ask whether such effort is justified for us today. Have we any reason, apart from pure historical curiosity or antiquarian interest, to study Maimonides with enthusiasm? Does his thought have any contribution to make to contemporary Judaism and to the resolution of the religious dilemmas of contemporary Western society? Is there at least some element of continuing relevance to general philosophic concerns or to specifically Jewish interests? These questions will be addressed more fully in the last chapter of this book. For the present we shall only survey the matter briefly.

The twelfth-century science on which Maimonides built many of his arguments is now out of date and, in certain respects, irrelevant. Traditionalists who are reluctant to admit that anything in Maimonides could be obsolete might take comfort from the fact that no less a rabbinic authority than Meir Leibush Malbim faced this issue squarely more than a century ago. In the introduction to his commentary on Ezekiel, Malbim discusses Maimonides' interpretation of the vision of the chariot in the first chapter of that book. As Malbim sees it, "Maimonides' interpretation has been refuted because the foundations on which he built it have been refuted. The astronomy, natural science, and ancient philosophy which were the foundations and supports of his interpretation have been completely undermined and destroyed by the scientific research which has developed in recent generations. This research has built its astronomy and structured its natural sciences on new foundations which are stronger and more reliable."[32]

We might well argue that not only Maimonides' science but also his philosophy and theology are completely obsolete. Recent philosophical developments in the Western world, especially logical positivism and linguistic analysis, cast grave doubts on the meaningfulness of many traditional philosophic questions and on the validity of their solutions. Similarly, the "new theology" claims to cut the ground out from under classical theological concerns and methods. What is left for a twelfth-century Jewish thinker to teach us today, if his science is wrong, and his philosophy and theology are open to the charge of meaninglessness or irrelevance?

One could certainly defend the view that the stance of contemporary philosophy is by no means the last word, and that there is much of continuing value in earlier metaphysical studies. However, to work out such a claim would require far more space than is available in this brief study. Abandoning that effort for the present, it will be more fruitful to concentrate on the significance of Maimonides for contemporary thought in the fields of ethics and the philosophy of religion, especially of Judaism. It seems to me clear that he has much of continuing interest and importance to teach us about these matters.

We can learn first, and most importantly, from Maimonides an uncompromising and fearless intellectual honesty in all matters having to do with religion. At a time when the forces of closed-minded intellectual timidity have managed to gain a position of some prominence in certain Jewish circles, the example of Maimonides is of great interest. While protecting the integrity of the system of Jewish law, he left room for the intellect to develop its own best understanding concerning the fundamental questions of faith. In his interpretation of the Bible he battled against literalist fundamentalism, finding his justification in the long-established tradition of nonliteral midrashic interpretation. The Law is necessarily fixed, because the integrity of society demands that the precepts of the Law must be obligatory. But the human effort to grasp the ultimate nature of things must, in Maimonides' view, never be totally constricted or suppressed. We can command patterns of behavior, and we rightly expect people to subordinate their private inclinations to legal norms. It is dangerous and self-defeating, however, to

32. Meir Leibush Malbim, *Commentary to Ezekiel* (Vilna, 1911), 3a.

24

command conformity in the formulation, understanding, or apprehending of ultimate philosophical or theological matters. Here the human mind must be left free to find its own way. If, by chance, we were to succeed in preventing people from thinking, we would also rob them of what is essential to their humanity. This is one of the topics we shall discuss more fully in the last chapter.

Just as we can profit from the model of Maimonides' intellectual openness, so can we learn much from him about the possibilities and the limits of reason in general. We can also profit from a careful consideration of the way in which he dealt with problems in ethical theory. These topics form the subjects of other sections of this study. The general question of what Maimonides has to say to our generation will be considered in our discussion of Maimonides and the challenge of modernity. In studying Maimonides properly we are engaged in more than a purely historical exercise. We open up valuable perspectives on some of the most aggravated problems of our own time. Moses Maimonides, when properly understood, is both one of the greatest teachers of Torah and a true guide of the perplexed.

2

The Range and Limits of Reason

One of the perennial problems in reading and understanding Maimonides is to determine the role of reason in his religious and philosophical thought. Much has been written on this subject, but very little that is well founded and helpful. Without a sound understanding of where Maimonides stands with respect to the role of reason, we risk overlooking critical moves that he makes, substituting preconceived ideas for careful study of the texts, and ending up with erroneous notions about his teachings. I shall, therefore, first survey the diverse accounts of this problem in the literature, and then turn to my own exposition of how Maimonides defines the role of reason in his philosophical understanding of religious faith.

We noted earlier that the famous Hebrew essayist, Aḥad Ha-ʿAm (the pen name of Asher Ginzberg), wrote an essay in observance of the seven hundredth anniversary of the death of Maimonides which he entitled "The Supremacy of Reason" (*Shilton ha-Sekhel*).[1] The deliberately chosen title accurately reflects his views about the place of reason in Maimonides' thought. For Aḥad Ha-ʿAm, reason and only reason is supreme in the works of Maimonides. In the thought of Maimonides, according to Aḥad Ha-ʿAm, "reason is the supreme judge; religion is absolutely subordinate to reason and cannot abrogate any of its decisions even in the smallest particular." He goes on to assert that Maimonides "did not stop short of the subjection of man—and of God, too, if one may say so—to the empire of sovereign reason. . . . One proof of reason is stronger than all the proofs of prophecy." In a brief, but intense, summary statement, he puts the matter this way: "Maimonides subordinated religion to reason. . . . From this point of view we may put the whole teaching of the *Guide* in a single sentence. Follow reason and reason only, he tells the 'perplexed', and interpret religion in conformity with reason: for to reason is the purpose of human life, and re-

1. *Aḥad Ha-ʿAm, Essays, Letters, Memoirs*, ed. and trans. Leon Simon (Oxford, 1946), 139–82. For the Hebrew, see *ʿAl Parashat Derakhim*, vol. 4 (Berlin, 1921), 1–37.

ligion is only a means to that end."[2] Although this may be the most extreme expression of this view, it is shared, in its essentials, by many other interpreters of Maimonides. Leo Strauss makes a particular point of opening his early study, *Philosophy and Law,* by noting that "according to Hermann Cohen, Maimonides is the 'classic of rationalism' in Judaism."[3] Careful attention must be given to the precise meaning that Cohen attached to this phrase, but this is not the place for that inquiry. What is of interest for us is that a professional philosopher of high rank seems to agree, in principle, with the judgment of Aḥad Ha-ʿAm.

It is not difficult to find examples of exactly the opposite view. One of the most striking, as we have already seen, is that presented by Aaron Kaminka, a well-known scholar of the late nineteenth and the first half of the twentieth century. In an essay written in connection with the world-wide celebration of the eight hundredth anniversary of the birth of Maimonides, Kaminka fiercely attacks Aḥad Ha-ʿAm's representation of Maimonides as someone who subordinates religion and all else to the rigorous demands of reason. Kaminka argues that the contrary is true. As he understands him, although Maimonides was an incomparable master of the science and philosophy of his time—disciplines in which the ultimate authority was reason—it was not science or reason which reigned supreme in his world, but religious faith. He subscribed above all to the sacred teachings of the Torah and found place for reason and its disciplines only insofar as they were consistent with and approved by the canons of religious faith.[4] Kaminka's way of understanding Maimonides is widespread, in particular among those who are anxious to defend Maimonides as a paragon of religious orthodoxy.

The citation of such sources gives evidence of widely differing ways of reading and understanding Maimonides, but it does very little to clarify the substantive issues. To discuss the subject fruitfully, we need first to clarify some major points. Just what is being asserted or denied when it is stated that Maimonides did or did not give absolute supremacy to reason? Furthermore, what are the philosophic and religious implications of one position or the other? Only after clarifying these issues can we hope to understand what Maimonides himself is saying on this subject. Until then, we shall not know how to go about reading Maimonides in a responsible way.

2. *Aḥad Ha-ʿAm, Essays, Letters, Memoirs,* ed. Simon, 158, 166, 172.

3. Leo Strauss, *Philosophy and Law* (Philadelphia, 1987), 3. For the original German, see Strauss, *Philosophie und Gesetz* (Berlin, 1935), 9.

4. Aaron Kaminka, "Ha-'Emunah veha-Bikkoret ha-Sikhlit be-Mif ʿalo shel ha-Rambam," *Ha'Aretz,* no. 4788 (5695), 17–18.

We should note first of all that the issue is formulated incorrectly. From the perspective of the history of philosophy it makes no sense to talk as if the options were either the absolute domination of reason or its absolute subordination. Even the most extreme rationalist is aware that there is a limit to the capacity of reason, and that there are some questions of the deepest interest and concern which reason cannot resolve. The same is true, incidentally, of the empiricist reliance on experience. Here too there are limits and a need to go beyond them. On the other hand, no one who seeks to deny the dominance of reason can ever do so completely; without the canons of reason operating at least implicitly in our thinking, no intelligible discourse is possible. For any sentence we speak to be intelligible to others, both speaker and hearers must take basic rules of reason for granted. If we do not, we are in a world in which nothing is fixed, nothing is stable, and nothing is intelligible.

Consider the case of classical rationalism. Its fundamental reliance on reason is meaningful only if it can transcend the limits of formal logic to tell us something we want to know about the world. Everyone acknowledges that logic depends on reason, that it is in fact the creation of reason. In the field of logic reason dominates absolutely. It is important to note that Maimonides set as a prerequisite for readers of his *Guide of the Perplexed* that they be fully trained in the fundamentals of logic. Logic is, however, only a tool for understanding the relationships between statements. It is purely formal and by itself tells us nothing about the world. We can determine with certainty that if two given propositions are true, and if they imply a certain conclusion, then that conclusion is also true. But logic alone can never establish the truth or falsity of the propositions themselves. When we assert, for example, in the standard textbook paradigm, that "all men are mortal" and that "Socrates is a man," we can be sure that it follows that "Socrates is mortal." This much we know by virtue of the formal relations of the propositions. What we do not know is whether it is true that all men are mortal or that Socrates is a man. Logic alone is insufficient to inform us. We need to appeal to some other reliable source for information about the mortality of all men and the humanity of Socrates.

Normally in a case like this, we would appeal to experience and to generalizations from experience. Yet classical rationalism always wanted to establish on a basis of reason not only our formal understanding of the relations of propositions to each other, but even more our knowledge of the way things really are in the world. This is to say that classical rationalism by its very nature is driven to carry the claims of reason and rational knowledge far beyond the limits of formal logic. For the major philosophers of the rationalist tradition, this goal is achieved by affirming certain fundamental claims about the world that are not derived from reason, but are rather an act of faith in the universal hegemony of reason.

Rationalist claims about the world rest on the affirmation that reality is itself a fully rational structure. Although this affirmation is not always explicit, it is certainly an implicit premise of all rationalist philosophies. For philosophers of this school, reason and reality are one or at least mirror each other. They hold that the real must be rational, and that the rational alone is real. The committed rationalist holds firmly to this position even when, as frequently happens, it leads to bizarre conclusions that run counter to all the evidence of our direct experience. Perhaps the point can be seen most clearly in the classic case of the paradoxes of Zeno.[5]

Although all of us, including presumably Zeno himself, regularly experience motion and change, Zeno denies that this common human experience gives us any knowledge of reality. In the real world, he argues, there is neither motion nor change, and therefore our experiences of the moving and the changing are illusory.

Let us take as an example just one of the paradoxes as it is formulated by an outstanding contemporary historian of Greek philosophy. He writes that "Zeno seems to have argued that an arrow which appears to be flying is really stationary because everything that occupies a space equal to itself must be at rest in that space, and at any given instant of its flight . . . an arrow can only occupy a space equal to itself; therefore at every instant of its flight it is motionless."[6] To reach such a counterintuitive conclusion and be able to affirm it as true, one must take the position that reason alone gives us a true understanding of reality. No set of sense experiences serves as sufficient ground for rejecting the conclusions of reason. Quite the contrary. Reason alone is determinative and, given the conclusions of reason, we can judge with total confidence that our sense experiences must be false or misleading. The arrow only appears to move, although in reality it does not. Reality must be distinguished from appearance, and the evidence of our senses must yield to the dictates of reason. What is neither questioned nor defended is the basic claim itself—namely, that reason alone is the key to a knowledge of reality. It might be said that this claim is affirmed as an act of

5. It is not necessary for our present purposes to determine if the paradoxes rest ultimately on an erroneous understanding of infinity, or if they are soluble. These questions have occupied students of these matters since classical antiquity, but they do not affect our present inquiry. We are interested in how a thinker like Zeno could hold to his seemingly strange position.

6. This is the formulation of the argument in W. K. C. Guthrie, *A History of Greek Philosophy*, vol. 2 (Cambridge, 1965), 93. For literature on Zeno see Guthrie's extended bibliographical note as well as his general bibliography.

faith, a faith held firmly despite the strange conclusions to which it some-times leads.

Even when the rule of reason leads to conclusions that are not offensive to our intuitive sense of how things really are, it can be shown easily that the rule rests on something other than reason itself. Consider the principle of noncontradiction, the most common and fundamental of all rational prin-ciples. It is normally taken to be not just a principle of logic, but a rule about how things must be in the world. That is to say, it is also a principle of on-tology. It asserts a doctrine that hardly anyone is inclined to deny—namely, that a given thing cannot be both P and not-P in the same respect and at the same time. Put differently, it is impossible for anything in the world to have simultaneously contradictory properties. In contrast with Zeno's paradoxes, this is a claim that easily commands our affirmation. We are all convinced that objects that are simultaneously all black and all white simply do not and cannot exist. There are no round squares in the world, or four-sided tri-angles. Nothing of that sort is possible in any world that the human mind might construct. So confident have we always been of these claims that me-dieval philosophers struggled mightily with the problem of whether an all-powerful God could make something with contradictory properties; they generally concluded that He could not. The usual way of expressing this idea is that what is logically impossible must be impossible in fact as well, even for God.

It appears that this claim about the world rests on a rule of reason. If we consider it carefully, however, we can see that we have no ground for con-cluding that this principle of logic is also a necessary truth about the nature and order of reality. In the last analysis the only reason we have for our confi-dence that the world must conform to our reason in this case is that we are incapable of conceiving or making sense of the alternative. Such alternate ideas, when expressed by a Lewis Carroll, charm us momentarily, but they do not command our assent. It may free the human imagination to say that you were so tired this morning that you got back into bed even before you got out, or that you hurried so fast that you met yourself coming around the cor-ner. We do not take such statements literally, precisely because we can form no idea of what they might actually be like in reality, or of the kind of world in which such things would make sense and be true.

What rule of reason, however, requires us to affirm that not only logic, but the world itself, is defined and determined by our reason? Is there any ground for the strongly and near-universally held view (at least in Western cultures) that, because the human intellect cannot conceive the existence of something possessing simultaneously contradictory properties, such exis-tence is necessarily impossible in reality? On what ground do we assume that the limits of the human mind are also the limits of reality? It is instructive to see that although we readily accept these limits as a negative and restrictive rule, we are generally reluctant to affirm its positive counterpart. We all are prepared to believe that what reason finds impossible—that is, the self-contradictory—cannot be the case in the world. We are far less certain that what reason finds logically necessary must be the case in the world.

The classic model is provided by philosophical reactions to proofs for the existence of God. Most modern philosophers are of the opinion that facts and states of affairs in the world are contingent, that is, that there are no necessary facts. From this it follows that there are no necessary existents, hence no God whose necessary existence can be known and demonstrated. The most instructive case is the resistance in the history of philosophy to the ontological proof for the existence of God. This proof argues from the claim that since I have an idea of the most perfect being it follows that this being must exist in reality. The ground of the argument is that a being that has every possible perfection including existence is more perfect than one that has every other perfection but lacks existence.

It is not our task to pursue the detailed analysis of the ontological argument, but we have here a paradigm case for testing the grounds on which rationalism rests. Carrying their rationalism to its final step, proponents of the ontological argument argue that if the idea of God's existence is a necessary idea in the human mind, then He must exist, since whatever is necessarily the case in the intellect must also necessarily be the case in reality. If we assert that there are things which we know necessarily cannot exist because the human mind finds them to be logically impossible, it seems at first to make equal sense to assert that there are things whose existence is necessary just because the human mind finds they are logically necessary. Yet the primary criticism of the ontological argument is that it makes the mistake of supposing that we can move from an idea in our mind to certainty about what must be the state of affairs in the world.

We see here that the doctrine that reason is an exact image of reality doesn't always work. We accept it when it agrees with our intuitive sense of what cannot be the case but are uneasy when it forces us to affirm something positive about the world. For the medievals, who believed that they had other fully valid proofs for the existence of God, rejecting the ontological argument did not necessarily have major consequences. Every other argument for the existence of God also asserts that what reason finds necessary must be the case in reality, since no philosophical argument rests on a claim of immediate, direct experience of God. It took the genius of Immanuel Kant to see that all proofs for the existence of God rest ultimately on the ontological argument. Thus, if we reject this foundational argument, as he did,

31

on the ground that we have no justification for supposing that any idea in our mind must be the case in reality, then we have made every other argument for the existence of God impossible.

If thinkers who hold this view would carry the logic of their own position forward, they would be forced to conclude as well that the law of noncontradiction need not apply to the world. It would then follow that although something is found to be logically impossible in our minds, we have no ground for concluding that such a thing cannot exist in reality. We all resist this mightily because its result would be chaos and the final bankruptcy of the intellect as a guide to reality. The idea that there is no necessary relationship between the human intellect and the order of the world generates chaos. It leaves us with the threat of never being sure that we know anything about anything beyond, possibly, our own immediate states of consciousness. An honest confrontation with the issues leads us to conclude that reason is indeed limited, and that we regularly transcend the limits because to do less would be intolerable. Maimonides provides us with a classic model of how to take reason to its farthest limits, how to recognize when we have reached them, and how to proceed at that point in a way that is intellectually honest and responsible while never failing to take the teachings of Judaism seriously.

It is worthwhile to take brief note of the fact that the problems of pure rationalism have their parallel in the structure of every attempt to establish a pure empiricism. David Hume, the classic model of the empiricist philosopher, taught us well that we cannot restrict ourselves to what we know from experience, despite his strong argument for the thesis that truths of reason are purely formal (or in Kantian terms, analytic) and that only experience gives us knowledge of matters of fact, that is, tells us about the world. A rigorous reliance on experience alone would leave us with a world of discrete and unconnected moments, and this could only be a world of unintelligible chaos. This is due to the fact that we have no experience of relations such as cause and effect—or of any other relations for that matter. Yet we regularly claim to have direct experience of such relations in our perceptions of the world, for without them there would be no intelligibility. Hume, however, argued that such relations are not known to us either by reason or by experience. He concluded that they are psychological constructs that we impose on our experiences, as a result of habit and built-in natural impulses, so that we can make experience coherent and stable.

The case of causal relations is the most instructive. Without such relations our experienced world would lack stability or reliability. To structure our experience and make it intelligible, we must not only remember the past and confront the immediate present, but also project into the future. Every scientific law rests on the confident premise that the future will resemble the past, as does every ordinary practical decision of the kind that we make in our daily lives. However, our assurance that there is a fixed order in the world that we can and do project into the future with confidence is neither a rule of reason nor a principle of experience. We affirm it as a necessary act of faith, because without it life would be unbearable. How would any of us live from one moment to the next without trusting in the reliability of our projections into the future? Such projections are presupposed by all the routine activities of our lives, to say nothing of the highly sophisticated work of scientists.

We are all secure in our convictions that the future will resemble the past, and that we can make reliable judgments about the future on the basis of our knowledge of the past, although we have no theoretical justification for this claim. Consider the implications of a phenomenon as commonplace as the standard tables of the times of sunrise and sunset for every day of the year, which are readily available for every area of the United States. These tables list the days from January 1 to December 31, but not the years. The compilers are certain, and so are we, that whether five years from now or fifty years from now, their tables will be accurate, and the sun will rise and set within milliseconds of the stated time on any given day. This is a classic example of how we transcend the limits of our empiricism just as we do those of our rationalism. In both cases we do what we must to preserve intelligibility and the practical conditions for living our lives.[7]

We can now see how unacceptable it is to speak loosely about the supremacy or subordination of reason in a thinker like Maimonides. A man of impeccable intellectual honesty, he was without peer in his acute under-

---

7. These subjects are discussed at length by Hume in his major philosophical works. The flavor of his discussions may be gained from a single passage. At the end of Book I of his *Treatise of Human Nature,* Hume makes the following observation. "After the most accurate and exact of my reasonings, I can give no reason why I shou'd assent to it; and feel nothing but a **strong** propensity to consider objects **strongly** in that view, under which they appear to me. Experience is a principle, which instructs me in the several conjunctions of objects for the past. Habit is another principle, which determines me to expect the same for the future; and both of them conspiring to operate on the imagination, make me form certain ideas in a more intense and lively manner, than others, which are not attended by the same advantages. Without this quality, by which the mind enlivens some ideas beyond others (which seemingly is so trivial, and so little founded on reason) we cou'd never assent to any argument, nor carry our view beyond those few objects, which are present to our senses. . . . The memory, senses, and understanding are, therefore, all of them founded on the imagination, or the vivacity of our ideas. No wonder a principle so inconstant and fallacious shou'd lead us into errors, when implicitly follow'd (as it must be) in all its variations." David Hume, *A Treatise of Human Nature,* ed. L. A. Selby-Bigge (Oxford, 1888), 265–66; cf. 633, 636.

standing of the issues before him and meticulously careful in his formulations. Only someone who fails to grasp both the complexity of the questions and Maimonides' depth as a thinker could suppose that he would resolve these problems with catchy slogans. Superbly sensitive to the methodological problems that he faced, Maimonides laid out for us an illuminating account of how to deal with them. He was committed to the principle that we must follow reason wherever it takes us, because intellectual honesty demands that we accept conclusions that reason has demonstrated to be true. He was often acerbic in his criticism of those who abandoned reason prematurely and contemptuous of those who thought it desirable to give pride of place to the irrational or the antirational. In an essay written late in life, he states his position against his opponents.

> Our effort and similarly the effort of the small number of wise [i.e., philosophically sophisticated] men is the exact opposite of that of the masses. The unreflective masses of the various religious communities find nothing, in their foolishness, which is more attractive and more satisfying than to conceive religion and reason as polar opposites which contradict each other. They account for all phenomena in a way that goes contrary to reason, and affirm that whatever occurs is a miracle. In this way they move as far away as possible from conceiving events as occurring within the order of nature, whether they be past events, about which we have been told, or events that are predicted to take place in the future. We, on the other hand, make every effort to unite religious teaching and reason. To the fullest extent possible we account for all events in the context of the order of nature. Only in those cases when we are taught explicitly that a particular event is a miracle and there is absolutely no possibility of giving any other account of it, only then do we feel forced to admit that it is a miracle.[8]

We see here the extent to which Maimonides gives priority to the rational and the natural. The principle is clear. We do not appeal to the supernatural or to the irrational until we have reached the point where we have no option. Yet Maimonides never tires of reminding us that there are limits to the capacity of human reason because it is finite and imperfect. Even though we recognize clearly that human reason cannot deal with all our concerns, it does not follow that when reason fails us, we can always choose to be agnostic. On

---

8. Moses Maimonides, "Treatise on Resurrection," in *'Iggerot ha-Rambam,* ed. Y. Kafih (Jerusalem, 1972), 87–88. For a less literal English version see A. Halkin and D. Hartman, *Crisis and Leadership: Epistles of Maimonides* (Philadelphia, 1985), 223.

the contrary, there are questions of an urgent nature about which we cannot choose to remain neutral. Sometimes these questions are of such importance to us that we feel forced to take a stand on them. Other times, not taking a stand is already to declare oneself on one side or the other of the issue. At this point reason must transcend itself; its demands force us to go beyond the limits of reason and to base ourselves on some other ground. For Maimonides this other ground is generally religion or, to be more precise, revelation. There are circumstances where it is not only legitimate to go beyond reason in this way, but even necessary and inescapable. Intellectual responsibility requires, however, that we shall always be controlled by one principle. We may go beyond reason when this is intellectually justified, but even then we may never take a position contrary to reason.

We can now readily see that the issue for Maimonides is not at all a matter of the exclusive supremacy of reason, or of religion, or of some other source of truth. His is rather a delicately balanced stance which affirms the claims of both reason and revelation, each in its proper sphere. Reason is supreme within the limits in which it can work authoritatively. No claims of revelation, no body of dogmas, no set of ideas or practices, even when supported by deeply rooted conventions, can supplant or be allowed to take precedence over reason and the insights to which it leads us. We must be open to the results of reason, whatever they may be and wherever they may lead. There is, however, a limit on the capacity of human reason, and there are questions to which our reason, operating exclusively by its own powers, cannot give us answers. At this point, where rational inquiry and demonstration have been pushed to their outer limit, every person is forced to appeal to some other source of truth. Even then reason still continues to exercise an important degree of control, because neither religion nor any other source of truth is acceptable if it forces us to affirm doctrines directly contrary to reason.[9]

Almost fifty years ago Simon Rawidowicz offered a somewhat different account of the limits of reason in Maimonides. His stress is not on the

9. This exposition of the position of Maimonides is very close in certain ways to that which was set forth by Leo Strauss in his early work. While I believe that Strauss continued to hold this position to the end, it becomes less and less explicit in his later writings on Maimonides. In *Philosophy and Law,* he states the point with admirable clarity: "There can only be an *interest* in revelation if one *needs* it. The philosopher needs revelation if he knows that his capacity for knowledge is in principle inadequate to know *the* truth. The conviction of the inadequacy of human reason to know *the* truth, i.e., the decisively important truth, is the condition of possibility for a philosopher's having an interest as a philosopher in revelation. The classic of Jewish rationalism in the Middle Ages, Maimonides, is imbued with this conviction" (44; see the continuing discussion through p. 49).

formal limits of claims to rational knowledge, but rather on the fact that, in Maimonides' thought, reason seeks to transcend itself by transforming itself into a deeply passionate search for and attachment to God. "If Maimonides' *'aql* [reason] were the *ratio* of the super-rationalist, as he is commonly described, it would never have been able to grow so infinitely from itself and to expand so as to conquer man and the universe, to surpass all the natural limits of 'rational' knowledge as to *turn* into *love* and 'passionate desire', as well as into an extraordinary dynamic link between God and man."[10]

This is a useful and perceptive extension of the points we have just made about the place of reason in the thought of Maimonides. Particularly instructive is Rawidowicz's subsequent observation that scholarly study of the thought of Maimonides will not take readily to claims that he limits the role of reason, no matter how well these claims are documented. He notes: "While this trend to re-discover the non-rationalistic elements of Maimonides' philosophy, or at least to keep the proper balance between the various motives in his system, in order to free it from a too one-sided rationalistic interpretation, may gain ground in the field of the history of Jewish philosophy, it will probably for a long time to come have to reckon with strong resistance. For Maimonides' 'rationalism' is too established an axiom—from the older generation till Samuel David Luzzatto on the one hand and Aḥad HaʿAm and his followers on the other—to yield its ground, or even to accept its modifications."[11] The trend of much Maimonidean scholarship since these words were written supports this prediction.

The issue has arisen again in a debate between two of the most respected contemporary scholars in the field of medieval Jewish philosophy. Raising the debate to a much higher level of technical philosophic discourse, they provide us with some reason to think that we may have moved beyond the period of narrow vision to which Rawidowicz referred. Shlomo Pines and Alexander Altmann take positions that are opposed, but not completely contradictory.[12] Pines is convinced—contrary, it would seem, to some of his own earlier views—that Maimonides limits human knowledge to what

10. Simon Rawidowicz, "On Maimonides' *Sefer Ha-Maddaʿ*," in *Essays in Honour of the Very Rev. Dr. J. H. Hertz,* ed. I. Epstein, E. Levine, and C. Roth, (London, 1942), 331. Reprinted in Rawidowicz, *Studies in Jewish Thought* (Philadelphia, 1974), 317.

11. Rawidowicz, "On Maimonides' *Sefer Ha-Maddaʿ*," in *Essays,* ed. Epstein et al., 332; Rawidowicz, *Studies,* 317–18.

12. See Shlomo Pines, "The Limitations of Human Knowledge According to Al-Farabi, ibn Bajja, and Maimonides," in *Studies in Medieval Jewish History and Literature,* ed. Isadore Twersky (Cambridge, Mass., 1979), 82–109, and Alexander Altmann, "Maimonides on the Intellect and the Scope of Metaphysics," in *Von der mittelalterlichen zur modernen Aufklärung* (Tübingen, 1987), 60–129.

Pines calls "terrestrial physics" while denying human beings any possible knowledge of the higher levels of being that are the subject of "celestial physics and metaphysics." This leads him to conclude that for Maimonides "the existence of the separate intellects is merely probable and . . . no way has been found to attain certainty with regard to this matter." He also recognizes that Maimonides holds that "human reason is incapable of discovering the truth" concerning the question whether the world is eternal or was created in time.[13] In his response Altmann takes issue with some of the conclusions that Pines draws concerning the significance of these limits of human knowledge for the definition of the ultimate end of humankind.

Pines supposes that we can conclude that Maimonides did not genuinely believe in the possibility of the human soul apprehending the highest metaphysical truths. Consequently he infers that the usual ideas about Maimonides' conceptions of the aim of human life and the nature of immortality are simply wrong. Even while vigorously denying these claims of Pines, Altmann is largely in agreement with Pines that for Maimonides there are limits to the capacity of the human intellect to know reality.[14]

Despite the recent work of Altmann and Pines, the widespread failure to recognize Maimonides' rigorous awareness of the limits of reason continues to be one of the mysteries of the history of Jewish philosophy. Maimonides, however, was clear and explicit about this matter, and one has only to read what he wrote in order to have a sound grasp of his position. Moreover, anyone who pays careful attention not only to what he wrote but to what he actually did as a philosopher will emerge with a full and clear picture. Let us first see what he himself said about this subject. In I, 31 of the *Guide*, he begins his discussion with the following statement:

> Know that the human intellect has objects of apprehension that it is within its power and according to its nature to apprehend. On the other hand, in that which exists there also are existents and matters that, according to its nature, it is not capable of apprehending in any way or through any cause; the gates of apprehension are shut before it. . . . Man's intellect indubitably has a limit at which it stops.

13. Pines, "Limitations," in *Studies,* ed. Twersky, 94, 97.

14. Altmann, "Maimonides on the Intellect," 110–11, 114, 117. We shall have occasion in later chapters to address extensively some of the specific topics that have been mentioned in connection with the Pines/Altmann debate. At present, it is sufficient to record that in their most recent work both scholars have taken note of the limits of reason in the philosophy of Maimonides. They have not, however, undertaken to explore the significance of Maimonides' position as a general framework for his thought. The remainder of this chapter will address this question.

There are therefore things regarding which it has become clear to
man that it is impossible to apprehend them (I, 31, p. 65).

This statement alone should be sufficient to make clear that Maimonides has
no doubt at all that human reason has limits and that it is important for us to
know just what those limits are.

Maimonides goes on to caution that "you should let your intellect move
about only within the domain of things that man is able to grasp. For in regard to matters that it is not in the nature of man to grasp, it is, as we have
made clear, very harmful to occupy oneself with them" (I, 32, pp. 69–70). It
is true, as Maimonides points out, that the emphasis on the limits of the
human intellect and the caution that it is important for us to know those limits
are already expressed in Scripture. He makes a particular point, however, of
bringing to our attention that this is not the controlling consideration for him.
"Do not think that what we have said with regard to the insufficiency of the
human intellect and its having a limit at which it stops is a statement made in
order to conform to Law. For it is something that has already been said and
truly grasped by the philosophers without their having concern for a particular doctrine or opinion" (I, 31, p. 67).[15] It is not primarily a matter of
religious dogma, but simply sound philosophy to know and have regard for
the limits of human reason.

To see and understand the full force and significance of the limits that
Maimonides imposes on reason, we must pay attention to the immense range
of authority that he gives to reason. One of the most difficult problems he,
along with all other students of the Bible, faces is the question of how to
understand biblical statements that speak about God as having corporeal
properties. From our current perspective, in which we take for granted the
notion that God has no physical properties whatsoever, it is not easy to understand a religious situation in which divine corporeality was in some
circles a respectable doctrine. The main source of uncertainty on this issue
arises from the corporeal language that the Bible frequently employs in what
would today be called God-talk.

Maimonides considered it to be one of his major responsibilities to root
out every vestige of corporeality in the Jewish way of understanding and

15. Similar points are made elsewhere in the *Guide* and in some of Maimonides' other
writings. An example of how these ideas are set forth in explicit language can be found in
Maimonides' letter to R. Ḥisdai Halevi, where he says: "I hold that the human intellect has a
fixed limit. So long as the soul is in the body, it is incapable of knowing that which is beyond the
sphere of nature [i.e., ultimate metaphysical truths]. Because the soul is embedded in the natural world, it is not able to see and apprehend beyond that world" (*Kovetz Teshuvot ha-Rambam
ve-'Iggerotav*, II, 23b).

thinking about God. In his view the theological error of those who believe that God is a body or has bodily properties is the most dangerous of all the errors we might make in our beliefs about God. He judges it to be even worse than idolatry. In his account of idolatry, he asserts that its error lies in the conviction that an idol is worthy of worship because "of its being an image of a thing that is an intermediary between ourselves and God," and not in the idol worshipper thinking that the idol is actually God. Perhaps Maimonides had an excessively favorable judgment of human intelligence, but it was, nevertheless, his stated view that, "in fact, no human being of the past has ever imagined on any day, and no human being of the future will ever imagine, that the form that he fashions either from cast metal or from stone and wood has created and governs the heavens and the earth" (I, 36, p. 83).[16] Yet even though they do believe in the existence of God, the error of the idolaters is so grave, they deserve to be put to death. "What then should be the state of him whose infidelity bears upon His essence, may He be exalted, and consists in believing Him to be different from what He really is? I mean to say that he does not believe that He exists; or believes that there are two gods, *or that He is a body. . . . Such a man is indubitably more blameworthy than a worshipper of idols* who regards the latter as intermediaries" (I, 36, p. 84; emphasis added). We see here the inordinate gravity with which Maimonides viewed even the smallest suggestion of corporeality with respect to God.

It is understandable that, with such a strong view about the extreme danger of the belief in divine corporeality, Maimonides would do everything in his power to root out this belief. So strong was his certainty that he formally classified as a heretic anyone who acknowledges the existence of only one sovereign being but affirms nevertheless that this being has a body and a physical form.[17] His critic, Rabad, in a frequently cited gloss to this passage, challenges this decision and says that "greater and better men than he [i.e., Maimonides], have accepted this doctrine" because of the way in which they understood scriptural statements and midrashic statements about God. Rabad certainly did not support the corporeal theory of the divine nature, but he was sensitive to the fact that anyone reading Scripture in a straightforward literal fashion could readily come to this conclusion.[18]

16. See also the account of the origin and nature of idolatry set forth by Maimonides in *H. 'Avodat Kokhavim*, I, 1, 2.

17. *H. Teshuvah*, III, 7.

18. It should be noted that there are variant readings of this Rabad gloss which temper somewhat the acerbic language, but they do not affect any substantive issues. That the threat of views concerning divine corporeality was real is evident from more than the comment of Rabad. Maimonides saw the widespread interest in *Shi'ur Komah* as a serious threat to correct doctrine

This is one of the important reasons that Maimonides is so greatly concerned in the *Guide* with teaching us how to read Scripture properly. On what did he base his certainty concerning the incorporeality of God, and how did he then deal with the plain language of Scripture? The key is, of course, that one must not read anthropomorphic passages literally. But how do we justify this rule, and how do we decide which passages to read literally and which figuratively or in some other nonliteral mode? What is the decisive evidence that establishes the correctness of the method and the conclusions of Maimonides' nonliteralist way of understanding biblical statements about God's bodily features?

Rabad was confident that Maimonides' conclusions were correct, but he felt a strong and protective sympathy for those sincere souls who remained with a literal reading of the biblical text. For Maimonides, however, the matter can be settled finally and definitively only by an appeal to reason. His guiding rule is that what reason finds incorrect and unacceptable cannot be the meaning of Scripture, no matter what it appears to say. In a move not unlike that of Zeno and the whole classical rationalist tradition, he in effect asserts that what reason finds to be impossible cannot be the case in scriptural reality. It follows that when Scripture speaks of the ultimate reality, it cannot intend to do so in a way that is a profound offense to human reason, because this would constitute an intolerable philosophical and theological error.

He argues the matter explicitly right at the beginning of the *Mishneh Torah*. Having established the existence of God as the fundamental principle of Judaism, he goes on to affirm that the doctrine of the absolute and unique unity of this God is necessarily true. He then shows that reason forces us to conclude that such a unity could in no way be a corporeal entity, because multiplicity is built into the very nature of the corporeal.

> This God is One. He is not two, nor more than two, but One; so that none of the things existing in the universe to which the term one is applied is like unto His Unity; neither such a unit as a species which comprises many units (e.g., sub-species), nor such a unit as a physical body which consists of parts and dimensions. His Unity is such that there is no other Unity like it in the world.
>
> If there were plural deities, these would be physical bodies; because entities, that can be enumerated and are equal in their essence, are

and therefore felt it necessary to attack the authenticity of this work against the views of a number of distinguished figures who accepted it, including Saadia Gaon, Judah Halevi, Abraham ibn Ezra, and others. One can also find many grossly anthropomorphic passages in the literature of the Hasidei Ashkenaz.

only distinguishable from each other by the accidents that happen to physical bodies. If the Creator were a physical body, He would have bounds and limits, for it is impossible for a physical body to be without limits.

That the Holy One, blessed be He, is not a physical body, is explicitly set forth in the Pentateuch and in the Prophets, as it is said "[Know therefore] that the Lord, He is God in Heaven above, and upon the Earth beneath" (Deut. 4:39); and a physical body is not in two places at one time.

Since this is so, what is the meaning of the following expressions found in the Torah: "Beneath his feet" (Ex. 24:10); "Written with the finger of God" (Ex. 31:18); "The hand of God" (Ex. 9:3); "The eyes of God" (Gen. 38:7); "The ears of God" (Num. 11:1); and similar phrases? All these expressions are adapted to the mental capacity of the majority of mankind who have a clear perception of physical bodies only. The Torah speaks in the language of men. All these phrases are metaphorical.

Since it has been demonstrated that He is not a body, it is clear that none of the accidents of matter can be attributed to Him.

This being so, the expressions in the Pentateuch and books of the Prophets already mentioned, and others similar to these, are all of them metaphorical and rhetorical.[19]

We have here a classic model of how Maimonides employs and gives authority to reason. To him it is eminently clear that if the sheer logic of the situation excludes even the possibility that God might have corporeal qualities, then it follows necessarily that He cannot and does not have such qualities. Consequently, we must read whatever Scripture seems to say literally in such a way as to conform with the requirements of reason. To do otherwise in this case is for Maimonides an instance of outright heresy.

This reliance on reason is underscored in his statement that Scripture states "explicitly" that God is not a physical body. The evidence he presents is not an explicit statement in Scripture, but a logical inference. Scripture says that God is in the heavens above and upon the earth below, but since no body can be in two places simultaneously, it follows that God is not a body. The rule of reason determines what Scripture must be saying. It is particularly striking that he treats the consequence of interpreting a scriptural statement in accordance with the demands of reason as if this were an ex-

19. *H. Yesodei ha-Torah*, I, 7, 8, 9, 11, 12. Moses Maimonides, *Mishneh Torah, The Book of Knowledge*, trans. Moses Hyamson (Jerusalem, 1965).

plicit statement in the text itself. For Maimonides it is evidently the case that whatever reason requires is what we must understand Scripture to be saying.

Another remarkable instance of his assigning such priority to reason should be enough to establish beyond any doubt the critically important role that reason plays in the system of Maimonides. Among the most aggravated questions with which he deals is the problem of whether the world is eternal, as the Aristotelians teach, or was created out of nothing by God, as many religious doctrines teach.[20] After having examined the arguments on both sides of the question, Maimonides concludes that neither the eternalists nor the creationists are able to demonstrate their thesis. In fact, he is convinced that this question is, in principle, incapable of a philosophically satisfactory solution. For this reason he considers it both desirable and justifiable to decide between these alternatives on nonphilosophical grounds. Yet he is deeply concerned that some of his readers may mistakenly suppose that he has abandoned reason in favor of a literal reading of Scripture. To prevent anyone from making this mistake, he says:

> Know that our shunning the affirmation of the eternity of the world is not due to a text figuring in the Torah according to which the world has been produced in time. For the texts indicating that the world has been produced in time are not more numerous than those indicating that the deity is a body. Nor are the gates of figurative interpretation shut in our faces or impossible of access to us regarding the subject of the creation of the world in time. For we could interpret them as figurative, as we have done when denying His corporeality. Perhaps this would even be much easier to do: we should be very well able to give a figurative interpretation of those texts and to affirm as true the eternity of the world, just as we have given a figurative interpretation of those other texts and have denied that He, may He be exalted, is a body (II, 25, pp. 327–28).

Why then does Maimonides not opt for the eternity thesis which would keep him in line with the scientific world view of the Aristotelians which he so much admires? Only for one philosophical reason, as he himself tells us: "That the deity is not a body has been demonstrated. . . . However, the eternity of the world has not been demonstrated" (II, 25, pp. 327–28).[21]

---

20. This problem is fully discussed in chapter 10. Here we consider only that aspect which is directly relevant to the subject of our present discussion.

21. In II, 23, p. 322, he puts it this way: "Do not turn away from the opinion according to which the world is new, except because of a demonstration. Now such a demonstration does not exist in nature."

According to his own testimony, if reason required it, that is to say, if it had been demonstrated, he would feel constrained to affirm the thesis of the eternity of the world. Furthermore, his general rule would then apply, and he would read the scriptural account of creation figuratively so as to conform to the teachings of reason. Since, however, there is no rational demonstration for the eternity thesis, he cannot be bound by a nonexistent rule of reason in this particular case. Recognizing that the Aristotelian version of the eternity doctrine would have disastrous consequences for Jewish religion, he affirms the doctrine of creation. He can do so only because the limits of reason leave the question open. It would be interesting to consider how Maimonides might have dealt with the religious problem confronting him if there were, in fact, a rational demonstration of the eternity of the world, but that would take us too far beyond the boundaries of our present discussion. At this point, however, it is important for us to see that he gives extraordinary force to the claims of reason even in those cases where he finally must decide that reason has nothing to say.

This positive emphasis on the sovereignty of reason is balanced, as we have already seen, by a careful exposition of the limits of reason. It is by no means true that human reason is always adequate for dealing with all questions that come before us for judgment and decision. Maimonides is just as vigorous and clear-headed in setting forth the limits of reason as he is in affirming its dominance within its proper sphere. His basic stance, as we have argued, is to confront the dialectical tension of affirming 'both/and' rather than 'either/or'. The affirmation both of the claims of reason and, at the same time, of that which stands beyond reason but still commands our assent requires a conscious effort to maintain a proper, although tense, balance. Much of my later discussion seeks to illustrate that the stance of Maimonides with respect to the role of reason is the model for the way in which he deals with a variety of topics in his systematic thought. However, it will be profitable even at this point to pursue the subject a bit further in a general way.

We see that, in confronting the question of divine corporeality, Maimonides was able to reach a firm conclusion even against the seemingly literal testimony of Scripture. As long as he had a sound rational demonstration that God cannot have bodily properties, the matter for him was settled absolutely. In contrast, the question of the eternity of the world or its creation could not be settled by reason at all. In this instance he takes a position on other grounds, while acknowledging that if reason were able to settle this question, he would follow its lead without hesitation. In both cases he takes a strong fixed position. In one instance, reason alone is his guide, and he requires the text of Scripture to be understood in accordance with the canons of the teachings of reason. In the other instance, reason cannot help him so he is guided by the seemingly plain meaning of the scriptural text.[22] He does not always come to such a firm conclusion. On some subjects he says openly that his own formulation is the best he can offer, but he adds that the door must remain open for others to find their own way of understanding the subject.

In this instance we have to distinguish between beliefs that are necessary for the preservation of Jewish religion, and thus of Jewish society, and beliefs about which we can permit and even encourage openness. Maimonides allows very little flexibility in the understanding of the halakhah, but permits considerable latitude in certain matters of doctrine. Even with respect to the latter, however, the crucial distinction is between the areas of necessary belief that cannot be left free, and the other topics that are open. The contrast is instructive. Maimonides took a step without precedent in Jewish religious thought when he set forth a list of articles of faith and proclaimed them obligatory for all Jews.[23] He then applied the full rigor of the law to this formulation and proclaimed the legal decision that belief in these articles was to be the criterion for determining whether or not a person was part of the community of Israel. Maimonides ruled that, even though he transgresses the law in other regards, a Jew who is firm in his belief in these articles is a full member of the Jewish people. He may well be a sinner, but there is no question about his belonging within *kelal yisrael* (the community of Israel). One who is in doubt about any one of these articles, to say nothing of one who denies any article directly, is explicitly excluded from *kelal yisrael*. He is a heretic whom one should despise and reject.[24]

Within the *Commentary on the Mishnah,* in which Maimonides has set forth this unyielding formulation of prescribed articles of faith, we also find him addressing issues of belief with openness and flexibility. In commenting

22. I am fully aware that many contemporary students of Maimonides do not believe that these matters can be dealt with in such a simple and straightforward way. They believe that an esoteric doctrine with respect to the eternity of the world hides beneath the surface teaching. I shall address this question in chapter 10, on the problem of creation and eternity. For our present purposes at this stage of our discussion, I believe that the formulation I have offered can stand.

23. For the most comprehensive discussion of the entire subject, see Menachem Kellner, *Dogma in Medieval Jewish Thought* (Oxford, 1986). In his introduction, Kellner states, "Maimonides was the first non-Karaite Jewish author systematically, self-consciously, and explicitly to posit specific beliefs which all Jews *qua* Jews had to accept."

24. *Commentary to the Mishnah,* Introduction to *Sanhedrin,* chap. 10 (*Perek Ḥelek*). The most reliable Hebrew translation is in the edition of Y. Kafih (Jerusalem, 1964). For English translations, see *A Maimonides Reader,* ed. Isadore Twersky, (New York, 1972), 422, and Kellner, *Dogma,* 16. This is not the place for a discussion of the problem concerning the status Maimonides assigned to these articles of faith in his later thought. Kellner provides an extended discussion and a comprehensive bibliography on this subject.

on a Mishnah in which there is debate about who will have a place in the world to come, Maimonides chooses not to take a stand among the conflicting views of the Sages. Instead he says, "I have mentioned to you a number of times that when there is any division of opinion among the Sages which does not affect any rule of practice, but is concerned exclusively with establishing an understanding of a point of doctrine, there is no need to decide in accordance with any one of them."[25]

The articles of faith are prescribed, but much else is open. In some cases the articles of faith are prescribed because they are rationally demonstrated propositions; in other cases, because they are expressly taught in the revelation in Scripture. Examples of the former are the existence of God, His unity, and His incorporeality. Examples of the latter are the days of the Messiah and the resurrection of the dead. In formulating this creedal statement, Maimonides applies a fixed and rigorous rule that determines which beliefs are necessary and thus absolutely mandatory. He also determines that a great many other matters of belief have the sanction neither of reason nor of revelation; in these cases he holds that individuals should be free to apply their own best understanding to the matter and reach their own conclusions.

When we are dealing with beliefs that are either rationally certain and/or necessary conditions for the survival of the community of Jewish faith, Maimonides considers it legitimate and desirable to impose them, even by the most forceful exercise of authority. In the case of the destructive doctrine of divine corporeality, for example, it is his view that, if rational argument fails to convince, then one should use the weight of superior authority with no hesitation. "For just as it behooves to bring up children in the belief, and to proclaim to the multitude, that God, may He be magnified, is one and that none but He ought to be worshipped, so it behooves that they should be made to accept on traditional authority the belief that God is not a body." He goes on to say that we should set forth the arguments and engage in the exposition of Scripture as far as this can be successful in any given setting. "If, however, someone's mind fails to understand the interpretation of the texts . . . he should be told: The interpretation of this text is understood by the men of knowledge" (I, 35, pp. 79–80, 81).

We have here a balanced tension between necessary beliefs that are to be imposed from above, if need be, and the whole range of beliefs that Maimonides treats as open to a variety of views. The major task is to determine which beliefs are necessary and to establish criteria for that necessity.

25. *Sanhedrin*, 10:3. It should be noted that this statement occurs in the commentary to the same chapter in which the rule about the articles of faith is set forth. See also the commentary to *M. Sotah*, 3:3 and *M. Shevu'ot*, 1:4 for similar statements.

This is a project in which he was engaged, in one fashion or another, throughout his life. From his early work in the Mishnah commentary until some of his last writings, he never turned away completely from concern with the formulation of a balanced tension between officially prescribed doctrines and freedom of thought. This preoccupation, in turn, was one aspect of the tension between his submission to the sovereignty of reason and his legitimate need to transcend the limits of reason. This situation has its parallel in the tension between the range and the limits of revelation, between the authority of revelation and its restraints.

In closing this discussion, we note that there are several areas of Maimonides' thought in which his teachings should be understood and interpreted in the light of this balanced tension between the opposed poles. This is the case with respect to much of his ethical theory. It is also true with respect to such important metaphysical issues as his treatment of divine causality, his treatment of prayer, and his treatment of the problem of creation vs. eternity which we have already considered briefly.[26] Nothing could be more misleading than to view Maimonides either as submitting exclusively to reason or as making religion (i.e., revelation) the sole and independent criterion of truth. Neither view is correct, and to hold to either view is to assure a misreading of Maimonides. Yet I am not suggesting that Maimonides offers us some kind of artificial synthesis of reason and revelation. This well-known textbook description of his method is a serious misreading. Maimonides is a thinker of absolute intellectual integrity and remarkable depth and clarity who struggles with the most complex questions. He is not ready to settle for externally imposed syntheses, and he is not prepared to affirm that he knows more than he does. He gives us, through his struggles, a classic and deeply moving paradigm of how one can be both a true philosopher and a faithful Jew. He yields to no one in his commitment to rational truth. He yields to no one in his discovery of the limits of reason. What he teaches us is how a single human being can encompass multiple worlds with uncompromising loyalty to each.

26. Each of these subjects will be discussed extensively in later chapters of this book.

3

The Esoteric Method

In the previous chapters we considered certain elements of the method for reading Maimonides well. We showed that no one can read and understand Maimonides properly who does not take into account the many facets of his work and thought. To try to reduce Maimonides to a single monochromatic plane is almost certainly to misrepresent him. The richness of texture that characterizes all his work, along with the range and complexity of the ideas and arguments, must always be in the center of the reader's awareness. We have shown that this is especially true with regard to the question of the role and authority of reason in Maimonides' thought. As we saw, it is a major error to assume, as some commentators have, that he gives exclusive dominance to reason or subordinates it totally to the demands of religion. Even forearmed with these cautions, the reader still confronts the unusual demands made by the works of Maimonides, particularly the *Guide of the Perplexed*. This book, as we have seen, is no ordinary work. It cannot be read as a simple, straightforward piece of philosophical discourse. In this chapter we turn to a study of how certain prominent contemporary scholars go about teaching us to read Maimonides.

Shlomo Pines and the late Leo Strauss have each contributed important studies on various aspects of Maimonides' thought, with Strauss concentrating in particular on the problem of how to read the *Guide*. They joined together in a most fruitful way to produce a new English version of the *Guide*, with Pines doing the translation and Strauss contributing an important introductory essay.[1] In reading the *Guide*, it is imperative not only to use a well-recommended translation, but to be aware of how much difference the translation can make in our conception of the work and in what we find in it. We shall study the Pines translation briefly to see how much our understanding of the text is affected by the quality of the translation we use. Even the

---

1. Moses Maimonides, *The Guide of the Perplexed*, trans. Shlomo Pines, with introductory essay by Leo Strauss (Chicago: University of Chicago Press, 1963). All citations of the *Guide* in the present book are to this edition; see chapter 1, note 6.

best translation is not a fully satisfactory substitute for the original, yet the simple reality is that most contemporary readers of Maimonides do not have access to the Arabic original, or even to the medieval or modern Hebrew translations. In the case of the *Guide of the Perplexed,* we face the added problem of the inordinate complexity of the work itself. Even if we use as good a translation as one can hope to have, or better yet, if we read the book in the original Arabic, we will still face the problem of how to understand such an esoteric text.

The publication in 1963 of Pines' new English translation of Maimonides' *Guide of the Perplexed* was an event of major importance to students of medieval philosophy and Jewish thought. The translation and the Strauss essay have set a standard against which to measure all other translations and aids to the study of the *Guide.* By common consent Maimonides is recognized as the greatest and most original of the medieval Jewish philosophers. Yet until the appearance of the Pines translation, his major work had been largely inaccessible to those without a command of Arabic and Hebrew, particularly to those who read only English. The *Guide* had been translated earlier into a number of other modern languages, most notably into French by Solomon Munk. Until the appearance of the Pines version, Munk's translation was by far the most responsible one in a modern language, and it still deserves to be studied seriously. Most of the other translations suffer from defects that distort the book and make it unintelligible.[2] These defects result in part from the translators' inadequate command of the necessary languages, and at least as much from their failure to understand in any depth the work that they were translating. As Pines puts it, "the *Guide* belongs to a very peculiar literary genre, of which it is the unique specimen."[3] Although Maimonides himself makes this eminently clear, most translators treat the *Guide* as if it were an ordinary book, with the inevitable consequence that both they and their readers are misled. Their translations are insensitive to both the nuances of the text and the overriding need for complete precision and accuracy in the translation. For a work of this kind, paraphrases simply will not do, nor are loose translations of common or technical terms acceptable. Pines approached his task with a superb

---

2. *Le Guide des Égarés par Moïse ben Maimon dit Maïmonide,* trans. S. Munk, 3 vols. (Paris, 1856; rpt. 1960). The two medieval Hebrew translations are in a special category which we do not take up here. The translation of Samuel ibn Tibbon, in particular, approximates the Arabic very closely and is indispensable for serious students of the *Guide.* My remarks about the Pines translation are directed particularly to readers who have neither sufficient Arabic nor Hebrew to manage on their own.

3. Pines, Introduction to Maimonides, *Guide,* trans. Pines, lxxix.

mastery of both the language and the contents of the text, and he made special efforts to note and take account of the peculiarities of this remarkable piece of esoteric writing.

We shall first discuss the Pines translation in order to understand how significantly it affects the possibility of reading the *Guide* with insight and intelligent appreciation. We shall then turn to an examination of the introductory essay by Strauss as the most important and influential model of a contemporary guide to the study of Maimonides. This will lead to an exposition of some of my own proposals for how to deal with the Maimonidean text.

The translation now available to us is so far superior that it should permanently replace that of Friedländer.[4] No translation can ever be a fully adequate substitute for the original text, but Pines' rendition of Maimonides' *Guide* comes as close to this aim as anyone could hope. He has managed to be remarkably faithful to Maimonides, avoiding the strong temptations to improve or emend which ensnare so many translators. Pines' intention was that his "translation should remain as close as is practicable to the original," and he has succeeded admirably. Where Maimonides is obscure, the translation deliberately reproduces the obscurity, and where Maimonides is awkward or ambiguous, the translation is equally so. Pines holds correctly that Maimonides wrote exactly as he intended, and that the English reader should be offered the book that Maimonides wrote, not a translator's revision of it. Neither felicity of style nor seeming clarity of thought were Pines' controlling purposes. He sought accuracy above all, and he achieved it.

The quality and significance of Pines' superb translation can only be fully appreciated when it is compared carefully with the earlier English translation by M. Friedländer that began to appear in 1881 and was long considered the standard English version of the *Guide of the Perplexed*. Some examples will show how far students have been misled when they have been forced to rely on Friedländer. His version adds phrases not in the original, drops phrases present in the original, misconstrues key passages, and mistranslates key terms. We can see here both the great value of Pines' work and the extent to which readers of a translation are at the mercy of the translator, particularly if they have no access to the original to check the text. The following examples, chosen from the Introduction and Part I of the *Guide,* are typical of what one finds throughout. They permit a useful comparison of the Pines (P) and Friedländer (F) translations.[5]

---

4. Moses Maimonides, *The Guide for the Perplexed,* trans. M. Friedländer, 2nd ed., rev., 7th impression (London and New York, 1942).

5. The numbers in parentheses refer to pages in the two translations.

1. Some of these terms are equivocal; hence the ignorant attribute to them only one or some of the meanings in which the term in question is used (P, 5).

Of these some are homonyms, and of their several meanings the ignorant choose the wrong ones (F, 2).

2. It is not the purpose of this Treatise to make its totality understandable to the vulgar or to beginners in speculation, nor to teach those who have not engaged in any study other than the science of the Law—I mean the legalistic study of the Law. For the purpose of this Treatise and of all those like it is the science of Law in its true sense (P, 5).

It is not here intended to explain all these expressions to the unlettered or to mere tyros, a previous knowledge of Logic and Natural Philosophy being indispensable, or to those who confine their attention to the study of our holy Law, I mean the study of the canonical law alone; for the true knowledge of the Torah is the special aim of this and similar works (F, 2).

These passages, occurring in Maimonides' "Introduction to the First Part," show typical errors of Friedländer in contrast with the accuracy of Pines. In (1), F has missed the point. Maimonides says that the ignorant are unaware of the range of meanings of key equivocal terms in Scripture, not that they consistently choose the wrong meaning. In (2), F adds the phrase "a previous knowledge of Logic and Natural Philosophy being indispensable," although it is not present in the original text. Moreover, F blurs the significant distinction between "the legalistic study of the Law" and "the science of the law in its true sense," that is, between *shari'a* and *fiqh*. Without this distinction it is impossible to understand the professed aim of the *Guide*.

3. Know that with regard to natural matters as well, it is impossible to give a clear exposition when teaching some of their principles as they are (P, 7).

Know that also in Natural Science there are topics which are not to be fully explained (F, 3).

Here, F renders "topics" in place of "principles" and misconstrues "it is impossible to," reading it "are not to be," that is, "ought not" in place of "cannot."

On some occasions F conveys exactly the wrong sense of a term and, in so doing, both obscures the meaning of the particular passage and misses crucial distinctions.

50

4. We saw also that if an ignoramus among the multitude of Rabbanites should engage in speculation on these *Midrashim* he would find nothing difficult in them (P, 10).

We have further noticed that when an ill-informed Theologian reads these Midrashim, he will find no difficulty (F, 5).

To identify this "Rabbanite" as a "Theologian" is a serious error. The whole point is that he is a legalistic student of the law who has neither training in, nor aptitude for, theology or metaphysics. He is not an "ill-informed Theologian"; he is no theologian at all. P recognizes this clearly; F's rendition misleads the reader.

At times F seems not to be familiar with standard terminology. In I, 17 and elsewhere, for example, he repeatedly contrasts Form with Substance, when the text reads Form and Matter. As usual, P's version is correct. At the end of I, 28 we see a similar instance of inattention to precise terminology.

5. The purpose of everyone endowed with intellect should be wholly directed to rejecting corporeality with respect to God . . . and to considering all these apprehensions as intellectual, not sensory (P, 61).

The primary object of every intelligent person must be to deny the corporeality of God, and to believe that all those perceptions . . . were of a spiritual not of a material character (F, 38).

P is both clear and accurate. F probably understood the passage, but what is the unwary reader to make out of a call for perceptions that are "spiritual" rather than "material"? P uses the terms "intellectual" and "sensory," which convey clear meanings to philosophically informed readers. F's terms have no recognized standing in philosophical usage. In a similar but more serious instance, we find F incorrectly using "exact sciences" where P and the text read "mathematics," for example, in I, 31.

On other occasions, F restricts certain terms to specific meanings where the text is not at all specific. For example, at the end of I, 36, P is faithful to the text when he speaks of "men who inquire into the truth and are engaged in speculation," while F reads into the text more than it says and translates this phrase as "true philosophers." Further on, at the beginning of I, 51, F again reads "philosophers" where P and the text read "men of science." Similarly in I, 59 (F, 83; P, 138), F speaks of "the lowest class of philosophers," but P correctly reads "a single individual among the pupils." In the very next sentence, the term "philosophers" does occur and is rendered properly in both versions, as is the case with respect to the phrase

51

"chief of the philosophers" at the beginning of I, 5. Precision and consistency obviously did not concern F. We have here a not untypical case in which four different Arabic terms are translated by F with the common term "philosopher," but P carefully renders each term by a different and exact English equivalent.

Then there are passages in which F exhibits surprising insensitivity in translating certain key terms. One wonders what confusions were generated for uninitiated students who struggled to understand the following passage in F's version.

> 6. If, however, the attribute were the essence of the thing of which it is predicated, the attribute would be either a tautology—as if you were saying that man is man—or the attribute would be a mere explanation of a term—as if you said that man is a rational living being. For being a rational animal is the essence and true reality of man, and there does not exist in this case a third notion, apart from those of animal and of rational, that constitutes man. . . . It is as if you said that the thing denoted by the term "man" is the thing composed of life and rationality (P, 112–13).

> If the attribute denoted the essence [*to ti ein einai*] of the object, it would be either mere tautology, as if, e.g., one would say "man is man," or the explanation of a name, as, e.g., "man is a speaking animal"; for the words "speaking animal" include the true essence of man, and there is no third element besides life and speech in the definition of man, . . . that is to say that the thing which is called man, consists of life and speech (F, 68).

In describing man as a "speaking animal," F generates needless confusion over a commonplace term in medieval Hebrew and Arabic usage. Following the ambiguity of the Greek term *logos,* which means both word and reason, Hebrew and Arabic usage described man by a similarly ambiguous term. Thus in medieval philosophical Hebrew man is often identified as *medabber,* i.e., the being who is endowed with the power of speech, but it is elementary that this term is to be understood as referring to man's rationality. It means *logon exein,* which is to say, having the power of reason. To translate it literally is to confuse and mislead the unwary English reader. P is clear and consistent on this point. In a footnote (P, 77), he points out that the Arabic adjective, *nutqiyya,* derives from a term that "means, like *logos* in Greek, both speech and reason." Wherever this term or its derivatives are used to speak of man's essence, P consistently renders it as "reason" or "ra-

52

tional." F, on the other hand, uses various terms, such as "speaking," "intellectual," and "having reason." In I, 34 (F, 47) he uses "intellectual"; in I, 51 (F, 68), "speaking"; and in I, 52 (F, 69) "has reason." It should be stressed that in all of these instances the Arabic text uses exactly the same term. Even if F was clear in his own mind about the correct meaning of the term "speaking animal," this translation fails to convey the sense of the text. Moreover, F misleads the reader when he adds Greek terms in the body of the text, even when they are in brackets. There is the suggestion that these are terms which Maimonides actually used or at least knew. There is no evidence that he did, in fact, know any Greek.

F not only mistranslates individual words or phrases, he also frequently gives an erroneous translation of an entire passage.

> 7. Furthermore his saying, "That I may find grace in Thy sight," indicates that he who knows God finds grace in His sight and not he who merely fasts and prays, but everyone who has knowledge of Him (P, 123).

> The words "That I may find grace in Thy sight," imply that he who knows God finds grace in His eyes. Not only is he acceptable and welcome to God who fasts and prays, but everyone who knows Him (F, 75).

Here F says that God favors primarily the man who fasts and prays, while adding that he who knows God is also acceptable. But the text reads just as P has translated it, namely that prayer and fasting alone do not make a man acceptable to God, but only true knowledge of Him. This passage caused severe attacks on Maimonides for seeming to suggest that God does not desire the ordinary worship of pious men and that such worship without intellectual apprehension is religiously insufficient. If we had only the F translation, it would be difficult, indeed impossible, to see here any ground for questioning Maimonides' orthodoxy. The reader of F can only be puzzled over why this conventionally pious statement should have generated religious controversy.

I have presented only a small selection of typical passages exhibiting the variety of errors in F that are corrected in P. On this basis, it must be evident that P must now be viewed as *the* English translation of *The Guide of the Perplexed*. It is superior not only to F, but also to the other translations in modern languages. Even the French translation of Munk, which is an acknowledged classic of pioneering scholarship, does not meet the standard of precision and consistency achieved by Pines. Translators of other classic works would do well to imitate his method and strive to meet his very high standards.

It should be evident from our discussion that accurate and sensitive translation of such a work as the *Guide* is an indispensable requirement if the book is to be at all intelligible to a reading audience that has no possibility of studying the original. This is a matter not of pedantry, but of vital necessity. These same concerns apply to every translation, but they are particularly urgent in the case of the *Guide*. This is a work in which every word needs to be taken seriously, in which the exact terms used by the author must be available to readers if they are to have any hope of penetrating the inner meanings that Maimonides set into his book.

Even with a translation of high quality or, what is far better, independent access to the original version, we still have the serious problem of the methodology to use in our approach to the works of Maimonides, and particularly to the *Guide*. Leo Strauss has done more than anyone in this century to provide us with a classic paradigm of a method for studying this esoteric work. Unfortunately, Strauss turns out to be of limited help to his readers. Although, as we shall see, his essay serves to sensitize readers to the subtlety and complexity of the *Guide,* it generates at least as many problems as it solves. Indeed, if the purpose of a commentary is to clarify the text on which it comments, then Strauss has a mixed achievement. He is always suggestive and stimulating, but his method fails to help readers unless they are already able to find their own way—and in that case the commentary itself becomes superfluous.

The story is told that after James Hutchinson Stirling published his massive volume, *The Secret of Hegel,* he was congratulated by some of his readers for having kept the secret so well. One has a similar feeling when studying Leo Strauss's introductory essay, "How to Begin to Study *The Guide of the Perplexed.*" It is brilliant, tantalizing, frustrating, and at times infuriating. To be understood at all, it should be read in conjunction with Strauss' other writings on Maimonides, particularly his essay, "The Literary Character of *The Guide for the Perplexed.*"[6] But even with this added help, much still remains obscure. For Strauss has not written (nor did he intend to write) a simple and straightforward introduction for the use of uninitiated readers. Rather, he has constructed an obstacle course designed to block the

6. Leo Strauss, "The Literary Character of *The Guide for the Perplexed,*" in *Persecution and the Art of Writing* (Glencoe, Ill., 1952), 38–94. First published in *Essays on Maimonides,* ed. S. W. Baron (New York, 1941), 37–91.

forward movement of all but the most skilled students of Maimonides' *Guide*. Ordinary readers are unlikely ever to get beyond this introductory essay to the text of the *Guide*. Even highly skilled readers will receive no clear and explicit analysis of the *Guide,* for if they succeed in finding their way through the Strauss essay, they will have clues, hints, suggestions, and some confusions—not a systematic and structured interpretation. Strauss has provided a kind of methodological introduction to reading this complex work, leaving to readers the task of interpreting the *Guide* for themselves. This, of course, is implicit in the title of his essay, which stresses that it is concerned only with how to begin the process of studying the *Guide*.

These comments are meant not as a criticism of Strauss, but only as a characterization of his introduction. It is exactly the kind of introduction he intended to write, and he says so explicitly at one point when he notes his "desire to give the readers some hints for the better understanding" of a particular section. It is quite clear that any readers who want more than hints will have to get the rest on their own. This deliberately obscure manner of introducing Maimonides' *Guide* is necessitated by the special way in which Strauss understands and reads this great work. Unlike most earlier interpreters, he takes seriously Maimonides' own instructions on how to read the *Guide*. It is strange that, despite the great pains Maimonides himself took to instruct and direct readers on how to read the *Guide,* his instructions have been largely ignored. Rarely does one find a work on Maimonides, a commentary on a portion of his book, or a systematic study of some aspect of his thought in which the author gives evidence that he or she is always conscious of Maimonides' admonition that the *Guide of the Perplexed* is a special kind of esoteric book. As a result, the book has been consistently misunderstood because it was not studied with the method that Maimonides himself set forth. It is to the credit of Strauss that he has taken Maimonides seriously. In his various writings Strauss reminds us that esoteric books must be read in a special way, and that Maimonides' *Guide* is a supreme example of such a book.

It may seem regrettable that Strauss has chosen to write interpretations that are as esoteric as the *Guide* itself, insisting that no other responsible mode of interpretation is open. "Above all," he writes, "an esoteric interpretation of the *Guide* seems to be not only advisable, but even necessary. . . . The interpretation of the *Guide* cannot be given in ordinary language, but only in parabolic enigmatic speech. That is why, according to Maimonides, the student of those secrets is required not only to be of mature age, to have a sagacious and subtle mind . . . and to be able to understand the allusive speech of others, but also to be capable of presenting things allusively himself."[7] Strauss has written an introduction that meets this standard, one that is most often cryptic and allusive, explaining basic points only by way of hints and hidden clues.

For readers, such an introduction poses a major dilemma. How seriously shall we take Strauss? Shall we deal with him as he deals with Maimonides? Strauss insists that Maimonides wrote each word of the *Guide* with such meticulous care that we must assume that there are no inadvertent slips or errors. Every seeming mistake, every apparently careless or inaccurate quotation, every internal contradiction—all are clues for skillful readers. To perceptive students they open up doors to the deeper and secret meaning of the *Guide*. This imposes a great burden on readers, who are never allowed to take the easy way in accounting for the peculiarities of the *Guide*.

Does Strauss write with the same care as Maimonides? When we find that Strauss in his introductory essay makes errors or seems to be careless, how shall we react? Are these merely the ordinary slips to which most of us are prone, or are they deliberate devices for testing and directing readers? Readers will have to make up their own minds. I believe, however, that it is most fruitful to study Strauss' essay as if it is both deliberately esoteric and perfectly constructed. Only then can we reach a sound judgment of it. In what follows I shall point out only a few typical instances of the various types of apparent errors made by Strauss. The burden of interpreting and evaluating this puzzling essay must be assumed by individual students in their own fashion.

The essay opens with an outline plan of the *Guide*. This outline is by no means a mere conventional résumé of its contents but an original and creative analysis of the structure of the book and the interrelations of its parts. Strauss first divides the book into seven sections, with deliberate emphasis on the significance of the number seven. He then tells us that, "wherever feasible, each section is divided into seven subsections" (p. xiii); but he never tells us directly at any point what considerations determine feasibility. This leaves us mystified by Section VII, which contains only two subsections and consists altogether of three chapters. Later (p. xliv) Strauss returns to this theme, stating that "for the general reason indicated, Maimonides desired to divide each of the seven sections of the *Guide* into seven subsections." We must note that the "general reason" has never been clearly indicated, nor are we told what prevented Maimonides from doing as he desired. It is proper to raise these points because, as Strauss himself reminds us

7. Strauss, "Literary Character," in *Persecution and the Art of Writing*, 56–58.

(p. xxx), "it is one thing to observe these regularities and another thing to understand them."

Strauss begins his discussion by quoting the last sentence of Maimonides' own Introduction to the *Guide* and ends his essay with the same quotation. But the two versions are not identical. In the second version the order of the last two clauses is reversed, and a phrase is omitted. The first version is an accurate translation of the original; the second is not. Moreover, neither is absolutely identical with the reading in Pines' translation. A similar "error" occurs (p. xxviii) when Strauss says that the first subsection (i.e., I, 1–7) begins and ends with the same word, "image." But while the first word of I, 1 is "image," the last word of I, 7 is "image" only in the English translation. In the original it is the Hebrew word *ketzalmo,* i.e., "according to his image," rather than *tzelem,* as in I, 1. Are these careless errors, or do they contain clues planted deliberately to test readers and lead them to the inner secrets of Strauss' interpretation?

In a suggestive discussion, Strauss touches on the crucial issue of Maimonides' treatment of the doctrine of the unity of God. But as usual he leaves us with unanswered questions. He makes the brilliant observation (which is obvious only after he calls it to our attention) that in the *Guide,* Maimonides quotes only once "the most important biblical text . . . 'Hear, O Israel, the Lord is our God, the Lord is One' " (p. xlvii). What he does not tell us is that Maimonides omits the words "Hear, O Israel," and quotes only the remainder of the verse. The same is true of the quotation in *Mishneh Torah, H. Yesodei ha-Torah* I, 7, to which Strauss also refers. Further on in the same discussion (p. xlviii), Strauss notes three instances in the *Guide* where Maimonides quotes from Deut. 4:35, "The Lord He is God; there is none else beside Him." In each of these instances, however, Maimonides does not quote the portion that Strauss cites, but only the first part of the same verse, "Unto thee it was shown," adding, "and so on." What might seem like small matters in an ordinary book must be taken seriously in a careful study of Maimonides' *Guide.* Does Strauss make these errors deliberately to test and teach us, or are they merely oversights?

There are passages in which Strauss tantalizes us with cryptic and mystifying observations. This is particularly true of the number symbolism which he suggests but does not work out in detail. For example, after noting (p. xxx) that I, 14 and I, 17 deal respectively with man and the prohibition against teaching natural science publicly, he comments that "14 stands for man or the human things and 17 stands for nature." A few lines further on, he notes that I, 26 is concerned in part with a principle for the interpretation of the Torah. This leads to the strange claim that since "26 is the numerical equivalent of the secret name of the Lord, God of Israel, 26 may therefore also stand for His Torah."

If we study this supposed symbolism, we are puzzled. No explanation whatsoever is offered for the association of 17 with nature.[8] But let us examine the other numerical symbols for which some hints of an explanation are offered. It is true that 26 is the numerical equivalent of God's name, but how can one justify a simple identification, by way of a common symbol, of God and Torah? Is there any evidence that Maimonides would have made such an identification? Our confusion grows when we consider the implications of 14 as the symbol for man. This is not a numerical equivalence at all, because the numerical value of *adam* (man) equals 45. But Strauss gives us a clue when he note that 14 is the numerical equivalent of hand (*yad*), "the characteristically human organ." Presumably this is the justification for using 14 as the symbol for man.

We have already taken note of the fact that in Maimonides' works the number 14 is also closely associated with Torah. The *Mishneh Torah,* Maimonides' code of Jewish law, also known as *Yad ha-Ḥazakah,* that is, "the mighty hand," is divided into 14 books. In his *Book of the Commandments,* Maimonides sets out "14 roots of the commandments." And in the *Guide* he divides all the commandments into 14 classes.[9] If 14 stands for man, then there is the strong suggestion that the commandments of the Torah are to be viewed as human rather than divine. This in turn seems to contradict the symbolism of 26, which is taken as identifying Torah with God, not with man. When we study I, 14 we are even more bewildered. The verses cited by Maimonides in that chapter all seem to suggest that except for rare individuals, man has little connection with God and hardly any superiority over the beasts. Perhaps 14 and 26 suggest the ambiguity of "Torah," as Strauss does when he speaks of Torah as "the true science of the law" in contrast to Torah as "the science of the law in the usual sense, i.e., the *fiqh. . . .* In contradistinction to the legalistic study of the law, which is

---

8. We might guess that part of the association is that 17 is also the numerical equivalent of *tov,* the Hebrew word for "good." We are told repeatedly in the creation story that God saw that his creation was good, and finally that it was "very good." It is likely that "good" in this context means something like "fully adapted to its proper end." (On this point, see *Guide,* II, 30, p. 354, and III, 13, p. 453.) This could well be identified with the order of nature. However, all this is conjecture, and we do not know for certain exactly what Strauss had in mind or, in turn, what he is hinting that Maimonides had in mind. Fascinating at such hints are, they carry with them certain inherent dangers. We can play the game of numerical symbolism almost without limit, and such games can result in bizarre ways of reading our texts. Once we give up the controls built into such a text, we risk totally uncontrolled and irresponsible interpretations.

9. This subject is discussed from another perspective in chapter 1.

concerned with what man ought to do, the true science of the law is concerned with what man ought to think and to believe."[10]

This is the distinction between the subject matter of the *Mishneh Torah* and that of the *Guide*. At one point Strauss calls the latter the *Torah for the Perplexed,* in contrast to the first Torah and Maimonides' own code, the *Mishneh Torah,* both of which are for the intellectually unsophisticated who are in their very nature unperplexed. There is, in all this, the daring suggestion that Maimonides viewed the original Torah as less connected with divine matters than his own new "Torah." This suggestion is developed by Strauss (p. xxxiii) when he argues that according to Maimonides some later prophets (e.g., Isaiah) achieved "a higher stage in the knowledge of God than Moses." Since "progress beyond the teaching of the Torah is possible or even necessary," he may also be making the daring suggestion that Maimonides himself has reached a higher level than the Torah or the prophets.[11]

None of this is stated explicitly by Strauss. In fact at times he seems to take a contrary position. What I suggest here is only one possible interpretation, which shows there is always a danger that our ingenuity can trap us into merely playing a game with the text instead of understanding the author's thoughts. The case before us holds such serious implications concerning the true views of Maimonides that it would have been better either to spell them out and defend them clearly and unambiguously, or else not to present them at all. It is counterproductive to deal with matters of such gravity only through hints and allusions.

Let us turn to still another problem in interpreting Strauss introduction. In his earlier essay, Strauss urges us to take note of "little words" in Maimonides' text that are readily ignored by the unwary although they profoundly affect the meaning. "Cannot miracles be wrought by such little words as 'almost', 'perhaps', 'seemingly'?"[12] Shall we in turn pay equal attention to Strauss' own use of such "little" words and phrases? He assures us, for example (p. xv), that "no one can reasonably doubt . . . that II, 32–48, III, 1–7, and III, 25–50 form sections." What is the force of "reasonably"? Since Maimonides explicitly cautions us not to take the apparent structure for the real structure of the *Guide,* it seems perfectly reasonable to doubt that the parts in question form sections. Does avoidance of seemingly "reasonable doubt" perhaps characterize simple-minded readers unprepared for the adventure of exploring the hidden levels of the *Guide?* The

10. Strauss, "Literary Character," in *Persecution and the Art of Writing,* 38.

11. On this topic see the suggestive study by A. J. Heschel, "Ha-he'emin ha-Rambam she-Zakhah le-Nevu'ah," in *Sefer ha-Yovel li-Khevod Levi Ginsberg* (New York, 1946), 159–88.

12. Strauss, "Literary Character," in *Persecution and the Art of Writing,* 78.

qualification "reasonably" opens up various possibilities, but charts no clear course for readers. We are put on our guard in similar fashion by such "small words" in contexts that seem to call for unambiguous statements, for example, cases of simple counting.

Speaking of "lexicographic chapters" (p. xxv), Strauss says that of the first forty-nine chapters of the *Guide* thirty are lexicographic, "whereas in the whole rest of the book there occur at most two such chapters (I, 66 and 70)." Why "at most" when simple counting should settle the issue beyond question? Is it perhaps because I, 66, which opens not with a term or terms but with part of a biblical verse, does not precisely fit his criterion of what constitutes a lexicographic chapter? "At most" seems to be an invitation, if not a challenge, to readers to check carefully the citations that Strauss lists and to catch him in a mistake. Later Strauss writes (p. l) that in I, 68–70 Maimonides "refers to philosophy, I believe, more frequently than in the whole discussion of Incorporeality (I, 1–49). . . . In the exegetic discussion of the divine names (I, 61–67), if I am not mistaken, he does not refer to philosophy at all." Since these are matters which it should be possible to settle fairly easily and exactly, we must give special thought to the intention of such expressions as "I believe" and "if I am not mistaken." Is this just a manner of speaking, or are these also tests and clues for Strauss' readers?

In certain cases Strauss raises a question without suggesting any direct answer. If there is an indirect answer, it is hidden deeply in the caverns that lie at the end of the tortuous paths that Strauss has laid out. Our attempt at an interpretation in these instances is further complicated by our uncertainty as to whether his apparent errors are deliberate or accidental. For example, he makes much of what he calls the "lexicographical chapters" in Part I of the *Guide*. He means by this term "a chapter that opens with the Hebrew term or terms to be explained in the chapter regardless of whether these terms precede the first sentence or form the beginning of the first sentence, and regardless of whether these terms are supplied with the Arabic article *al-* or not" (p. xxv). Strauss goes on to note carefully the exact number of each variety of such chapters and then asks why they occur in precisely these numbers and variations; but he never answers the question directly, for he holds that it is of major importance for students to know which are the right questions even if they cannot yet answer them satisfactorily.

What is troubling, however, is that the count Strauss makes is not accurate. Perhaps he is testing his readers to see if they check each detail. Strauss says (p. xxv) that "ten of these thirty lexicographic chapters begin with the Hebrew terms preceding the first sentence." This count seems correct according to the Arabic text used in the preparation of this translation. The ten chapters in Part I are 1, 7, 8, 9, 11, 18, 19, 22, 25, 30. Yet, surprisingly, when we consult the Pines translation, to which Strauss has attached his introduction, there appear to be twelve such chapters, rather than ten. In Pines' version, chapters I, 15 and I, 21 also begin with the Hebrew terms preceding the first sentence. It is true that there is some ambiguity; in the Arabic text the opening term in each of the other ten chapters is followed by a period, but not in I, 15 and I, 21. Is this a trap set for us by Strauss or a mere failure to coordinate introduction and translation, an important clue or an unimportant oversight?

This same disparity among the introduction, the Arabic original, and the translation can be found in other places. Perhaps the most striking is in a passage of crucial importance that distinguishes between Maimonides' treatment of the Bible and the Talmud. Strauss claims that "generally speaking," Maimonides "introduces biblical passages by 'he says' (or 'his saying is') and talmudic passages by 'they say' (or 'their saying is')." To Strauss this means that Maimonides is anxious to suggest "that in the Bible we hear only one speaker, while in the Talmud we hear indeed many speakers. . . . Yet in the first chapter of the *Guide* 'He' who speaks is in fact first God, then the narrator, then God, and then 'the poor one' " (p. xliii). According to Strauss' reading, we should expect to find "he says" or "his saying is" at last four times in I, 1. In the translation of I, 1, however, the expression "he says" does not occur at all, and "his saying is" occurs only once; but we do find, in addition, the expressions "Scripture says," "it is said," and "the scriptural dictum." These are fully justified as translations of the Arabic term that Strauss renders as "he says." Moreover, Strauss says that in this chapter the "he" who speaks is first God, then the narrator. Three verses are quoted after the translator's expression "Scripture says." These are the verses Strauss ascribes to the "narrator." Of these the first, Gen. 39:6, may be thought of as spoken by the narrator. However, the second verse, I Sam. 28:14, is spoken by Saul, and the third, Judg. 8:18, by Zebah and Zalmunna. (For readers who wonder about "the poor one," this refers to the quoted verse, "I am like a pelican in the wilderness" from Psalm 102, which begins, "A prayer of the poor one.") What are we to make of this doubly confusing situation? First, the speakers in the text turn out to be other than what Strauss claims. Second, the crucial point embedded in the phrase "he says" is in no way evident in the varied renditions of the translation. Again we are led to wonder whether these are mere human errors or mysterious clues to secret doctrines.

For reasons that should now be apparent, I have not attempted to give a systematic account of Strauss' interpretation of Maimonides. Strauss could well argue that an essay entitled "How to Begin to Study *The Guide of the Perplexed*" is literally only a beginning, and that he is not called upon to offer in such an essay final and systematic interpretations. Though it may be justified, this kind of an introduction leaves us unsatisfied. For Strauss exhibits so many brilliant flashes of insight and tantalizes us with so many acute observations that we can only wish that he had been willing to share his secret knowledge with all serious students of Maimonides.

I have chosen to discuss Strauss' method at such length because it is widely, and justly, considered to be one of the most important modern contributions to the study of Maimonides. We have seen, however, that with all its brilliance and ingenuity, it seems to do little to advance the cause of sound understanding, even for readers who are well prepared and sophisticated. If the only way to expound an esoteric text is by compounding and complicating the esotericism, then perhaps we should give up the effort altogether.

It has long been recognized, in both the Jewish and the general Western cultural traditions, that certain subjects are not appropriate for public discussion but must be restricted to a few specially qualified initiates. In ancient times the Mishnah set down such a rule in its teaching that the most esoteric of all subjects, the Chariot Vision of Ezekiel, may be taught to only one individual at a time. Even this is conditioned on that individual being "*hakham u-mevin mida'ato,*" that is, endowed with such great intellectual capacity and such perspicacity that he can figure things out by himself with little or no help. In expounding this passage the Talmud adds the qualification that one may only transmit to this special individual "chapter headings," leaving him to fill in all the rest on his own.[13] If we consider Maimonides' works to be in this legally restricted, esoteric category, then it is both improper and impossible to provide an adequate commentary. In that case, we may view Strauss, as he clearly intends, as one who is teaching us to read Maimonides in the way that the Mishnah authorizes the teaching of such an esoteric body of literature.

In principle this may seem to be the only proper approach to the study and exposition of the *Guide*. Maimonides himself addressed this question in his Introduction to the *Guide*. He was sensitive to the fact that in writing a book about these topics he was apparently violating rabbinic law, because a book is by nature a public document. He justified the need to produce such a document because of the great confusion about fundamental matters of religion that bedeviled his intellectually sophisticated contemporaries. It was, however, necessary to conform to the requirements of the law by writing the book in such a way that it is, in effect, being addressed only to the rare individual to whom the Sages authorized us to teach these subjects. Furthermore, it had to be written in such a way as to satisfy the restrictions set down

13. M. *Ḥagigah,* 2:1, and b. *Ḥagigah,* 13a.

by rabbinic law. After citing the talmudic rule, Maimonides goes on as follows:

> Hence you should not ask of me here anything beyond the chapter headings. And even those are not set down in order or arranged in coherent fashion in this Treatise, but rather are scattered and entangled with other subjects that are to be clarified. For my purpose is that the truths be glimpsed and then again concealed, so as not to oppose that divine purpose which one cannot possibly oppose and which has concealed from the vulgar among the people those truths especially requisite for His apprehension. (Introduction to the First Part, pp. 6–7).

If he was to conform to the law, Maimonides had no choice but to write his book in this esoteric fashion. Yet he did write the book and as a result exposed his teachings to the general reading public. In some societies such a book might be permanently removed from all public access, as was attempted by some forces during the anti-Maimonidean controversy, when a ban was pronounced on any general reading of the *Guide*.[14] In our society this is neither possible nor desirable. The *Guide* exists as a public document and is readily available. In these circumstances, it is important to provide the most responsible commentaries and works of interpretation. The purpose of such expository studies must be to help and guide readers, not to confuse them even further.

At stake in such an effort is whether the real Maimonides can be saved for the instruction of a contemporary generation of students of Jewish thought, or whether we must consign his work to a dimension so deeply hidden from access, even to the most thoughtful and intelligent readers, that he is effectively lost to us. It seems to me beyond all argument that Maimonides is much too important for us to accept passively the judgment that his real teaching is permanently inaccessible. Once we complete our study of the methodological problems that occupy our interest in the first part of this book, my efforts in the remaining sections will be directed to showing in concrete cases of central importance how Maimonides' thought can be penetrated and explicated in a responsible manner.

Before closing this part of the discussion, we need to address one more issue. There is a large and ever-growing literature on the problem of textual interpretation. We have a variety of schools occupied with such questions as how to read a text, what we can expect any text to convey, and whether the

14. For literature on the anti-Maimonidean controversy, see chapter 1, note 8.

meanings are in the text or supplied by the reader. Everyone today is familiar with such schools as the new critics, the structuralists, and the deconstructionists, among others. They have adopted complex technical names to characterize their varied approaches to reading a text, but few of their theories are really new, although they are certainly formulated and practiced with a sophistication that may have no precedent. The names may be new, but the hermeneutic concerns are very old. Since human beings began to write and to read, the problem of textual interpretation has always confronted them. Within the Jewish tradition the entire classical literature is in large measure one of textual commentary and interpretation. With or without today's highly developed technical jargon and polysyllabic terminology, the activity of interpretation is an enterprise that has always occupied serious and thoughtful readers. In the Jewish tradition this activity has never stopped.

I do not want to suggest that I am doing anything here to resolve the complex problems of the theory and practice of interpretation, nor do I presume even to offer a rigorous formal account of my own procedure. I should like, however, to characterize briefly my conception of how to go about the task of reading a text, even a text so special in character as that of Maimonides' *Guide*.

I begin with the most fundamental assumption, namely, that the author is serious and thoughtful, and has made a responsible effort to record his or her thoughts in such a way as to communicate an important message. This means, in turn, that we must relate to the work with the utmost seriousness. When we are reading major philosophers, we cannot allow ourselves to suppose that they say silly things or make elementary errors. The presumption must always be in their favor. If my reading of Plato or Maimonides turns him into an intellectual incompetent, then I have to assume that the fault is with me. At that point I have to go back again, read more carefully, think more rigorously, and do all in my power to arrive at a deeper and sounder understanding of the text.

This is not a fashionable concept in most contemporary academic circles. In the field of philosophy, for example, one can regularly hear college sophomores imitating their teachers with comments like "Plato went wrong here" or "Descartes simply muddled that argument completely." I am fully aware that there are writers who are neither serious nor thoughtful, but this hardly applies to the great literary figures or the great philosophers. One must work long and hard before finally concluding that Plato was silly or that Descartes was incapable of seeing an elementary logical fallacy. They were only human, and it is always possible that they slipped. However, readers earn the right to make such a judgment only if they know what it means to read a text with meticulous care and mature understanding, and if they have exhausted every effort to understand the author seriously in his or her own terms.

I am also aware that, even with the most careful preparation and the most responsible reading, we can never be absolutely certain that we have discovered what the author intended rather than reading into his or her work our own insights.[15] We know that interpretation is always exposed to this unavoidable hazard. It seems to me, nevertheless, that we can proceed with some confidence that it is possible to do the work soundly and responsibly.

To read any serious text well requires that a number of preconditions should be met by readers. First, they must approach it with as full control as possible of the requisite languages or at least with confidence in the reliability of the translation they are using, although it must be stated again that for purposes of serious scholarship no translation can be a fully satisfactory substitute for the original.[16] In the present case, however, we have already presented our evidence in favor of the remarkable faithfulness of the Pines translation of the *Guide*.

Second, good readers must know enough about the historical setting and context of the work to be able to relate to it appropriately. Third, readers must have a good grasp of the background and the intellectual resources that the author brings to the work. Every writer, even one such as Maimonides who speaks to all the ages, still lives inside a particular intellectual tradition and, in Maimonides' case, a particular religious and philosophical tradition as well. Readers must know and understand that background as it relates to

15. I recall vividly a lecture many years ago in Jerusalem in which a distinguished literary scholar was expounding some aspects of the work of Agnon. The eminent author was present, sitting in the front row. When the discussion began, Agnon asked for the floor and stated bluntly that the critic had ascribed to him thoughts and ideas that he never had and never expressed. The critic turned to him and said, "Mr. Agnon, you have not the vaguest idea of the true contents and meaning of your work." The critic may well have been right, but right or wrong, the exchange between author and critic was a striking moment exemplifying the problem of arriving at some supposedly correct interpretation of a text.

16. We see more and more today the phenomenon of people who parade under the banner of scholarship, posing as experts in fields where they do not have even the most basic linguistic equipment. Books and articles on the Bible, written by people who know little or no Hebrew, to say nothing of the related languages of the ancient Near East, are being published in respectable forums. It is common today for writers to make seemingly profound pronouncements about subjects in the field of rabbinic literature without having the training or the linguistic capacity to read even a few lines on their own. Midrash has now become a popular subject, widely talked about, quoted, analyzed, and explicated by "experts" who cannot read the text. The same is true of Kabbalah. Such a flowering of interest in Jewish subjects is pleasing, but regrettably is frequently not accompanied by the disciplined study required to turn amateurs into responsible scholars. This gives all the more reason to applaud the small but growing corps of students who are being trained properly in the classical disciplines of Judaic studies.

the work before them. Thus readers of the *Guide* must have a sound grasp of the rabbinic and philosophical sources and traditions out of which the work of Maimonides emerges. Otherwise, they will fail to understand terms, arguments, citations, and allusions that are essential to a responsible reading of the text.[17] Fourth, readers must learn to pay close attention to every detail of the text, to take the author's own directions seriously, and to follow carefully the clues and guideposts that the author has provided.

With this intellectual equipment serving them, readers should be able to do well in finding their way through the text. There is one final condition. Any reading of the text must be verified as far as possible by the internal evidence provided by the text itself. There is never a guarantee that a given interpretation is correct, but we can go far in building confidence in the soundness of our interpretation by scrutinizing with the greatest care the evidence that the text itself provides. I shall try to show, in what follows, that when we seek to interpret Maimonides, we need not be driven to either the extreme of irresponsible simplicity or that of an interpretive esotericism even more obscure than the work it seeks to illuminate. One can read even so elusive a work as the *Guide of the Perplexed* with the degree of care and understanding that the author expected.

In the chapters that follow, I aim at a balance between those studies which trivialize the *Guide* by ignoring its subtle hidden dimensions and those, like Strauss, which turn out to be even more obscure than the original. It is my conviction that it is possible to mediate between these extremes and to explicate Maimonides in a way that helps to make him intelligible, while paying full attention to the esoteric elements in his style and thought.

17. For the philosophical background of Maimonides' work, the translator's introduction by Pines is particularly useful (Maimonides, *Guide*, trans. Pines, lvii–cxxxiv). He provides a careful discussion of the philosophic sources of the *Guide*. There is, of course, a large literature dealing with many of these historical questions.

4

Maimonides' Method of Contradictions

A New View

To read the *Guide* well, we need to learn how to deal properly with perhaps the subtlest of all the methodological problems that it poses for us, namely, how to understand and interpret the contradictions that are presumably to be found throughout the book. We have already noted that we can grasp Maimonides' true doctrine in the *Guide of the Perplexed* only if we give most careful thought to the author's own instructions to his readers. Much attention has been paid by recent writers to the stress that Maimonides seems to place on the presence of contradictions in his book and on the correct way to resolve them. This concern is of the highest importance and is by no means only a recent preoccupation. Medieval commentators on the *Guide* were also fully attuned to the fact that the *Guide* is no ordinary book and that it must be read with special care. The medievals, like our contemporaries, were aware of the problem of contradictions in the book, and in the case of seemingly contradictory statements, they were concerned with determining exactly what Maimonides was affirming.

This was to be expected, since no author could have been more explicit in his instructions to readers. What is surprising is how much has been overlooked by both medieval and modern commentators and how much they take for granted that is in no way supported by the text. Maimonides demanded a close and careful reading which weighs the force and significance of every word, but with respect to the problem of contradictions the commentators have not given him such a reading. Maimonides requires his readers, and all who would deal with the subject matter of his book, to be thoroughly trained in the basic elements of logic and to make use of this knowledge as an indispensable tool for a correct critical reading.[1] Yet the commentators, both medieval and modern, have failed either to pay attention to certain elemen-

---

1. With regard to the obligation to read with meticulous care and to pay attention to every word, see *Guide,* Instruction, p. 15, and my comments and passages cited in the previous chapter. For the emphasis on the importance of logic as a necessary prerequisite, see *Guide,* Epistle Dedicatory, p. 3, and I, 34, p. 75.

tary logical principles and distinctions or to take note of the special terminology that Maimonides introduced into his discussion of the so-called method of contradictions. As a result, they have not confronted the text of the *Guide* in the way the author expects of his readers. Much that has been written about contradictions in the *Guide* turns out to be doubtful, if not simply wrong. Inattention to Maimonides' terminology and to the clues that he provides leads to misunderstanding and error.

Maimonides begins his instructions on this point in the following way: "One of seven causes should account for the contradictory or contrary statements to be found in any book or compilation" (Introduction to the First Part, p. 17). The most important point is that he speaks of "contradictory or contrary statements." We should note first that he is speaking about "statements" and then that he specifically refers to those that are "contradictory or contrary." Now as we shall show, these are technical terms in logic, and specifically in Maimonides' own logic. Yet no commentator addresses directly the significance of this sentence.

Consider the most obvious points. First is the important rule that logical opposition is restricted here to statements. We may confront other kinds of peculiarities or inconsistencies in this book, but they will not be of the logically formal type that occurs in the opposition of statements to each other. Second, Maimonides does not speak loosely or in a general way only about contradictions, but specifically mentions "contradictory or contrary statements." A commonplace of Aristotelian logic is adopted by Maimonides here, namely, that contradictories and contraries behave in quite different ways. Contradictories cannot both be true or both be false. If one is true, the other is necessarily false, and vice versa. Contraries cannot both be true, but may both be false, and subcontraries (which I believe he included here under the general term "contraries") cannot both be false, but may both be true. It is already evident how much error we hazard if we allow ourselves—as has been generally done, especially by contemporary commentators—to ignore these distinctions and to speak only about "contradictions" in the *Guide*, without taking note of the important differences in the logical behavior of contraries and contradictories.

That Maimonides was aware of the exact technical meaning of these terms is evident from his *Treatise on Logic*.[2] Since that treatise is devoted to an explication of logical terms, it does not deal directly with the way in which contradictories and contraries are related to each other. Yet, there can be no doubt that Maimonides was familiar with the relations between these types of statements as they were set forth in what came to be known as 'the

2. See Israel Efros, *Maimonides' Treatise on Logic* (New York, 1938), chap. 4.

68

square of opposition.' These relations had been set down by Aristotle in his logical works, and from there they entered into the logical tradition as standard items.[3] Most important for our purpose is to note that this same account of the relations of propositions within the square of opposition is present in al-Fārābi in his discussion of this topic in the logic of Aristotle.[4] We know that Maimonides held al-Fārābi in the highest esteem, especially as a logician; in a frequently quoted statement, he advises his translator, Samuel ibn Tibbon, to ignore all works on logic except those of al-Fārābi, which are alone of the very highest quality in Maimonides' opinion.[5] We can, therefore, be confident that Maimonides was thoroughly familiar with al-Fārābi's teaching concerning the opposition of propositions. When we add to this the fact that the relations of propositions as set forth in the square of opposition had become a standard part of logic in the intellectual world that Maimonides inhabited, there can be no doubt that he knew and accepted these rules as correct. It seems to follow as a matter of course that when we find statements in the *Guide* that are in any way inconsistent with each other, it is a serious mistake simply to classify them all loosely as contradictions. Yet this is in fact what the commentators, including even such close readers of the text as Leo Strauss and his followers, have generally done. We are required to determine in each case whether we are dealing with contradictories, contraries, subcontraries, or some other form of opposition or inconsistency. Failing to make this determination and to treat the problem before us in accordance with the rules of logic, we are almost certain to fall into error in our interpretation of the Maimonidean text.

When we study the work of Strauss, who more than any other contemporary scholar has made us aware of the importance of inconsistencies in the *Guide*, we discover to our great astonishment that he pays no attention to the rules of logic and to the basic logical distinctions essential for understanding Maimonides. He speaks only about contradictions and ignores the other forms of opposition and inconsistency. He emphasizes—no doubt with full justification—the importance of contradictions, but then sets down a rule

3. See Aristotle, *De Interpretatione*, 7, 17b17–37.

4. *Al-Farabi's Commentary and Short Treatise on Aristotle's De Interpretatione*, trans. F. W. Zimmerman (Oxford, 1981), 65–66. See also *Al-Farabi's Short Commentary on Aristotle's Prior Analytics*, trans. Nicholas Rescher (Pittsburgh, 1963), 55–57.

5. Moses Maimonides to Samuel ibn Tibbon, in *Kovetz Teshuvot ha-Rambam* (Leipzig, 1859), 28d. Cited by Pines in his Translator's Introduction to Maimonides, *Guide*, trans. Pines, lx: "As for works on logic, one should only study the writings of Abu Nasr al-Farabi. All his writings are faultlessly excellent. One ought to study and understand them. For he is a great man." Pines cites this from the version edited by Alexander Marx, *Jewish Quarterly Review*, n.s. 25, 371–428.

for dealing with them that ignores the canons of logic and Maimonides' own careful instructions. Strauss says, "Contradictions are the axis of the *Guide*. . . . While the other devices used by Maimonides compel the reader to guess the true teaching, the contradictions offer him the true teaching quite openly in either of the two contradictories."[6] He goes on to instruct us how to determine which of the contradictories Maimonides considered to be true. "We may therefore establish the rule that of two contradictory statements in the *Guide* or in any other work of Maimonides that statement which occurs least frequently, or even which occurs only once, was considered by him to be true."[7]

This claim may conceivably be a good general rule for reading an esoteric work, but it certainly does not conform either to the canons of logic or to Maimonides' own clear instructions. Students dealing with the complex subjects discussed in the *Guide* must take particular care to abide by the rules of logic and not to suppose that they know anything with certainty if it is not supported by logical evidence.

> For if you stay your progress because of a dubious point; *if you do not deceive yourself into believing that there is a demonstration with regard to matters that have not been demonstrated; if you do not hasten to reject and categorically to pronounce false any assertions whose contradictories have not been demonstrated;* if, finally, you do not aspire to apprehend that which you are unable to apprehend—you will have achieved human perfection. . . . If, on the other hand, you aspire to apprehend things which are beyond your apprehension; *or if you hasten to pronounce false, assertions the contradictories of which have not been demonstrated or that are* possible, though very remotely so . . . you will not only not be perfect, but you will be among the most deficient among the deficient (I, 32, pp. 68–69; emphasis added).[8]

6. Leo Strauss, "The Literary Character of *The Guide for the Perplexed*," in *Persecution and the Art of Writing* (Glencoe, Ill., 1952), 74.

7. Ibid., 73. In support of this thesis, Strauss offers Maimonides' procedure in the *Treatise on Resurrection*, where he relies on an isolated passage in the Book of Daniel against the many other scriptural passages that seem to speak against resurrection. Even if Strauss' reading of Maimonides on this point is sound (a claim I am not prepared to grant), it in no way establishes the rule he proposes.

8. That Strauss was familiar with this passage goes without saying. See, e.g., his reference to it in "How to Begin to Study the *Guide of the Perplexed*," in Maimonides, *Guide*, trans. Pines, xxxix. It is instructive that, despite his full awareness of this statement of Maimonides and others like it, he did not follow it but substituted instead his own rule for determining which of two contradictories Maimonides believed to be true.

Maimonides' own rule is stated here with sufficient clarity. In the case of contradictories, we can proceed correctly only if we know which of the two statements is true, since it follows necessarily that its contradictory is false. However, we can know with certainty which statement is true only if we base our claim on a rigorous demonstration. For Maimonides, demonstration is a strict logical category. It is not an esoteric procedure at all, but one well established in the philosophical tradition to which he belongs. I can find no justification whatsoever for substituting Strauss' rule for the one that Maimonides himself set down. Furthermore, when we are dealing with any case of inconsistent propositions, our first task is to determine the nature of the inconsistency. If they are contradictories, then we must determine whether either of them can be demonstrated to be true. If they are contraries, we need to deal with the possibility that they both may be false; if they are subcontraries, that they both may be true. In addition, as we shall soon see, there are in the *Guide* other modes of opposition or inconsistency which do not fit into any of these standard logical classifications, and these too must engage our attention.

Of special importance to us are not only those points of logic with respect to which Maimonides is in full agreement with the classical tradition, but even more those on which he differs from that tradition. Among these the most striking is his treatment of singular propositions. These are propositions that are neither universal nor particular in the standard sense of those terms, but instead have as their subject a single individual. Maimonides' examples of such singular propositions are "Zayd is an animal" and "Bekr is wise." In the history of logic, from the time of Aristotle on, singular propositions have been a source of trouble because they do not seem to fit precisely into any of the established classifications. Some logicians construe them as universal statements. Since the predicate is applied to the entire subject, they treat the subject in this case as a class having one member. Others treat singular propositions as particular statements because the subject is an individual. Among the Arab logicians, al-Fārābi classifies singular propositions as particular, while Avicenna classifies them as universal.[9] The debate has persisted for centuries, but here Maimonides goes his own way, taking an independent stand for which there is no clear precedent. He distinguishes singular propositions from all other types and makes a special point of not assimilating them to any other form of proposition. He tells us nothing at all, however,

9. Cf. al-Fārābi, *Short Commentary on Aristotle's Prior Analytics,* 53–54. On Avicenna see Ibrahim Madkour, *L'Organon d'Aristote dans le Monde Arabe* (Paris, 1969), 171: "Comme Aristote, Ibn Sina assimile les singulières aux universelles et les indéterminées aux particulières."

about how to integrate these propositions into the standard system of logic, nor does he give us any information about how to deal with cases of opposition between singular propositions. They evidently are not to be treated like standard cases of contradictories or contraries.[10]

This topic is especially important because all propositions that have "God" as their subject are singular propositions. If, as Maimonides tells us, the *Guide* has as its subject "the science of the law in its true sense," and this includes *Ma'aseh Merkavah* (i.e., metaphysics and theology), then it follows that the subject matter of the book must include extensive discussions about God, as it in fact does. Thus we face difficult problems of interpretation if we do not have a proper logical understanding of how to classify and deal with singular propositions. Whenever we have statements of which "God" is the subject, and the statements are in some way opposed or inconsistent, we have no straightforward rule for resolving the problem. Certainly we cannot with any confidence make use of Strauss' rule for resolving contradictions in Maimonides. It may well be that if the subject matter of "divine science," which is the way to the highest wisdom, can only be expressed in singular propositions, some mode of thinking other than ordinary logic is required of those who would master it.

Our suspicions are confirmed to some degree when we take note of an additional peculiarity in Maimonides' terminology. After setting forth his statement of the seven causes "which should account for the contradictory or contrary statements to be found in any book or compilation" (I, Introduction, p. 17), Maimonides goes on to discuss which of the causes are applicable to which types of books. He reviews briefly various types of sacred literature and then turns to the works of the philosophers and to his own work. Remarkably, he makes no reference to contradictions or contraries in the case of the works of the true philosophers or of his own work. Instead, he introduces a new term which Pines translates as "divergences." "As for the divergences [*ikhtilāf*] occurring in the books of the philosophers, or rather of those who know the truth, they are due to the fifth cause. . . . Divergences that are to be found in this Treatise are due to the fifth cause and the seventh. Know this, grasp its true meaning, and remember it very well so as not to become perplexed by some of its chapters" (I, Introduction, pp. 19–20).[11]

---

10. For a discussion of this subject see Efros, *Maimonides' Treatise on Logic,* 21–23. Discussing the importance of Maimonides' work in the light of the earlier logical teachings, Efros makes the wise observation that "perhaps the significance of our work lies not where it agrees . . . but where it shows discrimination in daring to disagree." At least with respect to his treatment of singular propositions, Maimonides does not follow an established school.

11. In the ibn Tibbon translation, we have the Hebrew cognate *ḥilluf,* but in the al-Ḥarizi translation this sentence is missing completely in the printed editions.

Of critical importance here is the fact that, both in the case of the works of the philosophers and (what is of particular interest to us) his own work, Maimonides makes no mention of the standard types of logical opposition. *He says nothing about the presence of contradictions or contraries in his own work,* although he begins this section with an account of how we are to explain any contradictions or contraries that we find in various types of literature. Shall we conclude that there are no contradictions or contraries in Maimonides' own book? Or is he directing our attention to other types of actual or seeming inconsistencies in the *Guide,* while telling us nothing about contradictions that we may find in his book? At this point, we cannot answer with any certainty, but it is clear that we must pay particularly close attention to this new term that he has subtly, and with almost no warning, introduced into the discussion. Since we know that Maimonides has written his book in such a way as to test the competence of his readers, it is reasonable to suppose that taking note of this new term and reflecting on its implications are part of that test. Few of the most eminent and justly respected of the medieval or modern writers on Maimonides have met this challenge.

The term "divergence" confronts us with special problems. In the history of logic before Maimonides, the term has no established use. It appears that only one of the earlier Arab logicians used the term at all, and his usage is so broad as to rob it of any technical significance.[12] The term is not used by al-Fārābi, upon whom Maimonides depended so heavily in the field of logic. We can only conclude that he has deliberately introduced a nontechnical term in order to make careful readers aware that in his book we must look for and deal with types of inconsistency that are not standard logical forms.[13]

12. Only the early logician ibn al-Muqaffa used *ikhtilāf* as a logical term. He used it, however, to mean opposition in general and also with qualifiers to mean the various types of contraries and contradictories. See F. W. Zimmerman, "Some Observations on al-Farabi and Logical Tradition," in the Walzer festschrift *Islamic Philosophy and the Classical Tradition,* ed. S. M. Stern, A. Houra, and V. Brown (Columbia, S.C., 1973), 530–31. It appears doubtful that the terminology of ibn al-Muqaffa would have influenced Maimonides.

13. In his logic Maimonides identifies a certain type of syllogism as *qiyas al-khalaf,* which is translated by Efros as "apagogic" syllogism. Two of the three Hebrew translators use the term *hekesh ha-ḥilluf.* See Efros, *Maimonides' Treatise on Logic,* chap. 7. This is a mode of argument that depends on *reductio ad absurdum* or *reductio ad impossibile.* Its source is in Aristotle's *Prior Analytics,* I, 29b1–10. This is of little help to us here, since it is nothing more than a mode of argument in which a conclusion is established by showing that its contradictory must be false. As we shall see in the discussion that follows, there are "divergences" of various types in the *Guide* that by no means fit this simple model. It seems therefore that Maimonides has something else in mind when he uses the term *divergence* in connection with the apparent inconsistencies in his own book.

I am inclined to believe that Maimonides has given us earlier clues intended to catch our attention and alert us to what lies ahead. Twice in his introductory remarks he uses forms of the term *ikhtilāf* and on both occasions specifically in connection with his own work. The translators have not taken care to convey the exact term that is used in Arabic. The first occasion is in the general introduction, where he notes that his book is written for "one who has philosophized and has knowledge of the true sciences." He instructs that type of reader in some of the oddities to expect in the *Guide* and explains that in certain chapters one should look for hints and clues of a particular sort. Then he adds, "Such a chapter may contain strange matters regarding which the contrary of the truth sometimes is believed" (I, Introduction, p. 10). The term translated as "contrary" is *khālāf,* and I believe that if we take seriously Maimonides' emphasis on the care with which he has chosen each word, we should be consistent and translate the expression as "that which diverges from the truth," rather than as "the contrary of the truth." The latter has a specific technical meaning, and Maimonides did not choose to use his own technical term for 'contrary', *taddād* or one of its derivatives.[14] It is interesting that in this early reference to what may be jarring to the attentive reader, Maimonides speaks of cases where people sometimes believe what diverges from the truth. We are not informed of the nature of this divergence, but the terminology itself is enough to alert us to the likelihood that he is not talking about standard cases of logical inconsistency.

The second case is also in reference to his book. Maimonides asks an oath of his readers not to offer their own explanations of the *Guide* to others. If they believe him to have said anything original, they should keep it to themselves. Moreover, he urges that a reader who thinks Maimonides is in error "should not hasten to refute me, for that which he understood me to say might be contrary to my intention" (I, Introduction, p. 15). Here again the term rendered as "contrary" is *khālāf,* which I believe would be better translated as "may diverge." In this case, ibn Tibbon does in fact render it by its Hebrew cognate, *ḥilluf.* Again Maimonides seems to be informing us that there are modes of inconsistency with his own intentions that are important and must command our attention, but which do not share the characteristics of contradictories or contraries. Finally, in his discussion of the reasons for

14. It is worth noting that ibn Tibbon in his translation does exactly the same thing when he renders the phrase *hefekh ha'emet.* In other contexts the term *hefekh* is used by him to mean "contrary" in the technical sense. Thus, he begins his version of the passage on the seven causes with reference to the causes of *hasetirah 'o hahefekh,* contradiction or contrariety.

inconsistencies in the Talmud, he speaks of "contradictions or divergences [*ikhtilāf*]" to be found in that work (I, Introduction, p. 19).

Before we turn to a discussion of cases of supposed contradictions, it may be instructive to note that among the medieval commentators Joseph Kaspi was perfectly clear about the distinction between contraries and contradictories.[15] In contrast, Shem Tov, in his comment on the opening of the discussion concerning the causes of contraries or contradictories in various types of books, makes the error of eliminating the distinction between the two. He says, "Contradictories and contraries are such that they cannot both be true, but it is possible that both should be false." Now it is correct that contraries are such that both may be false, but this is certainly not the case with respect to contradictories. This may explain in part why the comments of Shem Tov about particular cases of contradictions in the *Guide* tend to be singularly unilluminating. Furthermore, both Shem Tov and Efodi are careless in their quotations or paraphrases of Maimonides' carefully chosen language. Where Maimonides speaks about the "divergences" that may be found in his book, they substitute 'contradiction' (*setirah*) for the term 'divergence'. In this case, ibn Tibbon, who is not always meticulously careful in matters of terminology, correctly has *ḥilluf*.

Since Maimonides informs us that the divergences in his book are due to the fifth or the seventh cause, it is important to look carefully at his account of these causes. The fifth cause is purely a matter of didactic strategy. In teaching any given subject matter, the teacher must take account of the level of the student's knowledge and intellectual development. This requires the teacher at times to give an initial account that is not fully accurate, or even one that in some degree misrepresents a particular point. Later, when the student is ready to understand the subject at a deeper level, the earlier account is corrected. It is obvious that we have here not instances of genuine contradictions but only a teaching device adopted by the skillful teacher for the benefit of the pupil. No terms for the opposition of propositions are used in the discussion of the fifth cause; there is no mention of contradictories or contraries.

In the case of the seventh cause, however, we must pay very close attention to exactly what Maimonides says, since whatever genuine contradictions, contraries, or divergences we find in the *Guide* are, by the author's own testimony, due to this cause. As we study the brief paragraph carefully, however, we come to the frustrating conclusion that the author has told us

15. See *Maskiyyot Kesef*, 9, in *Shelosha Kadmonei Mefarshei Hamoreh* (photocopied edition, Jerusalem, 1961).

very little. Let us examine the text. "In speaking about very obscure matters it is necessary to conceal some parts and to disclose others" (I, Introduction, p. 18). We are not informed of the nature of the obscurity that we are dealing with here. Is it identical with the obscurity of subject matter that occupies us in the case of the fifth cause? Is it different and, if so, in what way? Maimonides does not clarify this point. Nor does he tell us what it is about that particular form of obscurity that requires us to conceal some parts and to disclose others. He goes on to say that sometimes "this necessity requires that the discussion proceed on the basis of a certain premise, whereas in another place necessity requires that the discussion proceed on the basis of another premise contradicting the first one." We are not told the nature of this "necessity" or how the author determines when to employ one premise or its contradictory. It is worth noting that, among the medieval commentators, both Shem Tov and Efodi cite the sentence about basing the later discussion on a premise that contradicts the first one, and then add their own words, *kefi ha'emet,* that is, "in accordance with the truth." In this way they add to what Maimonides actually says without any clear justification, thereby confusing the issue. Finally, we are cautioned that "the vulgar must in no way be aware of the contradiction; the author accordingly uses some device to conceal it by all means." Again we are given no understanding of why the contradiction must be hidden from the vulgar. What undesirable effects will it have if they should learn about the contradiction? Maimonides gives no help at all in clarifying this obscure account of the seventh cause.

The usual assumption is that we are dealing here with the exposition of doctrines that will seem heretical to all but the most highly sophisticated readers. According to this view, Maimonides' position is that we must not risk corrupting the simple innocent faith of the vulgar; hence, we must conceal from them any premise that would endanger their spiritual health. Moreover, we must never let them discover that we are basing our real doctrines on such seemingly dangerous premises. Finally, we must conceal from them the contradiction inherent in this entire procedure, otherwise we again risk corrupting them. While it is likely that Maimonides did mean something of this kind, we must nevertheless stress that the account of the seventh cause tells us nothing explicit about this matter. This account may be correct but, if so, it will have to be justified by an analysis of what Maimonides actually does in his book.

Let us turn then to an examination of some actual instances of 'divergences' in the *Guide* in the hope that we may be able to achieve a somewhat better understanding of this complex topic. We begin with some cases of alleged contradictions in the *Guide* noted by Strauss. In the course of his elaborate discussion of prophecy, Maimonides stresses the uniqueness of the prophecy of Moses, its incomparability to all other instances of prophecy, and the fact that we are not able to give a proper account of it. In this connection, he asserts: "As for the prophecy of Moses our Master, I shall not touch upon it in these chapters with even a single word, either in explicit fashion or in a flash" (II, 35, p. 367). Yet we know that he does in fact discuss various aspects of Mosaic prophecy. Strauss points out that in the *Guide* we are explicitly taught that unlike all the other prophets the prophecy of Moses had no element of the imagination in it, but was purely intellectual. On this basis Strauss observes, "Undoubtedly Maimonides contradicts himself regarding Moses' prophecy."[16] This is a typical instance of speaking about 'contradictions' loosely and with no regard for the technical meaning of the term. Whatever seems to have gone wrong here, it is not a 'contradiction' in any literal sense. How would Strauss go about even applying his own rule to the resolution of this "contradiction"?

What we have here is a statement, followed by an action inconsistent with that statement. Now a statement can be contradicted only by another statement, not by an action. This is why Maimonides was so careful to speak about the seven causes that "should account for the contradictory or contrary *statements* to be found in any book." Truth or falsity are exclusively properties of statements, never of actions. Consequently, it is misleading to speak about Maimonides' *action* as being in contradiction to his earlier statement. Admittedly, something is not in order here; however, it is not a logical contradiction, but a difficulty of another sort. I take this to be one instance of what Maimonides meant by "divergences." We have here an inconsistency that engages our attention by, in effect, stopping the smooth flow of the text. The author does something that he said he would not do. We are forced to stop, to reflect, to determine whether he has actually done what he said he would not do, or whether he only seems to have done so, and to try to understand what has happened here.

This is certainly not a case of hiding something from his readers by using esoteric rhetorical devices. Any reader, however unskilled, will soon realize that Maimonides does say a great many things about Mosaic prophecy, even after he has assured us emphatically that he will not say a single word about that subject. It may be that we see here an instance of the fifth cause. For didactic purposes Maimonides needs to make clear early on that no one can give a full and adequate account of Mosaic prophecy. It will be difficult enough to understand fully the account of the lesser levels of prophecy, but the unique prophecy of Moses transcends our capacity to under-

16. Strauss, "How to Begin to Study *The Guide of the Perplexed*," in Maimonides, *Guide*, trans. Pines, xxxvi–xxxvii.

stand. This point has to be stressed in a way that leaves no possible doubt. Yet even to characterize other modes of prophecy, we are forced to speak of them in contrast with the prophecy of Moses, and in this process we necessarily say something about Mosaic prophecy as well.

With enough understanding developed in the course of study and reflection, it will become clear to the reader that even when Maimonides does speak about Mosaic prophecy, he does not give any clear account of it. To take just one point, which Strauss also discusses, we find it difficult to understand the claim that there is no element of imagination in Moses' prophecy. He does, after all, employ metaphors and similes that are the work of the imagination. We might even say that when Maimonides appears to be speaking about the prophecy of Moses, he is not really doing so, because he says nothing that is fully intelligible. However we finally understand this inconsistency about the prophecy of Moses, it is certain that it is not a contradiction, but some other form of difficulty, one. that Maimonides includes under his term 'divergence'.

A similar case occurs with respect to Maimonides' treatment of prayer, where again Strauss claims to have found a contradiction. "The demonstrated teaching that positive attributes of God are impossible stems from the philosophers (I, 59; III, 20); it clearly contradicts the teaching of the Law in so far as the Law does not limit itself to teaching that the only true praise of God is silence but it also prescribes that we call God 'great, mighty, and terrible' in our prayers."[17] There is no question that something is not quite in order here, but it is not a formal contradiction. We have noted that an action cannot contradict a statement; the same is true of an imperative. Like actions, imperatives have no truth value and cannot be either true or false. But to contradict a statement is to assert its falsehood. Hence it makes no sense to speak of the Law's requiring a particular form of prayer as contradicting the statement that God has no positive attributes. Moreover, even if it were a contradiction, it would not be a contradiction internal to Maimonides but rather one between the teaching of the Law on the one hand and that of Maimonides on the other. We need to take a more careful look at the whole issue.

Admittedly, prayer constitutes a problem for Maimonides just because we can never say anything positive about God that is philosophically acceptable.[18] The intellectual ideal would be the worship that expresses itself only

17. Ibid., xlviii.

18. For a more extended discussion of this problem, see M. Fox, "Hatefillah b'Maḥashavto shel ha-Rambam," in *Hatefillah Hayehudit: Hemshekh Veḥiddush*, ed. Gabriel H. Cohn (Jerusalem, 1978), 142–67. A revised version of the substantive argument of that paper is contained in chapter 11 of the present book.

through silence. Yet not only are we commanded by the Law to worship God in certain fixed linguistic formulas, but the need of the human spirit is such that it cannot help but express itself in words. In allowing both the denial of divine attributes and the duty to pray within his system, Maimonides presents us not with a contradiction, but again with a form of divergence. The two parts do not go together smoothly, and the attentive reader is forced to reflect on the implications of this inconsistency. For the untutored masses the problem need not arise at all; they find no difficulty in speaking about God in positive terms or in affirming that He possesses positive attributes. The intellectually sophisticated will feel the problem once they have grasped the teachings of Maimonides concerning God's attributes.

How can thoughtful readers go about dealing with this inconsistency, which cannot be treated as simply a logical problem in which we have to determine which of two contradictories is true and which false? They can recognize it as a divergence explicable by the seventh cause. In the process they can gain insight into how Maimonides solves for himself the problem of prayer. It is clear that Maimonides might have chosen to affirm his doctrine of divine attributes and simply have rejected categorically all possibility of prayer. Or he could have maintained a stance of simple piety with regard to prayer and given up or remained silent about the doctrine of attributes. In holding to both simultaneously, he seems to affirm that there must be a place within a single system for the demands of both religious piety and philosophical truth. To present this complex notion directly to unphilosophical readers would involve the risk of tearing them away from the life of piety. If they recognize the inconsistency, they may never be able to return to the life of faith, but they will also not be intellectually qualified to lead the life of the worship of God through the intellect alone. Consequently, it is important to keep them from being aware that, although the religious act is based on the premise that one can speak meaningfully and in positive terms about God, the philosophical analysis denies that premise. For the philosophical reader, the discovery of the tension between the teaching of the Law and the teaching of philosophy will pose the problem of which should prevail.

Maimonides enunciates the ideal of a form of worship that makes no use of language, but he also recognizes that this presents an impossible demand not only for common people, but even for philosophers. His solution is to retain both the language of worship and the truth about divine attributes within a single system. These elements of the system live in dialectical tension, and it is a great art to keep them in balance. Yet as we reflect on the "divergence" between the requirement to worship and the requirements of philosophical truth within the work of Maimonides, we learn a profound lesson. Contradictions must be resolved if we know with certainty which of the contradictories is true and which false. Intellectual honesty leaves us no choice but to affirm the one and reject the other.[19] About this, Maimonides is absolutely uncompromising. When we do not have a genuine contradiction but, as in the case of prayer, a divergence between a religious commandment and a philosophically demonstrated principle, then Maimonides teaches us the great art of balancing the two. To know how to keep them in balance and to live with the tension is precisely what is required of the religious man who seeks and discovers philosophical truth. We should never forget that it is to just such a person that Maimonides addressed his great work.

Another type of divergence arises with respect to the principle that we have a duty to imitate God. Maimonides treats this as a duty that defines the ideal of human conduct. "For the utmost virtue of man is to become like unto Him . . . as far as he is able; which means that we should make our actions like unto His, as the Sages made clear when interpreting the verse, 'Ye shall be holy' " (I, 52, p. 118). This theme is repeated in the *Guide* and is the foundation of *Hilkhot De'ot,* which Maimonides construes as a fulfillment of the commandment to imitate the ways of God (*lehidammot biderakhav*). Yet he also repeatedly expresses the conviction that there is "absolutely no likeness in any respect whatever between Him and the things created by Him" (I, 35, p. 80).[20] How can we imitate God if there is absolutely no likeness whatsoever between God and man? The puzzle grows even more complicated when we realize that Maimonides extends this doctrine to include a denial of any relations between God and man. "There is no relation in any respect between Him and any of His creatures" (I, 52, p. 118).[21] Now, it is only with respect to actions that we are told to be like God, and we know that Maimonides was tolerant and open to the idea of predicating of Him attributes of action. But this does little to solve our problem since even imitating God's actions, rather than God Himself, still suggests that there is some relation of similarity between God and man. Furthermore, "likeness" and "similarity" are symmetrical relations. This means that if in any respect man is like God, then, at least in that same respect, God is like man.

By now it is no longer necessary to point out that there can be no contradiction between a statement and a commandment. Hence we do not have here a case of direct contradiction or contrariety, but a divergence of some

19. On the matter of total commitment to accept as true whatever is established by demonstration, see, for example, *Guide,* II, 25.

20. This theme recurs with frequency. See, for example, I, 55, p. 128, where Maimonides says that we must "of necessity deny, with reference to Him, His being similar to any existing thing."

21. See I, 55, p. 128.

sort. Yet it is immediately evident that the premise on which the commandment to imitate God rests is problematic. We must assume that the fact that we are so commanded presupposes that there is some meaningful way in which the commandment can be fulfilled. This point is made by the Sages when they tell us in what ways to imitate God. This, in turn, rests on the premise that there can be some likeness between human action and divine action, and in that respect some likeness between man and God. We might formulate this premise as "God is a being who has some similarity to man." It is opposed by the philosophical statement that "God is a being who has no similarity whatsoever to man." We see immediately the nature of our problem. We have two opposed statements, but they are singular propositions whose subject is "God," so we have no rule for dealing with them. Because Maimonides refuses to follow his predecessors in treating singular propositions as either universals or particulars, we have here a classic case of 'divergence'. There is something logically wrong, but we cannot characterize it accurately, and we have no device for getting it straight within the established rules of logic.

Perhaps some guidance is available to us from the fact that Maimonides, despite the vigor of his denial of relations between God and man, is nevertheless more tolerant of this kind of predication about God than of almost any other. He says, "Relation is an attribute with regard to which it is more appropriate than with regard to the others that indulgence should be exercised if it is predicated of God" (I, 52, p. 118). This indulgence would appear to be in some measure an opening to an understanding of our problem. We are again probably dealing with a case of divergence due to the seventh cause. The philosophic understanding of God rests on the premise of His absolute uniqueness. The religious understanding that aims at the ordering of the political community rests on the premise that man and God can resemble each other, since men are required to be God-like in their behavior. It is important to protect the vulgar from any awareness of the divergence between these two premises, since rejection of the religious premise invites socially destructive behavior. When the learned discover the problem, they will be able to rely on their training in logic to help them see that these two premises, not being contradictories, are not necessarily mutually exclusive. As is the case with prayer, they will recognize that they are dealing with the tension between an imperative of action and a philosophical conclusion. Although these rest on premises that are in some fashion opposed, we are not forced to reject the one in favor of the other. Here again the model is that of Maimonides himself, who exemplifies for us the way in which a Jew who is a philosopher finds his way through the divergence by balancing, in an ongoing tension, the demands of both worlds.

A particularly difficult problem arises in connection with the assertion that God is the cause of the world. This is certainly a commonplace of Maimonidean teaching. "God . . . is the principle and the efficient cause of all things other than himself" (I, 16, p. 42). "God is the efficient cause of the world, its form, and its end" (I, 69, p. 167). Such statements can be found throughout the *Guide*. Moreover, they represent a truth that Maimonides claims to have proved beyond question. The demonstrations of God's existence are essentially based on establishing that God is the ultimate cause of the world. This conclusion follows necessarily from a set of seemingly rigorous philosophical arguments. Yet it conflicts with other doctrines of Maimonides. Cause is a relation, and we have already seen how vigorously Maimonides argues against the claim that there can be any relations between God and the world. He not only argues against this claim but also believes he has demonstrated its contradictory. In that case it would appear that we have before us demonstrations for opposed propositions. One asserts that "God has at least one relation with the world, namely, cause." The other denies that God has any relation with the world whatsoever.

These are, of course, singular propositions, and it may thus be that they are neither contrary nor contradictory, but divergent. In that case we cannot resolve the problem by determining which is true and which is false. For the vulgar to discover that there can be any problem about understanding God as the cause of the world would be intolerable. Confronting these opposed propositions might only undermine their faith in God, the Creator. The learned, however, should not fall into this error. They should understand that discourse about God is not limited by the known rules of logic and that there may well be cases where it is permissible, even necessary, to affirm seemingly inconsistent propositions in which the subject is "God."

Maimonides thought in just such terms. We need only consider what he himself does with respect to the issue of God's providence and/or governance of the world—one of the most important and comprehensive of all cases of divine causality. It is complicated not only by the difficulty of arriving at an unambiguous account of Maimonides' views, but also by the problems we have just pointed out concerning any claims that might be made about divine causality. The difficulties are openly set forth by Maimonides in a passage that might well serve as a model for any commentator on this subject: "For the governance and the providence of Him, may He be exalted, accompany the world as a whole in such a way that the manner and true reality of this accompaniment are hidden from us; the faculties of human beings are inadequate to understand this. On the one hand, there is a demonstration of His separateness, may He be exalted, from the world and of His being free from it; and on the other hand, there is a demonstration that the influence of His governance and providence in every part of the world, however small and contemptible, exists. May He whose perfection has dazzled us be glorified" (I, 72, p. 193). We are in the situation in which we have demonstrations for opposed propositions that refer to God. In this passage Maimonides does not speak of contrary or contradictory propositions. He only notes the fact that he has proved with seeming validity both that God is completely separate from the world and that He is present in the world as its cause. If this is not a case of contradiction, then it is certainly a case of divergence. How shall we deal with it?[22]

Affirming opposed statements about God, even if they are not formally contradictory, is an offense to the intellect. Consistency is the very stuff of which all rationality is made. Yet Maimonides asks us to accept the claim that he has demonstrated inconsistent propositions about God. This is remarkably similar to what we find in the section of Kant's *Critique of Pure Reason* dealing with the antinomies. There too the claim is made that both a thesis and its antithesis have been demonstrated—a situation that is intolerable, but inescapable. For Kant this is one of the ways in which he establishes that metaphysics is impossible, although we have a natural disposition to do metaphysics which persists against all counterforces. This is the point of the opening sentence of the preface to the first edition of the first *Critique*. "Human reason has this peculiar fate that in one species of its knowledge it is burdened by questions which, as prescribed by the very nature of reason itself, it is not able to ignore, but which, as transcending all its powers, it is also not able to answer." The problem is that once we are dealing with that which transcends all actual and all possible human experience, we no longer have any control over the subject matter. That is why it is possible to demonstrate, or to seem to demonstrate, both a thesis and its antithesis when dealing with such subjects. Kant's solution, as implied in the title of his book, is to discover the limits of reason and then to effect the Copernican revolution of the intellect that is his special contribution to philosophical thought.

I do not want anachronistically to turn Maimonides into a Kantian, but I do believe that we are able to get some insight into Maimonides from a Kantian perspective. He too sees that once we come to talk about God, we no longer have the concepts and the controls necessary for philosophical clarity and reliability. Yet we are dealing with subjects about which we cannot afford to remain agnostic. We cannot say that we do not know and leave it at that, since in our lives we will behave and think in such way as to have taken

---

22. An extended discussion of the problem of divine causality will be found in chapter 9; the problem of the creation or eternity of the world is taken up in chapter 10.

a stand. There are times, as in the case of providence and divine causality, when we may even have to affirm inconsistent propositions, simply because we can neither refute them nor give them up. This is why Maimonides can only end his comments on this subject with an expression of praise to God: "May He whose perfection has dazzled us [i.e., left our intellects stunned] be glorified." It helps to remember that Kant, in full awareness of the implications of his work, informs us, "I have therefore found it necessary to deny *knowledge,* in order to make room for *faith.*"[23] It may be argued that Maimonides should not be credited with fully anticipating the Kantian revolution, but he did have an acute sense of the limits of human knowledge and of our human need to go beyond what is known in cases where demonstration is unavailable or impossible.

This becomes evident in a passage that has not sufficiently occupied the attention of students of the *Guide,* although it seems to overturn in one stroke much that Maimonides has repeatedly affirmed. It is generally recognized that Maimonides consistently treats the existence of God as a demonstrated truth. Having set forth the proofs for God's existence based on the premise of the eternity of the world, he concludes, "All these are demonstrative methods of proving the existence of one deity, who is neither a body nor a force in a body, while believing at the same time in the eternity of the world" (II, 1, p. 249). His strategy, as he tells us, is to show that we can prove the existence of God even if we begin from the premise of the eternity of the world; it appears then to be self-evident that we can prove his existence while affirming the creation of the world in time. Jewish tradition teaches that at Sinai, the first two commandments were heard by every one present. This is interpreted by Maimonides to mean that since the existence of God and His unity are demonstrated truths, they were apprehended by all the people without the mediation of prophecy for "with regard to everything that can be known by demonstration, the status of the prophet and that of everyone else who knows it are equal; there is no superiority of one over the other" (II, 33, p. 364). It would seem then that there is no question about Maimonides' conviction that the unity and the existence of God have been shown to be demonstrated truths.

Yet there is one striking passage in which Maimonides throws doubt on any claim to prove the existence of God, on the ground that such knowledge is beyond the limits of human experience and thus beyond the capacity of the human intellect. "For it is impossible for us to accede to the points starting from which conclusions may be drawn about the heavens; for the latter are too far away from us and too high in place and in rank. *And even the general*

---

23. *Critique of Pure Reason,* Preface to the Second Edition, B xxx.

conclusion that may be drawn from them, namely, that they prove the existence of their Mover, is a matter the knowledge of which cannot be reached by human intellects. And to fatigue the minds with notions that cannot be grasped by them and for the grasp of which they have no instrument, is a defect in one's inborn disposition or some sort of temptation. Let us then stop at a point that is within our capacity, and let us give over the things that cannot be grasped by reasoning to him who was reached by the mighty divine overflow [i.e., Moses] so that it could fittingly be said of him: With him do I speak mouth to mouth" (II, 24, p. 327; emphasis added).[24]

Here we seem to have an actual instance of a contradiction. One statement affirms that there are no proofs for the existence of God, while the other affirms that there are some proofs for the existence of God. A universal negative is opposed by a particular affirmative, and these are true contradictories. In that case, we would be forced to conclude that one is true and the other false, but we do not know which is which. Did Maimonides think that he had, in fact, demonstrated the existence of God, or did he think that his proofs were invalid and that no demonstration is possible? We seem to have no convincing answer to this question. If we were to invoke the criterion proposed by Strauss, we would conclude that Maimonides denies that it is possible to prove God's existence, since that statement occurs only once in the *Guide* while its contradictory occurs many times. Should this not lead us then to the decision that most of the philosophic conclusions drawn by Maimonides are also unsound, since many of them derive from the proofs for the existence and the unity of God? What, for example, about the strong defense of God's incorporeality against all literal readings of Scripture and the rabbinic aggadah? This doctrine depends directly on the proofs for God's existence and unity. If we follow the Straussian directive, we are likely to undermine the entire structure built by Maimonides and thus return to a prescientific, prephilosophical mode of religious thought. But this would turn the whole Maimonidean enterprise into an absurd charade for which we could find no intelligible purpose.

---

24. This is the translation of Pines, who notes that his version differs from that of ibn Tibbon. This translation is fully justified by the original text. Munk gives essentially the same translation and makes a point of noting that it follows the reading in all available manuscripts and is also translated this way by al-Ḥarizi. He suggests that the translation of ibn Tibbon is motivated by a desire to make this passage harmonize with all the statements that affirm proofs for the existence of God. In a recent study, Alexander Altmann takes the position that this is not a correct reading of this passage. He concludes, "For Maimonides the existence, unity and incorporeality of God constitute the *terra firma* of Divine science." See Altmann, "Maimonides on the Intellect and the Scope of Metaphysics," in *Von der mittelalterlichen zur modernen Aufklärung* (Tübingen, 1987), 117.

Here again it helps to give greater care to the logical analysis of the issues and closer attention to Maimonides' instructions. It is logically correct to construe the propositions in question as contradictories only if we formulate them with the term "proofs" as their subject. If, on the other hand, we decide that the correct formulation should have "God" as the subject, the entire situation is changed. Then they would read: "God is a being whose existence can be proved" and "God is a being whose existence cannot be proved." These are singular propositions which require a different analysis. We are now faced not with a set of contradictories, but with some form of divergence. We do not have any logical tools for dealing with this difficulty, but we can give some account of what is before us. Proving the existence of God is essential both for the entire philosophical structure that Maimonides wants to erect and also to protect the purity of faith from contamination by any element of divine corporeality. Without such proof there is no basis for the claim that Maimonides' nonliteral reading of anthropomorphisms in the Bible is correct, and that any literal reading is mistaken. Hence he has more than ample reason to use every intellectual device available to prove the existence of God. Moreover, this effort is fully supported by the great philosophical tradition of Aristotelianism with which Maimonides associates himself. Several proofs are presented, and their reliability is invoked over and over, in order to be certain that all segments of the population, learned as well as vulgar, are protected from the destructive effects of erroneous doctrines about God.

Yet at some point it must be made clear to those of true intellectual sophistication that, in the end, no argument for the existence of God is completely sufficient. We force the intellect to carry us as far as we can possibly go in acquiring a rational understanding of these ultimate things and rational certainty about them.[25] In the end, however, and at the most critical point, we are dependent on faith in the prophecy of Moses. This is made known in the isolated passage quoted above—a passage that escapes the attention of most readers and even evokes disbelief from some translators. This is a classic instance of a divergence that can be explained by the seventh cause.

There are other inconsistencies, particularly about God, that display basically the same structure. There is, for example, the tension between the doctrine that God acts out of free choice and the opposed claim that He acts out of an inexorable inner necessity. Maimonides construes the verse that God speaks to Moses, "And thou shalt see my back," to mean, "thou shalt

25. See the discussion of the general problem of the limits of reason as it relates to the proofs for the existence of God in chapter 2.

apprehend what follows from Me, has come to be like Me, and follows *necessarily* from My will—that is, all the things created by Me" (I, 38, p. 87; emphasis added). Here we have the explicit statement that all things created by God follow necessarily from His will. Yet elsewhere Maimonides identifies "the First Cause of all things, I mean God's will and free choice" (II, 48, p. 409). The tension between these two conceptions is present throughout the *Guide*. It is, of course, the tension between the God of Aristotle, who is the first cause that acts only out of necessity, and the God of Scripture, the creator of the world who acts out of complete freedom and in accordance with His own purposes. The divergence between the two notions is built into the fabric of Maimonides' thought. He needs the Aristotelian first cause to be able to give a scientific account of the world in which there is a fixed natural order. He needs the freely acting Creator-God to provide for biblical prophecy, divine commandments, reward and punishment—all the elements that constitute the religious understanding of humankind, society, and history. He has no absolute intellectual ground for affirming the one at the expense of the other. Instead he retains them both in an ongoing tension. The alert reader will recognize the problem, see quickly that because of the special character of singular propositions we do not have a standard form of contradiction or contrariety here, and then try to penetrate how Maimonides deals with this divergence.

A parallel instance occurs with regard to the tension between human freedom and God's foreknowledge. In discussing this subject in the *Mishneh Torah*, Maimonides begins by setting down human freedom as an absolute condition for any divine commandments to be binding on human beings. It is both a moral and metaphysical requirement that people have free will. At the same time it is also an absolute condition of God's knowledge that it include knowledge of all future events. These propositions appear to be mutually exclusive. If human beings are truly free, then no decision has been made about what they will do until they themselves make the choice. How then can God know in advance? If God does know in advance, how can there be any free choice? The only answer Maimonides can give is that divine knowledge cannot be understood on the model of human knowledge. In some mysterious way God can know future events without causing those events to occur necessarily. We do not understand how this works, but we know with certainty that God has foreknowledge and that human beings are free. He adds that this is not only a matter of religious tradition, but of established scientific knowledge as well.[26]

In the *Guide* the same tension emerges in a somewhat different form.

26. *H. Teshuvah*, 5:5, 6:5.

When the emphasis is on God's justice, the principle of human freedom is stated in absolute terms. It is set down as a fundamental principle of the Torah of Moses that "man has an absolute ability to act; I mean to say that in virtue of his nature, his choice, and his will, he may do everything that it is within the capacity of man to do" (III, 17, p. 469). When, however, the subject is God as cause of the world and the events in it, we have a quite different statement. Here we are given an account of the deity as "He who arouses a particular volition in the irrational animal and who has *necessitated* this particular free choice in the rational animal" (II, 48, p. 410; emphasis added). So we have both the assertion that human beings are absolutely free and that God necessitates each free choice.

The notion of a free choice necessitated by an outside force seems itself to be a contradiction in terms. We are again dealing with a subject with respect to which there is the claim that inconsistent propositions have been demonstrated. In *Hilkhot Teshuvah,* Maimonides is open and straightforward about the seeming inconsistency. He makes no effort to hide it, nor does he attempt to resolve it. In the *Guide,* he is less open, separating his various statements so that they may not be noticed by ordinary readers. He expects, however, that these opposed statements will be noticed by careful readers. The statements will engage their attention, and they will have to decide how to deal with the issue. With no ground for affirming one proposition and denying the other, their only option may be to do what Maimonides recommends in the *Mishneh Torah,* namely, to affirm both statements as true without being able to give an account of how it can be so.

Maimonides would be a far easier writer to understand if he had not strewn so many obstacles in our path. If he needed to include a deliberate collection of inconsistencies in his book, it would have been far easier to cope with them if they were all of a standard logical type. If he were dealing with ordinary instances of contraries, subcontraries, or contradictories, we would know how to approach them with the standard tools of Aristotelian logic. Things would be quite clear indeed if, in addition, we had certain knowledge as to which of the various propositions were true and which false. It is not just perversity on the part of Maimonides that he does not make things easy for his readers, nor is it simply deliberate esotericism. It is dictated, above all, by the nature of the subject matter with which he is dealing. This subject matter generates problems that do not yield neat and easy solutions, as the whole history of Western philosophy will bear witness. This is particularly true of discourse about God.

Maimonides had as profound a grasp of the complexities of this subject matter as any philosopher in our tradition. He was a thinker of rigorous honesty, and was incapable of self-deception. He knew full well the difference between probability and certainty, between demonstration and conjecture. He was clear about where knowledge ends and faith or commitment begins. As a result, he saw it as his obligation to present readers not only with his certainties but also with his doubts, not only with demonstrations but also with conjectures. The reader who is competent to follow the labyrinthine structure of Maimonides' argument and who pays close attention to his language and his instructions will emerge with a deep understanding of what Maimonides thought was philosophically or scientifically knowable and what was a matter of faith.

We may learn, above all, the high and sensitive intellectual responsibility that Maimonides practiced. The notion that the secrets of the *Guide* will be revealed to us by a simple method of discovering so-called contradictions, and determining in some mechanical way which of them he was affirming, stems from a failure to appreciate the depth of sophistication and the high level of seriousness with which Maimonides did his work. I believe that in this respect he was a profound and subtle disciple of Plato (whether or not he had actually read much Plato). In the *Phaedo* Plato sets forth a basic principle of philosophic method. Socrates evokes from his young friend Simmias the following remarkable summary of the true way of the philosopher.

> I think, Socrates, as perhaps you do yourself, that it is either impossible or very difficult to acquire clear knowledge about these matters in this life. And yet he is a weakling who does not test in every way what is said about them and persevere until he is worn out by studying them on every side. For he must do one of two things; either he must learn or discover the truth about these matters, or if that is impossible, he must take whatever human doctrine is best and hardest to disprove and, embarking upon it as upon a raft, sail upon it through life in the midst of dangers, unless he can sail upon some stronger vessel, some divine revelation, and make his voyage more safely and securely.[27]

We must not give up the search for rational demonstration or empirical evidence too soon. Neither should we suppose that nothing less than demonstration is ever useful as a guide to our thinking. The challenge is to settle for no less than demonstrative certainty whenever it is available. Lacking an ideal kind of answer, we must still exercise our full intellectual powers

27. Plato, *Phaedo*, 85CD. An extensive discussion of this question of Plato's philosophic methodology is contained in M. Fox, "The Trials of Socrates: An Interpretation of the First Tetralogy," *Archiv für Philosophie*, 6(3/4) (1957), 226–61.

to achieve the best answers we can. The answers will inevitably fall short of the ideal, but they will reflect the deepest understanding we can arrive at after sincere and intense struggle with the hardest and most important questions that human beings have to confront.

That this is the method to which Maimonides is committed is evident from all that he has written. He states so explicitly when he tells us that the man who aspires to perfection "attains a rank at which he pronounces the . . . correct opinions to be true; and in order to arrive at this conclusion, he uses the veritable methods, namely, demonstration in cases where demonstration is possible, or strong arguments where this is possible. In this way he represents to himself these matters, which had appeared to him as imaginings and parables, in their truth and understands their essence" (I, 33, p. 72).

PART II
ASPECTS OF MAIMONIDES' ETHICAL THEORY

5

The Doctrine of the Mean in Aristotle and Maimonides

A Comparative Study

The scholarly literature dealing with the interpretation of the philosophy of Maimonides moves between two poles. As we noted earlier, some scholars insist that Maimonides was in all significant respects a true and faithful disciple of Aristotle, or of the Aristotelianism that he knew through the Arabic sources. At the other extreme are those who argue that the Aristotelianism of Maimonides is only a surface appearance and that he was, in fact, not an Aristotelian at all in his actual philosophical and theological doctrines.

This difference of opinion is especially sharp in the discussions of Maimonides' ethics, particularly with respect to his doctrine of the mean. This doctrine is as prominent in the ethical thought of Maimonides as in the ethics of Aristotle. Without a sound understanding of this teaching of Maimonides, we cannot arrive at a correct understanding of his ethical theory. I shall show that we can grasp Maimonides' version of the doctrine of the mean only if we see it in direct comparison with Aristotle's. Our first question is whether we have any clear indication as to how Maimonides' teachings concerning the mean relate to the Aristotelian doctrine. The clarification of this issue is particularly important because, although many have discussed this subject, few have provided convincing ground for us to believe that they have examined the evidence with sufficient care.

One group of writers takes the position that the pure Aristotelianism of Maimonides' doctrine of the mean is so obvious that it does not even require discussion or evidence. Writing about Shem Tov ben Joseph Falaquera, Henry Malter says that "the Aristotelian ethics of the golden mean found in Palquera a disciple scarcely less devoted than his master Maimonides."[1] Joseph Gorfinkle, in his edition of the *Eight Chapters of Maimonides*, comments on the chapter "in which the Aristotelian doctrine of the

---

1. Henry Malter, "Shem Tob ben Joseph Palquera," *Jewish Quarterly Review*, n.s. I (1910–11), 160. See his extended footnote on 160–61. Malter preferred the spelling "Palquera" to the more common spelling "Falaquera." See also Henry Malter, *Saadia Gaon: His Life and Works* (New York, 1926), 257.

Mean . . . is applied to Jewish ethics." He argues that "although Maimonides follows Aristotle in defining virtue as a state intermediate between two extremes, . . . he still remains on Jewish ground as there are biblical and talmudical passages expressing such a thought."[2] Harry S. Lewis speaks of "the famous attempt of Maimonides to equate Jewish ethics with the Aristotelian doctrine of the mean." He goes on to affirm that "Maimonides derived his doctrine of the Mean from Greek sources, but it was quite congenial to the native hebraic spirit."[3] In his study of the ethics of Maimonides, David Rosin sees the doctrine of the mean as essentially Aristotelian in origin and character, despite some of Maimonides' deviations from the Aristotelian pattern. He says that Maimonides is in full agreement with Aristotle that actions are good if they follow the rule of proper measure and are in accordance with the mean that lies midway between two extremes.[4] Even those writers who like Rosin seek additional sources of Maimonides' doctrine of the mean in rabbinic literature take the position that these are supports that legitimate the Jewishness of the doctrine, but they do not claim that they are the sources from which Maimonides derived his position.

Opposed to these writers are those who deny that Maimonides' ethics are Aristotelian in any significant respect. We noted briefly in chapter I a typical voice from the traditionalist camp—that of R. Ya'akov Moshe Ḥarlap, who affirms with the greatest passion that no non-Jewish source can ever legitimately make any contribution to Jewish doctrine. After having discussed at great length various aspects of Maimonides' doctrine of the mean, Ḥarlap wants to protect his readers from the mistake of supposing that this doctrine has any non-Jewish origin. If the doctrine appears to be similar to the teachings of Aristotle, this is no more than an appearance, and we must understand it properly. Such a doctrine can enter Jewish teaching from the outside only if it has first been thoroughly Judaized—only if, like the convert, it has been reborn and has acquired a new, specifically Jewish, nature. "Whatever is taught by others cannot be presented as Jewish teaching unless it has first undergone conversion [*gerut*]. Just as it is possible to

2. *The Eight Chapters of Maimonides on Ethics,* ed. and trans. Joseph I. Gorfinkle (New York, 1966; rpt. of 1912 edition), 54.

3. Harry S. Lewis, "The Golden Mean in Judaism," in *Jewish Studies in Memory of Israel Abrahams,* (New York, 1927), 283.

4. David Rosin, *Die Ethik des Maimonides* (Breslau, 1876), 79. Throughout this book, and particularly in his discussion of the mean, Rosin repeatedly cites what he identifies as the Aristotelian sources of Maimonides' doctrines. For similar views with respect to the doctrine of the mean in Maimonides, see M. Wolff, *Musa Maimunis Acht Capitel* (Leiden, 1903), xiii–xiv.

convert souls, so is it possible to convert doctrines."[5] Ḥarlap claims that this is what happened with Maimonides' doctrine of the mean. It may appear to be similar to Aristotle's doctrine, but after having been converted, it is a totally new and uniquely Jewish creation.

Coming to the materials from a different background and perspective, Hermann Cohen also argues fiercely against the Aristotelianism of Maimonides' ethics. Cohen holds that Maimonides chose to give the appearance that he was agreeing with Aristotle only for tactical purposes; otherwise he would have opened himself to endless attack. In fact, says Cohen, Maimonides' doctrine is not Aristotelian at all. It is independent of Aristotle and not in agreement with him. If we were forced to affirm that Maimonides derived his ethics from Aristotle and was in agreement with him, we should then have to conclude that Maimonides had failed both as a moral philosopher and as a religious thinker.[6] Cohen later delineates carefully and in detail the ways in which he finds that Maimonides' doctrine of the mean differs from that of Aristotle.

My aim in this chapter is to present a fresh investigation of the question. I hold, however, that no responsible treatment can be offered of the relationships between Maimonides' and Aristotle's doctrines unless we first understand what Aristotle actually taught. In my view, conventional representations of the doctrine of the mean in Aristotle fail to grasp the

5. Ya'akov Moshe Ḥarlap, *Mei Marom: Mi-Saviv li-Shemonah Perakim le-ha-Rambam* (Jerusalem, 1946), 85–86. An even stronger statement is made by Shem Tov ben Abraham ibn Ga'on in his *Migdal 'Oz*. Commenting on the passage in *H. De'ot*, I, 4, in which Maimonides attributes the doctrine of the mean to the *ḥakhamim ha-rish'onim* (presumably, though not necessarily, the earlier rabbinic authorities), the *Migdal 'Oz* makes the following observation: "All the moralists [*ḥakhmei ha-Musar*] have taught this principle, which they stole from the teachings of our sages [*genuvah hi 'ittam me-'asher dareshu, z"l*]." Additional sources which make similar extreme attempts to find the doctrine of the mean in Jewish literature are cited in S. Rawidowicz, "*Sefer ha-Petiḥah le-Mishneh Torah*," in his *'Iyyunim be-Maḥashevet Yisrael* (Jerusalem, 1969), 429 n. 113 (reprinted from *Metzudah*, 7 [1954]). See also *Shemonah Perakim le-ha-Rambam*, ed. M. D. Rabinowitch (Jerusalem, 1968), 20–21, n. 9, and especially the quotation there from Holzberg.

6. This subject was discussed in chapter 1; see the references there in note 20. In his essay, "Charakteristik der Ethik Maimunis," one of Cohen's main purposes was to argue and provide evidence for the claim that Maimonides was not an Aristotelian. In striking contrast is the view of Husik who asserts, without any qualification, that in his ethics "Maimonides is an Aristotelian, and he endeavors to harmonize the intellectualism and theorism of the Stagirite with the diametrically opposed ethics and religion of the Hebrew Bible. And he is apparently unaware of the yawning gulf extending between them. . . . It is so absolutely clear and evident that one wonders how so clear-sighted a thinker like [sic] Maimonides could have been misled by the authority of Aristotle and the intellectual atmosphere of the days to imagine otherwise." Isaac Husik, *A History of Medieval Jewish Philosophy* (Philadelphia, 1944), 300.

fundamental philosophical ground on which that doctrine rests. I shall, therefore, set forth a careful interpretation of the Aristotelian position as the basis on which to make the comparison. My interpretation of Maimonides will then be directed to the double task of understanding him in his own right and of seeing him in comparison to Aristotle. Only in this way will we be able to grasp clearly the full significance of Maimonides' version of the doctrine of the mean as a principle of ethics.

Although the doctrine of the mean is among the most familiar and popular of Aristotle's teachings, it has been widely misunderstood and misrepresented, as a brief survey will reveal. This failure to grasp the essential elements in Aristotle's doctrine is evident in the standard criticisms to which it has been subjected. Some writers argue that the mean is no more than Aristotle's adaptation of the long established Greek folk rule, *mēden agan,* "nothing to excess." They deny that it is either a philosophical principle or based on one, seeing instead in Aristotle's doctrine nothing but a restatement of the common sense of the ages. A related but more pointed and serious charge is that, in the last analysis, the Aristotelian mean is nothing more than an affirmation of the proprieties of social convention. Typical of this approach is the statement of Theodor Gomperz charging that Aristotle's ethics rest on the view that "current opinion, when purged or corroborated by the settlement of real or apparent contradictions, is identified with absolute truth so far as concerns questions relating to the conduct of life."[7] Hans Kelsen expresses the criticism even more vigorously: "Although the ethics of the *mesotēs* (mean) doctrine pretends to establish in an authoritative way the moral value, it leaves the solution of its very problem to another authority. . . . It is the authority of the positive morality and positive law—it is the established social order. By presupposing in its *mesotēs* formula the established social order, the ethics of Aristotle justifies the positive morality and the positive law. . . . In this justification of the established social order lies the true function of the tautology which a critical analysis of the *mesotēs* formula reveals."[8] This criticism gains what may seem like solid support from Aristotle's admission that all judgment concerning the application of the doctrine of the mean to particular cases depends completely on the insight of the man of practical wisdom; but, the critics argue, that man has no standard to which he can appeal other than the conventional attitudes and values of his society.

7. Theodor Gomperz, *Greek Thinkers,* vol. 4 (London, 1929), 274.

8. Hans Kelsen, "Aristotle's Doctrine of Justice," in James I. Walsh and Henry L. Shapiro, *Aristotle's Ethics* (Belmont, Calif. 1967), 109.

The absence of any objective standard appears to be underscored by the fact that the Aristotelian mean is not determined arithmetically, and is thus not the same for all. It is, rather, a rule that must be applied only with full cognizance of the particular circumstances and the characteristic peculiarities of the individual in question. It is *pros hēmas,* determined in relation to the individual moral agent. This compounds the difficulty, since it would now appear that, in the doctrine of the mean, we have merely social convention adjusted to individual differences—a far cry indeed from a philosophical principle derived from a rule of reason.

Perhaps the most contemptuous of all the criticisms was made by Kant, when he wrote:

> The proposition that one should never do too much or do too little says nothing for it is tautological. What is it to do too much? Answer: More than is good. What is it to do too little? Answer: To do less than is good. What is meant by I ought (to do something or forbear doing something)? Answer: It is not good (contrary to duty) to do more or less than is good. If this is the wisdom we are to seek by returning to the ancients (Aristotle) as being precisely those who were nearer to the source of wisdom, then we have chosen badly to turn to their oracle. . . . For to be much too virtuous, i.e., to adhere too closely to one's duty, would be like making a circle much too round or a straight line much too straight.[9]

If these charges are justified, they are grave indeed, since they challenge what Aristotle himself claims explicitly. In his definition of moral virtue he includes the proviso that the choice in accordance with the mean is *hōrismenē logō,* determined by a *logos,* that is by a rule or principle of reason.[10] It is clear that Aristotle believes that he is offering a principle of reason, not just the arbitrariness of convention.

Yet the charges against Aristotle do not appear to be without foundation. He himself informs us early in the *Nicomachean Ethics* that the actions that are the subject matter of ethical reflection and choice "admit of much variety and fluctuation of opinion, so that they may be thought to exist only by convention [*nomos*], and not by nature [*physis*]." Near the end of the same book, he expresses the view that "what all think to be good, that, we assert, is good."[11] Moreover, he regularly invokes common opinion about moral matters and the good life as if it were clearly worthy of being consid-

9. Immanuel Kant, *The Metaphysical Principles of Virtue* (Indianapolis, 1968), 95 n. 10.

10. Aristotle, *Nicomachean Ethics* (cited hereafter as *N.E.*), ii, 1107a 1.

11. *N.E.,* i, 1094b 15–17, x, 1173a 1–2.

ered authoritative. In all this he seems to be admitting the very criticisms that are thought by many to be fatal to his position. What can we make out of the doctrine of the mean in the light of these critical attacks? In what follows I seek to answer that question by offering an interpretation of the doctrine of the mean that takes into account and copes with the difficulties that have been raised.

To grasp the doctrine correctly it is extremely helpful to reflect on the medical model which Aristotle uses repeatedly, namely, his recurring comparison between the process of attaining moral virtue and the work of the physician who brings patients to a state of physical health. The subject has been treated carefully and convincingly by Werner Jaeger, who concludes that in Aristotle's ethics the appeal to the medical pattern is so deep and pervasive that "in the light of it Aristotle tries to justify almost every step he takes in his ethical philosophy."[12]

The essential elements in the medical model are easy to discern. The practice of medicine has as its end the attainment of health for the patient. That end is given in and defined by the physical nature of the human patient. There is nothing arbitrary about physical health in general. It is the proper excellence of the body, which is gained when the body is brought to its highest degree of natural perfection. Insofar as it concerns the treatment of bodies in general, the practice of medicine involves a knowledge of principles that are fixed because they are the principles of a type of being that exists by nature and has its own nature. Yet these general principles alone are insufficient for the practice of medicine, which requires physicians to deal with particular cases, make practical decisions, and offer practical guidance for each individual case. Their prescriptions at best can be only approximately correct, never absolutely precise. Even if they know what foods are in general healthful, they are ineffective unless they are able to prescribe for each particular case a diet adjusted to the special needs and specific circumstances of the patient. It is here that their special art comes into play. Anyone who is modestly educated might be expected to know general rules of health, but only skilled physicians can be relied upon to diagnose individual cases and to apply the general rules to the particular needs of each patient. In their medical practice doctors must use the rule of the mean, as Aristotle repeatedly notes. As the work *On Ancient Medicine* (sometimes attributed to Hippocrates) expresses it, in the treatment of human ailments "it is necessary to aim at some measure."[13]

12. Werner Jaeger, "Aristotle's Use of Medicine as a Model of Method in his Ethics," *Journal of Hellenic Studies*, 77 (1952), 57.

13. *On Ancient Medicine*, ix.

If we follow Aristotle in thinking about ethics on the model of medical practice, then we can solve most of the problems his critics raise concerning the doctrine of the mean. Like medicine, ethics rests on a natural base. If there were not this base in human nature, which Aristotle considers to be fixed, there could be no talk of ethics as a practical *science*. At best it would be a fairly sophisticated art, but even as an art it could not proceed successfully if it had no fixed points of reference. Like medicine, ethics is concerned with knowledge not for its own sake but for the sake of action. This is what makes it *practical*. This practical element is carried out primarily with respect to individuals in particular circumstances, as is the case with medicine. To achieve this, the moral teacher (the *phronimos*) cannot rely only on his knowledge of human nature in general. He must have the capacity to deal with particular cases; and that is accomplished finally through *aisthēsis,* a kind of immediate perception of what is required in order to apply the general rules to a particular individual. In this situation, he cannot expect to achieve demonstrative certainty. At best he can offer the kind of informed judgment that emerges from the total combination of theoretical understanding, practical experience, and the special intelligence of the practically wise man, which is a capacity to deliberate well about such moral issues. Finally, his judgment will depend, in some degree, on *nomos,* the accepted patterns and attitudes of the society in which the individual lives. The doctor prescribing for a patient takes account of both the patient's particular situation with respect to physical health and development, and the patient's particular needs. Thus, when he prescribes for Milo, he must know not only that this patient has such and such specific complaints and that his physical condition is so and so, but also that he is a wrestler and wants to be restored to the state of health requisite for a successful wrestler. Similarly, the moral guide must know not only the particular moral situation of his client, but also his place in society and the norms of the society in which he must function. The norm of courage for a soldier at the battle front is likely to be different from what is proper for a professional chess player.

The critics have gone wrong in supposing that all Aristotle offers us is the social framework and the individual peculiarities of the moral agent. They have utterly ignored the crucial fact that his moral philosophy and, in particular, his doctrine of the mean are rooted in principles of nature. They have failed to see that Aristotle carefully introduces qualifications whenever he speaks of the conventional aspects of morality. The earliest passage in the *Nicomachean Ethics* dealing with this topic is a case in point. Aristotle stresses that we must not expect in ethics the same precision and degree of certainty that we expect in the demonstrative sciences. The subject matter of ethics and politics are *ta kala kai ta dikaia,* the fine or noble and the just, "but these conceptions involve much difference of opinion and uncertainty, so that they may be thought to exist only by convention and not by nature."[14] The stress is on the fact that "they may be *thought*" to be nothing more than convention, but those who think this are mistaken. For although they are, of course, in some measure dependent on convention, that is not the whole of the content or foundation of moral virtue. Let us then examine that natural foundation of moral virtue which has escaped the attention of Aristotle's critics.

Moral virtue, like any virtue (*aretē*), is concerned with the proper excellence of its subject, in this case man. Man's proper excellence is determined by man's proper end as it is given in nature. This is standard doctrine for Aristotle, found consistently in those of his works which deal with the question in any way at all. The principle is stated in *Metaphysics* v, 1021b 21–24, where he says that virtue (*aretē*) is a *telos*, the perfection of a thing by achieving its proper end. "And excellence is a completion [*telos*]; for each thing is complete and every substance is complete [*teleion*], when in respect of the form of its proper excellence it lacks no part of its natural magnitude." Note that the *aretē*, the excellence or virtue, is natural; it is determined by the nature of the thing. The same point is made in *Physics* vii, 246a 10–247a 20. "Excellence [*aretē*, i.e., virtue] is a kind of perfection [*teleiōsis*], since a thing is said to be perfect [*teleion*] when it has acquired its proper excellence, for it is then in most complete conformity to its own nature. . . . Excellence and defect are in every case concerned with the influences whereby their possessor is, according to its natural constitution, liable to be modified. . . . The same is true of the moral habits [*tēs psychēs hexeōn*, the states of the soul], for they, too, consist in conditions determined by certain relations, and the virtues are perfections of nature, the vices departures from it." These passages speak for themselves and merely reinforce what is stated in the *Nicomachean Ethics* on the same subject. The stress is on the *nature* of a thing, since for all things that exist by nature there can be no knowledge of their virtue except in terms of their nature.

That ethics is closely tied to nature is eminently clear, since human virtue is determined by human nature and this in turn requires a knowledge of psychology, the principles of the human soul. Aristotle sets out some of these principles in the *Nicomachean Ethics* as a first step in defining human virtue. Lest there be any doubt that psychology is a subject matter that is natural, one need only turn to the opening of *De Anima*, where Aristotle says explicitly that the knowledge of the soul admittedly contributes greatly to the advance of truth in general and, above all, to our understanding of nature.

14. *N.E.*, i, 1094a 16.

The particular problems of ethics arise because of the complex nature of man. To the extent that man is truly rational, it is easy for Aristotle to specify his proper end. Here the nature of rationality itself determines the end, namely, the use of reason for the knowledge and contemplation of that which is highest and most perfect. The most virtuous life for man would be one in which he would engage most completely in that supreme contemplative activity that is philosophical wisdom.

However, man is not a purely and perfectly rational being. He is a rational animal, an animal that has the capacity for being rational. This animal aspect of his nature must be given its due, but must not be allowed to control him; otherwise, man will be only animal and not rational at all. The problem then is to determine what it would be like for man's animal nature to be subject to the rule of reason to the fullest possible degree, and to discover the practical means by which this end might be achieved. True virtue for man will be the fullest realization of his *telos,* his proper end as a rational being— a life in which not only his contemplative powers but also his actions and passions are directed and controlled by reason. But what exactly does it mean to say that action and passion are controlled by reason? Aristotle's answer is that such a state can be defined formally as one in which action and passion are directed in accordance with the rule of the mean, and that this is what we all moral virtue.

The crucial question is then why we should consider the rule of the mean to be a rule of reason. Aristotle's answer is that the mean is the way in which nature and art normally achieve their goals of proper excellence, the realization of the proper end of each thing that exists by nature or is the product of art. To the extent that moral virtue has its foundations in nature, reason requires that it accord with nature. Otherwise it will not be virtue, that is, the proper excellence of man as man. If the end is to fulfill our proper nature as human beings, then virtue will consist in the fullest completion of that nature. If the nature of all things is to find their proper completion, *qua* natural, in the mean or the middle way, then this is also the way that reason requires us to choose in order to achieve moral virtue. For it is a rule, according to Aristotle, that rational beings act always with an end in view, and that they must choose the means requisite to that end. [15]

The principle that all things that exist by nature tend toward the mean, or middle way, in order to attain their proper perfection is common to various areas of Aristotle's thought and is by no means peculiar to his ethics. The simplest version of this point may be found in his discussions of the anatomical structure of animals. Over and over again he stresses that the middle is

15. Cf., *N.E.,* vi, 1139a 32–33.

the best. "Eyes may be large or small, or medium-sized [*mesoi*]. The medium-sized are the best." "Ears may be smooth, or hairy, or intermediate; the last are the best for hearing. . . . They may stand well out, or not stand out at all, or intermediately. The last are a sign of the finest disposition." "Now the tongue can be broad, or narrow, or intermediate; and the last is the best and gives the clearest perception."[16]

The principle that nature always seeks the middle way is set forth in more complex cases as well. For example, Aristotle holds that all motions of sensation begin and end in the heart. This is as it should properly be, he says, since reason requires that there should be only a single source, if possible, "and the best of places in accordance with nature is the middle" [*euphuestatos de tōn topōn ho mesos*]."[17] In this passage we see clearly how Aristotle ties together the way of reason and the normal way of nature, which tends always toward the mean.

Aristotle further expands and generalizes this doctrine when he propounds the view that nature always aims at the mean, always strives to overcome excess of every sort by counterbalancing it so that the mean is achieved. That is why the brain, which is cold, is continuous with the spinal marrow, which is hot. "Nature is always contriving to set next to anything that is excessive a reinforcement of the opposite substance, so that the one may level out [*anisazē*] the excess of the other."[18] Moreover, whatever comes into existence does so by way of the mean. In the process of generation opposites meet and are balanced, and form new creatures by way of the mean. "It is thus, then, that in the first place the 'elements' are transformed; and that out of the 'elements' there come to be flesh and bones and the like— the hot becoming cold and the cold becoming hot when they have been brought to the mean [*pros to meson*]. . . . Similarly, it is *qua* reduced to a mean condition that the dry and the moist produce flesh and bone and the remaining compounds."[19]

The principle that nature always follows the middle way is explicitly viewed by Aristotle as a rule of reason. This might be expected in view of the relationship between *logos* and *ratio,* between reason and proportion or due measure. As Aristotle puts it, "Everything needs an opposite to counterbalance it so that it may hit at the mark of proper measure and the mean [*tou*

16. Aristotle, *Historia Animalium,* i, 492a 7–8, 33–34, 492b 31–32.

17. Aristotle, *De Partibus Animalium,* iii, 666a 15.

18. Ibid., ii, 652a 31–32.

19. Aristotle, *De Generatione et Corruptione,* ii, 334b 25–30.

metriou kai tou mesou]. The mean, and not any of the extremes alone, has being [*ousia*] and reason [*logos*]."[20]

Since "art imitates nature," it is to be expected that the product of art will also conform with the rule of the mean, for art is defined by Aristotle as "concerned with making involving a true course of reasoning."[21] Consequently it too must follow the rule of reason that all things achieve their proper realization when they have been formed in accordance with the right measure, that is, with the mean, which stands at the proper point between excess and defect. The point is expressed charmingly by Aristotle in his discussion of the proper speed for narration in ceremonial oratory: "Nowadays it is said, absurdly enough, that the narration should be rapid. Remember what the man said to the baker who asked whether he was to make the cake hard or soft: 'What, can't you make it right?' Just so here. We are not to make long narrations, just as we are not to make long introductions or long arguments. Here, again, rightness does not consist either in rapidity or in conciseness, but in the happy mean."[22]

The principle is carried through consistently by Aristotle when he deals with what may be thought of as the highest products of art working in conjunction with nature, namely, virtuous men and good states. In his discussion of the various aspects of life in the city-state and of the constitution of such a state, he always considers the mean, or the middle way, to be the most desirable model. The structure and order of the state—which is, like the order of the life of the individual, the combined work of art and nature—mut be in accordance with the mean if it is to achieve its own proper perfection. As individuals men would also do well to seek no more than moderate amounts of all desirable things. For since the mean is always best, "it is manifest that the middle amount of all of the good things of fortune is the best amount to possess. For this degree of wealth is the readiest to obey reason."[23]

We have now established clearly that Aristotle's doctrine of the mean is not peculiar to moral virtue. In his system of thought, it is an overarching principle that encompasses the operations of the world of nature and the world of art. One cannot properly understand his treatment of moral virtue without seeing the mean in this wider context. Given this context, we can

20. *Part. Animalium*, 652b 17–20.

21. *N.E.*, vi, 1140a 20.

22. Aristotle, *De Rhetorica*, iii, 1416b 30–35.

23. Aristotle, *Politica*, iv, 1295b 3–7.

now turn to a more direct examination of the way in which Aristotle conceives the doctrine of the mean as the pattern in accordance with which moral virtue is formed.

As a first step, we must remember that Aristotle is fully explicit about the fact that there is a natural foundation for moral virtue. Introducing the discussion of moral virtue, Aristotle makes the point that it exists neither fully by nature nor fully contrary to nature but is a combination of nature and art. Virtue arises in us through habit as its efficient cause. This process of deliberate habituation, however, could not occur at all without a natural medium in which it took place and to which it was adapted. "The virtues therefore are engendered in us neither by nature nor yet in violation of nature; nature gives us the capacity to receive them, and this capacity is brought to its proper completion by habit."[24]

In a later discussion in the *Nicomachean Ethics,* Aristotle expands his treatment of this topic. There he makes it clear that, although all virtue is the product of a certain deliberate effort, it nevertheless has its origin and base in what is natural. What Aristotle calls natural virtue is the initial source of all true moral virtue. Natural virtue is our inborn capacity for the states of character that become, when properly developed, the moral virtues. Without this inborn capacity we could not become morally virtuous, for that aspect alone of our nature makes moral virtue possible. Just as cleverness is the natural base that, when developed properly, becomes practical wisdom, so, says Aristotle, is "natural virtue [*hē physikē aretē*] to true virtue [or virtue in the strict sense]. It is generally agreed that the various kinds of character are present in man by nature, for we are just, and capable of temperance, and brave, or have the other virtues from the very moment of our birth. Nevertheless, we expect to find that true goodness is something different, and that the virtues in the true sense come to belong to us in another way."[25] There are then two types of virtue in us: natural virtue, which has a potentiality for development in a way appropriate to man, and true moral virtue, which is the actualization of that natural potentiality. The model for the development of that potentiality is followed by all natures seeking their own perfection; it is, of course, the doctrine of the mean. Aristotle's insistence that moral virtue follows the rule of the mean is thus in no sense arbitrary. Following his own principles, it is a rule of reason. If the proper perfection of the moral part of our nature is specified by nature in accordance with its general rule that the middle is best and most complete, then reason requires that in seeking moral

24. *N.E.,* ii, 1103a 24.
25. *N.E.,* vi, 144b 1–2.

virtue we must employ as our guide and criterion the pattern that is the only appropriate instrument for attaining the end we desire.

If this is so evident, how shall we understand all the criticisms that accuse Aristotle of offering nothing more than a formalized approval of social convention? I believe the answer lies in the fact that the critics have ignored the natural foundations of moral virtue despite the trouble Aristotle took to make his position clear. They have been further misled by two other considerations to which we must now turn our attention.

The first consideration is that there is, of course, a social-conventional aspect to moral virtue. About this there can be no difference of opinion. What is at issue is the question of how we should understand this dimension of moral virtue, its nature, the function it serves, and the weight we should put on it. Man is not an animal who achieves the goal of self-development in isolation or solitude. For Aristotle man is a being whose development, excellence, and true humanity depend on society. Detached from all social relations and structures, man is barely human, if at all. Man is by nature a political animal, a creature whose nature requires that association of community with others of which the *polis* (the city-state) is a model. For this reason Aristotle considers the *polis* or, more widely, the forms of human society to exist by nature. Whatever the elements of human art that account for and cause the diversity of societies, society itself is natural, and only in society can man fulfill himself. Only in society, his natural setting, can man be humanly virtuous.

Aristotle is fully aware that, despite the natural basis on which human society rests, societies differ in their customs and value patterns, and moral virtue will always reflect the particular characteristics of the community in which a person lives. Yet this is not to say that moral virtue is only *nomos,* only convention and nothing more. Rather, moral virtue is the result of the development of natural virtue toward its proper end in the context of a particular social setting. In fact, the existence of society is dependent on man's natural capacity for moral virtue. "For it is the special property of man, in distinction from the other animals, that he alone has the perception of good and bad and right and wrong and the other moral qualities, and it is partnership [community] in these things that makes a household and a city-state."[26]

Without the natural capacity for morality there could be no human community at all. Given this capacity, there emerges a community in which moral virtue is possible. That virtue exhibits both the fixed elements that its

26. *Politica,* i, 1253a 16–19.

nature determines and the varying elements deriving from the diverse characteristics of particular societies. When the man of practical wisdom deals with moral issues, he is guided by his knowledge of the natural character of moral virtue, tempered by his knowledge of the standards of the society in which he lives. He is a model precisely because he has developed this combination of the natural and the socially conditioned to its ideal level. To understand Aristotle's conception of moral virtue, one must give full weight both to the natural and the social elements. Those who say that morality is merely *nomos* are mistaken. Those who say that it is merely *physis* are equally mistaken.

The second factor that has led Aristotle's critics astray is the inescapable particularity of each moral situation. If the rule of the mean is to be applied to an individual with full cognizance of his own particular level of development, the circumstances in which he finds himself, and the special characteristics of his society, how can there be anything more than only individual and private judgments? To the extent this is a sound criticism, it would appear to apply with equal force to any moral philosophy. The problem of moving from general moral principles to particular moral judgments is hardly peculiar to Aristotle. As a classic example, one need only think of the difficulties that interpreters of Kant suffer when they try to give an account of how he moves from the categorical imperative to particular moral judgments. The troubles that Kant's famous four examples have caused the commentators are sufficient to make the case.

Yet it seems that Aristotle is not without resources for dealing even with this aggravating problem. To begin with, let us note that he is fully aware of the problem. In the first chapter of the sixth book of the *Nicomachean Ethics,* he explicitly expresses his dissatisfaction with a moral rule that is general, unless one can show how it can be applied to particular cases. In many other places in the *Ethics* he repeats the same point—that judgments about conduct always deal with particular cases, and that it is especially difficult to apply the rule of the mean in an exact way to particular cases. Having laid down some procedural cautions for anyone trying to hit the mark of the mean, Aristotle recognizes that even if they are heeded, the cautions offer no guarantee of success. One should aim at the mean, guided by these rules, "but no doubt it is a difficult thing to do, and especially in particular cases; for instance, it is not easy to define in what manner and with what people and on what sort of grounds and how long one ought to be angry."[27]

The difficulty of applying the rule to particular cases results in judgments that can never claim to be absolute or exact. At best, they are

27. *N.E.*, ii, 1109b 13–14.

approximations, guidelines for conduct leading to proper self-development, never demonstrated certainties. The lack of precision is compounded by the dependence on social circumstances as well as individual particularities. This caused Aristotle to remark early in the *Nicomachean Ethics* that one should expect no more precision than the subject matter is capable of yielding. He stresses at several points that inquiry in this field can be carried out successfully only if one recognizes, as a condition of the inquiry, that it will yield conclusions that are far from certain or precise. "This must be agreed upon beforehand [i.e., before beginning to inquire into moral philosophy], that the whole account of matters of conduct must be given in outline and not precisely . . . matters concerned with conduct and questions of what is good for us have no fixity, any more than matters of health. The general account being of this nature, the account of particular cases is yet more lacking in exactness; for they do not fall under any art or set of rules, but the agents themselves must in each case consider what is appropriate to the occasion."[28] Nowhere does Aristotle claim that he is offering us a system that will result in precise, absolutely fixed, and reliable moral judgments. In fact, he says exactly the contrary over and over again, so that it is difficult to understand why his critics believe that they have discovered some secret dark failure in his treatment of these matters. Even general moral rules cannot be laid down with precision, he believes, much less judgments in particular cases.

According to Aristotle, such judgments rest with perception. The term he uses consistently is *aisthēsis,* which refers to a kind of immediate intuitive grasp of the particulars and a capacity to make a judgment concerning them. *Aisthēsis* is the only way in which we know particulars. It is one of the essential components of practical wisdom which, unlike scientific knowledge, is concerned with particular cases. "Practical wisdom is concerned with the ultimate particular, which is the object not of scientific knowledge but of perception [*aisthēsis*]—not the perception of qualities peculiar to one sense but a perception akin to that by which we perceive that the particular figure before us is a triangle."[29]

Here again Aristotle claims no certainty. On the contrary, he is fully aware that what he offers is both less than exact and less than certain. The development of the capacity of moral perception depends upon maturity and experience. There is no other source. Practical wisdom, although an intellectual virtue, is that part of the intellect dealing with opinion, not demonstrated knowledge. Its subject matter is not fixed but varies with indi-

28. *N.E.,* ii, 1104a 1–2.
29. *N.E.,* vi, 1142a 25–26.

vidual and social circumstances. Yet it is capable of making judgments and offering guidance, precisely because it brings together the range of knowledge, experience, and perception out of which alone any reasonably sound moral judgment might emerge.

The problem human beings face in their effort to attain moral virtue can now be readily formulated. Like all things that exist by nature, man has a fixed nature. This confers certain fixed ends, the realization of which constitute man's proper excellence. Unlike man, other things that exist by nature are without any independent power of choice and are moved by their internal principle of development in the direction of their proper ends only. Outside forces or internal defects may prevent their attaining their end. The healthy acorn will become a full-grown oak if it receives the nutrition it requires and if nothing invades it from the outside to prevent its natural course of development. Its nature, its internal principle of development, is fixed and can go only one way.

Things are not nearly so simple for human beings. They have a nature, but they also have the capacity to choose their own actions. They can, by their choice, either advance or frustrate their development in accordance with their nature. If man had no fixed natural disposition toward moral virtue, such virtue would not be possible for him at all. If he had only a fixed natural disposition, moral virtue would be unnecessary, for he would achieve his end automatically. However, man is in the middle. He has a nature, but he must choose to bring it to its full actuality. He must develop his own character in accordance with his true nature if he chooses to be human in the full and proper meaning of the term. It is at this point that he must cope with the problem of knowing exactly what kind of action to choose. Nature specifies man's proper end in a general way. It also specifies the criterion of virtuous character in a general way, namely, by the rule of the mean. However, this is insufficient as a guide to action in particular cases, and all action is particular. The components of the social framework, individual differences, and the special circumstances must all play a role in the decision. Here no precise rule can be specified. One can only appeal, within the context of a rule of reason determined by nature, to the perception and judgment of the man of practical wisdom.

Does it follow from all this that the doctrine of the mean is, as the critics claim, no more than an appeal to social convention, that it is utterly useless as a guide to moral action, or that it is merely an empty tautology? I believe that we have shown otherwise. The doctrine of the mean is not a matter of social convention. It is a rational rule, deriving from nature and showing us the general way to actualize a deeply fixed principle of nature. It is not a fixed or precise rule because it involves varying social circumstances and deals with a diversity of individuals, who must be considered in the context of their special personal and social conditions. Even this is not arbitrary, however, since man is by nature a social animal, and action is by nature always particular.

Perhaps the matter can be made clearer and the argument more persuasive by returning to the medical model. The work of physicians, seeking the physical health of their patients, deals to a large extent with what is natural. No one is ready to deny the natural aspect of the body and of bodily health. However, this is only part of the story. Health has to be achieved for individual patients in the light of their special circumstances and conditions, and of their particular constitutions and special possibilities. No diagnosis is foolproof. It can only claim to be probable, and it is never absolutely exact and certain. Similarly, no prescription is ever absolutely precise, nor is its anticipated effectiveness more than probable. All this is the case just because medicine must take account of the particular. As Aristotle never tires of saying, a proper diet for Milo may be all wrong for a sedentary scholar.

Despite its inexactness and uncertainty, we do not ordinarily condemn all medical practice as pointless. On the contrary, considering the built-in limitations of the subject matter, we see in it the best we can achieve. Even if we doubt the soundness of a particular doctor's diagnosis, or if we fail to be helped by his or her prescriptions, we do not conclude that the practice of medicine is a fraud. We do know what good health is, and we do recognize that, granted their limitations, physicians are nevertheless people of special knowledge and experience who can help us achieve that desirable goal. Similarly, Aristotle argues, we do know what a virtuous character is, for it is specified by our nature. Physicians of the soul may be harder to find than physicians of the body. It may also be more difficult for the former to lay out and justify their general principles and rules of practice, to say nothing of their judgments in individual cases. It is my contention, nevertheless, that I have explained why Aristotle believes that this difficult task is not impossible, and how it is that his critics have misunderstood him.

As we reflect on the relationship of Maimonides' doctrine of the mean to that of Aristotle, we are confronted by puzzles that demand resolution. It would seem on initial reflection that, of all the areas Maimonides wrote about, the ordering of human behavior should have presented him with the fewest problems. As an expositor of Jewish tradition and a master of the Law, he had a complete system of behavioral rules and norms ready-made for him in the halakhah. It would seem, then, that there should have been no need for him to seek beyond the halakhah itself for the principles and specific patterns of virtue and the good life—all the more so since, as we shall show later, Maimonides denied that there is any independent rational ground for morality. He rejected all claims that there is a natural moral law, holding instead that morality derives either from social convention or divine command. It is obvious that for Judaism only the latter source can be decisive.[30] Why then was it necessary for Maimonides to appeal to the doctrine of the mean at all? The elaborate and detailed principles and directions for the life of the Jew that he codified in his *Mishneh Torah* would seem to be sufficient to answer every need for the moral and religious guidance required to lead people to the virtuous life.

Furthermore, an appeal to non-Jewish sources would seem to be singularly inappropriate with respect to this subject matter in particular. It could be argued plausibly that, to the extent that Maimonides' Jewish theology required principles of natural science or metaphysics as a foundation, these might appropriately have been drawn from non-Jewish sources, since the biblical and rabbinic literature are relatively poor in these areas. This is surely not the case with regard to the area of human conduct. How strange than that in a treatise devoted to setting forth the principles and end of the good life, Maimonides begins by telling us explicitly that he drew his materials from non-Jewish as well as Jewish sources. In his foreword to *Shemonah Perakim* (*Eight Chapters*), he makes a special point of denying that the work contains any original ideas. All that is of consequence in the treatise has been gleaned, says Maimonides, "from the words of the wise occurring in the *Midrashim,* in the Talmud, and in other of their works, as well as from the words of the philosophers, ancient and recent, and also from the works of various authors." He immediately goes on to justify this procedure by invoking the principle that "one should accept the truth from whatever source it proceeds."[31]

The force of this open appeal to non-Jewish sources is even greater when we remember that these statements are contained in the introduction to a commentary on *'Avot,* a treatise that in its opening words takes great pains to establish its legitimacy by associating itself with the tradition whose source is in the Torah which "Moses received at Sinai."[32] My analysis of Maimonides' version of the doctrine of the mean will seek to resolve some of these puzzles. The primary concerns are to understand the doctrine pre-

---

30. The extended discussion of this subject will be found in chapter 6.

31. *The Eight Chapters,* ed. Gorfinkle, 35–36.

32. For the views of some traditional commentators who see the opening of this treatise as an attempt to underscore the independence of Jewish ethics from all external sources, see the comments of Bertinoro and *Tosafot Yom Tov, ad loc.*

cisely, see its similarities to and differences from the Aristotelian doctrine, and determine how it fits into the Jewish tradition.

With respect to the general nature of ethical inquiry, Maimonides holds views similar to those of Aristotle. Like Aristotle, he makes clear at the outset that he is concerned, above all, with the truly good life for man, and that his interest in individual actions and states of character is primarily because they are instrumental to the realization of the ultimate good. In the foreword to *Shemonah Perakim*, he makes a point of explaining that the treatise on which he is commenting contains a rule of life that "leads to great perfection and true happiness." In fact, one who puts into practice the teachings of *'Avot* can hope to be led even to prophecy. This ultimate human felicity comes to one who attains the knowledge of God "as far as it is possible for man to know Him," and the truly good life is that in which all human effort, thought, and activity are directed toward the realization of that goal.[33] The same ideal is developed in *H. De'ot*, III, and of course it constitutes a central theme of the *Guide of the Perplexed*, where it reaches its climax in the final chapters.

Maimonides also follows Aristotle in his view that achieving this ultimate aim of the contemplative life presupposes the achievement of moral virtue. Man is so constituted that he can devote himself to the highest intellectual activity only if he has first achieved the personal and social discipline included under the heading of moral virtue. The crucial question then emerges as to what specifically are the character and shape of the morally virtuous life. Here too in his initial approach Maimonides remains faithful to the Aristotelian pattern. Like Aristotle, Maimonides is primarily concerned not with individual acts but with states of character. Thus in *Shemonah Perakim* he introduces his discussion of the rule of the mean by distinguishing between good acts and good states of character: "Good deeds are such as are equibalanced, maintaining the mean between two equally bad extremes. . . . Virtues are psychic conditions and dispositions [*tekhunot nafshiyyot ve-kinyanim*] which are midway between two reprehensible extremes."[34]

The title of the section of the *Mishneh Torah* that deals with the mean is *De'ot*, and it is quite clear that the term is used to refer to states of character. This is obvious enough from the context and is confirmed in a passage in which Maimonides explicitly distinguishes *de'ot*, as states of character, from particular actions. In *H. Teshuvah*, VII, 3, Maimonides tells us that just as

33. *Shemonah Perakim*, chap. 5.
34. Ibid., chap. 4; *The Eight Chapters*, ed. Gorfinkle, 54–55.

one must repent for sins that involve a particular action, such as robbery or theft, so is one obligated "to search out his evil *de'ot* and repent of them, i.e., from such states as anger, etc."[35]

Aristotle had already defined virtue as a state of character or, according to another translation, "a settled disposition of the mind" that observes the mean.[36] Maimonides follows him here, as he does with respect to the view that our actions follow from the fixed states of our character; therefore what must concern us most is the development of the appropriate states of character, since that is the best assurance that our individual actions will also be virtuous. Finally, in what appears to be a thoroughly Aristotelian fashion, Maimonides also defines the good character as one that is determined by the mean and avoids the extremes. Given these general similarities, we must now ask what the main elements of Maimonides' doctrine of the mean are and how they compare with Aristotle's views as already set forth.

The fundamental distinction is the ground on which the mean rests. It is striking that in both *Shemonah Perakim* and the *Mishneh Torah,* Maimonides introduces the rule of the mean without any discussion of its origins or justification. He treats it rather as an established truth to which one need only refer but which does not require any evidence to support it. In both works he proceeds as if it were an established principle that good deeds and good states of character follow the mean between extremes. In the *Mishneh Torah* he opens the discussion with some empirical observations about the diversity of states of character that are to be found among men and then informs us that "the two extremes which are at the farthest distance from each other with respect to each state of character are not the good way . . . while the right way is the middle way." Not only does he offer no defense of this claim, but he goes on to say that because the mean is the right way, "therefore the early sages [*ḥakhamim ha-rishonim*] commanded that man should always evaluate and judge his own states of character so as to direct them toward the middle way."[37]

If we accept the view of most commentators that the reference is to the Sages of Israel—a view that seems plausible enough in this context—then

---

35. See also *H. Teshuvah,* IV, 5. Maimonides speaks of five modes of behavior which are addictive, so that one who does them will be inclined to repeat them and will find it more and more difficult to change his behavior. "These are all of them evil dispositions [*de'ot*] including, tale-bearing, malicious speech, an easily inflamed temper, etc." These actions all derive from defective states of character, i.e., *de'ot ra'ot.*

36. *N.E.,* ii, 1106b 36–37.

37. *H. De'ot,* I, 3, 4.

we have the remarkable situation of Maimonides telling us that the principle that the middle way is good is known as an independent truth, and that because it is known to be true, the Jewish religious authorities accepted it as their rule of conduct and character development. So far he would seem to be doing exactly what he says in his introduction to *Shemonah Perakim,* that is, relying on established knowledge without regard to its source.

There is evidence to support the view that Maimonides was convinced that the rule of the mean was a well-established basic principle of explanation in the sciences and in philosophy. He was explicit about this point in the *Guide.* In thoroughly Aristotelian fashion, he strongly supports the view that the order of nature is such that all things achieve their proper excellence when they reach the mean, which suffers from neither excess nor deficiency. The highest praise he can pay to the divine creation of the world is that it was guided by the rule of the mean; from this it follows that in the created world there can be no change in the fixed order of nature: "The thing that is changed, is changed because of a deficiency in it that should be made good or because of some excess that is not needed and should be got rid of. Now the works of the Deity are most perfect, and with regard to them there is no possibility of an excess or a deficiency. Accordingly, they are of necessity permanently established as they are, for there is no possibility of something calling for a change in them. . . . 'The Rock, his work is perfect' . . . means that all his works . . . are most perfect, that no deficiency at all is commingled with them, that there is no superfluity in them and nothing that is not needed" (II, 28, pp. 335–36).

Viewing the doctrine of the mean as a scientific principle, Maimonides treats it as fully established and needing no further evidence. He is explicit about the general rule that whatever is scientifically known, whatever is demonstrated, must command our assent. For such matters we do not need to look for confirmation in the official Jewish literature, nor should we be uneasy if on such matters the views of the Sages of Israel are contradicted by our contemporary knowledge. Here the Sages spoke not with the authority of the prophetic tradition but only as students of physics or metaphysics bound by the limits of their own knowledge and the general state of knowledge at their time.[38] It seems clear enough that this is one of the points Maimonides had in mind when he informed his readers in the foreword to *Shemonah Perakim* that he would seek the truth from whatever source it

38. For explicit comments on this point, see *Guide,* II, 8, and III, 14; Moses Maimonides, *Letter on Astrology,* ed. A. Marx, *Hebrew Union College Annual,* 3 (1926), 356; and *Kovetz Teshuvot ha-Rambam* (Leipzig, 1859), II, 26a.

could be found. Even with respect to the standards and rules of virtuous behavior, good character, and the good life for the faithful Jew, we need certain general principles of explanation, a general theoretical framework, in order to give a philosophical account of the subject. We also need a sound psychology on which to base our understanding of human character and its development. Without these theoretical foundations, our account of moral virtue, even of specifically Jewish moral virtue, will be incomplete and will lack an essential philosophical-scientific dimension. Moreover, no practical guidance toward the achievement of good character and the performance of good acts is possible unless we first have a sound theoretical understanding of human nature and the nature of the good in general. These are universal truths, in no way peculiar to the Jewish religious community. For such truths we may, nay we must, turn to the most reliable scientific authority we can find. So far as I can judge, this is the point of Maimonides' announcement that he seeks guidance wherever he can find it.

So far we might say without hesitation that Maimonides follows Aristotle or the Aristotelian tradition faithfully. However, when we move away from the general theoretical foundations to his specific way of understanding and applying the doctrine of the mean, the differences emerge sharply and clearly. Perhaps the most significant single difference is that, while Aristotle construes moral virtue as a case of art imitating nature, Maimonides teaches that the model of human virtue is the standard provided by the ideal of the imitation of God. The first of the eleven *mitzvot* set forth in *H. De'ot* is *le-hiddamot bi-derakhav,* and it is to the exposition and explication of this commandment of *imitatio Dei* that the first five of the seven chapters of *H. De'ot* are devoted. For Aristotle the imitation of nature was nothing more than a general indication that the good life for human beings, like the pattern of all natural excellence, should be one of perfect measure. Nature does not itself give us specific norms or standards of behavior, nor does it tell us what a virtuous character is, apart from its general principle that the middle way is the best. Given the imitation of nature as the only ideal, Aristotle had no choice but to fill out the specific details of the good life for man by appealing to the norms of society and to the judgment of the man of practical wisdom. Nature gives us only the form (i.e., the mean) and not the content of the moral life. It does not and cannot teach us what the rule of the mean specifically requires of us in concrete cases of human action or human character development.

In striking contrast, Maimonides works here fully inside the Jewish tradition. He follows what he considers to be sound philosophy and adopts the outer form of the mean as his theoretical base and principle of explanation. But the specific contents of the good life are defined for him not by the imitation of nature but by the imitation of God. Now, viewed as metaphysically ultimate, Maimonides' God is not truly knowable except through negative attributes; however, Maimonides does permit us knowledge of God through the attributes of action. We can know Him indirectly through His works in the world, and in this way we can speak meaningfully of *imitatio Dei* as the human ideal. This is why Maimonides is so careful to formulate the commandment as *le-hiddamot bi-derakhav*—because, strictly speaking, we can imitate His ways only, but not His nature. The God who is represented as Creator, who continues through His actions to make His presence felt in history as well as in nature, is a being whom man can meaningfully hold before himself as an ideal to follow.

As in the case of Aristotle's prescription for the imitation of nature, this general rule is insufficient as a guide to man. It must be made specific and concrete. For Maimonides this is achieved simply enough. According to his view the commandments of the Torah are, in fact, the specification of ideal behavior in conformity with the rule of the mean, and this is what is meant when we are commanded to imitate the ways of God. The structure of Maimonides' argument is clear and unambiguous, although it has often been ignored or misunderstood. First he gives us the theoretical principle that is generally known and acknowledged. Good action and good states of character are those that follow the middle way. So far we are in accord with all men who follow the way of scientific knowledge. Next, we face the question of what it means specifically to act in accordance with the mean. Here Maimonides answers—unlike Aristotle, for whom such an answer would have been meaningless—that we should imitate God. Finally, he faces the question of what divine behavior is like so that we can have a concrete model for imitation, and he answers that the rule of the Torah is the divine paradigm and therefore also the concretization of the middle way.

Maimonides is absolutely consistent in his adherence to this principle that the rule of the Torah is, in actual fact, the rule of the mean—that is, whatever the Torah commands *is* the middle way. No external standard measures the commandments to determine whether they accord with the mean. This is impossible, precisely because the only standard we have is that given by the commandments. In *Shemonah Perakim* he writes, "The Law did not lay down its prohibitions, or enjoin its commandments, except for just this purpose, namely, that by its disciplinary effects we may persistently maintain the proper distance from either extreme."[39] He goes on to stress that since "the Law of the Lord is perfect" (Ps 19:9), it is in its injunctions and prohibitions alone that man is given the proper standard of behavior. That is

39. *The Eight Chapters,* ed. Gorfinkle, 64.

why it is vice, and not virtue, to impose upon ourselves ascetic practices or disciplines of self-denial that go beyond what the Torah commands.

The same principle is set forth in *H. De'ot* and receives full expression in the *Guide,* where he argues that the Mosaic Law is absolutely perfect, the ideal and exact embodiment of true measure, the middle way in all regards.[40] Thus every law that deviates from it suffers from the fact that it moves away from the mean toward one of the extremes.

> For when a thing is as perfect as it is possible to be within its species, it is impossible that within that species there should be found another thing that does not fall short of that perfection either because of excess or deficiency. . . . Things are similar with regard to this Law, as is clear from its equibalance. For it says: "Just statutes and judgments" (Deut. 4:8); now you know that the meaning of "just" is equibalanced. For these are manners of worship in which there is no burden and excess . . . nor a deficiency. . . . When we shall speak in this treatise about the reasons accounting for the commandments, their equibalance and wisdom will be made clear to you insofar as this is necessary. For this reason it is said with reference to them: "The Law of the Lord is perfect" (II, 39, p. 380).

For the Aristotelian reliance on *nomos* as interpreted and applied by the *phronimos* (the man of practical wisdom), Maimonides has substituted the law of the Torah as taught by the Sages of Israel. The divine origin of this Law guarantees its perfection as a standard of behavior. All others fall short. Only the Torah "is called by us divine Law, whereas the other political regimens—such as the nomoi of the Greeks and the ravings of the Sabians and of others—are due, as I have explained several times, to the action of groups of rulers who were not prophets" (II, 39, p. 381). The Torah alone, according to Maimonides, can give us the true standard of the mean, because it alone can teach us concretely how to live the life of the imitation of God.

There is, however, more to be considered. We recall that the main interest in ethics is the development of virtuous states of character, not merely the performance of virtuous actions. The latter are derived from the former and are significant especially as outer evidences of a stable moral character. The passages cited make the Torah the standard of the mean in action, but it is obvious that Maimonides must also provide for the Torah as the standard of the mean with respect to states of character. This is, in fact, precisely what he does in *H. De'ot*. The ideal of *imitatio Dei* is concerned primarily with states of character, and these are dispositions described as generally in accor-

40. *H. De'ot*, III, 1.

dance with the middle way. "We are commanded to follow these middle ways which are the paths that are good and right, as is written, 'And you shall walk in His ways.' (Deut. 28:9). Thus have they taught with respect to this *mitzvah:* Just as He is called *ḥannun* [gracious], so shall you be *ḥannun;* just as He is called *raḥum* [merciful], so shall you be *raḥum.*"[41]

In the case of states of character Maimonides does not make a rule that the Torah standard specifies the mean in every case, but rather that whatever standard the Torah sets is the standard we are obligated to use as our norm, even in those cases where it clearly deviates from the mean toward one of the extremes. Thus in the very discussion in which he take the mean as the ideal Torah model of virtuous states of character, Maimonides proceeds to rule that "there are certain states of character with respect to which it is forbidden for a man to pursue the middle way."[42] Pride and anger are dispositions that should be avoided completely, as we have been specifically commanded. Aristotle also spoke of actions and passions for which the mean is an inappropriate rule. They are those, as he puts it, whose very names imply evil.[43] Here again Maimonides has a different ground on which he rests his cases of deviation from the mean. Not the name itself or some other supposedly self-evident ground, but the commandments of the Torah determine the cases in which we are required to abandon the mean. We know that there can be no proper moderation with respect to pride and anger, simply because we are so taught by various biblical verses and the explicit rulings of the rabbis.

With this background in mind we can also appreciate the difference between the medical analogy used by Maimonides and that of Aristotle. On the surface they seem similar, yet the foundations on which they rest differ significantly. In his various ethical writings Maimonides, like Aristotle, recommends that those in need of moral guidance seek out physicians of the soul. He views moral decay as a sickness of the soul, and those who treat it properly do so on the analogy of the therapy of the physicians of the sick body. So far, all is similar to Aristotle. Yet here too we find very important differences that result from the basically distinct foundations on which the doctrine of the mean rests in each case.[44]

---

41. *H. De'ot,* I, 5, 6. (From the manuscripts it seems clear that the end of I, 5, as we have cited it here from the printed versions, should really be the beginning of I, 6.)

42. Ibid., II, 3.

43. *N.E.,* ii, 6, 1107a 9–10. The problems that this Aristotelian passage has posed for the commentators are familiar, and this is not the place to review them.

44. The main sources for the moral-medical analogy in Maimonides are *Shemonah Perakim,* I (*The Eight Chapters,* ed. Gorfinkle, 38), III, IV (ibid., 62–63); *H. De'ot,* especially chap. 2; *Guide,* III, 34, pp. 534–35.

Both Aristotle and Maimonides require physicians of the soul to know how to take account of individual circumstances, and to advise in accordance with those circumstances. Both require physicians of the soul to have a sound understanding of human psychology; otherwise they will be incompetent to give guidance. Both agree on the practical rule that the morally sick soul is to be treated by being directed toward the extreme opposite of its present state, and that the aim should be to arrive at a stable state of character determined by the mean. Both consider the true physician of the soul to be a wise man. For Aristotle, he is the *phronimos,* the man of practical wisdom, and for Maimonides he is the *ḥakham,* the model Jewish scholar–teacher–man of piety. Maimonides advises that the proper way for sick souls to be healed is to "go to the *ḥakhamim,* who are the healers of souls, and they will cure their illness by teaching them to achieve the proper states of character, thereby bringing them back to the virtuous way."[45]

Despite all these similarities, the differences are of crucial importance. Aristotle's *phronimos* has only shifting conventional standards to guide him. Maimonides' *ḥakham* has the fixed discipline of the Torah as his standard. Of course, he must take account of the special condition of individuals and must tailor his advice to fit the special needs and circumstances in which individuals find themselves. Nevertheless, he is bound not by a conventional *nomos* but by a fixed Law, by commandments, and by principles held to be divine and thus unchanging. The divine-human ideal is set, and to be virtuous a man must direct himself to that ideal. Maimonides is fully aware of the variations and diversity of human temperament and of social conditions. Nevertheless his physician of the soul carries out his function by adhering rigorously to the fixed Law. He varies his advice for each individual only to move that individual closer to the one common ideal. Aristotle's mean, even when viewed as a principle of nature, always reflects something of the attitudes and values of the particular society in which it is invoked as the principle of moral virtue. Maimonides' mean permits no such variation because it is controlled by the ideal of *imitatio Dei,* and this in turn is concretized and fixed in the commandments and principles of the Torah.

It is revealing that this point, which is evident enough in the earlier works, comes out with striking force and clarity in the *Guide.* Here, where he deals with the Law as a primary force for the ordering of society, Maimonides openly shows his deviation from the Aristotelian norm. He first argues that men differ from each other in their temperaments and moral hab-

---

45. *H. De'ot,* II, 1.

its far more than any other living creatures, yet man, being by nature a political animal, must live in society. He then goes on:

> Now as the nature of the human species requires that there be those differences among the individuals belonging to it and as in addition society is a necessity for this nature, it is by no means possible that this society should be perfected except—and this is necessarily so—through a ruler who gauges the actions of the individuals, perfecting that which is deficient and reducing that which is excessive, and who prescribes actions and moral habits that all of them must always practice in the same way, so that the natural diversity is hidden through the multiple points of conventional accord and so that the community becomes well ordered (II, 40, p. 382).

He subsequently goes on to distinguish the application of the Law from the model of medical treatment. The Law is, he says, a divine thing, a perfect ideal not necessarily actualized in the life of each individual. Therefore, he argues against Aristotle that "in view of this consideration, it also will not be possible that the laws be dependent on changes in the circumstances of the individuals and of the times, *as is the case with regard to medical treatment,* which is particularized for every individual in conformity with his present temperament. On the contrary, governance of the Law ought to be absolute and universal, including everyone, even if it is suitable only for certain individuals and not suitable for others; for if it were to be made to fit individuals, the whole world would be corrupted 'and you would make out of it something that varies' [*ve-natatta devarekha leshi'urin*]" (III, 34, pp. 534–35; emphasis added).

With all the similarities between Aristotle's and Maimonides' doctrine of the mean, and with the especially striking similarity between the medical analogies of both thinkers, there is at the core a fundamental difference. On these matters Maimonides is controlled finally by the Jewish tradition, rather than by the principles of Greek philosophy. *Nomos* has about it an inescapable element of changing convention. Torah has an equally inescapable element of fixity and permanence. For this reason Maimonides holds that a Jewish thinker may freely adopt general theoretical structures and principles of explanation from the world of Greek thought, if he finds them to be scientifically sound and useful in setting the foundations for his own doctrine. If he is to remain loyal to his religious community, however, he may not substitute for the permanence of the Law and its divine-human ideal the shifting conventions of any society. (This view certainly held true for many Jewish thinkers of the Middle Ages, although it might well be challenged by some of our contemporaries.) Whatever the extent of Maimonides' possible deviation from orthodox Jewish theological norms in other areas of his thought, as claimed by some interpreters, when he dealt with the world of practice, the ordering of individual human life, and the life of society, Maimonides was consistently faithful to Jewish law. At this point he is no longer an Aristotelian but a Jew who stands fully inside the tradition.

The depth of this difference between Maimonides and Aristotle is underscored by the fact that they diverge significantly even with respect to their understanding of psychology and the nature of man. For Aristotle, the faculties of the soul that man shares with other animals are essentially the same in man as in the animals. Speaking of the nutritive faculty, for example, Aristotle says, "The excellence of this faculty . . . appears to be common to all animate things and not peculiar to man." For this reason he concludes that in his discussion he "may omit from consideration the nutritive part of the soul, since it exhibits no specifically human excellence."[46]

Maimonides categorically opposes this view. In his discussion of the faculties of the soul he makes a special point of emphasizing the fact that the human faculties, even when they carry the same name and exercise the same functions as the parallel animal faculties, are absolutely distinct and essentially different. As he puts it, "Our words concern themselves only with the human soul; for the nutritive faculty by which man is nourished is not the same, for instance, as that of the ass or the horse. . . . Although we apply the same term nutrition to all of them indiscriminately, nevertheless, its signification is by no means the same. In the same way, the term sensation is used homonymously for man and beast. . . . Mark this point well, for it is very important, as many so-called philosophers have fallen into error regarding it."[47] Little attention has been paid to this passage, but it seems to me to be of very great importance. Here Maimonides is saying explicitly that the standard psychology deriving from Aristotle, with whatever variations, is in error on a basic point. Man is not simply an animal in all respects, with the addition of the faculty of reason. Man is absolutely distinct from animals, even with regard to the faculties that constitute what we usually call his "animal nature." It is not our task here to take up the historical question of which "so-called philosophers" he had in mind when he used that rather acerbic expression.[48] We may well wonder whether it was possible that Mai-

46. *N.E.*, i, 1102b 2–12.

47. *Shemonah Perakim*, I (*The Eight Chapters*, ed. Gorfinkle, 39–40).

48. Rosin has an inadequate comment on this whole question. See *Die Ethik des Maimonides*, 48, note 1.

monides, with all his regard for Aristotle, should have included him among the so-called philosophers.[49] However troubling it may be to entertain this possibility, it is certainly clear that he contradicts his great Greek predecessor directly and rejects his views. In the last analysis it could not be otherwise: for if man is conceived as created in the image of God, he can no longer be understood as one more animal living in the order of nature. This affects the moral ideal and the medical analogy directly. In all respects, man is now viewed as different from animals, and his ideal end, *imitatio Dei*, encompasses not only his reason, but all his peculiarly human faculties. With such an understanding of man, physicians of the soul must be controlled by the divine norms. They are not training man on the analogy of training a dog or a horse. Rather they are directing a human soul, in its totality, toward the divine ideal.

As a result of this difference we can understand why Maimonides is so ready to deviate from the ideal of the middle way, while Aristotle holds to it firmly. Both acknowledge that moral virtue is only a propaedeutic to intellectual virtue, and thus to the life of ultimate felicity. For Aristotle, however, the life of moral virtue is, with minor exceptions, a life in accordance with the mean. Maimonides, on the other hand, regularly invokes the rule of the mean but just as regularly deviates from it. In the foreword to *Shemonah Perakim* he reminds us that the treatise to which this is a commentary is concerned with *ḥasidut*, the life of special saintliness, and that such saintliness "paves the way to prophecy." Therefore, if one practices the teachings of *'Avot*, one may hope to acquire prophecy. In short, the ultimate felicity is open to all who practice saintliness, and this is the subject under discussion in the treatise before us. Now saintliness is not simply a life in accordance with the mean but rather a deviation towards one of the extremes. Maimonides both recommends and defends this deviation at various points in his writings dealing with the good life in general, and even in those that deal specifically with the mean. It is especially significant, however, that he sets forth an ideal that is, in principle, no longer in any way similar to the balanced life of the Aristotelian middle way. In *Shemonah Perakim, H. De'ot,* and the *Guide* he repeats essentially the same line, namely, that all of a man's thought and activity, all his striving, and all his concern must be directed exclusively to the one single goal of the knowledge of God and fellowship with Him.

49. The standard older Hebrew translations read *harbeh min ha-pilosofim,* but there is no doubt, as is evident from the Arabic text, that the reading should be *mitpalsefim.* On this point see the editions of Gorfinkle and Kafih.

It is especially revealing that Maimonides sets out this ideal immediately after having discussed the doctrine of the mean, as if to make clear that the mean is not the true ideal at all. He considers it man's proper duty to devote himself to one goal only, namely, "the attainment of the knowledge of God as far as it is possible for man to know Him. Consequently one must so adjust all his actions, his whole conduct, and even his very words, that they lead to this goal. . . . So, his only design in eating, drinking, cohabiting, sleeping, waking, moving about, and resting should be . . . all to the end that man may reach the highest goal in his endeavors."[50]

It may well be that, as some scholars hold, Maimonides is here betraying neoplatonic influences on his thought. Our interest is not in tracing the possible sources and lines of influence but in recognizing how far Maimonides has moved from the Aristotelian line. He has in effect rejected the mean as the guiding principle and criterion of the good life, substituting for it a single controlling ideal: The good is that which leads to true knowledge and continuing contemplation of the divine being. Though Aristotle agrees, he does not counsel, as does Maimonides, that in ordering his life man should have this one concern only, that every activity, every choice, every state of character should be such as will move him effectively toward the ideal end. Maimonides holds that the mean may be a good general rule for this purpose, but it is not in and of itself the controlling consideration. Both in *Shemonah Perakim* and in *H. De'ot,* Maimonides cites in this connection the rule of the Sages, "Let all your deeds be done for the sake of God," and the verse that teaches, "In all thy ways know Him." This, rather than the mean, is decisive. Unlike Aristotle, Maimonides wants this extreme to be the practical rule for all.

Now we can see that the extreme opinions on both sides of the question of the Aristotelian foundations of Maimonides' doctrine of the mean are equally mistaken. There are both Aristotelian and non-Aristotelian aspects to Maimonides' treatment of this doctrine. It is impossible to support the view that there is nothing whatsoever of Aristotle in him; it is clear that the general form of his doctrine of the mean and much of his psychology are Aristotelian. It is just as impossible to defend the view that in Maimonides' version there is nothing more than a repetition of the Aristotelian teachings. As we have seen, there are deep and important differences. As heir, interpreter, and creative contributor to two traditions, Maimonides could not have been a pure Aristotelian in these matters. If Greek philosophy lived in him, and it did, the Jewish tradition and its Law never departed from the

50. *Shemonah Perakim,* V (*The Eight Chapters,* ed. Gorfinkle, 69); for almost identical language see *H. De'ot,* III, 2, 3; the same idea is set forth elaborately in *Guide,* I-II, 51.

center of his concerns. In dealing with the nature of man, the ideal of human existence, and the practical patterns by which human life should be ordered. Maimonides learned much from Aristotle but even more from the Torah. His remarkable achievement was that he not only knew what to choose and what to reject from the great philosophical and scientific traditions that he acquired in his culture; he also knew how to keep them in balance. In the fullest sense he was, even as a moralist, one of the most enlightened philosophers of his age and at the same time an uncompromisingly faithful Jew.

6

Maimonides and Aquinas on Natural Law

In our discussion of how Maimonides developed a strikingly independent and original approach to the doctrine of the mean, we saw that we cannot simply assimilate Maimonides to the Greek model even in the case of such a typically Aristotelian teaching. To understand Maimonides correctly we must always look for the distinctively Jewish dimension in his thought, which separates his position from that of the classical Greek and Islamic philosophical and scientific traditions which were important in forming his outlook. Indeed it is only possible to understand Maimonides deeply if we pay close attention to how he related to philosophical and scientific doctrines that were widely affirmed both in antiquity and during his own age. With all his regard for the great teachers of Greek antiquity and for their intellectual heirs among the Islamic thinkers, he never became an uncritical imitator. He knew well how to use effectively all that he learned from them without abandoning the teachings of the Torah that were always at the center of his thought. This is evident in every area of his philosophy where Jewish sources and traditions say something definite. It is particularly evident in his moral philosophy. In this chapter I propose to examine how Maimonides related to the theory that there is a natural moral law—an issue of great importance in the philosophic world in which he lived and of equal importance for an understanding of the foundations of Jewish ethics.

Classical Judaism and classical Christianity have profoundly differing views concerning the doctrine of natural moral law. In the sources of Judaism there is very little evidence of support for such a natural law doctrine, while in classical Christian thought natural law is strongly affirmed and plays a central role. Little has been done to explore the grounds of this difference or to explain its significance. After establishing the larger Jewish context for Maimonides' position by commenting on Jewish approaches to natural law as exhibited in biblical, talmudic, and philosophic sources, I shall turn to a direct examination of the teachings of Maimonides. To provide a fuller and deeper view of the complex issues Maimonides confronted, I shall then explain the contrast between the absence of any natural law theory in Maimonides with the major role assigned to natural law in the Christian philosophy of St. Thomas Aquinas.

The broad history of the *nomos-physis* conflict in Greek thought lies far beyond the limits of our present discussion, although we shall have occasion later to make reference to it. However, a clear idea of what we mean by "natural law" can best be gotten by considering some classical models. Whatever the earlier view of law in Greek thought, by the time of Euripides we already find reference to "the Law that abides and changes not, ages long, the Eternal and Nature-born."[1] This conception of law had become established more than fifty years later, as we can see when Plato speaks in defense of law and art "as things which exist by nature or by a cause not inferior to nature, since according to right reason [*kata logon orthon*] they are the offspring of the mind."[2] But it is in Stoic philosophy that natural law achieved its fullest and most influential form in the ancient world, and we will consider this conception of natural law in our present discussion. The versions of Cicero are the most familiar and most frequently cited as typical statements of the Stoic position:

> True law is right reason in agreement with nature [*recta ratio natu-rae congruens*]; it is of universal application, unchanging and everlasting; it summons to duty by its commandments, and averts from wrong-doing by its prohibitions. . . . We cannot be freed from its obligations by senate or people, and we need not look outside ourselves for an expounder or interpreter of it . . . one eternal un-changeable law will be valid for all nations and all times.[3]

> But if the judgments of men were in agreement with Na-ture . . . then Justice would be equally observed by all. For those creatures who have received the gift of reason from Nature have also received right reason, and therefore they have also received the gift of Law, which is right reason applied to command and prohibition.[4]

This conception of a law of nature that dictates principles of justice and mo-rality, a law deriving from reason and in accord with nature, which is universal, eternal, and unchanging, exercised enormous influence on Chris-tian thought. Yet though the main centers of Jewish learning were in contact with Hellenistic philosophy and Roman thought, Judaism, unlike Chris-

1. Euripides, *The Bacchae*, 895–97.
2. Plato, *Laws*, X, 890d.
3. Cicero, *De Re Publica*, III, xxii, 33.
4. Cicero, *De Legibus*, I, xii, 33.

tianity, never made such a theory of natural law a prominent feature of its teachings.

In the Hebrew Bible men are thought of as subject to direct and specific divine commandments. It is through God's revelation, mediated by the prophets, that men are taught to know what is right and wrong. Moreover, the vast majority of the biblical commandments are addressed specifically to the Jews. In established rabbinic teaching, only the smallest part of biblical legislation is universal law, intended for all human beings. All the rest, the hundreds of other injunctions and prohibitions, bind only the children of Israel. Nothing in the Hebrew Bible even approximates the Ciceronian idea of a natural law, which is addressed to all men by way of reason, and which prescribes right modes of human behavior.

In principle, there could not be such a conception in the Hebrew Bible, since there is no idea of nature, nor even a word for nature in that book. The Hebrew word *tev'a*, when it is understood to mean "nature," does not occur in the Bible or in the Mishnah. It makes its first appearance in medieval Hebrew usage, particularly in the works of the philosophers.[5] The idea of nature arises only with philosophical reflection. As Leo Strauss rightly points out, "the discovery of nature is the work of philosophy. Where there is no philosophy, there is no knowledge of natural right as such. The Old Testament . . . does not know 'nature'. . . . There is, then, no knowledge of natural right as such in the Old Testament."[6] Aristotle taught us to think of nature as that which is endowed with its own internal principle of motion. The natural world is thus self-developing and self-explanatory. In the Hebrew Bible the world and man are seen as created by God, sustained by Him and subject to His will, and this alone makes them intelligible. Biblical man has full powers of reason, but unlike Cicero the Bible does not teach that once man has reason he also has knowledge of the moral law. In ancient Hebrew thought there is only one source of the knowledge of good and evil—the commandments of God as they are revealed to man.[7]

5. See the note by Louis Ginzberg in Israel Efros, *Philosophical Terms in the Moreh Nebukim* (New York, 1924), 134–35. Cf. also Jacob Klatzkin, *Thesaurus Philosophicus Linguae Hebraicae ('Otzar Hamunaḥim Hapilusufiyyim)* (Berlin, 1928), vol. 2, 9–13. The absence of a term does not necessarily mean that the concept is absent from a particular culture. In this case, however, it seems clear that the Hebrew Bible lacks not only a term for "nature," but also the idea of a natural force that works independently of divine control.

6. Leo Strauss, *Natural Right and History* (Chicago, 1953), 81–82.

7. See Salo W. Baron, *A Social and Religious History of the Jews*, vol. 6 (Philadelphia, 1958), 5, 397 n. 168.

In the postbiblical rabbinic texts a few passages are frequently pointed to as supposedly teaching some conception of natural law. Properly interpreted, these passages in no way justify the claim that the sages of the Talmud advocated a natural law theory. They regularly and as a matter of course maintain the classical biblical teaching that divine commandment is the only ultimate source of law. Even positive human legislation is seen as legitimate and binding only insofar as it is an application or extension of rules or principles set forth in the divinely revealed law.

It is in this clearly set framework that we must see and understand such a rabbinic comment as: "'Mine ordinances shall ye do,' (Lev., 18:4). i.e., such commandments which, if they were not written [in Scripture], they should by right have been written, and these are they: [the laws concerning] idolatry, sexual immorality, bloodshed, robbery, and blasphemy."[8] There is no suggestion here that human reason could have known by itself that these acts are evil, nor is it suggested that they are not consistent with man's nature. What is asserted is only that, having been commanded to avoid these prohibited acts, we can now see, after the fact, that these prohibitions are useful and desirable. It is instructive that the passage goes on to contrast these rules, which civilized people have learned to value, with other ritual commandments that do not seem to serve any useful purpose. The conclusion is that both types of commandments bind and obligate the Jews because they come from God and that ultimately no fruitful distinctions can be drawn between them.

Much the same can be said concerning the passage in which we are told, "If the Torah had not been given we could have learned modesty from the cat, not to rob from the ant, chastity from the dove, considerate behavior to our wives from the rooster."[9] Those who interpret this statement as affirming a doctrine of natural law seem to me to miss a crucial point. R. Yochanan, who is credited with this statement, does not say that we would have known morally proper behavior by way of our unaided reason. He seems to be saying rather that without divine commandments we might have learned certain kinds of socially useful behavior by imitating various ani-

8. *Yoma*, 67b. The key phrase for our purposes is *din hu' sheyikatvu*, which is translated in the Soncino edition cited here, "they should by right have been written." I believe the translator was correct in using the ambiguous phrase "by right," without trying to specify whether this is a requirement of reason, a matter of social utility, or right in some other sense. What seems clear is that neither the context of this passage, nor the wider context of rabbinic thought, will sustain an interpretation that makes natural reason alone a sufficient and authoritative source of the rules of morality.

9. *Eruvin*, 100b.

mals. This view was expressed earlier in a famous bit of biblical counsel: "Go to the ant, thou sluggard; consider her ways and be wise." [10]

Neither the biblical nor the talmudic statements suppose that man would by himself have known what is good. Rather, having been taught by divine commandments to know good and evil, man can now look with admiration at certain animals which instinctively live in accordance with some of these divine patterns. By choosing to imitate these animals, natural man can make his life somewhat more decent and tolerable than it would be otherwise. By such imitation alone he could never arrive at ideas of obligation or commandment, certainly not at a theory of natural moral law. Furthermore, the logic of the situation makes it impossible to suppose that man could have learned rules of sound behavior only through independent observation of the behavior of animals. If there were no antecedent standard, how would man have known which animals to imitate and which particular behavior patterns of those animals to imitate? How would he have been able to decide that the chastity of the dove rather than the sexual habits of the rabbit were the appropriate model? Why should he have chosen to imitate the ant's respect for private property rather than the rapacious acquisitiveness of certain other animals? Unless we already know what constitutes good behavior through some other source of instruction, studying the life of the animals only informs us of a range of possibilities, but provides us with no criterion for choosing among them.

That so widespread a doctrine as natural law should have had some echoes in Jewish thought in the Middle Ages is not surprising when we consider the extensive and mutual interconnections among the works of Moslem, Christian, and Jewish medieval philosophers. What is remarkable is the almost total resistance to the theory of natural law in Jewish thought, a resistance emphasized by the small number of instances in which Jewish thinkers even approached such a theory. Let us consider briefly two medieval Jewish philosophers sometimes thought to hold a doctrine of natural law, Saadia Gaon (892–942) and Joseph Albo (1380–1444), respectively one of the earliest and one of the latest of the Jewish medievals. Joseph Albo is virtually the only medieval Jewish philosopher who uses the term *natural law* in the five hundred years that separate him from Saadia Gaon. Saadia, like some others, uses the expression, "the rational precepts of the Torah," to identify one of the classes of divine commandments, but he does not use the term *natural law.* Moreover, I shall show that, contrary to the views of

---

10. Prov. 6:6–8; cf. Prov. 30:25–31, where a number of animals are presented as models for human behavior.

many interpreters of his thought, he does not advance the idea of a moral law rooted exclusively in reason and binding on us independently of divine revelation.

For Saadia, to say that some of the divine commandments are rational is not equivalent to saying that reason knows them independently, or that reason alone can determine what is proper behavior for man. God alone is the source of the law. In addition to creating the human species, God "also endowed them with the means whereby they might attain complete happiness and perfect bliss . . . the commandments and prohibitions prescribed for them by God."[11] What Saadia seems to mean then by "rational precepts" is essentially the same as what we saw in the talmudic passages cited and discussed earlier. They are commandments for which we can produce good reasons from our own purely human standpoint. They have an obvious social utility or can, by reflection, be shown to serve purposes of which reasonable men generally approve. They are contrasted with precepts that are primarily ritual in character and are not understood by us through the principles of reason. A man might be expected to continue to observe the rational precepts even if he no longer believed in their divine origin. Once he learns of them, he can see that they are useful and that they help him achieve his own ends. The ritual precepts can command our loyalty only as long as we recognize that "the chief reason for the fulfillment of these principal precepts and their derivatives . . . is the fact that they represent the command of our Lord."[12]

But Saadia, concerned with appealing as far as possible to human reason, goes on to say, with regard to these ritual commandments, "yet I find that most of them have as their basis partially useful purposes." This seems to me to be strong evidence that he identifies the rational with the useful, but does not believe that utility serves as an independent and universal substitute for divinely revealed commandments. Having received the Law by revelation, we can now admire God's wisdom in commanding us to live in this advantageous way.

At the very end of the medieval period, Joseph Albo is the one Jewish philosopher who introduces the term *natural law* (*dat tiv'it*). His system of classification includes "three kinds of law, natural, positive or conven-

---

11. Saadia Gaon, *The Book of Beliefs and Opinions*, trans. Samuel Rosenblatt (New Haven, 1948), 137.

12. Ibid., 139–42, 143. For an extended discussion of this topic, see M. Fox, "On the Rational Commandments in Saadia: A Re-Examination," in *Modern Jewish Ethics: Theory and Practice* (Columbus, Oh., 1975), 174–87. Reprinted with minor variations in *Proceedings of the Sixth World Congress of Jewish Studies*, vol. 3 (Jerusalem, 1977), 34–43. Critics have disagreed with my views on this subject, but I have seen no counterarguments that are persuasive.

tional, and divine." He explains that "natural law is the same among all peoples, at all times, and in all places."[13] Yet, even Albo, coming as late as the fifteenth century and undoubtedly familiar with Christian thought and writing, does not really take natural law as a serious option.[14] He assigns it to the most inferior place in the hierarchy of types of law and makes clear his adherence to the traditional Jewish view that we are ultimately dependent on divine law. The scope of natural law is too limited to be useful. Its purpose is "to repress wrong, to promote right." But man's reason is not able, by itself, to spell out what is right and wrong. This is why neither natural law nor conventional positive law is satisfactory. All that natural man can rely on as a guide to good and evil are his own reactions of pleasure and pain, and these are so dependent on individual idiosyncrasies that they are completely unsatisfactory as moral guides.[15] We are thus left only with God's direct instruction, through his prophets, as ground for the distinctions between right and wrong. Reason cannot teach us to know what is good, nor can feeling guide and direct us. In spite of his minimal recognition of natural law, Albo is still a loyal Jew who can find no ground for moral law without divine revelation.

To understand fully this Jewish conception of law and to explicate the principles on which it rests, we must turn to an examination of the views of Maimonides. We have seen earlier that Maimonides is often described as a complete rationalist, but I shall show that he is most extreme in his rejection of all claims concerning a natural moral law based on right reason. However wide the extent of reason's authority may be in Maimonides' teaching, it does not extend to the realm of morals.

The clearest and most striking instance of Maimonides' approach to the doctrine of natural law can be found in his ruling with respect to the seven commandments of the Noahides. The rabbinic doctrine concerning these commandments is the most important early source that might be considered

13. Joseph Albo, *Sefer Ha-'Ikkarim (Book of Principles)*, trans. Isaac Husik (Philadelphia, 1946), vol. 1, 78. While Husik, on his title page, translates the title as *Book of Principles*, it would be more accurate to render it as *Book of Roots*. Husik does so himself in his Introduction, vol. 1, xvii. On this question, and for a general discussion of Albo's natural law theory, see Ralph Lerner, "Natural Law in Albo's *Book of Roots,"* in *Ancients and Moderns,* ed. Joseph Cropsey (New York, 1964), 132–47.

14. That Albo knew Christianity is evident from more than his participation in the famous disputation at Tortosa in 1413; in *Sefer Ha-'Ikkarim* he devotes a long chapter to a refutation of Christian charges against Judaism (Book III, chap. 25, 217–45).

15. Ibid., Book I, chap. 7, 79, 82, chap. 8, 87; Book III, chap. 6, 55–57, chap. 7, 58–60, 64.

as presenting a Jewish version of natural and universal moral law. Talmudic legislation had specified that there are seven commandments binding on all mankind. Mankind in general is referred to as the "children of Noah," since after the flood all humanity descends from Noah. These Noahide precepts include prohibitions against idolatry, blasphemy, murder, adultery, and robbery, and the commandment to establish courts of justice. These six are considered to have been given to Adam. A seventh was given to Noah, namely, a prohibition against eating a limb torn from a living animal.[16] The Talmud reads the first six of these commandments out of the verse, "And the Lord God commanded the man saying." The seventh is derived from the verse, "You must not, however, eat flesh with its life-blood in it."[17] It is understandable that those who seek a natural law in the classical Jewish sources would seize on these seven commandments of the Noahides as just such a law. They were presumably commanded to Adam, who is everyman, are universal in scope, and are binding on all mankind. These qualities are usually associated with natural moral law. However, there is no suggestion in the rabbinic literature that these laws originate in reason, are known to us directly through our reason, or obligate us because reason perceives them as binding duties. They are explicitly treated as divine commandments, on a par with all the other divine commandments.

We might have expected a philosopher like Maimonides to see in these precepts an opportunity to ground the fundamentals of morality in nature and reason. The fact is that he does just the opposite. In his *Mishneh Torah* Maimonides follows the established rabbinic ruling that gentiles who observe the seven precepts belong to the class of the "righteous of the nations of the world" (*ḥasidei 'ummot ha-'olam*), who are guaranteed a "portion in the world to come," that is to say, salvation. So far he is merely reproducing what had already been said by his talmudic predecessors. However, he adds another condition which is designed to eliminate any possibility of understanding the Noahide commandments as natural law. Let us study the exact language of the text:

Any man [i.e., any gentile] who accepts the seven commandments
and is meticulous in observing them is thereby one of the righteous

16. *Sanhedrin,* 56a–57a. For recent discussions of the Noahide commandments, see David Novak, *The Image of the Non-Jew in Judaism: An Historical and Constructive Study of the Noahide Laws* (New York, 1983), and Aaron Lichtenstein, *Seven Laws of Noah* (New York, 1981).

17. Gen. 2:16, 9:4. There is extensive discussion of the derivation of these seven laws in the Talmud, and some other scriptural sources are suggested, but these sources are those that are commonly and generally recognized.

of the nations of the world, and he has a portion in the world to come. *This is only the case if he accepts them and observes them because God commanded them in the Torah, and taught us through our teacher, Moses, that the children of Noah had been commanded to observe them even before the Torah was given.* But if he observes them because of his own conclusions based on reason, then he is not a resident-alien and is not one of the righteous of the nations of the world, nor is he one of their wise men.[18]

There are two points here of striking importance. First is the fact that for post-Sinaitic times Maimonides explicitly makes the salvific force of the observance of the Noahide commandments dependent on a belief in their divine origin as commandments known only by way of God's revelation through Moses in the Torah. However, even the pre-Sinaitic generations are considered to have been directly commanded by God, through Adam and Noah, to observe these precepts. Of particular interest is that Maimonides deliberately excludes the validity of any claim that these laws are known through reason or that they bind us because of purely rational considerations. One might have thought that it would be meritorious for a man to have achieved a basic knowledge of the rules of morality by way of rational reflection. But Maimonides denies to such a man all claims to special merit and, in the process, denies that there is or can be any natural moral law of the kind that Cicero had set forth.

The full force of this denial is evident in the second point that requires our special attention, namely, the final phrase in the quoted passage, "nor is he one of their wise men." Maimonides is here excluding a man who claims rational moral knowledge, not only from the circle of the pious and righteous who win salvation, but also from the circle of the wise. Much has been written about this last phrase in numerous attempts to show that this is a faulty reading and that the correct reading should be, "but he is one of their wise men." Considering the similarity of the formation of the Hebrew letters in the two Hebrew words, *velo'* and *'el'a*, "nor" and "but," it is easy to suppose a scribal or printing error. It is not possible to consider the relevant textual evidence within the limits of our present discussion. It is valuable, however, to note that the reading we have cited occurs in almost all the printed editions, including the first complete edition printed at Rome in 1480.[19]

18. *H. Melakhim,* 8:11, emphasis added.

19. For a discussion of the textual problem, see Steven S. Schwarzschild, "Do Noachites Have to Believe in Revelation?" *Jewish Quarterly Review,* 57, 4 (April, 1962), 301–3. The entire article, which is continued in the following number of *JQR,* is a valuable discussion of our topic. See also, on the textual and interpretative problem, Jacob Katz, *Exclusiveness and*

It is my view that a correct understanding of Maimonides will show why he could not affirm a theory of natural law, why he denied salvation to those who believed that they could have moral knowledge on purely rational grounds, and why he considered the latter neither pious nor wise. With respect to the last question, I shall not presume in any way to try to settle the problem of the correct reading of our text. I shall only give evidence that it would have been perfectly consistent with Maimonides' views, even necessary, for him to have denied that those who hold a doctrine of natural law are wise men, that is to say, good philosophers.

From his earliest work to the great book of his advanced years, the *Guide of the Perplexed,* Maimonides consistently denied that moral rules are based on principles of reason or that they are capable of demonstration. Already in his *Treatise on Logic,* written in his youth, he treats moral rules as not falling under the categories of truth and falsehood at all, so that it is simply a logical error to speak of moral rules as true or false. Instead he thinks of moral behavior as having to do with the beautiful and the ugly, and these are matters either of subjective taste or, as is usually the case, of established social convention. In short, Maimonides holds that moral claims are never open to rational argument or demonstration. They are "propositions which are known and require no proof for their truth." Unlike other such propositions that are indemonstrable but are certainly true, such as statements about immediate perceptions and the first principles of mathematics, moral rules are true only in the sense that in a well-ordered society they are generally accepted and not subject to doubt. They are "*conventions,* as when we know that uncovering the privy parts is ugly, or that compensating a benefactor generously is beautiful."[20] Society, properly governed, forms our tastes and

---

Tolerance (New York, 1962), 175–77. Both these writers hold that our printed texts are in error and adopt the reading *'el'a,* "but is," rather than our reading *velo',* "nor." They base their view on some of the manuscripts, quotations of the passage in works by other medieval authors, and, especially, on their understanding of what Maimonides' position must truly have been. It is only fair to note that most scholars share their view, and that it is supported by some manuscript readings. I shall argue, however, not from the manuscript evidence, which is at best ambiguous, but rather from the internal evidence as to what view Maimonides must have advanced.

20. *Maimonides' Treatise on Logic,* trans. and ed., Israel Efros (New York, 1938), 47; emphasis added. Efros seems to me to miss a crucial point when he translates the first sentence of chap. 8, "The propositions which are known to be true and require no proof for their truthfulness are of four kinds." In the ibn Tibbon version, the text reads, *ha-mishpatim asher yivad'u velo'yitztarekh ra'aya al 'amitatam,* "the propositions which are known and require no proof of their truth." This is an exact rendition of the Arabic text. Maimonides does not say that these are propositions which are "known to be true," as Efros puts it. They are, rather, types of propositions that we hold with a feeling of certainty, and in this sense we are convinced of their truth,

patterns of response in such a way that we have no doubt about such matters. However, this is not in any respect a matter of rational certainty or demonstrative evidence.

That this is a correct interpretation of Maimonides' position in the passage quoted is supported by a comment of Moses Mendelssohn. In his gloss on the term *conventions* Mendelssohn says: "These are matters which are incapable of being either true or false, but are only ugly or beautiful."[21] Mendelssohn goes on to argue that Maimonides is not speaking about the beautiful and ugly in general, but only about modes of human behavior that we consider to be of moral significance and that are so set by convention as to evoke fixed responses from us. These are our reactions to such behavior, in which we feel that what we are seeing or contemplating is beautiful or ugly, depending on whether it is socially approved or condemned. The soundness of this way of understanding Maimonides becomes evident when we move from the *Treatise on Logic,* his earliest book, to his treatment of the same topic in his later works.

In *Eight Chapters,* a treatise dealing with moral questions, Maimonides takes the same position. Moral evil is ultimately a matter of convention when considered from a philosophic point of view, and a matter of violating divine commandments when considered from a religious point of view. In his work on logic there was no proper place for any reference to divine commandments as the source of moral rules. Since that was a work of philosophy, or at least a propaedeutic to philosophy, it would have been inappropriate to introduce into it a purely religious element. Only at the very end of the *Treatise on Logic* does Maimonides give passing notice to the present state of affairs in which we are no longer dependent on the *nomoi,* i.e., the conventional laws of the philosophers, since we are in possession of God's commandments. "In these times we do not need all these laws and *nomoi;* for divine laws govern human conduct."[22] However, in *Eight Chapters,* which, as part of his commentary on the Mishnah, is a religious work, Maimonides deals directly and explicitly with morals as divine command-

---

i.e., they are not open to doubt. This is not the same as saying that we know them "to be true." In adding these words, Efros blunts the force of Maimonides' statement in a way that can easily lead to a basic misunderstanding of his position. Moreover, Maimonides says that they do not need to be established by *dalīl.* This term does not mean "demonstration" but something considerably less. It refers to the kind of evidence that, although short of demonstration, would incline a reasonable man to accept a given proposition as true.

21. Moses Maimonides, *Be'ur Millot ha-Higgayon,* with commentary by Moses Mendelssohn (Berlin, 1925), 38b. Mendelssohn's testimony is particularly important since his own views on this subject are almost totally contrary to those of Maimonides.

22. Maimonides, *Treatise on Logic,* ed. Efros, 64.

ments. But this does not turn them into rational laws available to man by way of natural reason.

> The evils which the philosophers term such . . . are things which all people commonly agree are evils, such as the shedding of blood, theft, robbery, fraud, injury to one who has done no harm, ingratitude, contempt for parents, and the like. The prescriptions against these are called commandments [*mitzvot*], about which the Rabbis said, "If they had not already been written in the Law, it would be proper to add them." Some of our later sages, who were infected with the unsound principles of the *Mutakallimūn*, called these rational laws.[23]

Here we have in a brief statement the main elements of Maimonides' ethical theory.

From the standpoint of the philosophers, morals are conventions, "things which all people commonly agree are evils." From the standpoint of the rabbis they are divine commandments. One thing is completely clear: in Maimonides' opinion, anyone who believes that moral principles originate in reason or are dictated by reason is suffering from a serious intellectual disease. The intensity of Maimonides' feeling about this matter can be seen from the nature of his attack. It is generally agreed that he is directing his criticism especially against Saadia Gaon. In other places, however, Maimonides speaks of Saadia with much admiration. He even goes so far as to say that were it not for him the Torah might have been completely lost.[24] This may explain the veiled reference, rather than a direct attack. Despite Saadia's merit, the fact that he spoke of rational commandments and thus opened the door even slightly to a theory of natural law is, for Maimonides, clear and incontrovertible evidence of his being "infected with unsound principles."

This theory of the nature of moral judgments came to full expression early in Maimonides' most mature and most profound speculative work, the *Guide of the Perplexed*. In I, 2 he answers a question put to him by an unnamed "learned man" concerning the punishment of Adam and Eve after their sin. In the course of his answer Maimonides explains that the true perfection of man is in his intellect, and that it is because he is endowed with

---

23. *The Eight Chapters of Maimonides on Ethics*, trans. and ed., Joseph I. Garfinkle (New York, 1912; rpt. 1966), 76–77. *Mutakallimūn* refers to the Islamic philospher-theologians, who developed the Kalām.

24. *Kovetz Teshuvot ha-Rambam ve-'Iggerotav* (Leipzig, 1859), II, 5a. Cf. David Kaufmann, *Geschichte der Attributenlehre* (Gotha, 1877), 503.

intellect that man is spoken of as created in the image of God. Only insofar as he has intelligence can man be commanded, since commands are never given to animals, which have no intellect.[25] "Through the intellect one distinguishes between truth and falsehood, and that was found in Adam in its perfection and integrity. Beautiful and ugly, on the other hand, belong to the things generally accepted as known [i.e., conventions], not to those cognized by intellect" (I, 2, p. 24).[26] As an example of the kind of conventional behavior that is bad only because of social decrees and commonly developed tastes, Maimonides again cites the case of one who uncovers his nakedness in public. For Adam, who was endowed originally with a perfect intellect and was free of all dependence on convention or taste, nakedness was not bad "and he did not apprehend that it was bad." This is evident from the biblical text where we are told that, though Adam and Eve were naked, they were not ashamed. After their sin, when they were robbed of intellectual perfection and reduced to dependence on conventions or feelings, they were embarrassed by their nakedness and covered themselves.

In this model case of man in the state of nature, there is no natural moral law at all according to Maimonides. Moreover, insofar as there is any law regulating human behavior even in that primal state, it is explicitly a divine command. It is worth noting that, in the biblical text, Adam is given no rational explanation for the command not to eat of the forbidden tree. He is simply warned that "on the day that you eat from it you will die." The force of the commandment rests with the wisdom and authority of God who commands; it is in no way dependent on its being grasped as obligatory by human reason. For Maimonides this must be the case, because morals are neither true nor false, while the intellect has as its proper subject matter only that which is capable of being either true or false.

In the light of this it is now clear why Maimonides denied that those who claim a rational knowledge of morality are wise men (if we accept the correctness of the reading in the printed versions). A wise man is one who, among other things, makes proper use of his faculties and understands what to expect from each subject. One of the marks of a well-trained mind, according to Aristotle, is that it knows how to distinguish between various

25. See the extended discussion and commentary on this passage in chapter 7.

26. Despite my praise of the excellence of Pines' translation, I have chosen in this passage to change it slightly in order to emphasize the point being made. Pines widely avoided using the terms *good* and *evil*, preferring *fine* and *bad*. In my opinion, *beautiful* and *ugly* convey the sense of the passage with less ambiguity. This translation is supported by the classic edition of Munk, who renders the terms in question by "le laid et le beau." Cf. S. Munk, *Le Guide des Egarés . . . par . . . Maimonide* (rp., Paris, 1960), vol. 1, 39.

types of subjects and never expects more precision than a subject is capable of yielding.[27] Maimonides knew his Aristotle well and had great regard for the Philosopher. As a follower of the Aristotelian teaching, he quite properly would refuse to recognize a man as wise who could be so confused that he would treat matters of convention or taste as if they were capable of rational demonstration. There is, in addition, a danger to society in such an error because it rejects sound moral authority in favor of pseudo-reason. Once it is clear that moral distinctions are not rational, and if they are no longer accepted on the authority of the temporal sovereign or of God, there is no longer any ground whatsoever for restraint in human behavior.

This leads us to consider Maimonides' explanation of law, its sources, and its purposes. All law must be understood as aimed at directing humankind toward the achievement of its own ultimate perfection. This perfection consists of the highest development of the intellect, leading to a rational knowledge of the "whole of being as it is" (*Guide,* III, 28, p. 512). However, no one can achieve this state of intellectual perfection in isolation. Man is a political animal whose natural habitat is in society. People cannot survive alone, but require the help of others. Moreover, even living in society, individuals cannot achieve the fulfillment of their highest intellectual potentialities unless their bodily needs are properly provided for. We therefore require a law that serves two purposes. First, it must order the life of the individual and the life of the community in a way that makes them receptive to correct opinions. Then it must communicate these correct opinions about ultimate matters so that even ordinary people will gain a substantial measure of true knowledge of the ultimate things. In a community that is under the governance of such a system of law, the truly gifted individual will emerge with the fullest and most profound grasp of the highest truths with respect to the whole of being as it is, thus gaining true salvation.

These two aims of law are not generally achieved by the positive law of secular societies. It is the special merit of "the true Law . . . which is unique—namely, the Law of Moses our Master" that it is directed toward the realization of both essential human objectives. It "has come to bring us both perfections, I mean the welfare of the states of people in their relations with one another through the abolition of reciprocal wrongdoing and through the acquisition of a noble and excellent character . . . I mean also the soundness of the beliefs and the giving of correct opinions through which ultimate perfection is achieved. The letter of the Torah speaks of both perfections and informs us that the end of this Law in its entirety is the achievement of these two perfections" (*Guide,* III, 27, p. 511). Thus all the command-

27. Aristotle, *N.E.,* I, iii, 1094b 12–28.

137

ments of Scripture and the rabbinic tradition are to be understood as aiming at these two goals. This means that every commandment has a reason, but it does not mean that we are necessarily capable of knowing or discovering the reasons that underlie the commandments. Maimonides subscribes to the view that it would be blasphemous to suggest that God, who is perfect, would issue commands that are arbitrary or capricious.[28] He thus makes an intense effort to discover reasons for the commandments that will fit into his general hermeneutic framework. This is, however, a speculative enterprise, which is only possible for us after the fact of our having been commanded, while it remains the case that the obligatory force of the commandments in no way depends on our knowing or understanding their reasons.

This is evident when we consider how Maimonides deals with the commandments in general. Those aimed at communicating correct opinions could, in principle, be known by anyone through skillful use of unaided reason. Those aimed at the propaedeutic task of ordering personal and social life so as to make possible intellectual perfection could not be known through the power of reason alone. Here we are dependent on the goodness and wisdom of God, who graciously taught us how to live in political communities that are properly ordered so as to provide the best conditions for the realization of human perfection. Given this understanding of the nature of the commandments in general, we can then look back at the individual commandments and seek to satisfy ourselves by gaining explanations of their utility.

This point is strikingly clear in Maimonides' discussion of the Ten Commandments. Following rabbinic tradition he says that at Sinai the people heard directly only the first two commandments: I am the Lord thy God; thou shalt have no other Gods before me. The remaining eight commandments, like the rest of the Torah, were brought to the people through Moses. Maimonides interprets this to mean that the first two commandments, which deal with the existence and the unity of God, are philosophical affirmations that can be known directly by human reason. We are not dependent on prophecy for our knowledge of these demonstrable truths, nor does the prophet have any special knowledge of them that is denied to others. "Now with regard to everything that can be known by demonstration, the status of the prophet and that of every one else who knows it are equal; there is no superiority of one over the other. Thus these two principles are not known through prophecy alone" (II, 33, p. 364).

These two principles, known by way of the intellect and open to rational demonstration, are essentially different from the remaining eight

28. See especially *Guide*, III, 25.

commandments. The latter, which are fundamental rules of common morality, are not demonstrable and are in no way derived from reason. Though we are speaking here of such basic rules as the prohibitions against murder, adultery, and theft, and the duty to honor parents, Maimonides does not regard them as binding because we see by way of reason that they are true principles. On the contrary, "as for the other commandments [i.e., the last eight], they belong to the class of generally accepted opinions and those adopted in virtue of tradition, not to the class of the intellecta" (II, 33, p. 364). It is difficult to imagine a more categorical rejection of natural law theory than that contained in this passage. The most common of the precepts, which are assumed to be essential for the life of any ordered society, are not thought by Maimonides to be derived from reason or in any way available to the unaided human intellect. Viewed philosophically, they are merely conventions which have won widespread acceptance and are enforced by the power of tradition.

If we were to leave the matter there, the entire fabric of civilized society would be threatened. Secular societies have no other source for such precepts than the will of the sovereign, the tradition of the people, or the conviction that these precepts serve a useful purpose. If this is the only ground of morality, then clearly such precepts cannot obligate rational individuals. Whenever they feel inclined to substitute their own judgment for conventional opinion, there is no good reason for them not to do so. If from their perspective it is not imprudent to violate the conventions, then clearly, as rational beings, they should feel themselves free to do so. The laws of such societies are *nomoi,* and there is a long history in Greek thought of opposition between *nomos* and *physis,* the merely conventional and the natural. Maimonides is faithful to classical Jewish tradition in holding that a merely conventional law is, in the last analysis, no law at all. If precepts do not bind and obligate us by way of our reason, then they can only become fixed obligatory rules as divine commandments. The Jews were favored by God with prophets, and particularly with Moses, the greatest of the prophets, through whom God's commandments were communicated to the people. Through divine law we have the principles of an ideal society in which personal and social needs, on the one hand, and correct opinions about the highest matters, on the other, are provided for everyone. This law is binding even with respect to moral matters that are not demonstrable, because it comes to us from God. Only such a law can be effective in leading man to the highest possibilities of human self-realization, "whereas the other political regimens—such as the *nomoi* of the Greeks and the ravings of the Sabians and of others—are due . . . to the actions of groups of rulers who were not prophets" (II, 39, p. 381).

Divine law, as received through the prophets, aims at the double objective of the welfare of the soul and the welfare of the body. The knowledge of ultimate truths is open to any man whose reason is sufficiently developed and who is motivated to engage in intense reflection about the nature of reality and the nature of God. Such men can arise only in a society so ordered that their kind of thinking has a place. Consequently they too need to have the benefit of the laws regulating personal and social behavior. For the large mass who are not impelled by nature and talent to metaphysical speculation, it is essential to establish both an ordered society and a system of correct beliefs. Beginning from the base of a properly ordered community and from beliefs that save them from hopeless errors, even ordinary people have some chance of achieving their own proper perfection. Without the special guidance of the divine law, however, the essential conditions for the movement toward true human perfection are lacking.

In a key passage Maimonides states succinctly and clearly his views about these fundamental matters:

> It has already been demonstrated that man has two perfections: a first perfection, which is the perfection of the body and an ultimate perfection, which is the perfection of the soul. The first perfection consists in being healthy and in the very best bodily state, and this is only possible through his finding the things necessary for him whenever he seeks them. These are his food and all the other things needed for the governance of the body, such as a shelter, bathing, and so forth. This cannot be achieved in any way by one isolated individual. For an individual can only attain all this through a political association, it being already known that man is political by nature. His ultimate perfection is to become rational in actu, I mean to have an intellect in actu; this would consist in knowing everything concerning all the beings that it is within the capacity of man to know in accordance with his ultimate perfection. *It is clear that to this ultimate perfection there do not belong either actions or moral qualities and that it consists only of opinions toward which speculation has led and that investigation has rendered compulsory.* It is also clear that this noble and ultimate perfection can only be achieved after the first perfection has been achieved. For a man cannot represent to himself an intelligible even when taught to understand it and all the more cannot become aware of it of his own accord, if he is in pain or is very hungry or is thirsty or is hot or is very cold. But once the first perfection has been achieved it is possible to achieve the ultimate, which is indubitably more noble and is the only cause of permanent preservation (III, 27, pp. 510–11; emphasis added).

140

We can see here the end of all true law, which is to bring men to both perfections. A true law must be clear about the order of importance and dignity of the two types of perfection, never confusing the instrumental good with the final good. Only the final good is rational. All the rest is aimed at establishing the conditions under which men can achieve the final good, but it has no intrinsic worth. There is no natural moral law. Divine law consists not only of true beliefs, but also of behavioral precepts by way of which people can be brought to the state in which it is possible for them to realize the final good. So important is it to have divine sanction for all the precepts by which personal and social life are ordered that the true law also commands us to accept certain beliefs without which the precepts might lose their force. "The Law also makes a call to adopt certain beliefs, belief in which is necessary for the sake of political welfare. Such, for instance, is our belief that He, may He be exalted, is violently angry with those who disobey Him and that it is therefore necessary to fear Him and to dread Him and to take care not to disobey" (III, 28, p. 512). This is necessary because reason alone provides no sanction for any set of moral rules.

Maimonides' categorical rejection of natural law does not entail holding that divine moral rules are irrational or opposed to nature. He is affirming only that moral precepts are not known by way of reason and are not capable of demonstration. Viewed by themselves, they would appear to be matters with respect to which one cannot logically affirm either truth or falsehood. So long as man does not live in society, as was the case with Adam, morality can be thought of merely as a matter of taste, and thus as purely subjective. Once human beings enter society—and historically they are always social and political beings—they can no longer afford to allow morals to be treated as purely private matters of personal taste. For the protection of society morals are reinforced with the power of convention, changing finally into law. But positive law suffers from two defects. First, it is only concerned with bodily welfare, but this is only instrumental to what really matters—the welfare of the soul. Second, it has no real sanction, since one can always question the wisdom or the beneficence of the human sovereign. This reduces the force of law to nothing more than the counsels of prudence. Plato demonstrated long ago that prudence is self-defeating, since the truly prudent man must ask what his true self-interest is and, in the process of this inquiry, is led to consider ultimate moral and metaphysical questions.

It is as an alternative to this untenable view of law that Maimonides understands the system of divine law that he sets forth. What reason cannot do alone is done for us by God through His prophets. What reason can do alone—namely, to know ultimate truths—is left open to every man, aided by the initially correct beliefs provided for him by Scripture. All the commandments, other than those that have to do with true belief, are useful and even necessary for the ideal ordering of the political community. Seen this way, we can say of them that, though they are not rational in the sense of being demonstrable, they are reasonable in the sense that we can give good reasons for them.

With this purpose in mind, Maimonides goes to great lengths in his *Guide* to expound the reasons for the commandments. He is concerned to show us that all the commandments are useful, in one way or another, as devices for helping us gain the ultimate perfection that is the true end of humankind (III, 31, pp. 523–24). No one could ever come, by way of rational reflection alone, to the conclusion that there is some particular set of moral rules that is correct and binding. On the other hand, having received the precepts and accepted them as divine in origin, we can, after the fact, recognize how valuable they are. Even in cases where we fail to find a satisfactory reason for given commandments, we continue to observe them; having acknowledged the divine origin of the entire structure, we can no longer justify selecting among the commandments in accordance with our individual private taste or judgment. Once we are prepared to deny the authority of prophecy to one commandment, however bizarre or obscure it may seem to us, we have effectively denied the binding force of the entire Torah.

For this reason, Maimonides lays extreme stress on our obligation to recognize the Torah, which has been transmitted to us, as complete and immutable. No one claiming today to be a prophet and proposing to change any law of the Torah can be recognized as legitimate. He is a false prophet who perverts the authority of Moses and in so doing undermines the authority of God's commandments.[29] Maimonides emphasizes that the Torah was given only once, that it is a work of divine perfection, and that we can hope to see the realization of the highest human possibilities only in a society that submits itself completely to the discipline of God's law.

Just as the commandments are reasonable without being rationally demonstrable, so are they in accord with human nature without being natural. The law takes account of natural qualities and is designed to cope with them. It does not demand what human beings are incapable of doing, and its commands are framed with an eye to what human nature requires for its own perfection. "Therefore I say that the Law, although it is not natural, enters into what is natural" (*Guide,* II, 40, p. 382). To take just one example, the laws of sacrifice, according to Maimonides, had to be given as a concession

29. Cf. *H. Yesodei ha-Torah,* 9:1; *H. Melakhim,* 11:3. On the latter see the striking correction of our received text by Y. Kafih in his edition of the *Commentary on the Mishnah* (Jerusalem, 1964), *Nezikin,* Introduction to *Sanhedrin,* X, 215 n. 77.

to accustomed patterns of pre-Sinaitic worship. To root out certain of these idolatrous patterns required accommodation to human nature: "For one could not then conceive the acceptance of [such a Law], considering the nature of man, which always likes that to which it is accustomed" (III, 32, p. 526). In this restricted sense Maimonides conceives of the law as natural, that is, as consistent with and attuned to human nature. There is no other or more significant sense in which we can find any version of natural law in Maimonides. This extreme position of Maimonides with respect to natural law is, of course, yet another reflection of the normative attitude of the classical Jewish tradition as it is formulated in the Bible, the rabbinic literature, and the works of the Jewish philosophers of the Middle Ages. In treating this topic in his characteristic way, Maimonides is prepared to carry reason as far as he possibly can, but he knows clearly when it is necessary to turn elsewhere because reason can no longer provide the guidance he seeks.

We saw earlier that the best way to understand the specific character of Maimonides' doctrine of the mean is to see it in comparison to Aristotle's doctrine. Similarly, one of the best ways to see the full force of Maimonides' views on natural moral law is to examine them in comparison to the classical Christian teachings on the subject. The ideal model for us is St. Thomas Aquinas, who provides a paradigm case of classical Christian thought on natural law. Aquinas is particularly appropriate, since Maimonides is often identified as the Jewish parallel to Aquinas. The supposition is that they faced similar problems and arrived at similar solutions, each within the framework of his own religious community. To the extent that this comparison has any validity, it is particularly illuminating for our subject. On some metaphysical questions, Maimonides and Aquinas are close, but when it comes to the foundations of ethics they are very far apart.

For the purposes of the present discussion we shall base our exposition of Aquinas on his Treatise on Law, contained in Part I-II of the *Summa Theologica*. We need to ask what the role of reason is in Aquinas' moral philosophy. We shall soon see that, although Aquinas is influenced by Maimonides at various points and quotes him in the Treatise on Law more than a dozen times, he nevertheless stands at the opposite pole from him with respect to the question of natural law.

This is immediately evident when we consider Aquinas' first remarks about law. The first question he considers is "whether law is something pertaining to reason," and he answers with an absolute and unequivocal yes. "Law is a rule and measure of acts, whereby man is induced to act or is restrained from acting. . . . Now the rule and measure of human acts is the reason. . . . Consequently, it follows that law is something pertaining to

reason." Any law, even that imposed by a sovereign power, is law only insofar as it is rational. "In order that the violation of what is commanded may
have the nature of law, it needs to be in accord with some rule of reason . . . otherwise the sovereign's will would savor of lawlessness rather
than of law."[30] What is true of positive law is true for Aquinas of all law; if it
is truly law, then it must follow a rule of reason.

All four kinds of law that Aquinas distinguishes—eternal, natural,
human, and divine—have this essential characteristic of being rational. The
eternal law is the work of the Supreme Reason and is thus fully rational. Of
more immediate interest for our purposes is Aquinas' theory of natural law.
First, he establishes that there is a natural law. Man is a rational creature, and
this creature has "a share of the eternal reason, whereby it has a natural inclination to its proper act and end; and this participation of the eternal law in
the rational creature is called the natural law." In striking contrast to Maimonides, Aquinas holds that the natural law is the source of the precepts of
morality and that moral precepts are all purely rational in character. "Now,
since human morals depend on their relation to reason, which is the proper
principle of human acts, those morals are called good which accord with
reason, and those are called bad which are discordant from reason . . . every judgment of practical reason proceeds from naturally known
principles . . . it follows, of necessity, that all the moral precepts belong to
the law of nature." Or, as Aquinas puts it in a somewhat different formulation, "all the acts of the virtues are prescribed by the natural law, since each
one's reason naturally dictates to him to act virtuously." This natural moral
law is universal, the same for all people everywhere and binding on all without exception. The natural law is universally known, except for some few
cases where reason has been "perverted by passion, or evil habit, or an evil
disposition of nature." Finally, human law is law only to the extent to which
it is derived from the law of nature. Any human law that in any way differs
from or opposes the law of nature is not law at all, but rather a distortion and
perversion of law.[31]

To appreciate the true significance of the profound opposition between
Aquinas and Maimonides in their theories of law, we need to consider the
one peculiar exception to his theory that Aquinas introduces. The one instance of law that is not natural and not rational (and, therefore, not binding)
is the Old Law, the law of what is for him the Old Testament. Some of its
precepts happen to accord with the natural law, and everyone is bound to
observe these just because they are natural law, but not because they are con-

30. *Summa Theologica*, I-II, Q. 90, a. 1, *ad* 3.
31. Ibid., Q. 91, a. 3; Q. 100, a. 1; Q. 94, a. 3, a. 4; cf. Q. 95, a. 2.

tained in the Old Law. All the rest is a peculiar kind of law. It is not natural, not in accord with reason, and is binding only upon the Jews of pre-Christian times.[32] To continue, after Christ, to observe any of the precepts of the Old Law because one believes them to have derived their binding force from the fact that they are contained in the Hebrew Scriptures would be a mortal sin. After the coming of Christ there is no longer any binding force to the Old Law, and to continue to treat it as if it were obligatory is tantamount to a denial of Christ.[33]

Aquinas has classified the law of the Hebrew Bible in such a way that its moral precepts are natural law and are binding exclusively on that score, while its ceremonial and judicial precepts are considered to be a peculiar legislation for the special purpose of prefiguring the coming of Christ. The ceremonial precepts may not be observed any longer under any circumstances. The judicial precepts may be observed if they seem to be useful, but only so long as they are not considered to have any obligatory element based on their biblical source. The strategy is to introduce a principle of selectivity into the law so that one can retain, on independent grounds, the moral precepts that are essential for the ordering of society, while rejecting all the rest of the biblical legislation. Maimonides could not admit any such principle of selectivity without undermining the obligatory force of the entire system of biblical and rabbinic law. His philosophy did not allow for a natural moral law. Consequently he had to argue for the absolute integrity of the whole received law and to treat it all as divine in origin and permanently binding. On theological grounds, it was essential for Aquinas to reject the Old Law. This left him no alternative but to find some principle by which he could retain those parts of the biblical law which are essential while dispensing with all the rest. The theory of a natural law, grounded in reason, serves this purpose.

In his elaborate scheme Aquinas is following closely the method and the logic of the New Testament. It is the inner need of Christianity that brings about not only the rejection of the Old Law, but also the appeal to natural law. The first step is evident in the way in which *Torah* is translated in the New Testament. In the Jewish understanding of the term, *Torah* is not reducible simply to *Law,* as the most familiar translations continue to render it even today. *Torah* is the totality of divine teaching, God's instructions for the ordering of human life and the achievement of final blessedness. The key terms in the Jewish tradition are *Torah* and *mitzvah.* The former is the whole body of divine teaching as contained in the sacred texts and in the normative

32. Ibid., Q. 98, a. 5.
33. Ibid. Q. 104, a. 3; cf. Q. 103, a. 4.

tradition. The latter refers to the specific and detailed commandments. Following the classical Jewish teaching, Maimonides shows that the force of these commandments lies in the fact that they are believed to be God's specific rules for humankind. The term *law* has a secondary and subordinate place in the entire Jewish system for ordering human life and society. The primary place is occupied by *commandment*.

Yet in the Greek New Testament, *Torah* is consistently and with few exceptions rendered as *nomos*.[34] Although *nomos* is the standard term for law, it has a set of associations calculated to undermine the authority and force of that which is presented as nomic. Originally, *nomos* is convention or custom that stands in opposition to *physis,* nature and the natural. The latter is fixed, orderly, intelligible, rational. The former always has about it an air of arbitrariness, a sense of local peculiarity rather than universal rationality. The shift from *Torah* to *nomos* in the Greek New Testament is of the highest significance, because it introduces into what were thought by the Jews to be fixed divine commandments a sense of something that is passing, temporary, and certainly not truly divine.

C. H. Dodd puts the matter with striking clarity when he says, "*Nomos* . . . is by no means an exact equivalent for Torah, and its substitution for the Hebrew term affords an illustration of a change in the ideas associated with the term—a difference in men's notion of what religion is. . . . *Nomos* is fundamentally 'custom', hardening into what we call 'law'. It does not necessarily imply any legislative authority. It is rather an immanent or underlying principle of life and action."[35] Later, speaking of the main elements of Hebrew law, Dodd adds, "The terms used all imply more or less directly a legislator, and this is true to the Hebrew idea. The fountain of all law for the Hebrews was God, whether the immediate human author of the commandments, statutes, and judgments was judge, king, or priest. . . . But *nomos,* for the most part, as we have seen, renders none of these term."[36]

Given the basic presuppositions of normative Christian doctrine, it was

34. For an extended discussion of this point, see C. H. Dodd, *The Bible and the Greeks* (London, 1954), 34–41. For familiar, but instructive, instances of *Torah* as *nomos,* cf. Matt. 22:36–40; Luke 10:26.

35. Dodd, *The Bible and the Greeks,* 25.

36. Ibid., 29–30. It is true that in the two instances cited Dodd is speaking about the Septuagint, not the New Testament. However, in his later discussion of *nomos* in the New Testament, the same point is made. Of Paul's use of *nomos,* Dodd says that "Torah by becoming *nomos* had entered into a new field of associated ideas" (37). For a discussion from another point of view, see Erwin I. J. Rosenthal, *Griechisches Erbe in der jüdischen Religionsphilosophie des Mittelalters* (Stuttgart, 1960), chaps. 2 and 3, "Torah und Nomos."

important to strip the Old Law of its authority and of its claim to being the immutable law of God. It is not my contention here that the translation of *Torah* as *nomos* was necessarily a deliberate polemical device on the part of the New Testament authors. Even if they were merely adopting a term already in common use, it nevertheless had the effect of making *Torah* appear to be the peculiar local customs of the Jews, rather than the permanent commandments of God.

A further element in the New Testament calculated to weaken the claims of the Old Law is the representation of that law as having been given not by God but by an angel or mediator. The law "was a temporary measure pending the arrival of the 'issue' to whom the promise was made. It was promulgated through angels, and there was an intermediary."[37] Aquinas, basing himself on this verse, argues that the Old Law was clearly imperfect and temporary, a kind of local *nomos*. This is why it was given through intermediaries: "It was fitting that the perfect law of the New Testament should be given by the incarnate God immediately."[38] As *nomos*, the law of the Old Testament can be viewed readily as having been limited to a particular time and place. The change of circumstances resulting from the coming of Christ makes that law no longer operative: "But now, having died to that which held us bound, we are discharged from the law, to serve God in a new way, the way of the spirit, in contrast to the old way, the way of a written code."[39]

Since the new law is not a written code, and since it does not explicitly include all the moral precepts of the Old Testament that Christianity wants to retain, these are regained through the device of natural law. The theory that there is a natural law prescribing moral behavior and binding all human beings is introduced in the New Testament and developed and elaborated in later Christian thought. The *locus classicus* for New Testament natural law theory is Romans 2:14–15:

> When Gentiles who do not possess the law carry out its precepts by the light of nature, then, although they have no law, they are their own law, for they display the effect of the law inscribed on their hearts. Their conscience is called as witness, and their own thoughts argue the case on either side, against them or even for them, on the day when God judges the secrets of human hearts through Christ Jesus.

37. Gal. 3:19. Cf. Acts 7:53.
38. *Summa Theologica*, I-II, Q. 98, a. 3.
39. Rom. 7:6.

147

It is hardly necessary to give further evidence that this Pauline statement concerning natural law is far removed from the standard Jewish view.[40]
What is of interest is to see where the internal logic of this position leads.
Beginning with a rejection of the Old Law, it substitutes for it a belief in a
natural law written on the hearts of all. This means that every individual
knows what is right and therefore that each can be his or her own judge. The
extreme version of this is the twice-repeated statement, evidently approved
by Paul, "All things are lawful for me."[41] Clearly, this cannot function as an
operative rule for ordering society, so it is necessary to introduce principles
of selection. This moves Paul to add that even though all things are lawful,
they are not all wise, healthy, or well advised. What we need is the capacity
to exercise our freedom from the law in a way that will still be good. We need
to reintroduce on some new ground the restraints cast off with the Old Law,
and to regain the positive guides to good behavior which are no longer available to us from the Old Law. Paul assures his Christian brethren that by
offering themselves completely to God, they will be so transformed that they
will be able directly to "discern the will of God, and to know what is good,
acceptable, perfect."[42] On another occasion he prays that the brethren at
Philippi, growing in Christian love, will "grow ever richer and richer in
knowledge and insight of every kind" and that they will thus gain "the gift of
true discrimination" (or, in another translation, that they will be taught "by
experience what things are most worthwhile").[43]

Thus we are finally led back to the full development of natural law
theory in a Christian thinker such as Aquinas. Here we are assured that
all conventional moral precepts are required by reason, known to all,
and universally obligatory. There is no room here for purely personal judgment or discrimination; that would inevitably undermine the foundations of
an ordered society. This moves Aquinas to affirm that everyone agrees
about the precepts of the natural law. But what shall we do with those
people who obviously do not agree? We simply announce that they are the
victims of a reason perverted by passion, or that they suffer from evil habits
or an evilly constituted nature. This is the way he deals in a paradigm case
with the Germans. "Theft, although it is expressly contrary to the natural
law, was not considered wrong among the Germans, as Julius Caesar re-

40. For a Christian comment on this claim, see Hermann L. Strack and Paul Billerbeck,
Kommentar zum Neuen Testament, vol. 3 (Munich, 1926), 88–89, *ad* Rom. 2:14–15.

41. 1 Cor. 6:12, 10:23.

42. Rom. 12:2. For another principle of selection, see Acts 15:19–21.

43. Phil. 1:10.

lates." Aquinas explains that since they did not recognize such an elementary principle of natural law, they obviously possessed a corrupt and perverted reason.[44] In this way we come back to the fixed norms of the law, while supposedly holding to a theory that every individual, through the agency of reason, is capable of being his or her own moral arbiter. All human beings are supposedly equally endowed with knowledge of the natural law, which is inscribed on their hearts, but some are apparently more equal than others.

St. Thomas Aquinas and Maimonides may be thought of as concerned with a common problem. Each needs to have a law that will regulate personal life and order communal life properly. Finding no rational ground for moral distinctions, Maimonides avoids the dangers of social chaos by turning to the Hebrew Bible and the rabbinic tradition. Here he finds all that human beings need to learn in order to live in such a way that they can move from the lower perfection of a decent bodily existence to the ultimate perfection of true metaphysical knowledge. This scheme of salvation is dependent on God's law to provide its essential external conditions. That law is viewed as absolutely authoritative because it is divine; it protects people from debilitating bodily passions; it orders the relations between them in society so as to prevent mutual destruction; it implants in even the most simple-minded correct opinions about the highest matters and protects them from serious theological error; and it frees human reason in everyone so that all can rise to the highest level of self-realization, to the knowledge of God that is true salvation.

On the other hand, as a Christian, Aquinas must reject the Law. Though

---

44. *Summa Theologica,* I-II, Q. 94, a. 4. It is fascinating to see how the same device is used by other writers on morals. It is a kind of truism that everybody accepts *my* moral rules or values. Whoever does not is obviously mad, wicked, or naturally corrupt. Thus, David Hume, denying categorically that reason is the source of moral rules, invokes in its place a moral sense with which all human beings are supposedly endowed. This must produce common moral sentiments which are "the same in all human creatures, and produce the same approbation or censure." When Hume confronts the undeniable fact that vast numbers of people have preferences different from his own, he dismisses them as mad. Thus, "celibacy, fasting, penance, mortification, self-denial, humility, silence, solitude, and the whole train of monkish virtues . . . are everywhere rejected by men of sense." Whoever approves of these "monkish virtues" suffers from perverted natural sentiments. Concerning them Hume assures us that "a gloomy hair-brained enthusiast, after his death, may have a place in the calendar, but will scarcely ever be admitted, when alive, into intimacy and society, except by those who are as delirious and dismal as himself" (*An Enquiry Concerning the Principles of Morals,* Sect. IX, Part 1). It would appear that there are inescapable hazards whenever one claims that a given rule of behavior is universally recognized as good.

he substitutes grace for law, he must still have some regulation of life in ordinary human society, for even the most faithful Christians are still fallible. He gains this end through the natural law, which takes the place in his system of Maimonides' divine commandments. It might be thought that there is really no significant difference, because Aquinas holds that "the natural law is promulgated by the very fact that God instilled it into man's mind so as to be known by him naturally." And he adds the view that "the light of natural reason, whereby we discern what is good and what is evil, which is the function of the natural law, is nothing else than an imprint on us of the divine light."[45] Yet although he speaks of the natural law as divine, the term has a vastly different force than its meaning in the Jewish teaching of Maimonides. For Aquinas, to call the law divine is simply to say that it is part of the eternal law, a part he claims is a natural possession of everyone by virtue of being human. When Maimonides speaks of the law as divine commandments, he relies on the claim of a particular historic event, the revelation at Sinai, as the source of our knowledge of the law.

Neither Maimonides nor Aquinas is prepared to accept a society where every man is his own judge and feels free to do whatever he chooses. Each responds to the problem in a way characteristic of his own religious community, reflecting genuine differences between Judaism and Christianity. If both Maimonides and Aquinas may be thought of as seeking the conditions of salvation, then their differences might be understood in the following way: For Aquinas, the Christian, salvation is neither by works alone nor by rational knowledge, but by grace. Natural law tells people how to behave, but it cannot lead them to their final and true fulfillment. For Maimonides, the Jew, salvation depends on good works, leading to a life devoted to the rational apprehension of the highest truth. There is no natural moral law, only the law of God, which teaches us to live our lives in such a way that we are worthy of our claim to have been created in His image. This, in turn, creates the circumstances under which we can develop our intellect so as to become as nearly divine as finite human beings can ever be.

In his moral philosophy, as in other areas of his thought, Maimonides clearly recognizes the possibilities and the limits of reason. Whereas reason cannot guide us, we must be ready to turn to other sources of instruction. Because he holds that moral judgments stand outside the realm of truth and falsehood, he concludes they are not among those matters determined by reason. In contemporary philosophic terminology we would say that Maimonides considers all moral statements to be noncognitive. As such they are

45. *Summa Theologica*, I-II, Q. 90, a. 4, *ad* 1; Q. 91, a. 2.

neither true nor false. If, then, we seek some stable moral order and guidance, it must come from the ultimate source that transcends the human intellect. God's teaching provides us with the indispensable standards and rules of behavior without which we cannot fully realize our own humanity. It is a teaching that *transcends* human reason, but being divine it can never be viewed as *contrary* to reason.

7

The Nature of Man and the Foundations of Ethics

A Reading of Guide, I, 1–2

Until now we have been dealing in a general way with issues of doctrine and methodology that are central to an understanding of the thought of Maimonides. In this chapter, we shall move to the task of addressing the text of the *Guide of the Perplexed* directly, continuing our studies of Maimonides' moral philosophy by considering carefully the subjects with which he opens his major philosophical work.

In I, 1 Maimonides is concerned with the precise interpretation of biblical terms that teach us fundamental principles about the nature of God and man. In I, 2 he addresses questions about the foundations of ethics and the place of morality in human life. This opening section of the *Guide* provides the essential theoretical framework for Maimonides' moral philosophy. My commentary on these initial chapters is intended to serve a double purpose. It will clarify the ideas and issues at the center of these chapters, thus providing the foundation for a deeper understanding of Maimonides' ethical theory. At the same time, although it is obviously not my intention here to provide a complete commentary on the *Guide,* the discussion will serve as one model of how to go about writing such a commentary.[1]

---

1. To follow the commentary in this chapter, readers should have before them the Pines translation of *Guide,* I, 1–2. One of the objectives of this commentary is to help clarify the meaning of the text for readers of this English translation. As noted in chapter 3, the Pines translation is a model of faithfulness to the original. Obviously, readers who have access to the Arabic text or to the Hebrew translations will want to follow them in this exercise.

Commentaries on the *Guide* began to appear not long after the book itself. Within a century several commentaries were available. The production of commentaries continued vigorously from the thirteenth through the fifteenth centuries, when it slacked off some, but did not stop completely. In the early part of the twentieth century, Yehudah ibn Shmuel Kaufman composed a detailed commentary in Hebrew in three volumes that went up to *Guide,* II, 24. A fourth volume, continuing through III, 13, has recently been published from the author's posthumous papers. No such commentary on the *Guide* has been produced in English, although there is an obvious need for one. A complete bibliography of commentaries on the *Guide* was recently published by Jacob I. Dienstag in *Gevurot ha-Romaḥ: A Festschrift for Moshe Ḥayyim Weiler* (Jerusalem, 1987), 207–37.

In producing this brief sample of a twentieth-century commentary, there are no earlier models that can be readily imitated. The major medieval commentaries presuppose more knowledge on the part of the reader than is possible today. Among the medieval commentaries, the later ones often build on the earlier, commonly quoting or paraphrasing extended sections from them. At the same time each commentator frequently is advancing some program of his own. However well they may have served the needs of their own time, none of these classic commentaries is a fully satisfactory paradigm for a contemporary commentary in English. In their own way, the more recent commentaries tend still to be largely medieval in style and structure.

More useful models are provided by the great commentaries on the Torah and on the Talmud. The classic model of what a commentary on the *Guide of the Perplexed* can and should be is provided for us by the commentary of Rashi on the Talmud. His goal is to lead the student through the obscurities and complexities of the text, and he does whatever is necessary to achieve that objective. He explains the meanings of terms and concepts. He corrects the text when necessary. He translates difficult words into the vernacular of his time and place. He structures the argument so that the student can follow its development with ease. In general, he is able to do this with a remarkable economy of language, restricting himself to glosses that are terse but clear, only occasionally allowing himself more extended statements. He provides a complete guide for the reader. For this reason all students of the Talmud to this day are heavily dependent on Rashi. For the past nine centuries, he has been the one absolutely irreplaceable and indispensable Talmud commentator.

A proper commentary on the *Guide,* which is a great desideratum, should ideally use Rashi as its model, providing readers with whatever help is needed for them to make their way through the text. It is in this regard alone that I allow myself to speak of Rashi as my model. He knew just what was needed to give the student of the Talmud the resources for making the text intelligible and grasping the line of the argument. I believe that, although the form of a commentary on the *Guide* must necessarily be different from that of one on the Talmud, the objective should be the same. He is my model in this sense alone. To allow oneself to speak of one's own work in the same breath with that of the greatest of all commentators is hazardous, since it suggests a lack of any sense of proportion. It should, therefore, be stated openly and clearly again that I invoke Rashi as my model only because he provides the best of all examples of how to make a commentary do its proper work. It is my hope that I can in a modest way begin to approach this goal of showing how a commentary on the *Guide* might go about making that book accessible to English readers in our time.

153

The Pines translation has dealt directly or indirectly with many of the textual and philological problems in the *Guide,* thus saving the contemporary commentator much of that work. I shall, therefore, concentrate on explicating the structure of the text, clarifying its ideas and arguments and, as far as possible, illuminating its obscurities. Unfortunately I cannot achieve this objective with a series of terse glosses. The subject matter and form of the *Guide* will not permit imitating Rashi in that regard. In contrast to the Talmud, the *Guide* is a deliberately esoteric book, and it demands a different kind of exposition. Often the necessary points can be made only by way of longer comments, because I am concerned here not only with clarifying the content of the two chapters we are studying, but also with exemplifying the method I believe is required for any serious study of the entire work. Further, contemporary commentators have to come to terms with a long history of earlier expositions of the *Guide.* For us today the range of originality is reduced considerably by the fact that we come so late in the history of the study of this work. I have learned much from the earlier commentators, and that will be evident to all those who are familiar with the literature. I will not burden readers with repeated references to these earlier writers. For those who know, it will be easy enough to determine what is original and what builds on the work of the great commentators of the past. For those who are not familiar with this literature, sources and origins are of little consequence.

COMMENTARY TO *GUIDE,* I, 1

The Superscript

Maimonides heads the first chapter of the *Guide* with a superscript consisting of a biblical verse: "Open ye the gates, that the righteous nation that keepeth faithfulness may enter in."[2] Readers of the *Guide* should never ignore the verses with which Maimonides heads the various sections of his book. These should not be thought of as mere adornments with no substantive significance, but should be studied with care to see what message the author is conveying to his readers. One might say that this is the first test of the competence of the readers. Readers who ignore these verses or fail to investigate the implications fully have already shown insufficient sensitivity to the text.[3]

---

2. Isa. 26:2.

3. In chapter 10, I discuss the significance of the verses that serve as superscripts over the three parts of the *Guide.*

The earlier commentators have properly called attention to the apparent connection between the end of the previous section and this superscript. In the last sentences of that section, Maimonides informs us that he will now begin to clarify the meanings of terms. He adds, "This, then, will be a key permitting one to enter places the gates to which were locked. And when these gates are opened . . . the souls will find rest therein." The reference to opening the gates makes the obvious connection with the superscript that follows. Yet cautious readers should immediately remember that in this book the seemingly obvious is not always what it appears to be, or that, at least, it is likely that there is more to the story than appears on the surface. Some commentators add one or another dimension to the fully apparent connections.

A dimension of the highest importance, however, has been overlooked. Maimonides has made it clear that to be able to read this book properly, one must have certain intellectual and scholarly qualifications. Among them is a high level of mastery of the standard body of rabbinic literature, including Talmud and Midrash.[4] It seems correct to suppose that Maimonides expected his readers to respond to a verse such as this superscript with the set of associations that would be in the mind of any properly trained talmudic student. Such a student would immediately think of the way in which this verse is construed in the Talmud. "R. Levi said, "The gates of Paradise are opened for every one who recites the response, "Amen," with all his power [i.e., with complete commitment], as Scripture states, "Open ye the gates, that the righteous nation that keepeth faithfulness [*shomer 'emunim*] may enter in." Do not read the text, *shomer 'emunim,* but *she-'omrim 'amen* [they who say, Amen].' "[5]

I believe that to skilled readers mindful of this talmudic passage, Maimonides is communicating a deeper message than simply the verbal connection between the superscript and the previous section. He is saying something important about his book—namely, that he is here opening gates through which one can enter Paradise. Those who are the truly "righteous nation" are the readers who master his doctrine fully and affirm it without reservation (i.e., answer amen to his teaching with all their power), and thus achieve a level of intellectual apprehension that assures them of the highest degree of salvation. From the beginning, readers are told how the author conceives his own work, and they are invited to participate in an effort

---

4. In addition to Maimonides' comments on this point in the opening sections of the *Guide,* see his statement in *H. Yesodei ha-Torah,* 4:13, concerning the need to master the standard Jewish curriculum before entering on philosophic speculation.

5. *Shabbat,* 119b.

whose rewards are the greatest and most precious to which a human being can aspire. The superscript tells readers what is at stake in their study of the *Guide*. It is not to be viewed as simply another book, but as a book that gives them the means to achieve the proper end of all Torah study.

This interpretation is strengthened if we note that the verse in question is quoted only once more in the *Guide,* and then in direct connection with *ma'aseh merkavah,* the chariot vision representing the highest metaphysical truth. Maimonides expects his readers to discover this fact and to note that he is promising to make available, to those who can follow him, insight into that subject matter whose mastery is the gate to salvation. Enter the gates that he is opening, see his vision, and say amen to it with all your power, and you will be among the spiritual elect. All this, and possibly even more, is the message contained in the verse with which he chose to open the text of Part I of the *Guide*.

The First Paragraph

Guide, I, 1 is a lexicographic chapter—that is, it begins with biblical terms requiring explanation. In this case the terms are *tzelem* and *demut, image* and *likeness,* the key terms contained in the verse spoken by God, "Let us make man in our image, after our likeness."[6] The immediate problem is apparent: What does it mean for God to say that He will make man in His own image and likeness? First we should note, as Maimonides would expect us to do, that the terminology of this verse is repeated. In the following verse we are told that "God created man in His image [*be-tzalmo*], in the image of God He created him." Further on in Genesis 5:1 we are told that "when God created man, He made him in the likeness [*be-demut*] of God." In its account of man's creation, Scripture uses these two terms both independently and together. This supports Maimonides' treatment of them as synonymous.

Only two verses further on, in connection with the birth of Seth, we are told that Adam "begot a son in his likeness after his image." We note at once that these terms, *image* and *likeness* are used to describe both the creation of man by God and the birth of a son to Adam, a son who is conceived and born in the normal way. This fact, not noted in *Guide,* I, 1, poses serious problems for us and requires explication. What is initially important, however, is just that the fact should be noted. Maimonides requires his readers to be aware of such matters even when he does not make any direct reference to them. An ongoing test of the readers' competence is built into the text of the *Guide*. Maimonides' immediate objective is to determine how we should

6. Gen. 1:26.

understand the key terms, *tzelem* and *demut,* and to establish exactly what the Bible means when it says that man was created in the image and likeness of God.

It is also apparent that from the very beginning Maimonides' greatest concern is to eliminate every vestige of the belief that God has corporeal properties. As every reader of the *Guide* knows, this is one of the main objectives of the entire book. It is, of course, aimed primarily at the masses and not at those who are sophisticated in their thinking about such matters, since anyone with basic philosophic training will already know that God cannot be conceived as having a body. Yet a problem is caused by the language of Scripture in which God is frequently spoken of in corporeal terms.[7] The first instance of such anthropomorphism seems to occur here in the story of the creation of man in Genesis. Maimonides knows that the terms *image* and *likeness* will most likely be understood initially by the average reader as referring to some kind of physical form. Let us proceed to identify the problems and clarify the issues which have been raised directly or by implication.

The first problem is raised directly by Maimonides. In the thinking of the masses the scriptural comparison between God and man leads directly to a corporeal notion of God. If man is in the image and likeness of God, and man is known to have a physical form, it seems to follow that God also has a physical form in some way similar to that of man. On the surface this conclusion seems reasonable enough. Yet Maimonides must show that it is completely wrong and must be rejected. It is a theological error to corporealize God in even the slightest degree, an error so serious that it justifies his claim that this is even worse than idolatry.[8] It is well and good to assert this categorically, but Maimonides owes his readers an explanation of how he arrives at his conclusion that God is a completely incorporeal being. He must also explain his method for reading Scripture in instances where it seems to contradict his views directly.

In the first paragraph he gives us only a brief hint, but it is extremely important for our understanding of his method. He informs us that we shall

---

7. In the *Mishneh Torah* Maimonides confronts the issue directly and with an ingenious argument. He asserts that Scripture states explicitly that God is not a physical body of any kind, since we are told that "the Lord, He is God in heaven above and on the earth below." (Deut. 4:39) Now, Maimonides argues, because no body can be in two places simultaneously, it is evident from this verse that God is not a body. What then shall we make of all the anthropomorphic expressions in the Bible? We must come to understand that they are never to be read literally (*H. Yesodei ha-Torah,* 1:8, 9). See the more extended discussion of this passage in chapter 2.

8. See the discussion of this subject in chapter 2.

later be given a demonstration of the fact that God must be incorporeal and that any claim with respect to His unity "can have no true reality unless one disproves His corporeality." Meanwhile readers are altered here to the fact that such a proof is an essential element in the program of the *Guide*. Moreover, it will become clear that such a proof is essential for us to be able to read Scripture correctly.

Maimonides takes the position that Scripture must always conform to the canons of reason. Therefore, once we have a rational demonstration that God cannot have any bodily properties, we know that Scripture must not be read literally when it makes statements about the hand of God, the eye of God, and so forth. For Maimonides, reason, within its limits, must be the controlling force in our thinking, and it is reasón that is decisive in teaching us the correct meaning of scriptural passages such as those we are considering here. Whoever reads Scripture literally, in opposition to the teachings of reason, is condemned to make fundamental theological errors. As expressed earlier, the rule Maimonides follows is that what reason finds incorrect and unacceptable cannot be the meaning of Scripture. It is clear that Maimonides deliberately chose not to introduce such a radical-sounding rule at this early point, but there is no doubt that it is a basic principle of scriptural interpretation for him.

A second point emerging in this paragraph is an introduction to another aspect of Maimonides' method of reading Scripture. He is keenly aware that we cannot read the biblical text responsibly unless we have full control of its language. As with most languages, one feature of biblical language is that terms often have multiple meanings. This is a commonplace often overlooked, especially when we are reading an ancient language. Think for a moment of the ordinary English word *pitch,* and consider the variety of its meanings. As a verb it can refer to putting up a tent, throwing a ball, or helping someone (as in "to pitch in"). As a noun it can refer to a musical tone, tar, a downward slope, a high point (as in "the pitch of success"), or the patter of a salesperson. In ordinary discourse or reading we are not troubled by this multiplicity of meanings. We carry the variety of meanings in our heads, even if we do not usually articulate them, and we determine from the context which meaning is intended in a particular statement that we hear or read. We are not likely to confuse a pitcher of water with a pitcher in a baseball game or the key of C with tar. Yet Maimonides claims that when it comes to reading Scripture, this is exactly what we do. We tend to treat the language as monochromatic, and we fail to respond to the range and richness of meanings of biblical terms. Consequently he stresses in I, 1 that one of the main burdens of his book is to teach us how to read scriptural terms with sensitivity to their multiple meanings. Otherwise we shall fail to understand the divine teaching correctly. His technique is to examine such terms, showing the range of their meanings from the contexts in which they occur and then showing us how to determine which meaning is intended in a given case. His prime interest, of course, is the clarification of terms that refer to God in corporeal language. He must show us, for example, that although our first thought is that *image* and *likeness* refer to physical form, this is an error. This is because these terms have more than one meaning, and we must know how to select the meaning that is appropriate when the terms refer to God.

Another urgent problem that confronts us in interpreting this opening paragraph and the whole chapter in which it occurs is the important requirement that we take account of what Maimonides omits, as well as what he includes. We can be sure that as a general rule he assumed that a competent reader would be immediately aware of certain other biblical verses that provide us with classic cases against which to test the interpretations he offers. When Maimonides ignores those familiar verses and instead uses fairly obscure cases as his examples, we need to ask what he is telling us by what he does *not* say, as well as by what he does say. It is not acceptable to suppose that he may simply have overlooked the obvious. We should always remember that he has given us ample evidence of his vast control over the biblical materials. For all practical purposes it is certain that biblical verses that occur immediately to readers like ourselves could not have escaped his attention. This is particularly the case when we recall the care with which the *Guide* was written. As a human being Maimonides was subject to error like everyone else. Our method of reading his book, however, presupposes always that he neither made simple mistakes nor was guilty of simple oversights. Only when we have exhausted every other possible explanation may we conclude that he erred. Even then we should treat this conclusion as tentative, as more probably a result of the limitations of our understanding than of his errors.[9]

A striking omission from his discussion is the first half of Genesis 1:26, which he quotes and then ignores, although it is a potential source of much

---

9. This respect for the author and the text should be a guiding principle of all serious reading. Indeed, when a great philosopher or writer of stature makes what appear to be obvious mistakes, we should always proceed on the assumption that the problem lies in our understanding rather than the author's competence. Only after long and careful reflection, and after having exhausted all other options, do we earn the right to say that Plato, or some other great thinker, offered an argument that is fallacious or explicated an idea stupidly. I commented on this matter earlier in chapter 3.

trouble. God speaks in the plural form and says, "Let us make man in our image, after our likeness." In a book that puts such heavy stress on the absolute unity of God, the use of the plural verb and pronouns should certainly be a cause of concern. Classical Jewish literature offers a variety of explanations for this troubling passage, ranging from the view that God is simply using the royal we to the view that, in His humility, God consulted the angels before He created man. In a later discussion, Maimonides himself cites some of these explanations and comments on them.[10] Why, then, does he ignore the problem here? I suggest that, in the context of the order of exposition that he set himself, it is premature for this question to be raised at this point. He has told us explicitly that we must disprove God's corporeality as a condition of establishing His unity. In the present chapter no such disproof is even attempted. Consequently, we are not yet prepared to deal with the issue of God's unity. Maimonides can assume that sophisticated readers will be aware of the problem, and that they will keep it in mind. At some later point they will have to learn how to read the verse in question correctly; one evidence of their competence is that they will not forget or ignore the problem. Readers who are so naive that they are not even troubled by the problem at this stage will suffer no injury to correct understanding, and they will be taught what they need to know when the proper time comes.

There is, however, another verse which Maimonides ignores here and which presents us with a far more serious problem. We have noted that Maimonides does not deal here with Genesis 5:3, which reads, "When Adam had lived 130 years, he begot a son in his likeness after his image (*va-yoled bi-demuto ke-tzalmo*), and he named him Seth." Now it is important to keep in mind that a few verses earlier we are also told of the birth of Seth, and there it is unambiguously clear that Seth was born in a natural way as a result of the conjugal connection of Adam and Eve. We have here an ordinary child, born in an ordinary way, about whom we are told that he was begotten in the likeness and image of his father. We would have every reason to construe the terms *tzelem* and *demut,* in this context, as referring to the resemblance of the son to the physical form of the father. This, in turn, could easily raise questions about the meaning of these terms when used with respect to Adam and God and, in the process, might well cause us to question the account that Maimonides will soon give up. Why then does he not address the issue here?

It is important to note that Maimonides does take up this verse later on in *Guide,* I, 7. (Another rule of method for reading the *Guide* is that, for verses he treats and those he ignores, we should always check to see if he has

10. See *Guide,* II, 6, pp. 262–65.

dealt with these same verses elsewhere in his book.[11]) In his discussion in I, 7, Maimonides is explaining the verb *yalod,* which means to bear children. He shows that the usage of this verb is not restricted to its simple literal meaning, but that it has a variety of figurative meanings as well. He then makes a particular point of construing Genesis 5:3 in such a way as to make certain that we will not read the terms *likeness* and *image* so as to ascribe to them corporeal meanings. When Scripture says that Adam begot Seth in his likeness and image, Maimonides interprets it to mean that Adam taught Seth and developed his intellectual powers to the point where he became truly human: "As for Seth, it was after [Adam] had instructed him and procured him understanding and after he had attained human perfection that it was said of him: And [Adam] begot [a son] in his own likeness, after his image. You know that whoever is not endowed with this form, whose signification we have explained, is not a man, but an animal having the shape and configuration of a man" (*Guide,* I, 7, pp. 32–33).[12] Just as God created Adam as a being with a fully developed intellect, so Adam can be said truly to create his son Seth only when he teaches him and brings about the growth and development of his intellectual powers.

A further explanation of the details of Maimonides' interpretation of the full significance of this doctrine is not required for our commentary on I, 1. It is enough that we should see that Maimonides is particularly careful to read the key terms in a noncorporeal way consistent with his interpretation of them in I, 1. He does not introduce this passage into the discussion at this point because it could only cause confusion for those who are not properly prepared. Sooner or later all readers must be made aware of Genesis 5:3 in order to be certain that they do not fall into the trap of misconstruing the statement concerning the birth of Seth by reading the key terms to refer to corporeal properties. The argument follows a certain graded order, doing no harm to those who do not discern the problem as early as I, 1 and, at the same time, relying on the sophistication of those who know and understand on their own.

11. This task is not particularly difficult. Most editions of the *Guide,* whether Hebrew or English, have an index of biblical passages cited. With only modest effort any reader can check out the places in the *Guide* where Maimonides deals with a given biblical verse. It is essential to do this if one wants to understand the *Guide* with any sophistication.

12. It seems very likely that Maimonides, as a sensitive reader of the biblical text, was reacting to the fact that in Genesis 4:25 we are told about the birth of Seth in natural terms: "Adam knew his wife again, and she bore him a son and named him Seth." The verse in Genesis 5:3 is now taken to give us information of a quite different sort. Eve gave birth to Seth in the ordinary meaning of the term. Adam "begot a son in his likeness and after his image" when he developed the boy's intellect.

One final point of interest requires our attention in this first paragraph. Why does Maimonides choose to begin with an account of the two terms, *tzelem* and *demut?* One part of the answer has already been given—that the fight against ideas of divine corporeality is one of his major objectives. Leo Strauss holds that he begins this battle with an account of these two terms because "that passage suggests to the vulgar mind more strongly than any other biblical passage that God is corporeal in the crudest sense."[13] It is not clear why this passage should be considered stronger than any other in its suggestion to the vulgar that God has corporeal properties. Explicit biblical statements about God's finger, hand, arm, or eye seem no less strong in their corporeality, as do such statements as that He smelled the sweet odors of the sacrificial offerings. I suggest that Maimonides begins here because it is the first explicit passage that implies corporeality, and it is a passage likely to be known to even the least educated of his readers. Furthermore, the terms in this passage make it possible for him to establish, at the very beginning, fundamental truths about the nature of man and the nature of God, truths that he could not establish in the same way were he to begin by considering other anthropomorphic passages in the Bible.

The Second Paragraph

The first part of the second paragraph appears to be fairly straightforward. Maimonides wants to show us that there is a standard term in biblical Hebrew for physical form. That term is *to'ar.* He cites examples to make his point, shows that *to'ar* is used regularly for physical shape and configuration, and in this way draws a clear contrast with the terms *tzelem* and *demut.* Most important is his added comment that the term *to'ar* is "never applied to the deity." Readers should always check out such a statement to be certain that it is accurate. If it should turn out that there is in fact some case of *to'ar* applied to God it would, of course, require careful consideration and explanation. We can be certain in such a case that Maimonides was testing his readers. I leave it to readers to settle the matter by their own investigation.

Maimonides now goes on to contrast *to'ar* with *tzelem.* Throughout this paragraph the focus is on the meaning of *tzelem* when it is applied to man. The term, he says, "is applied to the natural form, I mean to the notion in virtue of which a thing is constituted as a substance and becomes what it is. It is the true reality of the thing in so far as the latter is that particular being." Nothing is said about the term with respect to God, although the biblical

13. Strauss, "How to Begin to Study the *Guide of the Perplexed,*" in Maimonides, *Guide,* trans. Pines, xxvi.

passage says that God created man "in His image." We shall return to this point later. Let us first consider the account that Maimonides has given us of *tzelem*.

He introduces here the notion that *tzelem* is to be understood as meaning "natural form," which he then explains briefly. By this term he means the essence of a thing, that is, the set of properties that makes it what it is. He thus excludes all accidental properties, as well as properties that are unique, but not essential, to a particular being. The essential properties consist of that set without which the thing could not be what it is. This is a familiar enough notion to students of philosophy, and Maimonides states it here without any elaboration or explanation. In another flat statement, he then informs us, "In man that notion is that from which human apprehension derives. It is on account of this intellectual apprehension that it is said of man: In the image of God created He him." Again, this is a philosophical commonplace for those within the Aristotelian tradition. It is simply presented here as fact with no argument, defense, or explanation. Perhaps these ideas are set forth dogmatically because Maimonides requires his readers to have a certain level of philosophical training. For such people it is not necessary to comment on or defend elementary philosophical principles.

At the same time it confronts nonphilosophical readers with an inordinately difficult intellectual demand. They are instructed to set aside all their ideas of God as a corporeal being in favor of a being with no corporeal properties whatsoever. This runs counter to all common-sense human experience. Maimonides made a point of telling us in the first paragraph that such people would consider a God who is incorporeal to be nonexistent. They know only of corporeal existence and are unable to conceive of a mode of existence that lacks all corporeal properties. They are addicted to pictorial thinking, and when they think of something as an actual, or even a possible, existent they make mental images of that thing. A thing that, in principle cannot be apprehended through sensation or contemplated in our imagination is viewed by such people as something that does not and cannot exist at all. Yet Maimonides demands of even his most ordinary and least schooled readers—in fact, of every faithful Jew whether a reader of the *Guide* or not—that they believe in the existence of a God who is completely incorporeal. Furthermore, God alone is to be understood as true and independent being; all else that exists derives from Him and is constantly dependent on Him.[14] How is this demand to be met, when it goes so much against the grain of ordinary nonreflective experience? It is useless to require ordinary

14. This point is made explicitly in the opening section of the first book of the *Mishneh Torah* and is set forth in various places in the *Guide*.

readers to grasp the nature of God correctly unless they first have some easier and more accessible model with which to work.

That is why Maimonides concerns himself here with man. Philosophically trained readers will know at once that when Maimonides identifies the essence or natural form of man as the capacity for intellectual apprehension, he is simply reaffirming a well-established Aristotelian proposition. In that philosophical tradition man's rational capacity is taken to be his defining characteristic, the essential property without which he is not truly human. For nonphilosophical readers this unfamiliar idea opens up a whole new world. Although they may not yet have a clear understanding of what it means to assert that man's intellect is man's essence, such readers, since they do not conceive their own mind pictorially or in corporeal terms, have at least this intuitive awareness of the idea of a mode of being that is noncorporeal. They do have their own experience of human thought, and one can suppose that they will have some notion that thought is noncorporeal.

Thus two things are achieved. First, we have an opening from this point to the idea of God as a completely noncorporeal being, and this is already introduced into the discussion when we are told, "It is on account of this intellectual apprehension that it is said of man: In the image of God created He him." Like man in his proper nature, God too is incorporeal and may be thought of, in this respect, as similar to man's intellect. (Later this notion will be qualified and rejected as not literally accurate.) Second, we have been given a certain conception of what it is to be human, and this conception turns out to be critically important for much of the argument that follows.

The rest of the second paragraph goes on in a fairly simple fashion. Maimonides takes up instances of *tzelem* that on first reading seem to use the term to refer to some kind of physical form. He shows that, in each case, the term refers rather to the notion or the essence of the thing, not to its physical form. He leaves open, however, the option of treating *tzelem* in some of these uses as referring to shape or configuration rather than to idea or essence. In that case the term is a homonym that includes at least two different meanings. We must know, however, that in the verse we have been discussing the term refers to the essence of man, that is, his rational capacity.

The Third Paragraph

The third paragraph is, in many respects, the key statement in the first chapter. It may seem to be quite simple and straightforward, but it is in fact remarkably subtle and makes heavy demands on readers' ingenuity and understanding. Its apparent purpose is simply to interpret the term *demut* in a manner similar to the interpretation of *tzelem*. Toward this end, it is argued that *demut* "signifies likeness in respect of a notion," rather than any kind of physical resemblance of one thing to another. At this point Maimonides takes up cases of *demut* in its nominal or verbal forms which at first glance appear to suggest physical resemblance. He shows that this interpretation is not correct, but rather that the resemblance is with respect to an idea or a notion. For unwary readers nothing more will come out of this study of the term, and Maimonides does not want such readers to learn any more at this point. Careful and sophisticated readers, however, immediately face problems requiring thought and attention.

Indeed, this paragraph is a classic paradigm of a passage in the *Guide* in which Maimonides deliberately omits what is most important. He is unwilling to state openly what needs to be said, because ordinary readers are not yet prepared to understand and come to terms with the doctrine that he is teaching. This puts the burden on sophisticated readers of constructing independently the implicit but unspoken message. What first engages our attention is the fact that Maimonides has selected for consideration relatively innocuous instances of the term *demut*, in which it is easy to see that what is spoken of is, as he says, likeness in respect of a notion and not physical resemblance. Moreover, all but the last examples he cites seem to have no philosophical or theological significance. It all appears to be straightforward, but the reader who has even a modest control of the Bible will see at once how important are the instances of *demut* that Maimonides chose to ignore in this discussion.

He cites Ezekiel 1:26, but restricts himself to the portion of the verse that is least troublesome. Let us look at the entire verse, as Maimonides certainly intended we should do. "Above the firmament that was over their heads was the likeness of a throne, in appearance like a sapphire stone; and upon the likeness of the throne was a likeness as of the appearance of a man above upon it [*demut ke-mar'eh 'adam 'alav mi-le-ma'alah*]." Almost as if he wants to distract our attention, Maimonides cites the phrase, "the likeness of a throne," twice, but he says nothing at all about the far more troubling phrase that follows: "a likeness as of the appearance of a man above it."

Now we must remember the context of this verse. The first chapter of Ezekiel consists of the chariot vision, which is called *ma'aseh merkavah* in rabbinic terminology. All authorities, including Maimonides, agree that this vision contains the ultimate metaphysical insights that Judaism has to offer. It expresses in symbolic form the highest understanding of God we can hope to achieve. Both in rabbinic law and in the Maimonidean teachings, it is also considered to be the most esoteric body of doctrine in Judaism. Every phrase, indeed every word, is of the highest significance. Yet when the scriptural text speaks of a vision of the *demut* of the appearance of a man above the throne, it is not taken up by Maimonides as one of the examples of the term *demut* requiring interpretation. What shall we make of this undoubtedly deliberate omission?

This statement of Ezekiel is potentially very threatening. The entire thrust of the argument that Maimonides has made is to construe *demut* as referring to the notion, the inner idea, the essence of a thing, and not to any physical shape or configuration. Yet here we have the term used in a setting where it seems to refer to the physical shape of a man. That man is seen in the vision as located above the divine throne. This certainly suggests that the prophet may have represented the divine being in human form. It would seem very dangerous to leave this passage untreated here; it can readily lead us to conclusions about the meaning of *demut* and about the nature of God that are in direct contradiction to what Maimonides wants to teach us.

The physical image is made even stronger in the next verse when the vision describes what is seen above the loins of the man and below his loins. The last verse in Ezekiel 1 speaks of the radiance that surrounds the entire vision and says that it was "the appearance of the likeness of the glory of the Lord [*mar'eh demut kevod ha-Shem*]." Here we have *demut* used specifically with respect to God, and it refers to a visual image of radiant light. The problem this poses for Maimonides is obvious. We need to work out the implications of his decision to ignore in the present discussion these instances of *demut,* and to determine what he is saying to readers who notice the omission.

It seems clear that Maimonides was reluctant to introduce these particularly difficult verses at the beginning of his treatise. His readers are not yet prepared to deal with them properly, and they might only serve to corrupt the understanding of readers who are not well trained either in the Jewish materials, on the one hand, or in the disciplines of logic, natural science, and metaphysics, on the other. Yet there must be a way to address the issues for those who will see the problem on their own and are intellectually qualified to deal with it. This way is through those places in the *Guide* in which Maimonides considers the verses in question and sets forth directly or by implication his account of what they mean. It is particularly important to remember Maimonides' instructions to us concerning the proper method of reading his book. In his introduction he tells us specifically that no one topic is fully discussed in any one place. Readers are challenged to find the various places where a given topic is taken up, including those that are obscure or fragmentary, and to reconstruct the entire argument by putting the pieces together properly. Maimonides considers readers who are unable to do this to be intellectually unprepared to meet the challenge of reading the *Guide.*

166

Such readers do not satisfy the demand of the Mishnah that they must be able to follow the subject on their own once they are given the chapter headings.

When we follow through Maimonides' discussions of *demut,* we see a clear pattern. The first subject of direct interest for us is his treatment of the term *throne,* with which he deals briefly in *Guide,* I, 1. References to the divine throne would be troubling if they were taken literally. In the case of the verses from Ezekiel, which are a vision of the supernal world, naive readers might readily construe the term *throne* to mean the seat occupied by the divine being. This is why Maimonides makes a point in I, 1 of stressing that the likeness is "in respect of elevation and sublimity, not in respect of the throne's square shape, its solidity, and the length of its legs, as wretched people think." He discusses the term more fully in *Guide,* I, 9, where he concludes that *throne* is a metaphor for God's power and majesty. He does not cite the verse from Ezekiel among his examples, but the reasons for this are not germane to our present concerns. He does conclude the chapter with a general statement that goes far beyond his comment in the first chapter and is a guide to all the cases in which Scripture speaks of God's throne: "Hence the term 'throne' signifies, in this passage and in all those similar to it, His sublimity and greatness *that do not constitute a thing existing outside His essence,* as will be explained in some of the chapters of this Treatise" (I, 9, p. 35; emphasis added). It is important to note here that the stress is on two points. First is his obvious point that the meaning of *throne,* when used with reference to God, is symbolic and not literal. Second is the far subtler point that the term refers to His "sublimity and greatness" as purely internal to His nature and never as attributes that are external to His essence. Maimonides is laying the groundwork here for his account of God as a being in whom there are no separate attributes, no perfections other than His essence. This means that to speak of God's sublimity or greatness is simply one more way to call attention to the fact that He exists, but not to add anything whatsoever to our knowledge of Him. We shall see shortly that this point will be relevant for our understanding of the last sentences of I, 1.

We shall now turn to those passages in the *Guide* where Maimonides cites and takes up the expression, "a likeness as the appearance of a man." He cites the verse at the end of III, 2, but makes no direct comment on it. He also cites it in III, 7 in a group of other verses where his purpose is to distinguish the cases of similes in which the term *demut* is used from cases in which no such terms is used. Again, while the passage is of interest and importance, it is not particularly useful for our present purposes. The key citation is in I, 46. Maimonides has been discussing a variety of anthropomorphic terms in the Bible and has explained their significance when taken in a nonliteral sense with respect to God. He then turns to those parables where the language is particularly troubling and cites a Midrash on which he relies for guidance. The Midrash says: "Great is the power of the prophets; for they liken a form to its creator. For it is said: And upon the likeness of the throne was a likeness as the appearance of a man." The sages were expressing their awe at the fact that the prophet could permit himself to speak in such language about God, could permit himself to liken a created thing to its Creator. Maimonides construes their statement as being more than an expression of awe—as conveying a specific philosophical message. "They have thus made clear and manifest that all the forms apprehended by all the prophets in 'the vision of prophecy' are created forms of which God is the Creator. And this is correct, for every imagined form is created" (I, 46, p. 103). The image of a man above the throne of glory is now seen as a manifestation not of the divine being, but rather of a created form. Thus the likeness of a man seen in the prophetic vision is not to be thought of as in any respect similar to God Himself, but only as a created form whose splendor helps us think of the divine being.

The point is stated in a completely unambiguous way in Maimonides' discussion of the last verse of Ezekiel, which says of the refulgent light in the vision: "This was the appearance of the likeness of the glory of the Lord." He first expresses his own astonishment at the boldness of the symbolism. He says, "This is the most extraordinary comparison possible, as far as parables and similitudes are concerned; and it is indubitably due to prophetic force" (III, 7, p. 429). Here he is essentially repeating and underscoring what was said in the Midrash already cited. He goes on to make his position clear. He stresses that in the Ezekiel passage all the symbols are connected to the "likeness of the glory of the Lord [*demut kevod ha-Shem*]." He then points out, "Now the glory of the Lord is not the Lord, as we have made clear several times. Accordingly everything to which the parables contained in these apprehensions refer is only the glory of the Lord, I mean to say the Chariot, not the Rider, *as He, may He be exalted, may not be presented in a likeness in a parable*" (III, 7, p. 430; emphasis added). There are, then, no direct similes for God as He is in His own being.

We can now understand why in I, 1 Maimonides speaks of the meaning of *tzelem* and *demut* as they refer to man, but says not one word about them in reference to God. The reason is that nothing of this sort can ever be properly said about God. He is unique and incomparable. We may speak of His creations, including those most immediately derived from Him, but we cannot speak about God Himself. No discourse, direct or indirect, that has "God" as its subject can be admitted, for all such discourse is bound to be mistaken. This is why these verses are not open for consideration at the beginning of the *Guide*. At that early stage, uninstructed readers would only be confused by doctrines of such complexity and subtlety. The idea of a God concerning whom we can say nothing positive is utterly alien to them; it also seems to run counter to the Bible, which speaks of God frequently and in the most explicit language. Moreover, Maimonides himself makes many statements about God, or so it would appear. Readers with a philosophical education are prepared to come to terms with the doctrine of Maimonides. Either they are already sufficiently advanced to know how to find the appropriate guidance from other passages in the book, or they will be mature enough to defer their problems until they come to those passages and see how they cast light on what has gone before.

We can now return to the last part of I, 1. Exactly what does Scripture refer to when it tells us that man was created in the image and likeness of God? We have already answered that it refers to the human intellect, to man's capacity of rational apprehension. Now Maimonides, in closing this chapter, needs to refine the point. This power is what makes man human, that is to say, it is his essential property, the *sine qua non* of his existence as man. It is also unique to man among all the creatures in the sublunar world. There are beings of superior intellectual power in the supernal world but in the world below the moon, the world which we inhabit, no being other than man is endowed with such intellectual capacity. Most of this has been said before, although not quite so clearly. Now Maimonides adds two points of critical importance for a correct understanding of the subject and for a correct grasp of the argument that will follow. Let us consider the entire passage:

> In the exercise of this [intellectual power], no sense, no part of the body, none of the extremities are used; and therefore this apprehension was likened unto the apprehension of the deity, which does not require an instrument, although in reality it is not like the latter apprehension, but only appears so to the first stirrings of opinion. It was because of this something, I mean because of the divine intellect conjoined with man, that it is said of the latter that he is "in the image of God and in His likeness," not that God, may He be exalted, is a body and possesses a shape.

Note that Maimonides stresses initially not the quality of the human intellect, but the fact that the intellect operates with no physical/corporeal instruments. Here we have the particular way in which man in his essential nature may be compared to God. Man, *qua* man, is incorporeal. We can now see the full force of our earlier comments on this point. To apprehend correctly the nature of the human intellect is to understand man properly. It is also the best path we have toward a proper understanding of God.

We must, however, pay careful attention to the way in which Maimonides pulls back from the comparison in the very sentence in which he makes it. He emphasizes that the divine intellect is "in reality not like the latter [i.e., human] apprehension, but only appears so to the first stirrings of opinion." Despite all that has been said, he is now telling us that it is a serious mistake to compare man to God. All relations of similarity are reciprocal. If A is similar to B in some respect, then B is similar to A in that same respect. If man is in the likeness of God with respect to his intellect, then God must in this same regard be in the likeness of man. But this proposition is, in the view of Maimonides, not admissible. Here, in the first chapter, he can only allow himself to hint at the point in a passing expression at the very end of the discussion, because in the minds of his untutored readers it would undermine the whole argument of the chapter. We can, however, trace out the full argument from other sources.

Among the passages containing the term *demut* that were omitted from discussion in I, 1, the most remarkable is the statement of Isaiah, "To whom then will ye liken [*tedammeyun*] God? Or what likeness [*demut*] will ye compare unto Him?" Again he says, "To whom then will ye liken Me [*tedammeyuni*], that I should be equal?"[15] Here the nominal and verbal forms of the term *demut* are used by the prophet to deny any possible comparison between God and man. In the context in which he cites these verses as proof texts, Maimonides asserts, "One must likewise deny, with reference to Him, His being similar to any existing thing" (I, 55, p. 128).

In this statement, and others like it in the *Guide,* Maimonides has made clear that there can be no similarity whatsoever between God and any of His creatures, including man. What then is intended by the statement in Scripture that man is created in God's image and in His likeness? Shall we be forced to conclude that the account in Genesis is mistaken, and only the statement of Isaiah is correct?[16] This subject could not be discussed openly in the first chapter of the *Guide* for the same reason as some of the other topics we have noted. Until the ground has been laid it is dangerous and misleading to open up such an issue.

Yet, as we have seen, Maimonides does open the issue covertly and gives a solution intended to direct our thinking on this subject throughout our

15. Isa. 40:18, 25.

16. This may be part of what Strauss had in mind in his cryptic statements suggesting that Isaiah was a greater prophet than Moses. "We are thus induced to believe," he says, "that Isaiah reached a higher stage in the knowledge of God than Moses or that Isaiah's vision marks a progress beyond Moses'." See his comments in "How to Begin to Study the *Guide of the Perplexed,*" in Maimonides, *Guide,* trans. Pines, xxxiii.

study of his book. The key is in the last sentence of I, 1. Having said that human intellect cannot be truly compared to the divine intellect, Maimonides now seems to change his direction. There is a respect in which the comparison can be drawn. When Scripture says that man is "in the image of God and in His likeness," it is "because of the divine intellect conjoined with man." We have here a complex metaphysical concept which cannot be fully explicated at this point. Its main significance for our purpose, however, is fairly easy to state. The underlying theory, by no means original with Maimonides, is that true human knowledge occurs only when there is a conjunction of the human intellect with the divine intellect. This happens only at the point at which man has freed himself of all moral, psychological, and intellectual obstacles to pure rational insight and understanding. It is then that man transcends himself and becomes, as intellect, joined with the divine intelligence.

It is not necessary to explain here the complex system in which the divine intelligence moves down through the separate intellects to the agent intellect, which is the very last of the stages. It is enough for us to know that the purified human intellect, so to speak, breaks out of its bodily housing and is united with the agent intellect. This is what Maimonides means when he says that it is "because of the divine intellect conjoined with man" that man is said to be in the likeness of God. Some reflection will reveal that this is the same as saying that man is similar to God only at the point where he stops being fully man and is, instead, conjoined with the divine being. At that stage, we are no longer comparing man to God or God to man, but only God to Himself.

Read in this way, the verses in Genesis are in complete accord with the statements of Isaiah. God is truly incomparable. Not even man, the highest of the sublunar creatures, can be compared to God. When we are told at Creation that man is created in the image and likeness of God, we are being informed of the remarkable potential that man has for self-transcendence. He can, so to speak, leave his human form and elevate himself to the point where he is absorbed into the divine being. This, and this alone, is what is meant by the scriptural statements that speak of man as similar to God. Genesis has it right, and there is no reason to suppose that Isaiah excelled Moses in prophetic insight.

A final important point provides us with a transition to I, 2. Throughout the discussion in I, 1 Maimonides stresses the intellect as the essential property of man. At the close of the chapter he affirms, in a cryptic way, that man's highest fulfillment, the end toward which all his efforts should be directed, is the perfection of his intellect to the point where he transcends as far as possible the limits of his humanity. This doctrine, which climaxes the opening of the *Guide* and is taken up again in I, 2, seems also to be the main point of the conclusion of Maimonides' book, as eloquently expressed in the last four chapters of Part III. It is also expressed briefly by Maimonides in an earlier statement about the true end of man:

> His ultimate perfection is to become rational in actu; this would consist in his knowing everything concerning all the beings that it is within the capacity of man to know in accordance with his ultimate perfection. It is clear that to this ultimate perfection there do not belong either actions or moral qualities and that it consists only of opinions toward which speculation has led and that investigation has rendered compulsory (III, 27, p. 511).

This doctrine might be expected to trouble any thoughtful reader. Is it correct to say that a truly good man is one who has achieved the highest possible level of intellectual development? Can we accept Maimonides' outright rejection of "actions or moral qualities" as having nothing to do with ultimate human virtue? Certainly such statements are counterintuitive. If one were to ask within a normal Jewish setting what is it to be a good man or a good Jew, the answer would almost certainly focus on moral virtues and/or the fulfillment of God's commandments. However the answers might differ in detail, we can assume that a strong stress on morality and right action would be common to all of them. We can be equally certain that nobody who was not already under the influence of Maimonides or the classical philosophic tradition would answer that the good man is one with the most highly perfected intellect who uses that intellect to contemplate the highest and most perfect beings. Yet this is exactly what Maimonides says clearly, if allusively, in his words at the end of I, 1 and explicitly elsewhere in the *Guide*.[17]

That position requires a strong defense. It might seem ordinary enough within a philosophical tradition that derives from Plato and Aristotle, but it does not fit with commonly held Jewish views or with the popular views that one would find in societies that stand under the influence of Judaism or Christianity. We shall soon see that the reason for the subject matter of I, 2 is the need to establish the soundness of these claims in the preceding chapter about the true nature and end of man. Maimonides must show that he is espousing a doctrine that is not only philosophically sound, but also Jewishly authentic and correct. He opens the point up cautiously and with indirection in the first chapter so as not to distress or turn away his readers who believe

---

17. Students of the *Guide* do not need to be reminded that the last sentences of the book seem to go counter to the doctrine that moral virtue is purely instrumental to the highest value of the intellectual apprehension of God. The topic has been discussed repeatedly in the literature.

they correctly understand the Jewish tradition. Yet the subject cannot be ignored; there can be no serious discourse about axiological questions without first determining what is the essence of our humanity. To know what a good man is, we need first to know exactly what it is to be a man, to know what constitutes the essential element of our humanity. Maimonides establishes this point in I, 1, before he takes up directly in I, 2 the question of the foundations of ethics within the Jewish tradition.

Commentary to *Guide*, I, 2

The problem of chapter 2 is provided by a question that Maimonides says was posed to him "years ago." It is not relevant to know in particular who the questioner was or the circumstances under which he raised his question. From the nature of the question itself, and from Maimonides' response, we can learn all we need to know about the quality of intelligence and the level of understanding of the unnamed questioner. We have a situation similar to Plato's dialogues, where it is an important part of the readers' responsibility to understand all they can about the intelligence and character of each participant in the dialogue. In Plato the information is not usually given in direct fashion. But one can always find out whatever is necessary about each of the parties to the conversation by what he says, how he says it, and particularly by how he is answered by Socrates (in the vast majority of the dialogues in which Socrates is a major figure in the conversation). In the *Guide,* as well, a careful study of the question, of Maimonides' comments about the questioner, and of the reply that is given to him tells us all that we need to know about the questioner.

The First Paragraph

The first point to note is that the questioner is characterized in the first paragraph as "a learned man." In the standard Hebrew translation of Samuel ibn Tibbon this phrase is rendered somewhat ambiguously as *'ish ḥakham,* which might easily be read to mean "a wise man." Maimonides is precise and careful, however, in his choice of words. This questioner is not a wise man, but simply one who has a certain amount of learning.[18] A truly wise

18. See the comments by Lawrence V. Berman in "Maimonides on the Fall of Man," *AJS Review,* 5 (1980), 5. In this valuable article Berman provides his own commentary on *Guide,* I, 2. It has many important ideas and should be studied by anyone interested in this subject. I am grateful to Professor Berman (whose recent untimely death we mourn) for what I have learned from his effort, even though I believe that there is still a need for the type of extended commentary offered here as well as for a discussion of the many specific points on which my views differ from his.

man would be a sound philosopher/theologian. As will become evident very soon, this is not the case with this questioner. He may know a good deal about various sciences, but he lacks insight into and understanding of the highest science. Knowing this by virtue of the initial characterization of the questioner, we are put on our guard and are told with what care and critical judgment we must approach his question.

Maimonides then interrupts the flow of the discussion to make a statement about a point whose full relevance is not clear until we hear the question and follow his discussion of it. The point, however, is so important that he wants to stress it at the beginning of the discussion, before he has even set forth the question. The intended effect is to make certain that if readers get lost in the complex discussion that is to follow, they will, in any case, have learned the important truth which is now to be expounded, and which is directly connected to the discussion that has just been completed in chapter I. We ended our discussion of I, 1 with a clear statement about what is meant in Scripture when we are told that man was created in the image and likeness of God. We are now confronted with the disconcerting fact that the scriptural episode following the creation story has a statement that seems to offer a direct contradiction. We were just taught that man is godlike insofar as he realizes his capacity for the highest level of intellectual apprehension and contemplation. Yet in the Garden of Eden the woman is tempted with the statement, "Ye shall be like Elohim, knowing good and evil." The normal impulse would be to construe this to mean that "ye shall be like God, knowing good and evil." This seems to be a direct challenge to the doctrine set forth in the first chapter: it now appears that godlike qualities are associated with moral awareness, not with intellectual apprehension, and that they are acquired by the transgression of eating the forbidden fruit. Maimonides must address this threat at once, lest his entire structure collapse almost before its foundations have been set.

Our problem is shown to be of a type we have already confronted. We have been taught that words can have multiple meanings, and that it is essential to determine in each setting which meaning is intended. The key term here is *Elohim*. Maimonides begins by making the strong point that every "Hebrew" knows this term is equivocal, "designating the deity, the angels, and the rulers governing the cities." It is evident that by "Hebrew" he means, in this context, one who has a sound knowledge of the Hebrew language. Now it is, in fact, the case that anyone who has studied biblical usage with care must be aware of the range of meanings which the term *Elohim* carries. Moreover, a person who has even modest knowledge of rabbinic literature will have learned that the Sages of the Talmud often use that term to refer to judges. Here Maimonides is only bringing to our attention something that "every Hebrew" does know. Yet it is also the case that what should be well known may be readily overlooked or forgotten. Furthermore, although it is easy to read a text with the correct meaning of *Elohim* when the context leaves no doubt about its intent, what shall we do in cases that are not so clear? A key case is the one before us, where there is no way to be certain from the context which sense of *Elohim* is intended. Maimonides deals with this problem in two stages. The first is his appeal to the authority of Onkelos, whose Aramaic version of the Torah has official standing as the translation approved and quasi-canonized by the rabbinic authorities. In this initial paragraph he does no more than call to our attention that Onkelos understands the expression, "ye shall be as Elohim," in the verse before us to mean "ye shall be as rulers." For the untutored this is sufficient. It is only important that they should know the correct meaning of the term in this verse, and that they should accept that meaning as correct on the authority of Onkelos, if not on the authority of Maimonides. Whoever knows this much will be protected from the danger of a serious error. The second clarification of the term will emerge from the long discussion that is to follow. When we understand correctly all that is being taught in the episode in Eden, we will come to see that in the verse under discussion, the term *Elohim* could not possibly mean "God," but must refer to earthly rulers.

The Second Paragraph

The question to be discussed is formulated in the second paragraph. We should notice at the outset two small but important points. The first is that we do not have before us a question raised by someone who is puzzled and is honestly seeking an answer. This is not a neutral question posed by someone who sincerely seeks enlightenment. It is rather what Maimonides identifies as an "objection," and he calls the questioner an "objector." It is an attack aimed at the soundness and acceptability of Scripture itself. We can see why Maimonides feels called upon not only to reply with the clearest possible answer to the objection, but also to discredit the objector at the same time. Much is at stake. If the objection stands, it will appear that the teaching of Scripture is unworthy of the attention of serious people.

The second point to notice is the seemingly casual last sentence in the paragraph in which Maimonides states, "This was the intent and the meaning of the objection, though it was not textually as we have put it." In other words, we are told openly that we do not have before us the objection as it was phrased by the objector himself. What does Maimonides want to convey to us? This may be a statement of no special consequence, its only point being that Maimonides did not retain a stenographic transcript of a conversation that he tells us took place "years ago."

I believe there is more to it. My sense is that Maimonides tells us that he has himself reformulated the statement to make it as strong as possible. Because we are about to learn in the next few lines of this chapter that the objector is intellectually incompetent, we might conclude that he has put his objection poorly, and that a powerful intelligence could formulate it far more effectively. Maimonides wants to be certain that we are not left with the impression that he is fighting a straw man. He uses this subtle means to assure us that he has formulated the argument himself in the strongest way possible.

The perceptive reader is expected to discern, nevertheless, that even in its strongest form the objection reveals serious flaws in the thinking and understanding of the objector. The objector opens his attack with the assertion that the original intention in Creation was that man "should be, as the other animals are, devoid of intellect, of thought, and of the capacity to distinguish between good and evil." In this statement the shaky ground of the objection is immediately evident. No one who has paid close attention to the creation story is likely to conclude that man was intended to be like all the other animals. Scripture takes great care to establish that man is unique; he is different in his essential nature from all the other animals. Man is created in a special separate act of creation, and is associated from the beginning with the image and likeness of God. He is given dominion over all Creation, including all the animals. He is unable to find any partner for himself among the animals, so God must create for him a mate who, in her essential nature, will be like him.[19] Moreover, only man is commanded by God; this is not the case with respect to any other animal. This objector, who has failed to notice the striking distinctions that Scripture makes between man and all the other animals, and who concludes that man was intended to be like all the other animals, has shown already, by virtue of this alone, how poorly he has read and understood the scriptural text.

The objector's assertion that man was intended, like the animals, to "be devoid of intellect, of thought," is potentially a challenge to the doctrine of *Guide,* I, 1, where the major stress is on man's intellect as his defining property. Hence it is clear that what is really at stake in this debate is the question of what it means to be human. Moreover, the objector identifies the intellect with "the capacity to distinguish between good and evil." This, however, is the very point at issue in the debate. Maimonides argues vigorously against the claim that the true mark of intellectual development is the ability to dis-

19. See Gen. 2:18–24.

tinguish between good and evil. The whole debate turns on this point. In formulating the objection he has alerted us to the issues so that we know what to look for in the discussion that follows.

The objector goes on to assert that the capacity to distinguish between good and evil is "the noblest of the characteristics existing in us; it is in virtue of it that we are constituted as substances." Even if we grant his claim about the nobility of our moral capacity, it is not self-evident that it is "the noblest" of human faculties. Again, that is the very point at issue. Moreover, the questioner makes an elementary error when he asserts that our moral capacity is what makes us human. He confuses unique properties with essential properties. Moral capacity may be a *unique* property of human beings, a property that no other animal shares. It does not follow from this that it is an *essential* defining property, a property without which we are no longer human. Opposed thumbs are also a uniquely human property, yet no one wants to argue that a being who lacks opposed thumbs is, by virtue of that alone, not truly human. A person may have been born without arms, or with hands that lack thumbs. Such a person lacks a unique characteristic of human beings, but that in no way affects his or her essence as human. This is an elementary philosophical point which the objector does not understand, since he seems to think that all unique properties are necessarily essential properties. When we consider any unique property of man, we have to determine if it is only unique, or both unique and essential.

The objection, clearly formulated in the statement, needs no further elaboration. The objector argues that, before his sin, man lacked moral capacity, while we face the remarkable paradox that after his sin his punishment consists in his having acquired that noble capacity. It would seem then that the consequence of his sin is to make man a far nobler and more exalted being than before. If this reading of the scriptural text is correct, something is seriously wrong. Man's sin has generated for him the greatest possible reward, rather than the most serious punishment. Maimonides must now directly address this objection, which threatens the foundations on which his whole axiological system rests and, at the same time, threatens to destroy our confidence in the Bible as a source of divine wisdom and truth.

The Third Paragraph

Except for the final sentence, the long third paragraph constitutes the rest of the chapter. It contains the entire counterargument and sets forth in detail the major philosophical points that Maimonides makes. Its beginning is an open attack on the character and competence of the objector. Readers who have failed to infer, from the nature of the objection, that the objector is intellectually incompetent, now have it spelled out for them.

Three separate points are made in the attack. The first is that he is among those "who engage in theoretical speculation using the first notions that may occur to you and come to your mind." This shows a basic intellectual superficiality and incompetence. Philosophy and theology are exacting disciplines which require intense thought and concentration, the constant sifting of ideas, ongoing critical reflection, and a relentless review of what one thinks has already been settled. By the form and quality of his objection, however, the objector shows that he has no understanding at all of what is required of a person who purports to philosophize seriously. This man takes the first idea that comes into his head, and makes it the basis for his attack on the scriptural account of man.

The second point is that the objector has no idea of what is involved in reading a serious text properly. He has, in effect, accused Maimonides of not reading Scripture carefully. It appears to him that the Maimonidean account of the nature of man, which is based on an interpretation of the terms *image* and *likeness,* ignores the strong counterevidence of the Eden episode. Maimonides responds with the accusation that the objector thinks he can understand a book as complex and subtle as the Bible "while glancing through it as you would glance through a historical work or a piece of poetry."[20] We can see the superficiality of that reading in the fact that, in his opening comment in the previous paragraph, the objector speaks about "the clear sense of the biblical text." He supposes that the difficult and complex creation story has a clear and evident meaning that is available to any reader on a first casual reading.[21] This by itself shows that he does not know how to read Scripture properly. The Bible has to be read with the closest attention to

20. This is not the place to discuss Maimonides' seemingly negative attitudes to history and poetry. Every reader of his works knows that he employed history as a useful tool for understanding the origins and purposes of the commandments, as well as for an account of how the Torah was transmitted and the halakhah developed. Yet he seems to have had no respect for history as an independent discipline, and certainly did not put it in a class with philosophy or theology. He seems also to have had no respect for poetry, at least not as an art that engaged the intellect in a deep way. When Maimonides shows his contempt for the objector as someone who reads the Bible as he would history or poetry, he is saying what we might say if we condemned someone for reading the Bible with the same thought and attention that he gives to the daily newspaper. For a study of Maimonides' views on history, see Salo W. Baron, "The Historical Outlook of Maimonides," *Proceedings of the American Academy for Jewish Research,* 6 (1934–35), 5–113.

21. Berman points out that the objector is represented as resting with "the apparent meaning," while Maimonides himself is concerned with the "inner meaning" (Berman, "Fall of Man," 6 n. 10).

every word and every phrase. It has to be read as the Sages of Israel read it over the generations, as Maimonides himself reads it in the *Guide,* not as a work that can be understood casually and without serious intellectual effort. One must always seek its inner meaning and not rest satisfied with its apparent surface meaning. Like every other serious book, the Bible has layers of meaning that we must penetrate and uncover. We shall soon see how the careless incompetence and superficiality of the objector's reading is reflected in his failure to achieve a proper understanding of the Eden episode.

The third point is that this objector is much given to the pleasures of the body at the expense of the development of his intellect. He is occupied with "drinking and copulating," not with thinking and studying. As we shall see, this is exactly the danger to which man becomes exposed when he chooses to reject God's commandments. This objector shows himself to be the kind of being that he imagines man was originally intended to be, one not different from the animals in any essential.

Having discredited the objector, Maimonides now begins his substantive reply, which consists of his own interpretation of the Eden episode. He begins by recalling and expanding slightly what was already established in the first chapter. "For the intellect that God made overflow unto man and that is the latter's ultimate perfection, was that which Adam had been provided with before he disobeyed. It was because of this that it was said of him that he was created 'in the image of God and in His likeness.' " We have here a reaffirmation of what we learned earlier. Man is essentially defined by his intellect, which alone makes him human and is the ground for his distinction from all other animals. That is the correct interpretation of the key verse concerning the creation of man. Added to this reaffirmation is a brief allusion to the source of this intellect and the way man acquires it. It is the "intellect that God made overflow unto man." We are given no account here of the doctrine of the overflow. That is a complex matter that is left for later exposition, especially in II, 11–12. It is enough here to know that the ultimate source of the human intellect is God, and that it is by way of the overflow that the divine intellect is connected to its human counterpart. So far we have only a counteraffirmation to the claims of the objector. This will have to be tested against a critical examination of those claims.

The next two sentences add a crucial element to the argument. Although there will soon follow a carefully crafted account of the noncognitive status of all moral judgments, Maimonides does not hesitate to assert that only by virtue of his intellect is man "addressed by God and given commandments. For commandments are not given to beasts and beings devoid of intellect." For any being to receive commandments, certain necessary conditions must be fulfilled. Foremost is that the commandments must be understood. We do not command inanimate objects because they are incapable of grasping the command or responding to it. The same is true of animals. Lacking language, and lacking the power of conceptualization that is a necessary condition for the use of language, animals cannot understand commandments or be bound by them. Trained domesticated animals may be taught to respond to certain vocal stimuli, but they are not intelligent beings who grasp and understand a commandment.[22] Only man can be commanded, because among all living things on earth, only man has the power to understand the commandment initially, retain it in memory, and apply it to particular circumstances. This makes the possession of intellect a necessary condition of being commanded, but it does not follow from this that the *content* of the commandments is derived from or dictated by the intellect. Only rational beings can be commanded, but Maimonides is unswerving in his conviction that the contents of the commandments are neither derived from nor dictated by reason.

This introduces us to one of the most deeply debated questions in moral philosophy. From classical antiquity on, there has been a line of thinking which holds that moral distinctions are founded on principles of reason. From this point of view, as we noted in our discussion of natural law, notions of good and evil, right and wrong, are thought to be determined by and accessible to the intellect in essentially the same way as principles of mathematics are.[23] This way of thinking may be identified primarily with Plato and those who follow him. For Plato, all knowledge is of one order, and in principle good and evil are knowable in the same way as we know any other truths. The school of Aristotle, on the other hand, taught that there is a distinction between the theoretical and the practical sciences. The former derive from first principles that are known intuitively to be true, and they yield conclusions whose certainty is demonstrated. The latter are established, as Aristotle puts it, by *nomos* not by *physis*—that is, they are derived from convention or humanly instituted law, rather than from principles of reason or the fixed order of nature.

Maimonides allies himself with the Aristotelian camp, but takes an even stronger stand on the fundamental issues than most Aristotelians. He denies categorically that we can know moral distinctions by way of the intellect. The reason is that the intellect is concerned only with truth and

22. The commentators point out that in II, 48 Maimonides takes up cases in Scripture in which it appears that animals, and even inanimate objects, are commanded. Those cases are explained there in a way that does not conflict with his flat statement here that commandments are not given to animals.

23. See chapter 6 for an extended discussion of another aspect of this subject.

falsehood. This includes the knowledge both of first principles, whose truth is apprehended immediately by reason, and of such scientific truths as are established by reason through its grasp of the necessary order of nature. (There is no discussion here of the epistemological status of particular matters of fact which are known only through direct experience.) Reason is concerned with the realm of the cognitive. However, according to Maimonides, moral distinctions are noncognitive. We do not treat them as true or false, but rather as "beautiful and ugly." These "*belong to the things generally accepted as known, not those cognized by the intellect.*"[24] The critical point here is that moral distinctions, like aesthetic distinctions, are noncognitive. It is inappropriate to speak of them as true or false in the same way that it is inappropriate to speak of matters of taste as true or false. Something is clearly wrong with the judgment that the sentence, "Chocolate ice cream is the tastiest of all foods," is true or false. We recognize this to be a matter of taste and invoke the ancient principle, *de gustibus non disputandum est.* In these areas, we all acknowledge that the intellect has no control, because we are dealing with matters about which it is fully legitimate for individual tastes to differ. No principles of reason are operative here, and the intellect does not determine our judgments concerning matters of taste. The statement about the tastiness of chocolate ice cream must be understood as a strong expression of the speaker's preferences, not as a claim about an objective fact. We are unable to demonstrate that someone who says that chocolate ice cream is not the tastiest food is wrong in the way that we can demonstrate the error of someone who draws a logically invalid conclusion from the premises of an argument.

The same holds for even the most sophisticated aesthetic judgments. Even when we invoke principles of aesthetic criticism in judging works of art, we are aware that they derive not from fixed rules of reason, but from individual taste which, however cultivated, makes its judgments in accordance with the norms of a particular society. In Maimonides' view the same applies to moral distinctions. They "belong to the things generally accepted as known," which is to say that they are established by convention or common consent, not by rational intuition or demonstration.

With this background, Maimonides is now ready to address directly the situation of Adam and Eve in the Garden of Eden. At the time of his creation, man was in a state of the highest perfection possible to him. Maimonides expects us to recall, without his mentioning the point, that when God com-

24. Emphasis added. I also discuss this subject in chapter 6, where I explain my preference for the translation "beautiful and ugly" against Pines' rendition of "fine and bad." Both make the same philosophical point, but I believe it is clearer with my proposed translation.

pleted His work of creation, He gave it His full approval. "And God saw all that He had made and found it very good."[25] This means that everything God had created was perfect after its kind. The first man was then all that it is possible for a man to be. He realized fully the potentiality of his humanity. Nothing less would be appropriate for that which God had created. In his pristine state Adam was a model of what it is to be truly human. He was a being of fully developed intellect whose life was exclusively formed and shaped by that intellect. "He had no faculty that was engaged in any way in the consideration of generally accepted things, and he did not apprehend them." As a being whose life was centered on intellectual apprehension and contemplation, there was no place in his life or thought for concern with conventions or arbitrary laws. After Eden, when man entered the realm of history, these came to be necessary devices for controlling society and for reducing in individuals the distractions of the imagination, the dangers of the passions, and the arousing powers of sensation. Convention and restrictive law have no place, however, in the life of a man who is totally preoccupied with rational reflection and contemplation.

This point is made in the biblical account by calling attention to a paradigmatic case. Man and woman are both naked, but they are not ashamed. This means that they did not respond to their own nakedness either by becoming sexually aroused or even with the most minimal moral concern.[26] Maimonides construes this to mean that, as beings preoccupied with the life of the intellect, they simply were not involved in the passional dimension of human experience which is represented by nakedness. This is the best possible evidence that such matters are not concerns of the intellect, otherwise these beings of perfected intellect would also have taken notice of them and responded to them. If conventional morality were established or verified by the intellect, rational beings could not simply ignore the fact of their own nakedness. Scripture itself makes this clear in the contrast it draws between the lack of response to nakedness before the Fall and the intense concern with it afterwards. In their original state: "The two of them were naked, the man and his wife, yet they felt no shame." After they had sinned: "Then the eyes of both of them were opened and they knew that they were naked; and they sewed together fig leaves and made themselves loin cloths." Moreover, Adam explains to God that he hid from Him because his nakedness made him afraid to appear before the divine being.[27]

Before examining the details of Maimonides' exposition of the sin and

25. Gen. 1:31.

26. See *Guide*, III, 8, p. 434, for a further discussion of this point.

27. Gen. 2:25, 3:7, 3:10.

fall of Adam, we need to deal with a prior question. Why is man commanded not to eat of the tree of the knowledge of good and bad? What is there, even in Adam's pristine state, that causes God to impose this restriction on him? He has, after all, been given explicit permission to eat of every tree in the garden. He has also been given dominion over all the earth and the creatures that inhabit it. Why then this one small restriction? And why is this restriction so severe that Adam is told by God that he will die on the day that he eats the fruit of the forbidden tree? These are questions any thoughtful reader of the Bible must raise, questions that must be raised again by any reader of Maimonides' exposition of the Eden episode in the chapter before us. Yet, Maimonides does not raise these questions for us. His silence serves as a test of the reader; it is clear that one cannot fully grasp his exposition without having settled these questions. Our task is to determine just what Maimonides wants us to see as the background and context for his specific response to the objection with which the chapter began. Let us then undertake to set forth what Maimonides wants us to keep in mind.

The fundamental point to remember is that even the first man in his pristine state was not a pure intellect. He was, after all, housed in a body and therefore was potentially subject to the desires and passions of the body. It is a root characteristic of man *qua* man that he is forced to choose what kind of being he wants to be. Neither animals nor angels have this burden. An animal is what it is at birth and becomes what it becomes by virtue of the natural realization of the potential present in it. Its line of development is predetermined, and it is either aided or obstructed by outside forces impinging upon the animal but over which it has no control. The young horse does not have the option of deciding that it wants to become the most perfect horse possible, and then striving toward that goal. Angels are also created in such a way as to be fully what they are.

Man alone has the freedom to choose and the inescapable burden of choosing his own direction and his own destiny. It is true that outside forces beyond his control may impede him from realizing his goal, but in the largest measure his destiny is in his own hands. Maimonides never ceases to give voice to his conviction that freedom and choice are essential elements in our humanity.[28] Man alone can decide whether he wants to bend all his efforts

28. See especially the extended discussion in *H. Teshuvah*, chaps. 5, 6. Maimonides sets forth there in detail the centrality of human freedom for the whole structure of Judaism. He acknowledges that there are some very complex philosophical puzzles posed by human freedom, puzzles for which he does not claim to offer a satisfactory solution. His conviction concerning human freedom is not simply a yielding to the demands of religion, but is based no less on the testimony of the sciences, including philosophy. In *H. Teshuvah*, 5:5, after acknowledging the problems posed by the affirmation of human freedom, he makes the following

toward the realization of his true self, his rational capacity, or whether he wants to live the life of the passions of the body and the imagination. Animals have no intellect and angels have no bodily passions, so neither of them is open to such a choice.

The one restrictive commandment given to man, by granting him his freedom and imposing on him the need to choose, serves to define for him this aspect of his humanity. The reader of the Bible is given information not transmitted directly to Adam. We are told that when God planted the garden in Eden, He "caused to grow every tree that was pleasing to the sight and good for food."[29] This description probably has two purposes. It informs readers over all the subsequent centuries that to our ordinary, post-Eden human sensitivities the trees of the garden would be attractive and tempting. In the immediate context of the story, it tells us that Adam will be tested by this attractiveness. As a living being, he must have nourishment, so the fruit of the garden must at least arouse his minimal interest. The question is whether it will do more than that, whether he will be tempted to give priority to the physically attractive over the attractions of the life of the intellect. This option is made available to him as a result of God's commandment. He is given freedom to eat of all trees but one. This is the most minimal restriction possible, and one that certainly imposes no special hardship. To resist the restriction is to violate God's commandment, and this in turn is to bankrupt the intellect. The commandment has defined for Adam his only fixed duty. He has been able to grasp it as a commandment, and he knows its source. He also understands that, as God's commandment, it is to be obeyed. What now confronts Adam and Eve is the need to make a choice; they are forced to exercise their freedom and to decide in the process what kind of beings they want to be.

At this point the key event occurs, and Maimonides has left it in his account in such a way as to impose on his readers a serious demand to fill in the lacunae. This is again a case where what he does *not* choose to tell us is critical for an understanding of what he does tell us. He stresses the statement made in connection with eating the forbidden fruit: "And ye shall be like Elohim, knowing good and evil." This is the statement that the objector misconstrued. Nowhere does Maimonides remind us of the critical point that this statement is made by the serpent whose purpose is to tempt Eve into sin.

---

statement: "Yet we do know beyond doubt that a human being's activities are in his own hands and the Almighty neither draws him on, nor decrees that he should act thus or not act thus. It is not religious tradition alone by which this is known. It is also supported by clear proofs furnished by science" (Hyamson translation).

29. Gen. 2:9.

The objector may have overlooked this fact and paid the price of his profound misunderstanding. The competent reader, however, must keep it in mind and explore its significance. Such a reader will remember at once that the Talmud identifies the serpent with Satan, which is the evil inclination in man, the *yetzer ha-ra*ʿ, which is in turn the angel of death.[30] It is clear then that, contrary to the objector's supposition, this statement should not be construed as an assurance of great reward. Correctly understood, it conveys the dire threat that is present each time man yields to his own evil inclination. The serpent/evil inclination wants to pull man away from his pristine state, from the ideal life of the intellect to a life of the passions and imagination. He promises that in violating God's commandment, man will become like Elohim, which we now understand to mean like those rulers who set standards of behavior by way of convention in response to the drives of human passion and the distractions of the imagination. This is a projection into the future, because there is not yet any example of such a ruler before them. The serpent is offering them an alternative to the godlike life they now have, and they have to decide which direction they want to choose. God said that if they eat from the tree they will die. Eve remembers this point and cites it. The serpent assures her that they will not die but will become, like Elohim, involved in the passional life. From the divine perspective this is, of course, a kind of death. It is the killing of the dominance of man's rational soul and supplanting it with the appetitive animal soul. It is death in the sense that Adam will no longer be the paradigm of the fully realized man, but will have become instead a denizen of the animal kingdom, always having to decide whether to struggle for the realization of his humanity. The tempting perspective of the serpent is that this is really an affirmation of life, rather than a mode of death. The life of pure intellectual contemplation seems dull and uninteresting to those who follow the way of passion. For them, the life of the intellect is a kind of living death, and true life is the satisfaction of bodily desires.[31]

It is important to note that the temptation is directed initially to Eve, rather than to Adam. Although Maimonides makes it seem that some neutral

---

30. See *Baba Batra*, 16a.

31. One is reminded of the scene in Plato's *Phaedo* in which Socrates has explained that the philosopher is a person who is always seeking death. He is seeking the final separation of the soul from the body so that he can live the life of pure intellectual contemplation without the distractions of bodily sensations, passions, and needs. At this point his young friend Simmias observes with good-natured humor that in the view of most people philosophers are already half-dead. In rejecting all concerns of the body while concentrating their whole effort on the life of the mind, they are perceived by ordinary men as being as good as dead. See Plato, *Phaedo*, 64 A–C.

voice says the words, "that the tree was good for food and that it was a delight to the eyes," he expects us to remember that it is specifically said of Eve that she perceived the tree this way. Moreover, he does not quote the last clause in the verse, which says that, in addition to seeing that the tree was good for food and a delight to the eyes, she also saw that "the tree was desirable as a source of wisdom." It is imperative, however, that we be aware of this clause, and that we know how to interpret it correctly based on what Maimonides teaches us in this chapter. To Eve it now appears that the true way of wisdom is to satisfy the passions. The forbidden tree offers her that opportunity, and it is therefore perceived by her as opening up a new world with a far more attractive life and a superior set of values. From her perspective, it is "a source of wisdom." What escapes her is that this is the destructive wisdom of the serpent, the wisdom of Satan who is the evil inclination, the false wisdom that offers death rather than life.

We need to see how Maimonides understands the significance of the fact that it is Eve, rather than Adam, who initially yields to the temptation. Later in the *Guide* it becomes clear that, according to Maimonides, the female is used figuratively to represent matter, in contrast with form, which is symbolized by the male.[32] After explaining the literal use of the terms *man* and *woman* (*'ish, 'ishah*), he observes that "the term 'woman' was used figuratively to designate any object apt for, and fashioned with a view to being in, conjunction with some other object" (I, 6, p. 31). This refers to matter whose nature is that it has no form of its own and is always open to being formed by its union with another object. In the discussion in I, 17 he makes clear that privation is always "conjoined with matter." This means that matter suffers from a lack, an absence of definitive qualities that invites other forces (i.e., forms) to enter and give it its particular character. To complete the picture, it should be noted that, from the time of her creation until the end of the Eden episode, the woman has no proper name, but is referred to regularly by all as *'ishah*, "woman." Only when they are about to be expelled from Eden is she given her proper name, Eve. Maimonides is surely aware of this and is calling to our attention that it is the woman, symbolizing matter, that is most subject to temptation. It is she who suffers privation and seeks to fill in what is missing.

We already know that man's form, his essential property, is his intellect. The temptation of Eve is then the temptation of matter that lusts after other forms. The Eden story expresses figuratively the existential situation of man as a being who is always at risk of becoming less than the perfected

32. "Thus Plato and his predecessors designated Matter as the female and Form as the male" (*Guide*, I, 17, p. 43).

intelligence that he might be. He is driven to choose between achieving the highest possible actualization of his potential as an intellect or permitting his matter to be formed, instead, by the animal passions. In the *Mishneh Torah* Maimonides sets forth his account of the world of the angels (i.e., the separate intelligences). There are ten degrees, from the highest level nearest to God to the lowest level, which is that with which man makes conjunction. "To the tenth degree, belongs the form of those termed *'Ishim*. They are the angels that commune with the prophets and appear to them in the prophetic vision. They are called *'Ishim* [men], because their rank approximates to that of the intelligence of human beings."[33] This is the referent of the verse from Psalms that he quotes: "Thou has made him but little lower than Elohim." Man, at his best, is almost one with the angels (which is the meaning of *Elohim* in this verse). He has been given the capacity to elevate himself to a life of the mind so pure that he nearly transcends his bodily limitations and transfers himself to the world of the separate intelligences. Adam and Eve chose to give up that exalted state of being in favor of a life governed by desire, passion, imagination.

Once they changed their status, they changed the order of their lives in two regards. First, they shifted from a life concerned exclusively with the contemplation of necessary truths to a life preoccupied primarily with matters of opinion, a life whose intellectual concern is with conventions, with teachings "generally accepted as known." The life of the pure intellect has as its object what reason apprehends to be necessarily the case. This is the realm of the true and the false, the realm of knowledge. The punishment for their sin was not an arbitrary penalty imposed upon them by God for disobeying Him. It was rather the inevitable consequence of their choice. They chose to transport themselves from that heavenly realm, symbolized by the Garden of Eden, in which they lived a near angelic existence, to the world of man as we have known it ever since. As Maimonides puts it:

> Accordingly when man was in his most perfect and excellent state, in accordance with his inborn disposition and possessed of his intellectual cognitions—because of which it is said of him: Thou hast made him but little lower than Elohim—he had no faculty that was engaged in any way in the consideration of generally accepted things, and he did not apprehend them. So among these generally accepted things even that which is most manifestly bad, namely, uncovering the genitals, was not bad according to him, and he did not apprehend that it was bad. However, when he disobeyed and in-

33. *H. Yesodei ha-Torah*, II, 7 (Hyamson translation).

clined toward his desires of the imagination[34] and the pleasures of his corporeal senses—inasmuch as it is said: that the tree was good for food and that it was a delight to the eyes—he was punished by being deprived of that intellectual apprehension. He therefore disobeyed the commandment that was imposed upon him on account of his intellect and, becoming endowed with the faculty of apprehending generally accepted things, he became absorbed in judging things to be bad or fine. Then he knew how great his loss was, what he had been deprived of, and upon what a state he had entered.

The first loss then is clearly abandonment of the pure life of the intellect and absorption in conventions, modes of behavior that are generally accepted. It is the shift from a life of metaphysical speculation to a life of concern with the ethical. The realm of ethics is not a realm of true knowledge. It is not concerned with truth and falsehood, but only with generally held opinions.

This leads us to understand Adam's second loss, which follows from the first. Once he has left the realm of the intellect, he has made himself subject to all the drives of the passions which are normal for man in his new state. These drives need to be controlled and directed if there is to be an orderly society. In his pristine state Adam had no concern for, and no involvement with, the ethical. He lived on a higher plane in which, as Maimonides says, even the most extreme moral improprieties (when things are viewed from a conventional standpoint) were irrelevant to him. If one's life is lived in the realm of the intellect, then even total nakedness and the exposure of the private parts are of no moment. Such matters concern us only when they affect us. Only when nakedness generates lust does it need to be controlled. The same applies to all that is conventionally thought to demand moral rules for control of human behavior. We do not regulate property, for example, until there is a desire for possession, a lust for ownership, that causes individuals to protect their own against invasion by others.

In Eden there was no such problem. All man's wants and needs were provided for without having to claim private ownership. "Of every tree of the garden you are free to eat." There is no concept of private property, of competition for goods, of protecting what is mine. For one who lives in the realm of the intellect, none of this is in any way relevant. "The earth is the Lord's and all that it holds, the world and all its inhabitants."[35] He provides

---

34. It should be noted that elsewhere Maimonides identifies the imagination with the *yetzer ha-ra'*, the evil impulse. See *Guide*, II, 12, p. 280.

35. Ps. 24:1.

for all Adam's needs, and man is free, if he chooses, to live a life devoted to learning, thought, and contemplation.

Once man has left this state, however, it becomes necessary to regulate human behavior in all these areas. As the point is expressed in *Pirke 'Avot,* if it were not for the control exercised by governments, men would swallow each other alive.[36] When the life of man is controlled by his passions and imagination, then it is essential that there be a strong power regulating all human activity. We need rules of behavior to prevent men from destroying each other and themselves. These are the rules that constitute conventional morality.

Contrary to the claims of the objector, and also of many important philosophers, Maimonides holds that reason itself provides no grounds for ethical principles. Reason tells us nothing about good and bad. Where then shall we discover such principles? As we saw earlier, Maimonides holds that moral rules are at best principles generally held to be correct. They are the conventions of individual societies which in the course of social history turn into fixed laws. Such laws are, in Maimonides' view, nothing more than well-established and officially authorized conventions. There is about them an element of the arbitrary, an element of individual taste that never approaches the certainty of rational principles.

In the chapter under discussion, Maimonides does not develop further his views on the epistemological status of the principles of ethics, because this is not relevant to his argument. He only wants to respond to the objection that was raised, and to show that acquiring a concern with the realm of moral judgment is not an advancement for man but a tragic mark of deterioration. Yet he does, of course, know perfectly well how threatening it is to the order of society if we have nothing more than convention on which to base our distinctions of good and bad. Whatever the condition of man in prehistory, we no longer live in that idyllic state. As soon as man leaves the Garden of Eden, he is confronted with the first instance of homicide. Soon the catalogue of human crimes expands and grows to catastrophic proportions. If moral distinctions are no more than arbitrary conventions, on what basis can we judge any action to be wrong? The answer is that the generally accepted rules usually provide the elementary protection needed by all human beings in order to survive. Nevertheless, it surely is the case that once these conventions are questioned we can offer no rational defense of them. We can only appeal to such passions as self-interest or to the threat of punishment. In Maimonides' view there is only one law that is not arbitrary or conventional, and that is the Law of the Torah, which is the Law of God. That Law, as we

36. *Pirke 'Avot,* 3:2.

saw earlier, is concerned not only with the welfare of the body but, above all, with the welfare of the soul. The Almighty, in his grace, has taught us, in His revealed Torah, how we should live our lives. Once man has left Eden and entered the realm of history, he needs to be guided toward living the best possible life.

One purpose of the divine Law is to create the best possible social order so as to protect men from themselves and each other, to assure justice, and to prevent violence. This purpose is, however, only instrumental to a higher purpose: to make it possible for all to be so secure, and to live lives so well ordered, that they can turn their attention away from the concerns of this world of desire and passion and devote themselves to the life of the intellect. The aim is, in effect, to return mankind as closely as possible to the ideal state of the original Adam. This is how Maimonides conceives the messianic age, the final redemption of man in history. It is an Eden-like time in which all our needs will be provided for, all our passions will be stilled, and even the animals will no longer be driven by passion or desire. In such a state human beings will again devote all their energy and interest to the highest level of pure intellectual contemplation.[37]

He sets forth this same ideal in the last chapters of the *Guide*. Even before the messianic age, each man should aim at transcending all earthly concerns so that he can devote himself exclusively to the life of the intellect at its highest and most perfect level.[38] With this the objector has been fully answered, and his objection has been refuted.

More important than the refutation of the objector is the doctrine that has been set forth by Maimonides. He has provided us with a clearly formulated axiology, a system of values in which the supreme end of man is the most complete life of the intellect that it is possible to achieve. Maimonides has shown us that since moral rules are noncognitive, they cannot be true or false and therefore cannot be the concern of the intellect. If all ethical distinctions are purely conventional, then it is a matter of special importance that we have the divine ethical teaching that alone can save us from the arbitrariness of social convention and positive law. Adam's fall consisted in his deterioration from a being located in the realm of reason to one located in the realm of the passions.

This change of direction in the life of Adam and Eve is the last major point that Maimonides takes up in this chapter. He deals with the verse that

37. See the last paragraphs of the *Mishneh Torah*.

38. This is the main thrust of the last four chapters of the *Guide*. We have already remarked (note 17) that there is a well-known problem concerning the very end of the last chapter, which seems to move the ideal back from the intellectual to the moral realm.

says that after their sin, "The eyes of them both were opened, and they knew that they were naked." He stresses that we are told that they *knew* that they were naked, not that they *saw* that they were naked. "For what was seen previously was exactly that which was seen afterwards. There had been no membrane over the eye that was now removed, but rather he entered upon another state in which he considered as bad things that he had not seen in that light before." He supports his interpretation by a brief study of the term *pakoaḥ* to show that it is used regularly to refer not to physical sight, but rather "to uncovering mental vision." His reading of Scripture serves to justify completely his understanding of the Eden episode.

The final step in the argument of this chapter is to show that the correctness of the reading that Maimonides has offered us is clearly evident from later passages in the Bible and from the way these passages are understood in the rabbinic literature. The first passage is a verse from Job. "He [Adam] changes his face and Thou sendest him forth."[39] The commentators are aware, as every reader should be, that behind the reading of this verse, which Maimonides gives us, lies a readily accessible Midrash. There the verse from Job is used as a proof-text for the assertion that God had so endowed Adam that he could have remained permanently in his original state, but he chose to turn away from God and follow the direction set by the serpent.[40] As it is summarized here in Maimonides' account:

> For *panim* [face] is a term deriving from the verb *panoh* [to turn], since man turns his face toward the thing he wishes to take as his objective. The verse states accordingly that when man changed the direction toward which he tended and took as his objective the very thing a previous commandment had bidden him not to aim at, he was driven out of the Garden of Eden. This was the punishment corresponding to his disobedience; it was measure for measure.

Thus we find in a verse from the book of Job and in the midrashic understanding of that verse, a verification of Maimonides' interpretation of the Eden episode. This conception of the fall of Adam is now summarized by Maimonides as occurring at two levels. First, he would no longer enjoy the physical comforts that were his in the Garden of Eden. In place of the choicest of foods, which was Adam's normal diet in Paradise, he is now condemned to eat a diet of coarse and tasteless foods. In place of having

39. Readers should note that this verse is from Job 14:20, and that the first word of that chapter, to which all the rest refers, is "Adam."

40. See *Genesis Rabbah*, XVI, 1; XXI, 4.

delicacies available at all times with no effort or labor on his part, he is now condemned to work hard in order to acquire his bare subsistence. It must now all be earned by the sweat of his brow.

The second and more important dimension of Adam's fall, as we know from our whole preceding discussion, is the fall from the world of the intellect to that of the passions. This is also verified by Maimonides through a later scriptural verse which he introduces in a cryptic way in the next to last sentence of the chapter. Having cited a variety of biblical verses to support the picture of Adam's fall as physical degradation, he adds, "And it also says in explanation of this story: 'Adam, unable to dwell in dignity, is like the beasts that speak not.'" Clearly, it is his intention that we see in this verse from Psalm 49 a statement that Adam fell from the high dignity of the life of the intellect to the low estate of the beasts who lack any powers of reason. This is why Pines translates the last phrase of the verse as he does, although most translations read "is like the beasts that perish."

The translation, "that speak not," is also given by Rashi in his commentary to Psalms, although this was certainly not Maimonides' source. However, the translation can be justified linguistically.[41] In his Arabic text, Maimonides quotes the verse in Hebrew, so we have no incontrovertible evidence of how he read it. Yet we can infer that Pines is correct in rendering it this way, since it is the best way of drawing the essential distinction between men and animals. The latter "speak not," which is to say that they do not have the *logos,* the word that reflects the power of reason. Read this way, the verse sustains the view that Adam's fall was a plunge from the life of reason to the life of the irrational animal passions.

We should take for granted that Maimonides also expected his qualified readers to recall at once the last verse of this same psalm, a verse differing from our verse primarily in one word that is crucial and illuminating. Instead of saying that Adam is unable to *dwell* in dignity, it says that Adam does not *understand* his dignity. This verse should be read as an interpretation of the earlier verse. It tells us that Adam's fall from his state of special dignity is directly connected with a failure of intellect. He chose to exchange the life of the intellect for the animal life of the passions.

If we have any doubt that this is how Maimonides wants us to read these verses, we should consider the only other time in the *Guide* that he cites this verse from Psalms. In his discussion of divine providence, Maimonides associates the degree of providential protection of each person with the degree

---

41. In his commentary to Isa. 6:5, where the term *nidmeti* occurs, Kimhi reports that his father construed it to mean *nishtatakti,* "I have been silenced," i.e., "I have been deprived of the power of speech."

of his or her intellectual development. The lowest of all are those who have failed to attain even a minimally satisfactory degree of intellectual development. Of such people Maimonides makes the startling statement: "As for the ignorant and disobedient, their state is despicable proportionately to their lack of this [divine intellectual] overflow, and they have been relegated to the rank of the individuals of all the other species of animals: 'He is like the beasts that speak not.' For this reason it is a light thing to kill them, and has even been enjoined because of its utility" (III, 18, p. 475). Anyone who does not attain intellectual development is no different in essence from an animal. Without reason functioning within, such a person is simply a beast in the physical form of a human being. Harsh as it sounds to our ears, Maimonides holds that the life of such a person has little more worth than the life of an animal, and that it is permissible, even required, to kill such a being when it serves a useful purpose, just as it is permissible to kill an animal for a useful purpose. We cannot pursue here the grounds and the implications of this judgment. What matters in the context of our discussion is the fact that Maimonides confirms here our understanding of how he reads the verses from Psalms. In his view they are an affirmation that fallen man is no longer the dignified being who lives the life of the mind, but the degraded animal-like being who is a child of imagination and passion.

Before closing our discussion of this chapter of the *Guide*, we need to consider one more verse that seems germane to our subject but which Maimonides ignores. Just before Adam and Eve are driven from the Garden of Eden, we are told, "And the Lord God said, 'Now that the man has become like one of us, knowing good and bad, what if he should stretch out his hand and take also from the tree of life and eat, and live forever.' "[42] Maimonides does not cite this verse or explicate it anywhere in the *Guide*, although as we shall see he does take it up in some other works. This verse seems germane to a discussion of the issues central to *Guide*, I, 2, and we need to investigate both why it is omitted and how Maimonides understands it. The verse poses two major problems for us. First, it asserts that man has become godlike in that he now knows good and bad. This seems to run counter to what we have already learned about Maimonides' view that good and bad are noncognitive and are, therefore, not properly objects of the intellect. At first glance it seems to support the objections of the questioner whom Maimonides has sought to refute. What shall we make then of the explicit statement in this verse? Second, what does it mean to say that if man eats of the tree of life he will live forever? In God's original commandment to Adam He did not prohibit him from eating of the tree of life, only of the tree of knowledge of good

42. Gen. 3:22.

and bad. Why does He now resist the idea that Adam might eat of this tree, which had all along been permitted to him, and thereby gain eternal life? What kind of eternal life is meant? Does it mean that Adam would become "like one of us," a supernal being no longer bound by his physical limitations and his finite nature? Whatever the answers to these questions, this verse certainly seems to pose serious problems for the interpretation of the Eden episode Maimonides has presented.

These problems, in my opinion, cause him to omit the verse from the discussion at the beginning of the *Guide*. For unsophisticated readers the verse might present insuperable obstacles; they do not yet have the knowledge and level of understanding required to interpret this verse correctly and to integrate it with the rest of the account of the Garden of Eden. It is highly unlikely that such readers will introduce the verse into the discussion on their own and raise the difficult questions that it generates. For that reason it is best left in silence until a time when readers have developed sufficiently to raise the appropriate questions on their own. For sophisticated readers, the answer to the problem is available in the two places in his other writings where Maimonides cites and interprets this verse. Such readers will be able to find their own way and will presumably study the relevant passages so as to understand Maimonides' teaching. The silence about this verse in the *Guide* is a typical Maimonidean challenge to his readers' skill and competence.

The verse is cited by Maimonides in his Mishnah commentary, and again much later in the *Mishneh Torah*.[43] The approach is essentially the same in both contexts. The later version reads as follows:

> Free will is bestowed on every human being. If one desires to turn toward the good way and be righteous, he has the power to do so. If one wishes to turn towards the evil way and be wicked, he is at liberty to do so. And thus it is written in the Torah, "Now that man has become like one of us, knowing good and bad" (Gen. 3:22), which means that the human species had become unique in the world—

---

43. See *The Eight Chapters of Maimonides on Ethics,* trans. and ed. Joseph I. Gorfinkle (New York, 1912; rpt. 1966), 92; and *H. Teshuvah,* 5:1. For an extended discussion of this verse in the context of Maimonides' thought, see the Hebrew article by Warren Zev Harvey, "Maimonides on Genesis 3:22," *Da'at,* no. 12 (Winter, 1984), 15–21. Among the issues Harvey raises in this article is the problem of how to interpret the Hebrew word *pen,* which is normally translated as "lest" and seems always to carry a negative connotation. The New Jewish Publication Society translation, which I have used, overcomes this problem. Harry Orlinsky, in his *Notes on the New Translation of the Torah* (Philadelphia, 1969), 65–66, shows that on purely linguistic grounds his translation is correct, and that *pen* need not necessarily have a negative connotation.

there being no other species like it in the following respect, namely, that man, of himself and by the exercise of his own intelligence and thinking, knows what is good and what is bad, and there is none that can prevent him from doing that which is good or that which is bad. Since this is the case, "What if he should stretch out his hand, etc."[44]

It is clear that we need to determine the correct meaning of this passage and to decide if it is consistent or inconsistent with the doctrine set forth in *Guide,* I, 2.

On the issue of free will there is obviously no problem. We saw that this doctrine is implicit in the fact that man is commanded by God, and that he is free and able to violate the commandment as Eve and Adam in fact chose to do. What does generate a problem is the statement that construes Genesis 3:22 to mean that man, through his own intellectual powers, is capable of knowing the good and the bad. This seems to run directly counter to the doctrine that moral principles are noncognitive. A closer reading of Maimonides' teaching on this subject, however, will resolve the problem. The great error is to construe the terms *good* and *bad* as used here in a moral sense. In his comments on the creation story, Maimonides states explicitly that the repeated statement that God saw that His work was good has no moral implications whatsoever. This should be apparent with only a little reflection. What possible moral sense could there be to the statement that God found the vegetation good, or that He found the birds and the crawling creatures good? It is immediately evident that some other sense of the term *good* is intended here. Maimonides explains these passages to mean that "He only says that He brought every part of the world into existence and that its existence conformed to its purpose. This is the meaning of this saying: And God saw that it was good [*tov*]. . . . And good [*tov*] is an expression applied by us to what conforms to our purpose" (*Guide,* III, 13, p. 453). Elsewhere, also in connection with the creation episode, he says that "the meaning of the words, 'that it was good,' is that the thing in question is of externally visible and manifest utility for the existence and permanence of that which exists" (II, 30, p. 354). The good is understood here as the useful, that which is effective in achieving some specified purpose.

This is what Maimonides is saying about the state of man as depicted in Genesis 3:22. Man is not, and in his present state cannot be, identical in nature with the supernal beings. He is identified by God as "*like* one of us," but not simply *as* "one of us." He is like the supernal beings in that he has

---

44. *H. Teshuvah,* 5:1. I have largely followed the Hyamson translation with some minor adjustments, including rendering the biblical verse according to the NJPS translation.

intelligence, and one of the marks of intelligent choice and behavior is knowing how to select the means required to realize some particular goal. The divine wisdom manifests itself in the fact that all Creation is perceived as so ordered as to actualize its proper purpose. In the case of all other beings, however, their actions are totally determined by nature; hence, there is no element of intelligence in what they do. Man is a free being, capable of making genuine choices among the options open to him. He is endowed with the capacity to choose the appropriate means to serve his ends, and this is the evidence of his practical intelligence. In this respect, he is represented as being like the supernal beings. The point is not at all that moral good and evil are themselves known immediately by reason, but only that an intelligent man can choose instrumental goods that will serve his ends.

The problem, of course, is that we have no knowledge of ends that are intrinsically good, no knowledge of which ends we should try to realize other than whatever happens to strike us as pleasing. This is precisely why we need the teachings of the Torah to save us from total moral relativism. The Torah specifies both which ends are desirable in the eyes of God and are, therefore, no longer arbitrary, and which means (i.e., the divine commandments) are required to realize those ends. This is Maimonides' point when he observes that "since it is an essential characteristic of the very being of man that he should choose good or bad acts as he pleases, it becomes necessary to teach him the ways of the truly good, and to command him and caution him, to punish and reward him."[45] Because in the world of practice the human intellect can only select means in the light of whatever ends one seeks, it is essential for the Torah to instruct us with regard both to the ends that are the true fulfillment of man and of human society, and to the means requisite for their realization.

The tree of knowledge from which man ate deprived him of the privilege of living in the world of pure intellect, which had been his state up to that point. Man is now dependent either on human law and convention, on the one hand, or else on divine commandment, on the other, to set forth a value system that can form his life. In the former case the values are arbitrary; in the latter case they become objective and mandatory because of their divine origin. We saw earlier that the Torah, as Maimonides understands it, is concerned with the welfare of the soul, and that the welfare of the body is subservient to that higher end. The soul fulfills itself when it turns away from the world of human practice to the world in which it contemplates the highest and most perfect being.

45. *The Eight Chapters*, ed. Gorfinkle, Hebrew, 47. I have deviated here from the Gorfinkle translation in the interests of greater precision.

This was the world in which Adam found himself originally. Like all other created things, he was a perfect instance of his species at the time of his creation and, therefore, above the need to make the choices and decisions inescapable for any human being subject to the drives of the imagination and the passions. When he sinned against God and gave up thereby his uniquely privileged status, man was thrust into the world in which imagination and passion are factors with which he must constantly contend. From that point on man was condemned to struggle to recover his pristine ideal state. Yet man alone among all creatures can know the possibility of that pure life of the intellect that is the realization of the human ideal: the realization of the image of God in man. Almost all the philosophical commentators, certainly Maimonides among them, understand the "tree of life" to refer to the apprehension of those highest truths, an apprehension that alone confers immortality on man. In this light we can understand the verse to mean that since man had the intelligence to discern which means would bring him to the ends he sought, it was now possible, when Adam was still so near in time and place to the state of intellectual purity, that he might have sought to return to his original condition quickly and painlessly. But he had forfeited that option, so he had to be banished from the garden, thrust into the world of ordinary experience, and left to struggle throughout his lifetime to return to his original ideal state. That state is no longer a free gift of God automatically realized in man by virtue of his humanity. It is the goal that human beings can apprehend only through intense effort. Adam who is banished from Eden—that is, man who has entered into the order of history—must engage in an ongoing struggle to overcome all those obstacles that prevent him from knowing and realizing his proper end with ease. Maimonides' reading of Genesis 3:22 thus turns out to be completely consistent with everything that he says in I, 2 of the *Guide*. He leaves it to his readers, however, to discover the problem and solve it by reference to his earlier works and whatever else in the *Guide* turns out to be helpful.

The final element in our text, the last sentence in *Guide,* I, 2, closes with a laudation of the Almighty. "Praise be to the Master of the will whose aims and wisdom cannot be apprehended."[46] Note that God is identified here as the "Master of the will." This is a way of telling us at the outset that we cannot hope to penetrate completely the secrets of the universe. In some way they stem from God's will, which is inscrutable. Later in the *Guide*

---

46. It should be noted that a number of chapters of the *Guide* close with a prayer, and there are also some chapters that contain a prayer in the body of the text. It would be most important to study all of these prayers to see what they can teach us about Maimonides' method. It would also be extremely valuable to work out clearly not only when and where these prayers occur, but why

Maimonides makes the point more than once that the only answer to the question of why things are as they are rather than some other way is that God willed it so. This is only a way of saying that we cannot give a rational account of such matters, or demonstrate their rational necessity, but can only point to the facts of divine creation and divine choice. We are being reminded in this praise of God that we cannot answer fully the question of why Adam was made as he was while the animals were made as they were. We can only say that God willed it so.

We must also take note of the last part of the sentence. This Master of the will is one "whose aims and wisdom cannot be apprehended." There are several important points here. First, we cannot grasp His aims, that is, we do not understand and cannot give a satisfactory account of God's purposes in making things as they are. Second, we do, nevertheless, recognize that these purposes are neither arbitrary nor capricious. They are always derived from God's wisdom. In fact, as readers of the *Guide* will learn later in the book, His will and His wisdom are one but, whether considered under the rubric of will or under the rubric of wisdom, this divinely created reality transcends all human understanding. This is the third point in the hymn of praise, namely, that God's ways "cannot be apprehended." After all that has been said in the first two chapters of the *Guide* about the way in which man resembles God, after all that has been said in praise of the human intellect, even to its being capable of conjunction with the divine intellect, it is, nevertheless, the case that no human being can hope to penetrate the inner secrets of the divinely created world order. Much as we learn and much as we know, even more is left obscure and unknowable. Let science and philosophy advance as far as they possibly can and should. In the end it will turn out that all that we grasp in our understanding is never sufficient to explain the divine will and wisdom which underlie the universe.

With this we have come to the end of our commentary on chapters 1 and 2 of Part I. We have seen how these chapters establish the foundation for the Maimonidean value system which, according to his teaching, stands at the center of Judaism. We have also seen what would go into the enormously challenging task of producing a chapter by chapter, paragraph by paragraph commentary on the *Guide of the Perplexed*.

---

they occur where they do, what form they take, and what purpose they serve. This is more than we can undertake here. We shall simply try to understand this prayer in the context of the chapter which it concludes.

8

Maimonides' Views on the Relations of Law and Morality

One of the central issues in Maimonides' moral philosophy that still requires clarification is the problem of the relationship between law and morality. Maimonides is uniquely important in the history of Jewish legal thought. He, more than any other figure, took the protean materials of the Talmud and the other primary sources and gave them the form and structure that to this day provide the framework for serious analyses of Jewish law. Even those who reject many of Maimonides' specific legal decisions cannot afford to neglect his formulations and reformulations of the talmudic materials. His modes of categorization, organization, and classification are fundamental to all later studies in Jewish law. We still employ the conceptual structures that he first developed. We can hardly conceive the discipline we call Jewish legal thought without the foundations laid by this greatest of all post-talmudic Jewish thinkers. His views concerning the relationship between law and morality are therefore of the highest importance.

Before we turn to an examination of Maimonides' views on this subject, however, we need to consider the topic in a larger context. The problem is critical for an understanding of any developed legal system, and is by no means peculiar to Jewish law or to the thought of Maimonides. It has a long history, and it occupies a central place in contemporary studies in the philosophy of law.[1]

The extreme position of absolute legal positivism treats law and morality as totally separate, so that the legality of a law is in no way affected by the fact that it is judged to be immoral. Hart cites three great legal philosophers—Austin, Gray, and Kelsen, respectively—on this subject: "The existence of law is one thing; its merit or demerit another." "The law of a state is not an ideal but something which actually exists . . . it is not that which ought to be, but that which is." "Legal norms may have any kind of

---

1. An excellent comprehensive discussion of the issues can be found in H. L. A. Hart, *The Concept of Law* (Oxford, 1961), chap. 8, "Justice and Morality," and chap. 9, "Laws and Morals."

content."[2] This means that the law is seen as a self-contained system whose legitimacy depends only on the authority and legitimacy of the legislator. It is not subject to external criticism on moral or any other nonlegal grounds. From this point of view, laws may be imprudent, inexpedient, or even immoral without this having any effect on their legal status.

In contrast to this doctrine of legal positivism is the position of Thomas Aquinas that we discussed earlier.[3] From his natural law perspective, he argues that in any positive legal system no law is genuinely law unless it accords with the natural law, that is, with the canons of the moral law. "The force of a law depends on the extent of its justice. Now in human affairs a thing is said to be just from being right, according to the rule of reason. But the first rule of reason is the law of nature. . . . Consequently, every human law has just so much of the nature of law as it is derived from the law of nature. But if in any point it departs from the law of nature, it is no longer law but a perversion of law."[4] Thus the legitimacy of any law is determined by whether it accords with the rules of morality, and a law that does not accord with these rules is not just a bad law—it is no law at all.

Opposed as these two positions are, they have one feature in common. Both start from the premise that the positive law is manmade. The legal positivists take the position that the law as law is purely the act of the legislator; it follows from this that there is no room within the legal system for moral criticism of the law. If moral criticism has any legitimate role, it is external to the legal system and does not affect the legal system internally. Moral opposition to a given law may serve to generate social pressure for bringing about a change in that law but, for the legal positivists, neither the original law nor its substitute are, *qua* law, concerned with or determined by moral issues. Aquinas and the natural law theorists who follow him also consider the positive law to be legislated by the sovereign human legal authority, but hold that it must depend for its legitimacy on its accord with the natural moral law. This latter is a necessary condition of its being a law at all.

Similar positions that developed within Islamic thought may appear to be more immediately relevant since Maimonides was well schooled in the Muslim thinkers. In an excellent summary study, George F. Hourani has provided us with a clear statement of the issues and the alternate positions.[5] In the early centuries of Islam two parties developed.

---

2. Hart, *Concept of Law,* 203.

3. See chapter 6.

4. *Summa Theologica,* I-II, Q. 95, a. 2

5. George F. Hourani, *Reason and Tradition in Islamic Ethics* (Cambridge, 1985).

The party of rational opinion (*ra'y*) held that in deciding questions of Islamic law and morals judges and lawyers might make their own rational judgments independently of scripture, in cases or aspects where scripture gives no guidance. The other party, more strictly traditional, held that legal judgments can be based *only* on scripture and Traditions, or derived from them in certain approved ways such as analogy (*qiyas*). . . . Shafi'i worked out in a very thorough way the theory of a positive law, based entirely on Islamic revelation and Traditions; and he states his primary principle in his maxim that justice is nothing but obedience to the revealed law (the *shari'a*).[6]

This second position is based on the conviction that only God can determine what is right and wrong and only He can set down rules for human behavior: "The main objection they raised against rationalist ethics was that independent human reason implies a limit on the power of God; for if man could judge what is right and wrong he could rule on what God could rightly prescribe for man, and this would be presumptuous and blasphemous."[7]

Hourani goes on to comment on the rationalist reaction, which held that divine commands do not by themselves determine the right. The rationalists argue that men are capable of knowing what is right and wrong through their own powers of natural reason and are able to arrive, through the use of reason, at correct moral judgments. This knowledge then serves as a criterion of the moral soundness of the law given by God. These rationalists hold that, otherwise, there is the danger that we would be subjected to patently immoral commandments, "such as that God could then make lying right for men if He wished to do so, simply by commanding men to tell lies. And then if He wished He could punish them for not lying—or again, if He wished for lying."[8] The opposing side countered with the claim that there is no knowledge of right and wrong apart from God's revelation, hence, whatever God asks of us is by definition right.

Maimonides undoubtedly learned something about this problem from the Islamic thinkers and from other moral and legal philosophers, but his position is not fully in accord with any of them. We shall attempt here to explicate Maimonides' position and to see whether it fits into some classical Jewish pattern. For this purpose, we must first understand how the relationship of law and morality is dealt with in the Bible and in the rabbinic system of law developed from the Bible, which Maimonides subsequently codified.

6. Ibid., 16.

7. Ibid., 17.

8. Ibid., 18.

According to biblical teaching, there is only one true legislator for the people of Israel, and that is God Himself. This internal biblical teaching is adopted by the rabbinic tradition and elaborated to include a wide body of legislation, all of which is understood to be divine in its ultimate origin. God gave the Israelites an elaborate set of detailed commandments contained, according to rabbinic tradition, in the two Torahs: the written and the oral. Furthermore, the Sages teach us that, under the rubric of the Noahide commandments, God also issued basic legislation to all the other peoples of the world.[9]

In the Bible we find that God issues some commands that seem to be an offense to our ideas of common morality and, even more, to the spirit of His own teachings. God requires Abraham to obey the instructions of his wife, Sarah, to banish Ishmael and Hagar, his son and concubine, from his home, and send them into the wilderness. Although Abraham's sense of right is offended, he does as he is told.[10] God instructs Abraham to offer up his son, Isaac, as a sacrifice on Mount Moriah. In this case Abraham does not even question the rightness of the commandment, although many generations of Bible readers have found this episode morally troubling. Yet Abraham, the man of faith, does not question, but simply hastens to do the Lord's bidding.

Later on, the Israelites are commanded that when they enter the land and conquer it, they must utterly destroy every vestige of the idolatrous cults that prevail in Canaan. There is to be no mercy.[11] They are also commanded to make war relentlessly on the inhabitants of the land and "not let a soul remain alive."[12] It is true that the biblical text explains and justifies these commands which require the conquering Israelites to destroy the peoples of Canaan and their cults. This is not simply a call for wanton destruction with no reason, but is represented as a necessary step in order for the Israelites to be able to begin their new life of true service to the one God. Nevertheless, for many modern readers these passages generate great discomfort, agony, and even revulsion, because they seem to be so contrary to what we usually understand by Jewish morality. Yet there is not a word of internal criticism in the Bible about these commands. The reason is clear. The Bible knows only God as the source of all notions of right and wrong. There is no definition of the good except His teaching and His will. Consequently, even when His

---

9. The question of the way the Jewish legal system relates to the status and authority of the positive law of non-Jewish nations and governments is not germane to our present discussion. This topic is separate from the question of the contents and status of the Noahide laws.

10. Gen. 21:9–14.

11. Exod. 34:11–16; Deut. 12:1–3.

12. Deut. 20:15–18; see also Deut. 7:1–5.

commands strain or offend our individual moral sensibilities, we have no choice finally but to affirm that what He requires of us is truly good and right. The Bible could not accommodate the idea that God is morally deficient, or that He makes demands of man that are morally wrong. Within the biblical framework, He alone teaches us what is virtuous; there is no standard other than that which He has given us. A God whose commandments are evil would not be truly God.

This certainty, that God alone is the author of the right and the good, makes it permissible to question Him in cases of seeming injustice but never to reject Him or His commandments. Men may stand against God in their search for enlightenment and in their own commitment to His principles of justice and mercy. This is what makes it possible for Abraham to object severely to the apparent injustice of the divine decision to destroy Sodom and Gomorrah. When he asks, "Will You sweep away the innocent along with the guilty?" and adds the rebuke, "Shall not the judge of all the earth deal justly?"[13] there is no element of blasphemy in his question, nor is he appealing to an independently known moral standard. His criticism of God is that He seems about to violate the very standards He Himself has set. It is as "judge of all the earth" that God has taught us the principles of justice and has demanded of us rigorous adherence to those principles. This is the point of Abraham's challenge—a challenge that is satisfied when God immediately agrees that justice will, of course, be done. If there are righteous men in Sodom, the city will be saved in their behalf or, at the very least, they themselves will be spared. The moral standard in this case is both given by God and observed by Him.

Even in the moments of their greatest bitterness and despair, the biblical prophets did not question that God alone is the source of our knowledge of right and wrong. They affirmed that He is truly righteous, although we sometimes find it difficult to understand the justice of His ways. Jeremiah makes his charges, asking with pathos, "Why does the way of the wicked prosper?" but he first states that he knows that ultimately God will be proved right.[14] Even Job, who comes closer than anyone to a direct denial of God's justice, is finally reconciled once he confronts the divine majesty. He still has no answers, but his faith in God as the source of right and as the practitioner of the right has been restored. "Indeed," he says, "I spoke without understanding of things beyond me, which I did not know."[15] He recognizes that without the divine moral standard, there is no standard at all. In all these

13. Gen. 18:23, 25.
14. Jer. 12:1.
15. Job 42:3.

biblical cases, there are not two separate spheres—law and morality—which have to be brought together in some intelligible relationship. There is only the sphere of God's teachings that sets forth the Law and in this process defines what is moral.

The rabbis regularly confront cases that seem to suggest the existence of an independent morality, and it is instructive to consider briefly two such instances to see how they fit them into the pattern. The biblical condemnation of Cain for killing his brother presents us with a problem. There is no evidence in the biblical text that Cain has ever been instructed that murder is wrong yet he is held responsible for the killing. Some modern students of the Bible assert that this proves that the Bible presupposes some kind of natural moral standard, known by the human intellect independently of direct divine commandments. This view is rejected in the rabbinic tradition. The rabbis addressed this problem by invoking the doctrine that the first six of the seven Noahide commandments had already been given to Adam, and that the rule against murder was included.[16] Cain should have known that it was forbidden to take his brother's life, not because he was expected to grasp this as part of the natural law, but because God had explicitly issued the prohibition against murder.

Another biblical case that can illuminate the rabbinic approach to our subject involves not only a seemingly independent morality, but even a supererogatory morality. When Abraham's servant went to seek a wife for Isaac, he set down criteria that would identify the woman worthy of joining his master's family. The mark of fitness would be that the young lady would offer to draw water from the well to give drink to the servant and to his camels. It is generally agreed, and the text certainly bears this out, that the servant was looking for a woman who was kind, gentle, warm-hearted, and ready to put herself to any trouble to serve the needs of a weary, wandering stranger and his animals. Yet in Abraham's instructions to the servant not one word was said about this matter. Abraham only stressed that the girl should not be chosen from among the local Canaanite women, but should be brought from his original home, "the land of my birth."[17] Where then did the servant get the standard of *hesed*, of gracious kindness to those in need, that he now demands of the prospective wife of Isaac? Was it through his independent grasp of this virtue? Did he have moral knowledge and moral criteria that were not the teachings of the law, but simply arrived at through his own rational or intuitive moral sense? Furthermore, it would appear that

16. *Sanhedrin*, 56ab.

17. For the entire episode see Gen. 24.

he demands a standard of behavior that is a higher level of moral action, a supererogatory standard which is aspired to but not commanded.

We may have here a case in which there is a clear suggestion that law and morality are not coterminous in the teachings of the Bible. Two points need to be made in response to this challenge. First, it would appear that there was no need for Abraham to instruct his trusted servant about this matter. His own behavior had long since provided the servant with a model of hospitality to the stranger. It is not by chance that the later tradition regularly identifies Abraham as associated above all with the virtue of *ḥesed*. His behavior, as reported in Scripture, is a model of this virtue. He is concerned always for the welfare of the stranger, does much to help the needy, and puts himself to great trouble and even much personal discomfort to provide warm hospitality to any traveler he can find. I suggest that Abraham finds it necessary to instruct his servant only on the one point about which he cannot be expected to know his master's mind, namely, that the wife of Isaac must not be a local woman but should come from his birthplace. On all other matters the servant, who is specifically identified as *zekan beito,* the senior servant of his household, can be fully expected to know and understand his master's values. Not only does Abraham fail to mention that Isaac's wife should be kind and hospitable, he says nothing about any of her other desirable qualities.[18]

Furthermore, the obligation of *ḥesed* is not considered by the rabbinic tradition to be a supererogatory duty at all. It is treated by the Sages as a specific commandment that is part of the Law. There are differing views concerning which one of the 613 commandments is the general category that includes *gemilut ḥasadim,* acts of kindness, but there is apparently universal agreement among the rabbinic authorities that it is commanded and is not just a matter of voluntarily choosing to do more than the Law demands.[19] Even for Abraham the general commandment of *gemilut ḥasadim* would be viewed as obligatory, not purely self-motivated. There is a rabbinic tradition that the Torah was taught to the patriarchs even before it was given at Sinai, and that Abraham fulfilled all the commandments to be given in the later

18. In fact, both the Talmud and the Midrash note that the servant may have acted rashly when he specified only the quality of *ḥesed* as the mark of the divinely chosen wife for Isaac. The kind and hospitable woman may also have had a great many ugly deficiencies. It was only through God's goodness that Rebekah turned out to be a woman endowed with all desirable qualities. See *Taʿanit,* 4a; *Gen. Rab.,* 60, 3.

19. Some authorities classify it under the heading of the duty to love our neighbor as ourselves. Others see it as part of the commandment of *imitatio dei.* In general, they consider hospitality to the stranger to be included in this general obligation. See *H. 'Avel,* 14:1.

revelation.[20] It would seem then that, at least from the perspective of the rabbinic tradition, the servant's criterion of virtue is part of the Law and not an independent rule of moral behavior.

With this background, we can now turn to the discussion of how Maimonides dealt with the problem of the relationship between law and morality in the hope that we may succeed in illuminating this fundamental aspect of his moral and legal philosophy. This investigation is important not only for what it may teach us about Maimonides, but also for what it has to teach us about the larger context of the philosophy of Jewish law.

We have already seen that in modern legal theory much effort is devoted to the task of exploring and clarifying the relationship between law and morality. It should be kept in mind that even those who follow the line of the Islamic rationalists and Thomas Aquinas, that all true law rests on morality, have not thereby solved their difficulties. Such a theory of natural law only pushes the problem back one step, because we are now forced to ask about the foundations of morality itself. If the law rests on morality, we must ask: Whose morality? What justifies any particular moral claim? On what theoretical grounds does morality rest? These are difficult questions that we tend to avoid because they threaten to shake the foundations of our systems of law and morality. Yet all serious legal thinkers and moral philosophers know that these questions cannot be ignored if we are to reflect honestly and soberly on the problem of law and its relationship to morality. Appeals to natural law do not by themselves solve the problem, because the point at issue is whether the theory of natural law is defensible.

In contemporary studies in Jewish legal theory, the problem of the relationship between law and morality has assumed an increasingly important role. The general question of the place and function of moral rules within Jewish law has been much debated and lies beyond the limits of the present discussion.[21] We restrict ourselves here to an examination of this issue with-

20. See, for example, the statement in the *Baraita* which concludes the last *Mishnah* in *Kiddushin*. See also *H. 'Avel*, 14:2, where Maimonides gives credit to Abraham, viewed here as a figure in the Jewish legal tradition, for formulating some of the specific rules of the obligation to extend hospitality to the stranger.

21. The following is a sampling of studies that have attracted attention in recent years: Saul J. Berman, *"Lifnim Mishurat Hadin,"* *Journal of Jewish Studies*, 26 (1975) and 28 (1977). Elliot N. Dorff, "The Interaction of Jewish Law with Morality," *Judaism*, 26, no. 4 (1977). Marvin Fox, "Maimonides and Aquinas on Natural Law," *Diné Yisrael*, 3 (1972); revised version in chapter 6 of this book. Marvin Fox, "Law and Ethics in Modern Jewish Philosophy," *Proceedings of the American Academy of Jewish Research*, 43 (1976). Marvin Fox, "The Doctrine of the Mean in Aristotle and Maimonides: A Comparative Study," in *Studies in Jewish Religious and Intellectual History*, ed. S. Stein and R. Loewe (Tuscaloosa, Ala., 1979); revised version in chapter 5 of this book. Lenn Evan Goodman, "Maimonides' Philosophy of Law,"

in the thought of Maimonides. We have seen that the distinction between the legal and the moral does not accurately reflect the way in which these matters are dealt with internally by the Jewish legal tradition. If we are to understand correctly a medieval Jewish thinker such as Maimonides, we must not make the mistake of imposing on him categories and distinctions that he did not recognize. As a halakhic authority, Maimonides was fully attuned to the nuances of the Jewish legal system, and he understood well that the category "morality" is not an independent element in that system. This is not to say that there are no moral elements or moral concerns in the halakhah. Quite the contrary. All students of Jewish law know how pervasive these moral concerns are. The key question is whether these concerns are an independent force in the law, a force resting on independent sources and sanctions, or whether they are simply part of the internal structure and methodology of the halakhic system itself.

Our discussion starts from the premise that, for Maimonides, there is no independent moral dimension in the halakhah. We established earlier that Maimonides does not recognize reason or natural law as providing the foundations of morality. We now need to address the question of whether he holds that the law itself, even if viewed as divinely given, is in any way dependent on extralegal moral principles.[22] Our discussion will examine the evidence provided by Maimonides' legal works, primarily the *Commentary on the Mishnah* and the *Mishneh Torah*. Throughout this study I shall use the term *morality* to refer to those principles and values commonly identified today as the ethical teachings of high Western culture and religion in general and of Judaism in particular.

Before turning to the substantive question, we must first consider a prior methodological issue, namely, whether we can learn anything about the

---

The Jewish Law Annual, 1 (1978). David Weiss Halivni, "Can a Religious Law Be Immoral?" in *Perspectives on Judaism*, ed. Arthur Chiel (New York, 1978). Norman Lamm and Aaron Kirschenbaum, "Freedom and Constraint in the Jewish Judicial Process," *Cardozo Law Review*, 1 (1979). Aharon Lichtenstein, "Does Jewish Tradition Recognize an Ethic Independent of Halakha?" in *Modern Jewish Ethics*, ed. M. Fox (Columbus, Oh., 1975). Nachum L. Rabinovitch, "Halakha and Other Systems of Ethics: Attitudes and Interactions," in *Modern Jewish Ethics*, ed. M. Fox (Columbus, Oh., 1975). Shmuel Shilo, "On One Aspect of Law and Morals in Jewish Law: *Lifnim Mishurat Hadin,*" *Israel Law Review*, 13 (1978). Moshe Silberg, *Ḥok u-Mussar be-Mishpat ha-'Ivri* (Jerusalem, 1952). Moshe Silberg, "Law and Morality," *Talmudic Law and the Modern State* (New York, 1973), chap. 6. Walter S. Wurzburger, "Law as the Basis of a Moral Society," *Tradition*, 19 (1981).

22. The paper by Aharon Lichtenstein, "Does Jewish Tradition Recognize an Ethic Independent of Halakha?" in *Modern Jewish Ethics*, ed. Fox, has generated considerable discussion around this topic. It merits close study for the way in which Lichtenstein formulates the issues.

independent thought of Maimonides from his works of commentary and codification. Is Maimonides simply collecting existing materials and organizing them without giving us any clue to his own views? Or do his commentaries and code reveal his own system of thought? It is generally agreed that Maimonides is far more than a mere compiler. Isadore Twersky points out that Maimonides' "task was one of collecting and systematizing authoritative sources and hallowed traditions, and this inevitably entailed a large measure of interpretation as well as selection."[23] Elsewhere, Twersky calls to our attention the fact that "when asked by the Lunel scholars about a provocative halakhic formulation . . . Maimonides confidently replied that originality of interpretation was a fact of scholarly life."[24] There are a few instances in which Maimonides explicitly identifies a legal decision as his own view in direct opposition to other authorities, but these represent only the tip of the iceberg as far as his originality goes. As commentator and codifier, he selects from the vast body of earlier sources, decides which of a number of opinions or rulings to adopt, frequently gives his own interpretation of the meaning or significance of a law, and shows the perceptive reader his own way of understanding the law and its values. Consequently, when the materials of code and commentary are used judiciously, they constitute indispensable sources for the original thought of Maimonides.

From a study of code and commentary we conclude that, in Maimonides' legal work, there is no consistent pattern of giving independent place or authority to what we call the moral dimension. In fact, it is difficult in Jewish law to find any distinction between law and morality. As David Halivni has pointed out, a biblical or rabbinic law cannot be viewed within the system as immoral.[25] To consider a law as both a divine commandment and immoral is a contradiction in terms. What God commands must be good; otherwise the commander is not God. For this reason we can find no clear distinction in the halakhah between moral commandments and ritual commandments. Both come from the same source, and both fully obligate those to whom they are addressed. This is why, even in our own time, classical teachers of the Law repeatedly make the point that when the Law offends our individual moral sense, we must set aside our own judgment in favor of the Law. Otherwise we would be rejecting the divine teaching and the divine

23. Isadore Twersky, *Introduction to the Code of Maimonides (Mishneh Torah)* (New Haven, 1980), 60–61.

24. Ibid., 56.

25. Halivni, "Can a Religous Law be Immoral?" in *Perspectives on Judaism,* ed. Chiel.

mandate, and giving priority to human judgment over that of God.[26] Maimonides makes a similar point when he argues that the Law is concerned with the general welfare and, consequently, it may at times be injurious to the interests of particular individuals. In an important passage he states:

> The Law was not given with a view to things that are rare. For in everything that it wishes to bring about, be it an opinion or a moral habit or a useful work, it is directed only toward the things that occur in the majority of cases and pays no attention to what happens rarely or to the damage occurring to the unique human being because of this way of determination and because of the legal character of the governance. For the Law is a divine thing; and it is your business to reflect on the natural things in which the general utility, which is included in them, nonetheless necessarily produces damages to individuals. . . . In view of this consideration also, you will not wonder at the fact that the purpose of the Law is not perfectly achieved in every individual and that, on the contrary, it necessarily follows that there should exist individuals whom this governance of the Law does not make perfect (*Guide*, III, 34, p. 534).

There are widely held contemporary notions concerning what is loosely called Jewish ethics, or the moral principles of Judaism. Spokesmen for these views tend to identify Jewish ethics with what they view as enlightened principles of liberal humanism. Each tends to assert with near dogmatic certainty that his or her particular account of Jewish ethics represents the true and authentic teachings of Judaism. It is then easy for them to dismiss as inauthentic, or obscurantist, whatever within Judaism does not fit their model. We recognize that these accounts of Jewish ethics have a certain appeal because they seem to make Judaism consistent with what we take to be the highest ideals of Western culture. If we accept these contemporary notions concerning Jewish moral principles as sound, then Maimonides' thought will be for us a maddening paradox. His code seems to move between the extremes of high moral sensitivity and a total disregard for ordinary principles of morality. He sets down some laws that many contemporary Jews would view as an offense to morality, and he does so without comment, apology, or attempt at moral justification. At times he merely reproduces the primary sources without further elaboration; at other times he adds to those sources comments, explanations, or observations which are

26. For a striking contemporary discussion of this point see Ḥazon 'Ish, *'Al 'Inyanei 'Emunah, Bitahon, Ve'od* (Jerusalem, 1954), 21–43 and *passim*.

contrary to commonly held notions of Jewish ethics. So long as it is the Law, Maimonides records or explicates it without either hesitation or apology. These supposedly negative elements in his codification and commentary exist, although they are often ignored by those who find them unsettling.

To study the question of the relation between law and morality in Maimonides' thought, we shall begin by considering selected examples so that we have some concrete evidence before us. In some instances the primary sources explain a particular law as based on moral considerations. Yet instead of adopting the moral explanations set forth by the Sages, Maimonides rejects them in favor of strictly nonmoral interpretations. A striking case occurs in his interpretation of the Mishnah's prohibition of a prayer in the form, "May Thy mercies extend to a bird's nest." The reference is to the biblical law that requires us to send away the mother bird before taking her baby birds from the nest. It is perfectly natural to construe this law as rooted in moral feeling. It is reasonable to suppose that we are instructed to send away the mother bird in order to save her the agony of seeing her children robbed from her nest. In fact, in a nonlegal context in the *Guide*, Maimonides offers just this interpretation. There the only consideration that he sets forth is compassion for the mother bird and the development of compassionate feelings toward human beings. "If then the mother is let go and escapes of her own accord, she will not be pained by seeing that the young are taken away. . . . If the Law takes into consideration these pains of the soul in the case of beast and birds, what will be the case with regard to the individuals of the human species as a whole?" (III, 48, p. 600).

In his legal works, however, Maimonides takes a different line. Here he records the rule of the Mishnah and goes on to explain that we must not pray in this fashion because it would suggest that God's command concerning the mother bird was motivated by compassion. Maimonides rejects this notion and insists that this commandment is simply *gezerat ha-katuv*, a divine decree. He adds the argument that if the underlying rationale were the feeling of compassion, that same feeling should deny us the right to slaughter animals for food.[27] In rejecting the moral explanation, Maimonides is following one of the opinions recorded in the talmudic discussion on this Mishnah. We must note, however, that another opinion is expressed in that same discussion—one that sustains the moral interpretation and that he might have adopted. Maimonides, the philosopher, sees in this law a con-

27. Commentary to *M. Berakhot*, 5:3; *H. Tefillah*, 9:7. We later give some consideration to the problem of the difference between the seemingly moral concern in the *Guide* and Maimonides' clear reluctance to introduce purely moral considerations into the legal context of the code or commentary.

cern for developing in us compassion for living beings. Maimonides, the commentator and codifier, rejects out of hand a readily available moral explanation of the law. It is almost as if he is saying that morality should not serve as a formative force in determining the law.

We find other cases where Maimonides took no notice of a readily available moral interpretation of the law. The Torah teaches, "You shall not plow with an ox and an ass together."[28] The Torah gives no explanation for this prohibition, nor does the Mishnah, which codifies it.[29] Some later commentators explain this as a ruling motivated by humane considerations. If animals of different species are teamed together, it causes great discomfort to the weaker of them. As ibn Ezra puts it in his commentary on the Torah, "God shows compassion to all His creatures, since the power of the ass is not as great as that of the ox." In his commentary on the Torah, Abravanel cites ibn Ezra approvingly. Predictably, Hertz, who regularly seeks out moral explanations of the law, gives this same explanation in his Pentateuch commentary. Yet Maimonides does not suggest such an explanation of this law. In his commentary to *M. Kilayim* 8:2, he simply says that it is God's commandment and quotes the biblical verse. Similarly, in the *Mishneh Torah*, he records the law without any explanatory comment.[30] Finally, in the *Guide*, where we sometimes find Maimonides giving moral explanations that he did not include in his legal writings, he provides an explanation of a quite different sort. The prohibition against teaming together diverse species is "due to the possibility that if the two are brought together they might sometimes copulate" (III, 49, p. 609).[31] Surely, if Maimonides considered the moral explanation important, he was as capable as other commentators of formulating it on his own.

In another case he rejects a ruling of the Mishnah that is explicitly moral in purpose. In the case of a childless widow, the Torah requires that her husband's brother should marry her. If he does not want to marry her, there is a ceremony of release which then frees her to marry anyone else whom she chooses. In earlier rabbinic law, *yibbum*, levirate marriage, was originally considered preferable to *ḥalitzah*, the release of the levir from his obligation. The latter was interpreted as a concession on the part of the Torah and, as

28. Deut. 22:10.

29. *M. Kilayim*, 8:2.

30. *H. Kilayim*, 9:8.

31. If one follows through the entire preceding passage it might be possible to squeeze out of it a quasi-moral explanation. However, it is not the simple humane concern with the welfare of animals that we find in ibn Ezra, but a fear of arousing sexual feelings in the man who attends the animals and observes their behavior.

such, was distinctly the less desirable of the options. At a later time, changed social circumstances caused the rabbis to revise their ruling and to give preference to *ḥalitzah* over *yibbum*. The reason given in the Mishnah is a purely moral one. So long as *yibbum* was performed with the honest motivation of fulfilling a divine commandment, it was a commendable act. In later times, however, social conditions changed and the motivation of the levirs was no longer pure. Their decision to marry the deceased brother's widow was not motivated by their desire to fulfill a *mitzvah*. Instead they were attracted by the wealth or the beauty of their widowed sisters-in-law. Such marriages were held to be grossly improper, and the Sages ruled that under these circumstances *ḥalitzah* was to be preferred.[32] One talmudic sage even went so far as to equate such a wrongly motivated levirate marriage with incest and suggested that the child of such a marriage borders on being a *mamzer,* one who has the same illegitimate status as the child of an adulterous or incestuous union.[33]

Maimonides rejects the ruling of the Mishnah and follows other opinions that treat these levirate marriages as fully legitimate. He rules that *yibbum,* the consummation of the levirate marriage, is still preferable to *ḥalitzah.* He argues that the death of a husband who left a childless widow automatically removes the incest prohibition from her marriage to his surviving brother. Therefore, he says, such a "marriage is permissible, even if the levir consciously intended that it should not be for the purpose of fulfilling a *mitzvah.* Consequently, the law is that *yibbum* takes precedence over *ḥalitzah* in all such cases."[34] We have here one more case in which Maimonides did not take advantage of the readily available opportunity to base the law on moral considerations or to interpret it in moral terms. Even though he had a clear talmudic precedent that would have given support to a seemingly moral position over against a purely legalistic one, he opted nevertheless for the purely legal ruling as he understood it, rather than for a morally tempered version of the law.

Let us examine some other cases in which Maimonides fails to give any standing to widely accepted moral principles. If there is any single value commonly thought to be central to Jewish morality, it is the doctrine of human dignity—that all human beings, by virtue of their humanity, are worthy of respect and of humane treatment. Man is created in the image of God, and as bearer of the divine image every person is held to be uniquely precious. One would expect then that the legal writings of Maimonides

---

32. *M. Bekhorot,* 1:7.

33. *Yevamot,* 39b.

34. Commentary to *M. Bekhorot,* 1:7; see also *H. Yibbum,* 1:2.

would consistently and unequivocally reflect this moral ideal. However, even a cursory examination of the materials forces us to recognize that such is not the case. I commented earlier on the extent to which his selection, arrangement, and emphases in his legal works reflect his own original contributions. His specific formulations, the language he uses, the force and pungency of some of his comments, all tell us a great deal about his own thought. We also know that many times when Maimonides is silent and makes no comment, he is using another means to convey an important teaching.

There are striking examples of legislation in which Maimonides seems to deny all claims to innate human dignity. For example, the prohibition, discussed earlier, "Thou shalt not plough with an ox and an ass together," does not include a similar restriction on teaming together a man and an animal. In fact, the Mishnah explicitly permits teaming together man and animal.[35] Maimonides simply records this ruling without special comment and states that a man may be teamed with any animal for ploughing. He expresses no concern over the indignity to a human being that this implies, and sees no need either to mitigate the ruling of the Mishnah or give it a morally acceptable explanation.[36] One might have expected him to find some way to blunt the effect of this rule that seems so degrading to human beings, but he leaves it in silence.

In another case, the Law requires that one who has injured another person must compensate him in various ways. The compensation includes *boshet,* payment for the humiliation and embarrassment the injured person suffered. A Mishnah rules that in determining the extent of payment for *boshet,* we take into account the social position of the injured party. In that Mishnah, R. Akiba argues that even the poorest and most degraded members of society must be treated as dignified human beings, capable of embarrassment, and are thus entitled to compensation for their humiliation.[37] Maimonides, however, takes the position of the Mishnah literally and rules that the norms of fixed compensation for embarrassment apply only to people of recognized social standing. In explanation, he tells us that there are types of people not worthy of any such consideration. "There are vulgar human beings who have no concern for their own embarrassment [i.e., have no sense of self-worth]. They constantly degrade themselves in a variety of ways." For a penny or two they voluntarily make themselves ob-

---

35. *M. Kilayim,* 8:6.

36. Commentary to *M. Kilayim,* 8:6, citing *Sifre* to Deut. 22:10; *H. Kilayim,* 9:10.

37. *M. Baba Kamma,* 8:6.

jects of scorn by the lowest elements in society.[38] These people border on the subhuman in Maimonides' opinion and are, therefore, incapable of shame. Hence, they are not entitled to any compensation for *boshet*. While R. Akiba seeks to protect even such people from embarrassment, Maimonides apparently feels that, being beyond feelings of embarrassment, they are unworthy of humane concern.

The Law requires a wife to perform certain household and personal services for her husband. This is part of her duty as agreed to in the marriage contract. A wife who refuses to perform these services may be coerced by law, but Maimonides goes even further. He adds, in a comment that may well reflect the norms of the society in which he lived but seems to have no identifiable rabbinic source, that she may be coerced even by whipping.[39] His contemporary critic, Rabad, expresses astonishment and notes that he has never heard of it being permissible for a man to whip his wife to force her to carry out her household responsibilities.[40] Here again we have a case in which Maimonides seems not to be concerned with the dignity of persons.

Perhaps the most striking case of all is one that exhibits the tension between the command to love our fellow Israelites and the obligation to reject or even despise them under specific conditions. Maimonides formulates the former command in touching language. "Every person is obligated to love every member of the community of Israel as he loves himself, as Scripture teaches, 'Thou shalt love thy neighbor as thyself.' Therefore each of us is bound to praise his neighbor and to exercise the greatest care for the protec-

38. *H. Ḥovel u-Mazzik*, 3:8–11.

39. *H. 'Ishut*, 21:10.

40. See Rabad *ad loc*. One should note that, although Rabad finds the idea of whipping a wife to force her to fulfil her household duties a strange notion, he himself offers an only slightly less disturbing alternative that he believes to be generally accepted and acceptable. He proposes that the rebellious wife should be given only the most meager amount of food and that her other needs should also be attended to in the most minimal way to force her to do her duties. Although Rabad claims never to have heard of legal permission to beat a wife who rebels, it is evident from some of the other standard commentaries on the *Mishneh Torah* that the practice was known and approved in certain places; it is not a pure invention by Maimonides. In the thirteenth century, wife beating among Jews was apparently a known phenomenon that required special rabbinic intervention. R. Peretz b. Elijah, one of the most important of the Tosafists, issued a special edict restraining husbands from beating their wives and instituting penalties for noncompliant husbands. The edict begins with the statement, "The cry of the daughters of our people has been heard concerning the sons of Israel who raise their hands to strike their wives. Yet who has given a husband the authority to beat his wife? Is he not rather forbidden to strike any person in Israel?" See Louis Finkelstein, *Jewish Self-Government in the Middle Ages*, 2nd printing (New York, 1964), 216–17, and the discussion in M. Güdemann, *Ha-Torah ve-ha-Ḥayyim be-'Artzot ha-Ma'arav bi-Yemei ha-Beinayyim* (Warsaw, 1897), 193–95, 216.

tion of his property, just exactly as one would protect his own property and seek his own honor."[41] Elsewhere, Maimonides includes such duties as visiting the sick, comforting mourners, burying the dead, and providing for the needs of brides under the general rubric of the commandment to love our neighbors as ourselves. He adds, "Everything that you want others to do for you, you should do for your brother in Torah and *mitzvot*."[42]

At the same time, Maimonides sets forth certain situations in which we are commanded to reject our fellow Jews, even to despise them. In the passage where he formulates the obligatory principles of the Jewish faith, he rules that to be considered a member of the community of Israel (*kelal yisrael*) one must accept, without question, all thirteen of the articles of faith which he has outlined. Whoever accepts these articles, even though he sins, is a member of the community whom we must love and deal with compassionately. One who denies or doubts any one of the articles of faith, however, has thereby automatically excluded himself from the community of Israel. Such a person is a heretic, "and it is our duty to despise him and to destroy him. Concerning him the Psalmist said, 'O Lord, You know I hate those who hate You, and loathe Your adversaries.' "[43]

It is particularly instructive that Maimonides feels no need to temper or mitigate this call to hatred of the heretic. Many later authorities felt pressed to reinterpret the obligation that the Law imposes on us to hate certain categories of Jews. They were apparently ill at ease with the seeming immorality of such hatred and sought ways to make it morally palatable. For example, R. Shneur Zalman of Lyady, the founder of Ḥabad hasidism, explains in the *Tanya* that even when we are commanded to hate fellow Jews, "there still remains the duty to love them also, and both are right: hatred because of the wickedness in them; and love on account of the aspect of the hidden good in them, which is the Divine spark in them. . . . Compassion destroys hatred and awakens love."[44] In contrast, Maimonides feels no moral need to explain, justify, or explain away the commandment to hate Jews who are deficient in the correct principles of faith. They have willingly forfeited their status within the community of Israel and constitute a danger to the spiritual health and integrity of the Jewish people. In his devotion to a higher end, Maimonides issues a ruling of unmitigated severity against those who would undermine the foundations of Jewish faith.

41. *H. De'ot*, 6:3.

42. *H. 'Avel*, 14:1.

43. End of the discussion of the articles of faith in his introductory essay to the commentary to *M. Sanhedrin*, 10.

44. *Likkutei 'Amarim*, 32.

It is instructive to contrast this ruling with another in which there is a combination of concern for both the spiritual and physical welfare of those whom we may well be bound to hate and reject. The Torah has explicit legislation making it obligatory for a Jew to extend help to an animal that has fallen under the weight of its load, irrespective of whether the owner is a friend or an enemy.[45] From the talmudic sources it is clear that there is a double concern here—compassion both for the suffering animal and for the owner unable to cope with the situation by himself. The Talmud considers a case in which one meets up with two such animals, both in need of help. If one belongs to a friend and one to an enemy, the law is that the animal of the enemy should be helped first "in order to subdue his evil inclinations," that is, to help turn the enemy into a friend.[46]

In his code, Maimonides records this ruling, using essentially the language of the Talmud and initially adding nothing new. He goes on, following the line of that same talmudic passage, to rule that the enemy about whom we are speaking is not a gentile, but a fellow Jew. At that point he engages in an added reflection of his own. He asks how it is possible for one Jew to consider another Jew his enemy when we are commanded not to hate our brothers in our heart.[47] He answers, following another talmudic source, that this is a case in which, despite this man's repeated efforts to influence his fellow to refrain from a particular transgression, the sinner stubbornly continues to go his own way. It is a duty to feel hatred for him and to consider him an enemy until such time as he repents and abandons his sinful ways.[48] At this point Maimonides adds his own elaboration. He rules that, although the owner has not yet repented, if he seems to be stunned and confused because of the state of his animal and the load under which it has fallen, "one is obligated to help him load or unload, and not leave him possibly to die. For he might tarry because of his property and meet with danger; the Torah is very solicitous for the lives of Israelites, whether of the wicked or the righteous, *since all Israelites acknowledge God and believe in the essentials of our religion.*"[49] Here Maimonides is careful not to equate an ordinary sinner with a heretic. We deplore his sinfulness, and in ordinary circumstances are free to give expression to our pain, but when this man's life may possibly be at stake he has a full claim on us. He may be a sinner, but we presume that as

45. Exod. 23:5; Deut. 22:4.

46. *Baba Metzia*, 32b.

47. Lev. 19:17.

48. See *Pesaḥim*, 113b.

49. *H. Rotzeaḥ*, 13:14; emphasis added. Twersky, *Introduction to the Code,* 289, speaks of this passage as "Maimonides' new and highly sensitized interpretation of the law."

a Jew, he has not lost his faith in "the essentials of our religion." In the latter case he poses so severe a danger to the community that we must overcome any natural sympathy we may have for him and reject him. In the present case, however, we must overcome our inclination to reject him because of his sinfulness and extend to him our fullest measure of help and concern. Despite his sin, he is still a faithful Jew and merits our love.

All this is applicable so long as the sinner is alive and there is still hope that he will repent. However, Maimonides extends no such sympathetic concern to the wanton sinner after his death. He follows, and also elaborates, a rabbinic ruling that treats the death of such a sinner as no occasion for mourning. The earlier sources speak in a general way of those who have separated themselves from the community. Maimonides in his code expands and defines this term:

> Those who separate themselves from the community, that is, those who have removed the yoke of the commandments from their necks and are no longer included within the community of Israel in the fulfillment of the commandments, in honoring the festivals, in attending the synagogue and the house of study, but conduct themselves as if they were totally free of all such obligations, and similarly heretics or informers, we do not observe the rites of mourning for any of them. Instead their brothers and other relatives should clothe themselves in white and wrap themselves in white, and eat and drink and rejoice, because enemies of the Holy One, blessed be He, have perished. It is concerning such cases that Scripture says, "O Lord, You know I hate those who hate You and loathe your adversaries."[50]

The sinner who, by virtue of his death, is beyond redemption on earth no longer commands our sympathetic understanding. So long as he is alive and we believe that he is still firm in his devotion to the essentials of the faith, we can continue to hope that he will repent and abandon his sinful ways. Once that hope is no longer present, Maimonides follows the sources in ruling that the deceased sinner is an enemy of the Lord: we view his death with the same

---

50. H. 'Avel, 1:10. The verse cited at the end is Ps. 139:21. The primary source on which Maimonides elaborates here is Semahot, 2:10. See also Sanhedrin, 47a. We should note that there appears to be an inconsistency between Maimonides' position in the commentary on the Mishnah, where he affirms that we continue to love the sinner so long as his faith in the essential principles of Judaism is firm, and his view in these last cases that the sinner merits our hatred just for his sinfulness, even if he is not a heretic or an unbeliever. The problem is made more acute by the fact that he cites Ps. 139:21 as his proof-text in both cases. I am unable to offer a completely satisfactory solution to this problem.

joy that we might feel over the death of any enemy who threatens our spiritual security and integrity. It should be apparent that what controls Maimonides' rulings in these cases is not some independent set of moral values, but a clear perception of what the Law demands of us. Whatever our personal feelings may be, it is the Law that dictates whom we should view as our enemy.

A last and most telling instance makes the point with great force. Maimonides codifies the law holding that in a monetary dispute between a Jew and a non-Jew the Jew may choose to have the case judged by whichever legal system gives him the advantage. If the non-Jewish system is more advantageous, he may choose it, or he may choose the Jewish system if that will be better for him. Maimonides feels a need to respond to this legalization of an apparent inequity between Jew and non-Jew, one that in some modern opinions borders on dishonesty. His justification, however, may be more offensive to common morality than the law itself. He reassures us that we need feel no compunction, saying, "Let this not appear to you problematic, just as it is not problematic that we slaughter animals (for food) even though they are not guilty of any wrongdoing. The reason is that a being who does not possess the perfection of human virtues is not truly a member of the category 'human' at all. The purpose of such beings is simply to serve the needs of those who are truly human."[51] There could hardly be a more explicit denial of the intrinsic value of man as man, or a more severe rejection of the doctrine of the natural dignity of all men.

We learn from the *Guide* that Maimonides in his maturity continued to distinguish between those who are truly human and those who, in his opinion, are merely human in their physical form but lack any true status as men. In his theory of providence he takes the position that divine providence reaches individuals in accordance with the level of their intellectual development.

> Accordingly divine providence does not watch in an equal manner over all the individuals of the human species, but providence is graded as their human perfection is graded. . . . As for the ignorant and disobedient, their state is despicable proportionately to their lack of this overflow [i.e., divine providence], and they have been relegated to the rank of the individuals of all the other species of animals. "He is like the beasts that speak not" [Ps. 49:13, 21]. For

51. Commentary to *M. Baba Kamma,* 4:3. For a different explanation, which is in the nature of a moral justification for the seeming inequity, see *H. Nizkei Mammon,* 8:5. For still a third approach, see *H. Melakhim,* 10:12.

this reason it is a light thing thing to kill them, and has been even enjoined because of its utility (III, 18, p. 475).

A similar picture is drawn in his famous parable of the palace in *Guide*, III, 51. There he identifies those most remote from the apprehension of God as "all human individuals who have no doctrinal belief, neither one based on speculation nor one that accepts the authority of tradition. . . . The status of those is like that of irrational animals. To my mind they do not have the rank of men, but have among the beings a rank lower than the rank of man but higher than the rank of apes. For they have the external shape and lineaments of a man and a faculty of discernment that is superior to that of apes," (III, 51, pp. 618–19). These judgments are hardly consistent with the widely held view that there is in all human beings, however lowly, an innate dignity and an intrinsic worth that make them worthy of respect and cause them to be valued for themselves.

These cases of seeming unconcern with commonly held moral values are balanced by numerous passages in which Maimonides exhibits the greatest moral sensitivity. He codifies established laws that are morally elevated, makes independent rulings that reveal profound moral concern, and adds explanatory comments to his codification of established laws that express the most exquisitely delicate moral feelings. Let us consider some examples of his moral sensitivities.

We find a direct contrast with our last cases in a moving passage in the *Mishneh Torah* where he opens up to all mankind, not just to the Jewish people, the possibility of the highest levels of development along with the rewards that accompany such development. He first explains why the tribe of Levi has no share in the land distributed to the Israelites, and why they are also exempt from certain civic responsibilities, such as military service. They are consecrated to the service of God and to the life of study which will make them qualified to teach His Torah to the people. Maimonides goes on to extend this opportunity for joining the intellectual and spiritual elite to all mankind. In an eloquent coda to the laws of the sabbatical year and the jubilee year, he says:

> Not only the tribe of Levi *but every single individual from among the world's inhabitants*, whose spirit moved him and whose intelligence gave him the understanding to withdraw from the world in order to stand before God to serve and minister to Him, and to know God, and who walked upright in the manner in which God made him, shaking off from his neck the yoke of the manifold contrivances which men seek—behold this person has been totally

> consecrated, and God will be his portion and inheritance for ever
> and ever. God will acquire for him sufficient goods in this world just
> as He did for the priests and the Levites. Behold, David, may he rest
> in peace, says, "The Lord is my allotted share and portion; You con-
> trol my fate."[52]

In this case we have a remarkable universalism that appears to be in tension
with the seemingly exclusionist elitism which we saw earlier. The specific
virtues of the priests and Levites are now represented as an option open to all
mankind—not only the consecrated tribe of Levi, not only Jews, "but every
single individual from among the world's inhabitants." This is not, however, a change of perspective, nor is it the introduction of apparently new and
lofty moral ideals into the literature of the law. It is nothing more than a consistent expression of the views that Maimonides regularly advances. For him
the only true fulfillment of human potential is in the life of the mind and the
spirit, the life whose focus is the service, knowledge, and contemplation of
God. This mode of self-realization is open to any human being with the requisite moral and intellectual virtues. Such persons are challenged to use their
natural capacities well so that they can become what men truly ought to be.
At the one extreme we have those who achieve no moral or intellectual development at all. Such beings are not truly men, and thus Maimonides rules
that they have no claim on us to be treated in the full sense as men. At the
other extreme we have those persons who consecrate all their powers to the
knowledge and the service of God. Such persons are the ideal models of
what it is to be human. Jew or non-Jew, they are "totally consecrated." The
issue is not at all a contradiction between a rigorous and inhumane elitism,
on the one hand, and an open loving universalistic humanism, on the other.
It is rather a clearly drawn philosophical distinction between opposed human
types, one occupying the lowest end of the scale and the other the highest.
Anyone familiar with the teachings of Maimonides will recognize that, however sharp his language in the one case and however gentle and admiring in
the other, he is simply stating doctrines that he affirms consistently throughout his works.

Let us consider some other cases in which he seems to make moral considerations the deciding factors in the law. He explains the somewhat
puzzling laws of *temurah* (the rules governing the substitution of a noncon-
secrated animal for a consecrated one) as motivated by the purpose of saving
men from their own impulses of greed and meanness of spirit. At that point

---

52. *H. Shemittah ve-Yovel*, 13:13; emphasis added. The verse is Ps. 16:5.

he issues a general pronouncement to the effect that most of the legislation of the Torah is divine counsel aimed at bringing us to a state of refined character and virtuous action (*letakken hade'ot u-leyasher kol hama'asim*).[53] Thus he argues that the primary purpose of the entire law is moral. This general pronouncement, which has its counterpart in the *Guide of the Perplexed,* serves as a framework for much of the legislation he codifies and expounds.[54] For example, the same Maimonides who rules in one special legal context that there is a whole class of men who are subhuman and are by nature impervious to insult and shame rules elsewhere that insulting even the most ordinary member of the Jewish community is "a major sin" and adds that whoever is guilty of this sin is nothing but a "wicked fool."[55]

Maimonides shows a remarkably sensitive concern for the needs of the poor, their feelings, and their dignity. No codifier or decisor in Jewish law has exceeded him in zeal for protection of the needy, or in eloquence in legislating their cause. He repeatedly insists, for example, that festival celebrations must be characterized not primarily by involvement in our own pleasures, but first and foremost by providing food and meeting other needs for the deprived members of society. He teaches that true rejoicing on the festivals consists in the satisfaction that comes from helping those in need. In an especially sharp phrase he says, with open contempt, that a festival whose rejoicing is characterized by eating and drinking well, while giving no thought to the poor, is not *simḥat mitzvah,* rejoicing in the holiness of divine service, but *simḥat kereso,* nothing more than vulgar pleasure in filling one's belly.[56]

In another case, he sets down the rules for receiving converts into the Jewish faith. Then he adds the requirement that they must be cautioned concerning the severity of the sins of neglecting to leave the gleanings, forgotten sheaves, and the corner of the field for the poor, or of overlooking the tithe

---

53. *H. Temurah,* 4:13.

54. *Guide,* II, 39, 40; III, 27; III, 33, where he states that "to the totality of intentions of the Law, there belong gentleness and docility; man should not be hard and rough."

55. *H. Ḥovel u-Mazzik,* 3:7.

56. *H. Yom Tov,* 6:18. For other instances of this same principle see *H. Megillah,* 2:17; *H. Mattenot 'Aniyyim,* 9:4; *H. Ḥagigah,* 2:14. For some general instances of his attitudes to the poor, see *H. Mattenot 'Aniyyim* throughout and *H. Malveh ve-Loveh,* 1:1–3. This theme recurs with regularity throughout the *Mishneh Torah.* Often Maimonides is reflecting in these rulings the general orientation of the primary sources, and to that extent he is not completely original. The language in which he formulates these rulings, however, and the form he gives them testify to his deep concern with providing for the needy and maintaining their dignity.

for the poor.[57] His concern with charity is so deep that he makes awareness and acceptance of these commandments a condition for valid conversion.

One of the highest Jewish duties is *kiddush ha-shem,* sanctification of the divine name. This duty is fulfilled not only through the extreme self-sacrifice of martyrdom, but each time a Jew behaves in a way that reflects glory on the God of Israel. Maimonides stands watch over all behavior that may be formally in accord with the law, but that might bring about moral contempt for Jews and thus profane the name of their God. He faithfully codifies all legislation that seems to deny to non-Jews (or, at the very least, to idolators) the same advantages the law extends to believing Jews. Yet, after expressing himself on this subject openly and sometimes severely, he hastens to introduce the strong qualification that none of this permissive legislation is operative in any case where it may lead to *ḥillul ha-shem,* the desecration of the name of God.[58] In a similar vein Maimonides stresses the absolute duty to be meticulously honest in all one's dealings, maintaining rigorously correct weights and measures and all other modes of correctness in business transactions. These obligations extend equally to transactions with Jews or gentiles.[59] Anything less would profane God's name. Here again a supreme value principle determines the law.

In some cases the value scheme even requires us to restrict our own rights so as to protect others from wrongdoing. A classic instance is that of respect for parents. Maimonides sets forth the whole range of laws that give parents almost unlimited claim on the respect of their children. These laws apply to children of any age. He then adds a strong restraint that he formulates in an original manner. "Even though we have been commanded with respect to honoring parents, it is forbidden for parents to impose a very heavy yoke on their children and to demand of them every detail of honor

---

57. *H. Issurei Bi'ah,* 14:2. Maimonides, of course, bases his ruling on *Yevamot,* 47ab, which already sets down this requirement for the instruction of converts. In this respect he cannot be credited with originality. It is significant, however, that he decided to include it in his ruling. We are aware that he had no hesitation, even in this instance, about adding to or subtracting from the formulation in the Talmud. In *Tur* and *Shulḥan Arukh Yoreh De'ah,* sec. 268, this requirement is no longer included in the formula for instructing converts. On the other hand, it is retained by Meiri in *Bet ha-Beḥirah, Yevamot* 47a (189), and in *SeMaG,* Negative 116. Maimonides may well have retained it in the light of his ruling that these agricultural gifts to the poor are required even outside the land of Israel by rabbinic ordinance (see *H. Mattenot 'Aniyyim,* 1:14). In any case, it is clear that in this instance he took the opportunity to include in the instruction of converts their specific responsibilities to the poor, a rule of conversion procedure that was not followed by all authorities. For a discussion of this matter see Twersky, *Introduction to the Code,* 425, 474 n. 292, 475 n. 295.

58. See, e.g., *H. Gezelah,* 11:1–4.

59. *H. Genevah,* 1:1–2; 7:8; *H. Mekhirah,* 18:1.

which is due. So as not to put a stumbling block in their way, it is proper that parents should ignore failures of respect and forgive their children for them."[60] The deep concern is to prevent situations in which children will be so provoked by the excessive demands of their parents that they might violate the laws requiring them to treat their parents respectfully.

A different kind of moral concern is expressed in those laws condemning behavior that undermines social order. Most destructive of human society is the murder of the innocent. In recording the laws concerning murder, Maimonides follows the primary sources closely, adding comments of his own that underscore his special moral concern. Here Maimonides teaches that murder is uniquely destructive. Although there may be transgressions that, from a purely technical, legal perspective, are more severe, from the perspective of man and society no crime exceeds in its destructive effects the crime of murder. It threatens the civilized community as no other crime does. For this reason, he believes, the Torah was more deeply concerned with preventing murder than with any other sin.[61] Here again a system of moral values is expressed in Maimonides' unique formulations.

This same concern also takes the form of justifying unusually severe measures of punishment when they are needed to protect society from destructive forces. In various places Maimonides records laws that permit the imposition of severe penalties, including death, on transgressors who cannot be brought to justice under the strict rule of law. Although they cannot be convicted and punished by the judicial system, they pose such a threat to society that the Law permits nonjudicial means of penalizing them.[62] Speaking, for example, of the severe threat posed by those who seek to lead the people into idolatry, Maimonides justifies nonjudicial penalties with the argument that "cruel treatment of those who would mislead the entire nation into the worship of vanity is compassion to the world."[63] In the *Guide* he generalizes the same point with the statement, "Pity for wrongdoers and evil men is tantamount to cruelty with regard to all creatures" (III, 39, p. 554).

Finally, we should note among the moralistic elements in Maimonides' codification of the Law all those cases he labels *middat ḥasidut*. These are supererogatory rules that are not legally enforceable, but are nevertheless principles of conduct instituted by the Law that define the behavior of the truly pious. For the most part they consist of denying oneself privileges that

60. *H. Mamrim*, 6:8, 9.

61. *H. Rotzeah*, 1:4; 4:9.

62. *H. Sanhedrin*, 18:4–5.

63. *H. Sanhedrin*, 11:5. For some other instances of great severity, see, e.g., *H. Malveh ve-Loveh*, 1:4; 1:6; *H. Sanhedrin*, 20:4.

the Law permits in those cases where, to claim the privilege, would involve seemingly improper behavior. Maimonides rules, for example, that, apart from the specific laws of family purity, there are no restrictions on sexual behavior in marriage. Every form of sexual expression mutually desired by husband and wife is permitted. Nevertheless, he adds, true piety requires men to discipline themselves so as to avoid vulgarizing the conjugal relationship. That relationship should be imbued with the spirit of holiness and not be reduced to unrestrained animal lust.[64] Similarly, the truly pious exercise restraint in asserting even their just claims to property. Even though the Law is on their side, where there is any slight question, they will return lost articles and forego other property rights that the Law grants them.[65] In the case of slaves, who are the property of their owners, the Law permits one to work them mercilessly. Yet Maimonides teaches that *middat ḥasidut* requires the owner to be compassionate and gentle with his slaves. He should never impose the yoke of excessively heavy labor on them. He should treat them as cherished members of his family, not as insensitive labor machines.[66] In the *Guide,* he explains the reasons for a law concerning slaves in a way that stresses its value for generating desirable character traits in us:

> The commandment given in His saying, "Thou shalt not deliver unto his master a slave" (Deut. 23:16), besides manifesting pity, contains a great utility—namely, it makes us acquire this noble moral quality [that is, pity]; namely, it makes us protect and defend those who seek our protection and not deliver them over to those from whom they have fled. It is not even enough to protect those who seek your protection, for you are under another obligation toward him: you must consider his interests, be beneficent toward him, and not pain his heart by speech. . . . If this law is imposed upon us with regard to the least of men and the lowest in degree, namely, the slave, how must you act when a man of great worth seeks your protection! What an obligation must you have with regard to him! (III, 39, p. 554).

64. *H. Issurei Bi'ah,* 21:9. One is reminded here of the well-known comment of Naḥmanides that it is possible to be a *naval bireshut ha-Torah,* a person who observes all the specified rules, but who is at the same time crude, vulgar, and tasteless. This is why, according to Naḥmanides, we have the commandment, "Ye shall be holy," making it a duty not only to observe the law, but to do so with sensitivity and refinement. See his Commentary to Lev. 19:2.

65. For some instances see: *H. Mattenot 'Aniyyim,* 4:8; *H. Gezelah,* 5:10; 11:17; *H. Mekhirah,* 12:12; *H. Shekhenim,* 14:5.

66. *H. 'Avadim,* 9:8.

We should not overlook the fact that this sensitive moral concern is identified by Maimonides as part of the Law, not as some kind of independent moral rule.

There is no need to multiply examples. From the materials that have been presented, we see that the range of Maimonides' treatment of moral issues in the Law extends from what seems to be the deepest moral sensitivity to an apparently complete indifference to moral issues. The same codifier who enjoins us to treat even the Canaanite slave with the compassion that human dignity demands, also teaches us that there are circumstances in which a wife may be whipped if she fails to do her household tasks. The Maimonides who treats man as an exalted being also considers some Jews virtually subhuman and thus incapable of shame or embarrassment. What then is the relationship between law and morality in Maimonides' legal works?

To understand the position of Maimonides, we must first recognize that the question is poorly formed. It wrongly presupposes that Maimonides acknowledges that there is a distinction between the legal and the moral. He might grant such a distinction within those systems of law that he contemptuously dismisses as "the *nomoi* of the Greeks and ravings of the Sabians" (*Guide*, II, 39, p. 381). Conventional law, which has been created by men, is subject to imperfections. Such law might in fact be in conflict with principles of morality that are also affirmed by the society in question. But "the Law of the Lord is perfect," and it aims at leading all men who abide by it to realize their own human perfection.[67] When we judge the Law by our own standards of morality, we make the error of attempting to reduce the divine perfection to our finite capacity to know and understand. Using conventional moral standards, we may be inclined to judge that some divine laws are morally elevated and others are morally degraded.

Maimonides rejected all such external evaluations. As codifier it was his task to set forth the whole of the Law without regard to personal sentiments. While he is completely confident that the divine Law, in all its details, is the perfect instrument for promoting human welfare, he acknowledges that he cannot always provide a fully satisfactory explanation of the way in which each particular law serves that end. Yet, he neither praises the Law for being morally sound nor criticizes it for being morally deficient, since the only morality we know is that which is set down in the Law. In studying Torah we can achieve some insight into its value structure, and,

67. Ps. 19:8. This verse is cited by Maimonides in *Shemonah Perakim*, 4, and in *Guide*, II, 39, in support of his claims for the perfection of the law.

following this insight, we must try to remain faithful to Torah values as we extend the Law to new circumstances. At the foundation of all Maimonides' work in this area is the principle that, when we deal with divine Law, we must not treat law and morality as separate categories since the divine Law alone is morality.[68] This is one more evidence of how deeply rooted he was in the teachings of the biblical and rabbinic traditions.

68. I do not fully agree with the statement formulated by Twersky on this subject. He writes that "all the laws are a springboard for the highest morality and perfection which emanate slowly and steadily from them. Just as one embraces reality in order to transcend it, one adheres to the law in order that it may enhance one's perception of the good and the true and induce behavior which transcends the letter of the law. In short, law alone, in a formal sense, is not the exclusive criterion of ideal religious behavior, either positive or negative. It does not exhaust religious-moral requirements" (Twersky, *Introduction to the Code*, 428). It seems to me that Maimonides is saying that the Law is the instrument that refines our sensitivities and forms our character so that we will behave virtuously even in those areas where the Law is silent. The point of this is not that we should finally transcend the Law and substitute for it our own moral insights and feelings, but that we should extend the Law, applying it, in accordance with its own teachings, to areas not covered by formal legal prescriptions.

PART III
SOME PROBLEMS OF METAPHYSICS AND RELIGION IN THE THOUGHT OF MAIMONIDES

9

Maimonides' Account of
Divine Causality

We have considered so far some problems in Maimonides' moral philosophy, both for their intrinsic importance and as models of the way in which he
deals with fundamental issues. We turn now to the consideration of his treatment of several metaphysical questions that stand at the center of his thought
and are closely interconnected: divine causality, creation and eternity, and
prayer. Concerned primarily with a proper understanding of his specific
teachings in these three areas, we shall also discover in each case a paradigm
of how these individual teachings express aspects of the unified system of
his thought.

I shall also use these cases as models of how to go about reading Maimonides. From the beginning, I have been particularly concerned to underscore the fact that, in the case of Maimonides—more than for most other
philosophers— a sound method of reading constitutes by itself one of the
major intellectual challenges. I have tried to show that one can explicate this
method partly through abstract discussions of methodology, but far more
fully and effectively by concrete exemplification.

Since ancient times, philosophers have struggled to produce a clear and
coherent account of causality. They were concerned to learn what a cause is
and how the process of cause and effect works.[1] They tried to understand the
mechanics of causation as well as its logic. To this day we have no definitive
and universally accepted solution to the problem of causality. For many medieval philosophers the Aristotelian analysis and explication of causation
was taken to be sound and definitive. Maimonides knew and accepted the
causal theory of Aristotle, as is evident throughout his writings.[2] It is equally

1. The problem of causality was already a concern of the pre-Socratics, and continued to
occupy the attention of Plato, Aristotle, and their successors. Most medieval philosophers discuss it, and in modern times it is central in the philosophies of Hume and Kant, among others.
The problem continues to occupy the attention of contemporary philosophers, as is evident in
the wide literature on the subject still being published.

2. For cases of the standard Aristotelian account of causation in the works of Maimonides,
see *Treatise on Logic*, chap. 9; *Guide*, I, 69.

clear, however, that Maimonides had confidence in the reliability of Aristotle only so far as his theory was applied to the sublunar world. With regard to the supralunar world, which transcends all human experience, Maimonides believed that neither Aristotle nor any other human teacher had provided reliable guidance. The language of Maimonides is explicit on this point. He says with regard to Aristotle that

> all that he has explained to us regarding what is beneath the sphere of the moon follows an order conforming to that which exists, an order whose causes are clear. One can say of it that it derives of necessity from the motion and powers of the sphere. On the other hand, one can say of all that he has stated with regard to matters pertaining to the sphere, that he has assigned no clear cause with regard to this, and that the matter as he sets it out, does not follow an order for which necessity can be claimed (*Guide*, II, 19, p. 307).[3]

Maimonides holds that when we deal with the problem of causation in this sublunar world which we inhabit, we can fully rely on the teachings of Aristotle as our guide. When we deal with ultimate divine causality, however, we move to the world of the supralunar, which is on a different plane of reality. Here we can no longer rely exclusively on Aristotelian teachings. In Maimonides' view, to understand God as the ultimate cause of the world is to penetrate beyond time and space to the absolute beginning of all created being. Here Aristotle is no longer helpful.

A brief consideration of certain aspects of the Aristotelian account of divine causality will immediately make evident the nature of the problems confronting Maimonides. In speaking of the First Cause, Aristotle tries to apply to it the same general rule of causation that he developed for the sublunar world. In his view, it is a basic principle that the source of any motion must be "together with that which is moved by it (by 'together' I mean that there is nothing between them). This is universally true wherever one thing is moved by another."[4] Aristotle is here formalizing a common human experience. What is called 'the efficient cause' in standard Aristotelian terminology is the immediate force that brings about motion and change. In our experience this process is one of pushing and pulling, that is, the force that

---

3. Elsewhere he says that "everything that Aristotle expounds with regard to the sphere of the moon and that which is above it is, except for certain things, *something analogous to guessing and conjecturing*" (*Guide*, II, 22, pp. 319–20; emphasis added). See also *Guide*, II, 24, pp. 326–27. Less explicit statements to the same effect occur repeatedly in the *Guide*.

4. Aristotle, *Physics*, VII, 2, 243a33–35. See the extended discussion of this topic in *Physics*, V and VI.

brings about the motion must be in direct contact with the object that is moved. As it is put in the familiar classroom example, the second billiard ball moves only when it is struck by the first, which communicates to it its motion. On this model, seemingly long distance causation is always understood to involve a series of intermediate causes that stand between the primary cause and the final effect. Each of these causes is in direct contact with the effect that follows, down to the last cause that brings about the last effect.

This principle—that the cause of motion must be in direct contact with that which it moves—seems to work well enough when we apply it to phenomena in the world of our ordinary experience. It becomes deeply problematic, however, the moment we seek to apply it to the operations of the ultimate cause of all existence. The First Cause has peculiar characteristics not found in other ordinary causal agents. Aristotle teaches that, unlike other causes, the First Cause has no parts or magnitude, and it does not move or change in coordination with the motion or change it causes in its objects. It is obvious that this conception of the First Cause, or Prime Mover, creates serious difficulties for us when we try to explain the process of ultimate causation in accordance with the model we have established for the sublunar world. Nevertheless, in his discussion of this subject in the *Physics,* Aristotle tries to be faithful to his general rule that the mover must be in contact with the moved object. The First Mover, he teaches, causes and sustains the motion of the spheres. Without that continuing causal action there would be no ongoing rotation of the spheres, and, as a consequence, the entire world process would come to an end. But how does a causal agent, which has no parts or magnitude and does not itself move, bring about the motion of the spheres? In our image the first billiard ball must itself be in motion in order to bring about the motion of the second billiard ball. This image does not work for a nonmaterial Unmoved Mover. Aristotle does not seem troubled by this problem and does not address it directly. He simply concludes his discussion of this subject with the observation that the First Mover occupies the circumference of the outer sphere, and that from there it causes the rotation of that sphere that in turn imparts its motion to all the other spheres. "The things nearest the mover are those whose motion is quickest, and in this case it is the motion of the circumference that is the quickest, *therefore the mover occupies the circumference.*"[5] He does not address at all the puzzling question of how we can understand the idea that a being which has no parts or magnitude occupies a particular physical place. In his treatment of this subject in the *Metaphysics,* Aristotle seems to shift

5. *Physics,* VII, 10, 267b9; emphasis added.

his ground. There he puts the emphasis on the First Mover as the final cause that draws the world to it by its power of attraction. The perpetual motion of the spheres is caused by their desire for the First Mover, which Aristotle now has no hesitation in calling "God."[6] In the philosophical tradition that stems from Aristotle, this view was generally accepted as a satisfactory explanation for the way in which the First Mover imparts motion to the spheres, thereby causing all motion and all change in the entire universe. It does not take much thought, however, to recognize that the explanation doesn't work out satisfactorily. By itself, it provides no solution to our problem, since it is well established that final causes cannot move anything without an efficient cause to initiate the motion. If we stay with the image of desire as a cause, we need simply appeal to our own experience to recognize that while a mental state has a role (however difficult to explain) in causing a person to move, it cannot do so unless there are physical forces that can bring about the motion. A person who suffers from total paralysis may have an intense desire to walk out of her house, but the desire alone is not sufficient to cause the motion of her body. If the efficient cause of motion is absent or not operative, the desire to achieve a certain end, that is, the final cause, cannot by itself initiate motion.

Most contemporary scholars tend to sweep this problem under the rug. In an important and widely acclaimed book on the history of philosophy, F. C. Copleston assures us that Aristotle could not mean that God moves the world by physical action since this would require change in God. He acts only as final cause, that is, as the object of desire that moves the world. This account is put very clearly and neatly, but how this process works is never explained.[7] In another case, one of the most eminent Aristotle scholars, W. D. Ross, is more forthright in recognizing the problem. But then he seems to want to solve it with a wave of the hand. He first assures us that the account in the *Physics* is not to be taken seriously. Ross says that when Aristotle speaks of the First Mover as being on the circumference of the universe, he is merely using "an incautious expression which should not be pressed." He then asserts, although he presents no evidence to support his claim, that the only true view of Aristotle is that the First Mover operates exclusively as final cause. When Ross addresses the question about the need for an efficient cause, since final causes cannot move by themselves, he seems to think that he has solved the problem simply by asserting that "God is the efficient

---

6. *Metaphysics*, XII, 7, 1072a19–b30.
7. F. C. Copleston, *A History of Philosophy,* vol. I (London, 1946), 314–15.

cause by being the final cause, but in no other way."[8] This is a fine rhetorical flourish, but it contributes nothing toward the solution of the problem.

It is far more difficult for Maimonides than for Aristotle to give a satisfactory account of God as cause of the world. Since Aristotle affirms the doctrine of the eternity of matter, he requires only a First Mover, not a Creator God. Even so, as we have shown, he comes to grief when he tries to account for the way in which this First Mover does its work. Maimonides rejects the doctrine of the eternity of matter. He also associates himself with the teachings of the Torah concerning God. Consequently, he requires a God who is creator *ex nihilo,* who is involved in both the order of nature and the order of history, who commands, rewards, punishes, and in some way exercises providential care over His creatures. Whatever Maimonides' esoteric doctrine may be about these matters (and we will discuss this problem in chapter 10), he must be able to make his esoteric and exoteric views coherent and intelligible. In some way he is required to make sense out of the biblical God as Creator. Moreover, he is required to do this without ever deviating from his affirmation that God is absolutely incorporeal, immutable, eternal, and completely unlike anything in the created world. For Maimonides Aristotle's problems are compounded many times over.

The doctrine that God is the cause of the world is a recurrent theme in the writings of Maimonides. It appears in his youthful works and continues to have a central place in the teachings of the major works of his maturity. In his formulation of the first article of faith he states that we are required to affirm the existence of God, and to recognize that He is the cause of all that exists in the world. Similarly, he opens the first section of the first book of the *Mishneh Torah* with the statement that the most basic of all principles is that we should know that there exists a First Being who alone brings everything else into existence.[9] Yet, although the idea that God is the cause of the world is a commonplace in the writings of Maimonides, it is most difficult to find a clear and coherent account of how this ultimate causal agent operates. Like other philosophers, Maimonides provides reasonably satisfactory accounts of how human, and even inanimate, causal agents do their work. When we seek an account of how God causes the world, however, we face a mass of confusions, seeming contradictions, and a murky obscurity that contrasts strikingly with the superb clarity of which Maimonides is so capable when he chooses.

---

8. W. D. Ross, *Aristotle's Physics* (Oxford, 1936), Introduction, 93–94.

9. *Commentary to Mishnah,* Introductory Essay to *Sanhedrin,* 10, the first article of faith; *H. Yesodei ha-Torah,* I, 1–5. See also *Sefer ha-Mitzvot,* Positive Commandment 1.

It is my aim here to reconstruct and expound Maimonides' views on this subject, and to try to bring some order into the apparent chaos of his teachings, concentrating attention primarily on the *Guide of the Perplexed,* where the full range of the subject is treated in all its complexities. Before we can address the problem directly, however, we need to decide just what we are seeking when we ask for an account of Maimonides' theory of divine causality. Aristotle had already taught that, in knowing the cause of a thing, we come to know something important about its nature. "Knowledge is the object of our inquiry," he says, "and men do not think that they know a thing till they have grasped the 'why' of it (which is to grasp its primary cause)."[10] In later discussions of this subject, it becomes clear that there are at least two senses in which we can speak of knowing the "why" of a thing. It can mean that we come to understand the mechanical process by which that thing comes into being. Alternately, it can mean that we come to know the reason that lies behind a given thing's coming into being and having its particular nature.[11] In this latter sense, we deal with cause not simply, or even primarily, as a mechanical process, but as an intelligible explanation for any given state of affairs in the world.

In turning to an examination of Maimonides' account of divine causality, we shall pay particular attention to whether he provides an explanation of cause in either or both of these senses. A close study of the relevant texts reveals that Maimonides is fully aware of the complexity of the problem of divine causation. In his works of commentary and codification he simply affirms the fact of God as cause of the world without attempting to give any explanation. We have already noted that he begins his listing of the articles of faith with the affirmation that God is the cause of all existing things, and that he also begins his *Mishneh Torah* with essentially the same assertion. In that work he expands on the implications of this assertion, but he makes no effort either to explain the process of divine causation or to give a full account of the intellectual means by which we can come to understand God as the ground and explanation of the existence of the world. He provides readers with an extensive summary of the main theses of physics and metaphysics as they apply to the order of the world, but he does not include in his text an account of the workings of the divine cause.

Only when we turn to the *Guide of the Perplexed* do we find extended discussions of causality in general and divine causality in particular. When these discussions are subjected to a careful reading, however, they seem at

10. *Physics,* II, 3, 194b19–20.

11. For one of the best contemporary discussions of this point, see Gregory Vlastos, "Reasons and Causes in the *Phaedo,*" in *Platonic Studies* (Princeton, 1973), 76–110.

first to obscure more than they clarify. Maimonides appears to say a variety of things which are not consistent. As is his usual practice in the *Guide,* he deals with the subject not in one place, but in many. He presents us sometimes with extended discussions that seem to belabor the obvious, and at other times compresses complex and important ideas into a sentence or two. All this, of course, is in full accord with his own description of his method as set forth in his Introduction to the *Guide.* In what follows I shall attempt to offer an account of Maimonides' teachings on divine causality that grapples with the wide range of his statements and to construct a coherent exposition that is fully supported by the texts themselves.

The thesis advanced here is that we have in the *Guide* three separate, but related, accounts of divine causality. One is the explanation of divine causality in accordance with the requirements of physics. This is a physical, or more precisely a quasi-physical, treatment of the subject. The second exposition is in accordance with the requirements of metaphysics. The third is a religious account of divine causality. These three versions of Maimonides' treatment of this topic are not set forth as separate individual statements, nor are they directly identified with the labels I have attached to them. Maimonides spreads them throughout the *Guide,* sometimes separating them, sometimes intertwining them, but always, I believe, fully and consciously aware of the fact that each account will have to be disentangled from the others by alert readers who are able to penetrate to the depths of his teaching. Here, as in so many other cases, he is testing his readers by constructing an obstacle course that will sort out those who are ready to be admitted to the inner levels of his thought from those who are not.

The account according to physics is directed to the least sophisticated audience. It addresses the level of understanding of people who are able to think about ultimate questions only in pictorial images, those who have not yet mastered the high degree of abstract thought that is essential for all serious philosophical and theological reflection. The account according to physics is concerned, above all, to establish that God is the efficient cause of the world. It is more accurate to call it "quasi-physical" because, for Maimonides, there can be no compromise with the principle that God is in no sense a physical being. While this latter point is stressed repeatedly by Maimonides, there is enough left of the seemingly physical in this account to appeal to the level of understanding of those whose thinking about these matters still relies in some degree on the faculty of imagination. At this level of the discourse, Maimonides allows himself to come near to giving us a pictorial account of the subject.

We saw earlier that in Aristotle's teaching a basic principle of physical causation is that bodies act upon each other only through direct contact, which is to say that physical causation is conceived, above all, as a kind of pushing and pulling. As Maimonides expresses the point, "It has been made clear in natural science that every body that acts in some manner upon another body does this only through encountering it or through encountering something that encounters it" (*Guide,* II, 12, p. 277). In keeping with this image, he explains that God causes all motion and all change in the world, and that He brings all this about by rotating the spheres. The universe is conceived as an organic whole in which every internal motion derives from the motion of the heavens, and it is God who ultimately moves the heavens by keeping the outer sphere in permanent motion (*Guide,* I, 70, p. 172; I, 72, p. 191; II, 1, p. 246). The motion of the outer sphere is communicated to the other spheres and ultimately produces all motion in the world. In the *Mishneh Torah,* it is stated explicitly that God "directs the sphere with a power that has no end or limit, with a power that never ceases to operate, since the sphere revolves perpetually, and it is impossible that it should revolve without a power that causes it to revolve." He then adds the carefully phrased qualification that "He revolves the sphere without a hand and without a body."[12] It is significant that Maimonides makes no attempt at this point to explain the process by which this motion is accomplished without any physical contact between the divine mover and the sphere that is moved. Nowhere in the first four chapters of the *Mishneh Torah,* where this topic is discussed, does he expand on the physical account of divine causation, nor does he introduce the metaphysical account. In this work, which is directed to a general readership with no special training in natural science or philosophy, he simply states dogmatically that God is the ultimate cause of the rotation of the spheres, and that His work is done in His own unique way, "without a hand and without a body." Since all of this is set forth in the context of an explication of the commandments to know God, to love Him, and to fear Him, there is no need to raise philosophical problems or generate philosophical puzzles. All this changes when we move to the parallel discussion in the *Guide*.

In the quasi-physical account of divine causation in the *Guide,* some ambiguous passages come very close to speaking of the divine cause in a physical image, as Aristotle did. Maimonides dwells on biblical expressions such as "the rider of the heavens" and "the rider in the aravoth," which he associates with the ultimate power that dominates the highest heavens and causes their rotation (*Guide,* I, 70).[13] With all his caution not to ascribe to God physical characteristics in these passages, he nevertheless seems to ap-

12. *H. Yesodei ha-Torah,* I, 5.
13. Maimonides is commenting on Deut. 33:6 and Ps. 68:5.

236

proach closely the use of physical imagery. Once it has been established that God is the efficient cause of the rotation of the heavens, it follows easily enough that He is by virtue of that fact also the efficient cause of the entire world, more specifically, "He is the principle and the efficient cause of all things other than himself" (I, 16, p. 42). In this quasi-physical mode, Maimonides tends to concretize the images in a way that makes them more readily accessible to those who think of divine causality in physical terms. In speaking of the wonders of which God is the cause, he adds, "I mean the maker," as if to stress this physical image for his readers (I, 28, p. 59; cf. I, 34 and I, 69). This image of God as maker recurs in the *Guide* and serves well to advance the physical account of causality.

One is reminded here of the second biblical account of the creation of man, which is in striking contrast to the rest of the creation story. In the first creation story we are given no corporealized imagery to help us understand the creation process. We are just informed that "God said, 'Let there be . . .' and there was . . . ." In this version we have a process that is completely mysterious because it has no counterpart in human experience or in the physical world we inhabit. Creation seems to be *ex nihilo* and thus transcends the capacity of both the human imagination and the human intellect. This process has no analogue in the physical world. We are not informed of the prior existence of raw materials out of which the world is made. We are not told that God, through a recognizable process of physical causation, brought about certain effects. Instead we are left with what is to us a totally unintelligible account in which things come into being from a state of nonbeing, directly as a result of God's will. He speaks, and the world comes into existence.

In contrast, the second account of Adam's creation describes a kind of mechanical process with which we can identify, even though we cannot explain it fully. The work of creating man begins by making use of apparently already existing raw materials, and it is carried out in accordance with a causal procedure that seems intelligible because it is similar to our own experience of how things are made. "The Lord God formed man from the dust of the earth. He blew into his nostrils the breath of life, and man became a living being."[14] This version presents us with a picture that we can grasp, and with a mechanical process to which we can relate readily, even though we

14. Gen. 2:7, New Jewish Publication Society translation. It is obviously not my intention to give any consideration to the question of how the two creation stories relate to each other, or of whether they are a single unified account or are derived, as some would have it, from different documents. These matters lie beyond the limits of this book. The rabbinic midrashim, the standard medieval commentators, and modern Bible scholars have all treated this question from a variety of perspectives.

still cannot fully explain just how the dust turns into an intelligent living being. In his quasi-physical account of divine causation, Maimonides does something similar. He gives us a picture that ordinary, philosophically untutored persons can take hold of and to which they can relate.

In setting forth his detailed account of God viewed as the efficient cause of the world, Maimonides in one version dwells on the argument that begins from the observed fact that there is motion in the world and arrives finally at God as the first cause of all motion. He presents a fairly standard form of this argument, showing that whatever moves is moved by something else, which in turn is moved by something else, until we finally arrive at a First Mover. In this particular passage, Maimonides simply follows out the analogy, without being careful to add the qualifications that would make certain that we do not confuse God's action with any other form of moving. Having explained the chain in which one action derives from another, he concludes, "In this way every action that occurs in Being is referred to God, as we shall make clear, even if it is worked by one of the proximate efficient causes; God, considered as efficient cause, is then the remotest one" (I, 69, p. 168; see also I, 72 and II, 1). We have here a seemingly physical explanation of the causal process, with God as the ultimate source of all motion. No effort is made at this point to qualify or restrict the explanation, although elsewhere Maimonides does much to make certain that this image is not construed so literally that God is thought to generate motion in the same way as physical forces generate motion.

Maimonides helps the reader even further in this effort to provide a pictorial image of the causal process. In his final step in this quasi-physical explanation he introduces the idea of the overflow as an explanation of how the process of divine causation takes place. He specifically identifies this image as a device to help us grasp the idea of God as efficient cause, to give our imagination the help it needs; otherwise the notion of a noncorporeal efficient cause of the corporeal world remains hopelessly obscure (II, 11 and 12). We shall discuss more fully, in the context of our exposition of the metaphysical account of divine causation, the significance of the image of the overflow and the problems it poses. For the present, it is sufficient to note that the image is itself physical/pictorial and thus serves well as the climax of the physical account of God as cause of the world.

We shall shortly set forth in detail the cluster of problems that make it impossible for Maimonides to be satisfied with the physical account of causality. For the moment, however, we should note that he makes a special point of telling us early on that the idea of divine causality is not accessible to the comprehension of ordinary people. The "discussion concerning His creation of that which He created, the character of His governance of the world" are classified by Maimonides as among "the mysteries of the Torah and the secrets constantly mentioned in the books of the prophets and in the dicta of the Sages" (I, 35, p. 80). This is to say, that our subject is not one that can be expounded directly and in straightforward language. We must expect then that the quasi-physical version of divine causation, which is in fact fairly direct in its language and quite free in its use of corporeal images, will not be sufficient to its subject. It cannot be the final and correct account of God's causal activity, although it may be as far as many people can go toward an understanding of this subject. I suggest that at least part of the mystery and secret is just the fact that we do not know, nor can we understand or provide a satisfactory account of, the process by which God as physical cause brings the world into being. When the physical account is read carefully, it does not actively misrepresent the truth. In certain ways, it points to a dimension of the truth—namely, that all being is derived from God. It does, however, use sufficient physical imagery so that ordinary readers will feel relatively comfortable, although they may well ignore (at their peril) the explicit and implicit cautions not to literalize the images. In this quasi-physical account we see how Maimonides attempts to give us the feeling that we have an intelligible explanation of the mechanics of divine creation. Such images as the divine overflow or God rotating the spheres lend themselves to being understood literally as pictures of the process of divine causal action.

Once these images are seen to be inadequate and misleading, it is understandable that Maimonides must undertake a second account that is more philosophically sophisticated. In this account he is no longer in the position of catering to the intellectual limits of those for whom metaphysics is strange territory. In the metaphysical account Maimonides strives to overcome the problems that make the quasi-physical account unsatisfactory. Here he offers us not a description of the mechanics of creation, but rather an exposition of the philosophical considerations that force him to assert that God is the ultimate ground for all explanations of the existence and order of the world.

The first step in this account is to reject any idea or image of physical contact between God, the cause, and the effects that flow from Him. In so doing, Maimonides openly abandons the effort to adapt Aristotle's rule of physical causation to the action of God as cause. "For God . . . is not a body. . . . And accordingly He . . . does not draw near to or approach a thing nor does anything draw near to or approach Him, . . . inasmuch as the abolition of corporeality entails that space be abolished; *so that there is no nearness and proximity, and no remoteness, no union and no separation, no contact and no succession*" (I, 18, p. 44, emphasis added; see also II, 12, p. 279). Stated here simply and straightforwardly is the explicit denial that the

Aristotelian rule applies to divine causality. We are no longer operating in a world in which causes and effects must be physically contiguous. We need to look now more closely at Maimonides' own statement on this subject, cited earlier. "It has been made clear," he says, "in natural science that every body that acts in some manner upon another body does this only through encountering it or through encountering something that encounters it." A careful reader will take note that he is speaking specifically about "natural science," the realm of physics. But we shall soon see that divine causation is not a subject of physics, although it has important effects on the physical world and is therefore an indispensable foundation for natural science. In addition, he is speaking about how *bodies* work as causes. Of course God is not a body. Furthermore, God is immutable. Therefore, His causal action, unlike all ordinary physical causation in the world of our experience, is not one in which change in the effect is accompanied by a concomitant change in God, the cause (I, 11). In this respect, divine causality is unique, because in all other cases a change in the effect presupposes a change in the cause. Such a statement gives full notice to readers who are following the text carefully that the physical account must be unsatisfactory as an explanation of divine causality. God is not a body, and His mode of causation is not encompassed within the realm of natural science. It is now fully clear that the metaphysical account of causation will have to reject any propositions seeking to make divine causation intelligible on the model of physical causes.

The basic principle on which the metaphysical account rests is that there is absolutely no motion whatsoever in God.[15] This widely recurrent theme can be seen in its full force by examining a single key passage. Maimonides points out that motion is an attribute of corporeality. Hence once we deny that God is corporeal, we must necessarily deny all motion in Him. The terms in the Torah suggesting that God moves are to be understood non-literally according to the rabbinic principle that "the Torah speaks in the language of man." Because there is no way to express adequately in human language the truth about the nature of God, the Torah uses language that on the surface is immediately understandable, but is at the same time multi-layered in its meaning and heavily allusive. The burden is on the reader, and Maimonides was, of course, a model of a careful and perceptive reader of Scripture.

At this point in his discussion, Maimonides lists a group of eleven verbs of motion sometimes applied to God. The list includes "to descend, to ascend, to go, to stand erect, to stand, to go round, to sit, to dwell, to go out, to come, to pass." He notes, "There is no doubt that when corporeality is abol-

15. For some selected discussions of this point, see *Guide,* I, 21, p. 51; II, 1, p. 246.

ished, all these predicates are likewise abolished" (I, 26, p. 57). What is particularly significant is the fact that he has discussed ten of these eleven verbs earlier. In each case he has established that, when they refer to God, they do not connote movement. The new verb added in this list is *savav*, which carries the double meaning of "turning (or going) around" and "causing."[16] The intended connection between these meanings is not difficult to work out. The very force that is responsible for the rotation of the spheres, the power that turns them, is of course the true and ultimate cause of all that exists and all that happens in the world. It is instructive that Maimonides has added this verb to his list almost surreptitiously, placing it in the center so that it is surrounded by those verbs for which the point of nonliteral meaning has already been made. On the one hand, it is hidden by all the others so that those who read casually will not be likely to notice it. On the other hand, for those who know how to read the *Guide* properly the central position of this verb will be instructive. It will alert them to recognize not only that *cause* is to be treated like the other verbs that were discussed before, but that it is the key to the understanding of all the others.

A careful reader will also note another peculiarity in Maimonides' list. The other ten verbs are all applied to God in Scripture. They occur in contexts in which there is genuine danger that they may be read literally and thus produce a conception of God as a being endowed with corporeal properties. There are only four instances in the Bible in which some form of the verb *savav* is used with God as the subject, but not one of those instances offers any serious danger of being construed in corporeal terms.[17] If Maimonides chose to include this verb under these odd circumstances, it is evident that he wanted to bring something important to our attention.

The perceptive reader is expected to be sensitive to the problem of divine causality, to note and follow the clues that Maimonides has provided, and to conclude that *cause*, when applied to God, may only be understood in some nonliteral, nonphysical sense. If we understand why this must be the case with respect to *cause*, we shall then understand correctly what it means

16. Pines' translation, "to go round," does not convey the ambivalence of this term. I suspect that Pines chose to translate as literally as possible and to leave to the reader the task of determining what might underlie the inclusion of this verb in the present list. It should be noted that not all the verbs that Maimonides discusses in the *Guide* as applied to God are listed here. It is beyond our present purpose to explore the reasons for his inclusion of some and exclusion of others, but it should be noted again that this is typical of the kind of problems the careful reader has to face. The addition of *savav* to the list is noted by Kafih in his translation (Moses Maimonides, *Moreh ha-Nevukhim [Guide of the Perplexed]*, trans. Y. Kafih [Jerusalem, 1972], I, 26 n.17).

17. The four cases are Exod. 13:18, Deut. 32:10, Ezek. 7:22, Ps. 32:7.

to assert this of all the other verbs in the list, and why corporeal discourse about God must not be taken literally. Once we come to this point, it follows that we can give no physical/mechanical account of the way in which divine causation works. At best, we can hope for an explanation of divine cause that will serve as an intellectually satisfying ground for our understanding of the origin of the world. This account, like the physical one, is based ultimately on the arguments from motion that force us to the doctrine of a first unmoved mover. Once he demonstrates the existence of God, as well as His eternity, immutability, and incorporeality, Maimonides is forced to some corollary conclusions. Chief among these is that divine action can only be accounted for, if at all, in the metaphysical mode, never in the purely physical mode. The main features of this metaphysical exposition can now be made clear.

The first step is to establish that God does not act or create through the use of any instrument external to Himself: "However, God, may He be exalted, does not require an instrument by means of which He could act, for His acts are accomplished exclusively by means of His will alone" (I, 23, p. 53). How then shall we understand His creative activity? Maimonides' first level of response, as we see from the statement quoted, is that He accomplishes His acts through His will alone. This initial approach is designed to make the idea of noncorporeal, divine causation seem to be in some degree intelligible to human understanding. Although we find it difficult to give a fully satisfactory account of human will, we do believe that we experience directly the working of will within ourselves. It provides us with a model that serves as an analogy to the working of God's will as a creative/causal force. Maimonides is soon forced, however, by the logic of his position to move away from this level of explanation. So long as we appeal to God's will or intellect as the source of His causal power, we are still using the language of positive divine attributes. We learn quickly, however, why neither this kind of language, nor the idea behind it, is an acceptable way to think or talk about God. At this point Maimonides shifts from will as the explanatory principle to the idea that all of God's creative actions flow directly from His essence: "There does not exist in Him anything other than His essence in virtue of which object He might act, know or will" (I, 46, p. 102).

Note that we do not have here any attempt to illuminate the process by which God's essence creates the world. All we know is that a proper understanding of God's unity, and all that it implies, forces us to abandon such notions as will or intellect as the source of His creative power. In their place we appeal to the most fundamental of all ideas, the essence of God as the ground of all that exists outside of Him. In this way we preserve the absoluteness of the divine unity and incorporeality.

242

> We, the community of those who profess the Unity by virtue of a
> knowledge of the truth . . . we do not say that there is in Him a su-
> peradded notion by virtue of which He posseses power, and another
> by virtue of which He possesses will, and a third one by virtue of
> which He knows the things created by Him. His essence is, on the
> contrary, one and simple, having no notion that is superadded to it in
> any respect. *This essence has created everything that it has created*
> *and knows it, but absolutely not by virtue of a superadded notion* (I,
> 53, pp. 122–23; emphasis added).

Subsequently, Maimonides presents a definitive argument in favor of the thesis that we cannot distinguish between essence and existence in God. That being the case, we can now affirm that God's existence is sufficient causal explanation for all that exists in the world. We are back to the formulation of the opening lines of the *Mishneh Torah,* which assert, "He brings all that exists into existence and all that exists from the heavens to the earth and all that is between them exists only by virtue of the truth of His existence."[18] God is here understood to be the logical and metaphysical ground of all being, although we are given no account whatsoever of the process by which He causes the world to come into existence and then continues to sustain it. Maimonides has given us a highly abstract, nonpictorial, philosophic account whose main thrust is that once we understand (as far as human beings are capable of understanding) what God is, we will also understand that all else that exists flows from the very fact of His being. We have here a causal account that makes no pretense whatsoever of giving us an explanation of the processes by which God creates and sustains the world. It is, rather, a causal account that fulfills the Aristotelian standard of grasping the cause as the "why" of a thing. It is an understanding of God, not as the cause in the sense that one ball causes the motion of another, but rather as the reason, the logical/metaphysical ground on which all being rests.

In this metaphysical account the motion of the spheres is no longer explained through the notion of God functioning as physical efficient cause,

18. This use of the term, *the truth of His existence,* has many parallels in both the *Mishneh Torah* and the *Guide.* In *H. Yesodei ha-Torah,* I, 3, Maimonides distinguishes all the created beings from God by virtue of their dependence on Him, and concludes that "His truth is not like the truth of any one of them." It is quite clear that *truth* in this usage means "the true reality" of a thing. The connection between truth and being is made by Aristotle: "It is right also that philosophy should be called knowledge of the truth . . . so that which causes derivative truths to be true is most true. Therefore the principles of eternal things must always be true; for they are not merely sometimes true, nor is there any cause of their being, but they themselves are the cause of the being of other things, so that as each thing is in respect of being, so is it in respect of truth" (*Metaphysics,* II, 993b20–30).

but rather in accordance with the standard Aristotelian doctrine of God as final cause. Here it is explained that the spheres are moved continually by their unceasing love of the deity and by their desire for Him. "Furthermore . . . the sphere has a desire for that which it represents to itself and which is the beloved object: namely, the deity, may His name be exalted. He [Aristotle] says that it is in this manner that the deity causes the sphere to move, I mean to say through the fact that the sphere desires to come to be like that which it apprehends" (II, 4, p. 256).[19]

The discussion of divine causation reaches its climax in the image of the overflow. This image plays a role in both the physical and the metaphysical accounts of divine causation. The plenitude of divine being overflows its own limits, so to speak, and in that process brings into being the separate intellects, the spheres, and through them the entire created world. In his formulation of the workings of the divine overflow, Maimonides tries to eliminate any purely physical element while preserving the pictorial image and making the doctrine useful in the metaphysical account of divine cause.

> Considering that the effects produced by the separate intellect are clear and manifest in that which exists . . . it is necessarily known that this agent does not act either through immediate contact or at some particular distance for it is not a body. Hence the action of the separate intellect is always designated as an overflow, being likened to a source of water that overflows in all directions and does not have one particular direction from which it draws while giving bounty to others. (II, 12, p. 279).

The operation of the separate intellect as cause is modeled on the operation of God as cause. What stands out first is that all physical causal process is eliminated from consideration. Then the causal action is described as nonspecific. That is to say, it is a kind of generalized cause that grounds the whole of being, rather than a particular cause that explains the coming into being of some particular thing.

Neither the account according to physics nor that according to metaphysics is fully satisfactory. In the course of his discussions of various topics in the *Guide,* Maimonides provides us with the full range of arguments showing these accounts not to be fully satisfactory. Insofar as the physical and metaphysical accounts are derived from Aristotle, Maimonides has al-

---

19. We noted earlier the significant fact that this explanation is not offered in the discussion of the rotation of the spheres in the *Mishneh Torah.*

ready made their limitations clear. As we have already seen, Maimonides considers Aristotle to be reliable only with respect to the generation of things in the world beneath the sphere of the moon. With respect to all that occurs in the heavens above, the absolute beginning of things and the causal process that begins with God, neither Aristotle nor any other man has more than the smallest measure of knowledge: "the deity alone fully knows the true reality, the nature, the substance, the form, the motions, and the causes of the heavens" (II, 24, pp. 326–27).[20] We also saw earlier that, in what seems to be the most startling reversal of his usual position, Maimonides goes so far as to assert that we cannot even be sure that our proofs for the existence of God are sound, insofar as they are based on the argument that motion in the world can only be explained by the existence of a First Mover. It is important to repeat here the statement quoted in our discussion in chapter 4:

> For it is impossible for us to accede to the points starting from which conclusions may be drawn about the heavens; for the latter are too far away from us and too high in place and in rank. And even the general conclusion that may be drawn from them, namely, that they prove the existence of their Mover, is a matter the knowledge of which cannot be reached by human intellects (II, 24, p. 327).[21]

Maimonides' advice at this point is that we should not try to penetrate into this realm, which so far exceeds our intellectual capacity.

It is now clear that the account of divine causality according to physics is necessarily inadequate. If from the fact of motion we cannot prove even the existence of God, and if anything we say about the supralunar realm is utterly without sound intellectual foundation, then no physical or quasi-physical explanation of divine causation can be reliable. Similar difficulties confront the metaphysical explanation as well, but they are only the beginning. We need only consider some of the specific additional problems in order to grasp the depth of the mystery confronting us. Maimonides asserts repeatedly that there is absolutely no likeness whatsoever between God and His creatures (see, for example, I, 35, p. 80, and I, 56). Not only is there no resemblance between God and creatures, but no relation whatsoever, not even the relation of similarity, can properly be predicated between them: "In view of the fact that the relation between us and Him . . . is considered as nonexistent—I mean the relation between Him and that which is other than He—it follows necessarily that likeness between Him and us should also be

---

20. See the discussion of this point in note 3, and in the text to which it refers.
21. The question of the correct translation is discussed in chapter 4.

considered nonexistent" (I, 56, p. 130). So far does this restriction go that even such a term as *existence* can only be predicated of God and creatures equivocally. Maimonides adds that, "the terms 'knowledge,' 'power,' 'will,' and 'life,' as applied to Him . . . and to all those possessing knowledge, power, will, and life are purely equivocal, so that their meaning when they are predicated of Him is in no way like their meaning in other applications" (I, 56, p. 131). It is hardly necessary to point out that for philosophers cause is often the prime paradigm of relation, and if there is no relation between God and the world, then every conventional understanding of divine causality is seriously called into question.

To appeal at this point to the image of the overflow is not helpful. It may be the best image of which we are capable, but it is in its very nature inadequate. If we treat the image literally, we have fallen prey to a gross error. Even as metaphor it simply will not serve us as a satisfactory explanation of God's causal activity.

> For we are not capable of finding the true reality of a term that would correspond to the true reality of the notion. For the mental representation of the action of one who is separate from matter is very difficult, in a way similar to the difficulty of the mental representation of the existence of one who is separate from matter. For just as the imagination cannot represent to itself an existent other than a body or a force in a body, the imagination cannot represent to itself an action taking place otherwise than through the immediate contact of an agent or at a certain distance and from one particular direction (II, 12, pp. 279–80).

No image will work, not even the overflow image, which is the best of which we are capable. It is limited by its dependence, *qua* image, on human imagination, and this means that it can represent cause only in some quasi-physical mode. Once we have rejected that mode, the overflow image is very restricted in its usefulness.

This rare intellectual honesty and rigor, so characteristic of Maimonides, forces him to the realization that divine causality is a topic (like a number of others) about which we finally can only confess our intellectual incapacity. All he is able to do at that point is to acknowledge God's transcendent being and contrast it with man's worldly limitations. Thus he exults at one point, in almost lyrical language: "Glory then to Him who is such that when the intellects contemplate His essence, their apprehension turns into incapacity; *and when they contemplate the proceeding of His actions from His will, their knowledge turns into ignorance;* and when the tongues aspire to magnify Him by means of attributive qualifications, all eloquence turns into weariness and incapacity" (I, 58, p. 137; emphasis added).[22]

This incapacity makes necessary the third account of divine causality, which we have called the religious account. If neither natural science nor divine science can provide us with a satisfactory exposition of God as cause of the world, then we may legitimately seek guidance and instruction from the text of revelation itself. This is just what Maimonides advises his readers to do. As he puts it, "Let us then stop at a point that is within our capacity, and let us give over the things that cannot be grasped by reasoning to him who was reached by the mighty divine overflow so that it could be fittingly said of him: With him do I speak mouth to mouth" (II, 24, p. 327). In the religious account of divine causality we are provided with a statement of what God does, but no explanation of how He does it. The picture drawn under this heading is a fairly conventional one consistent with the biblical account. It may be conventional, but it is carefully formulated and carefully wrought.

The basic principle of this account is that the first cause of all that exists is "God's will and free choice" (II, 48, p. 409). We can seek no further explanation for why the world is as it is, rather than being different, other than the fact that God chose to make it this way.

> Thus we are obliged to believe that all that exists was intended by Him, may He be exalted, according to His volition. And we shall seek for it no cause or other final end whatever. Just as we do not seek for the end of His existence, may He be exalted, so do we not seek for the final end of His volition, according to which all that has been and will be produced in time comes into being as it is (III, 13, pp. 454–55).

The Creator God is the source of all existence. He not only created the world, but also continues to sustain it. His Creation is produced intelligently and purposively (II, 19, 21, 25). He operates continuously with uninter-

22. Later Maimonides notes another paradox having to do with causality. He observes that God's providence and governance, which are modes of divine causation, presuppose that there is some sense in which He is in the world, and this is opposed by the fact of His absolute transcendence. This passage was cited in chapter 4, in a somewhat different context, but it speaks so directly to the subject of our present discussion that it is worth citing again: "On the one hand, there is a demonstration of His separateness, . . . from the world and of His being free from it; and on the other hand, there is a demonstration that the influence of His governance and providence in every part of the world, however small and contemptible, exists. May He whose perfection has dazzled us be glorified!" (I, 72, p. 193).

rupted power, both as the Lord of nature and the Lord of history. As Lord of nature He has created the world in complete freedom and controls the natural order to suit Himself. He can change the order of nature should He choose to do so, although He rarely has reason to make such a choice. From the contrary opinion that the order of the natural world is necessary, "very disgraceful conclusions would follow. . . . Namely, it would follow that the deity, whom everyone who is intelligent recognizes to be perfect in every kind of perfection, could, as far as all the beings are concerned, produce nothing new in any of them; if He wished to lengthen a fly's wing or to shorten a worm's foot, He would not be able to do it" (II, 22, p. 319). As Lord of history He exercises providential care over mankind. Human affairs concern Him, and human behavior matters to Him.[23] Consequently, He commands man to live in accordance with His law; He rewards virtue and punishes vice.[24] The whole of Creation bears witness to His wisdom and His goodness (III, 25, pp. 503-6).

This manner of speaking generates some serious philosophical problems, and Maimonides is fully aware of the need to be cautious in terminology and modes of expression. Yet he is completely forthright about the threat to religious faith that is posed by a pure Aristotelian account of these ultimate things. His point in this mode of discourse seems to be that, since we have no language adequate to our subject, and since no exposition, scientific or philosophical, is adequate, we must choose the way of revelation. Its language and theses are no worse, if no better, than those of physics and metaphysics. It is thus that we serve the best interests of humankind in this world and in the world beyond.

There are those who will ask, with understandable interest, what Maimonides' true position is. Which of these three accounts of divine causality does he accept and which does he reject? The question is complicated by the fact that he does not give us three discrete theories. In the *Guide* the parts are intertwined and entangled in the most complex way. I have tried here to follow Maimonides' instructions in the effort to separate the parts and reconstruct the arguments as separate and coherent units. This allows us to be confronted with the full force of the internal tensions and the complexity of the puzzle that Maimonides has bequeathed to his readers.

The first step in answering the question is to recognize, against the

23. See, e.g., I, 24, 25, 37, 44, and the extended discussion of providence in III, 17-21, and III, 51.

24. On the law and commandments, see the extended discussion in III, 25-50. Reward and punishment are one of the articles of faith.

views of some eminent contemporary interpreters, that Maimonides was both a dedicated philosopher and a fiercely loyal Jew.[25] He categorically refuses to give up philosophy, affirming repeatedly that a rational man is bound to acknowledge the force of demonstrated truth. Anything less would be intellectually dishonest. This means that the claims of revelation are regularly subjected by him to philosophic judgment and criticism. When philosophy has spoken with demonstrative certainty, as in the case of divine corporeality, it establishes definitive guidelines for reading Scripture correctly.[26] Our problems arise precisely at the point where science and philosophy are no longer able to guide us. When we are facing the ultimate questions that speak to matters transcending our sublunar world, our intellect alone is insufficient. Yet there are some issues about which we cannot simply remain agnostic. We are forced to choose among the options open to us. Here religion is viewed by Maimonides as the one true teaching on which we can rely.

In some cases, as with divine causality, no one account is fully satisfactory. Each version has its own value, but none is completely adequate to its subject. At this point we find that Maimonides chooses deliberately a kind of dialectical tension as the only appropriate stance. All three accounts have much that is valuable, and each suffers from serious limitations. The comfortable way might well be to give exclusive right to one of them and to reject the others. In Maimonides' eyes this would be an instance of what Plato, in a famous phrase, called the "safe but stupid answer."[27] Instead, Maimonides has chosen, in this instance as in many others, the far more difficult way of living with the tension between the philosophic/scientific view of the world, on the one hand, and the Torah/religious view, on the other. Each has its convincing aspects, and each has its limitations. Maimonides teaches us that the price one pays for choosing to be both a philosopher and a Jew is that one sometimes must affirm the theses of both in the fullness of their tense opposition. In the best of worlds one achieves a balance between the dialectically

25. The major proponent of the view that philosophy and Judaism are mutually exclusive is Leo Strauss, and his position is vigorously supported by many of his disciples. Strauss holds that since the *Guide* is "devoted to the explanation of the secret teaching of the Bible . . . the *Guide* is not a philosophic book." He goes on to argue that since Maimonides himself "is an adherent of the law, he cannot possibly be a philosopher." "The Literary Character of the *Guide of the Perplexed,*" in *Persecution and the Art of Writing* (Glencoe, Ill., 1952), 42–43; rpt. from *Essays on Maimonides,* ed. Salo W. Baron (New York, 1941), 41–42.

26. See the opening of *Guide,* II, 25 and the whole set of lexicographic chapters which teach us how to read correctly biblical terms that seem to ascribe corporeal properties to God.

27. Plato, *Phaedo,* 105C.

opposed elements. Sometimes the tension is permanent and irresolvable. In the case of the problem of divine causality, Maimonides provides us with a model of how to live with this irresolvable tension, moving back and forth between the poles and all the time preserving both intellectual and religious integrity.

10

Creation or Eternity: God in Relation to the World

In discussing divine causality in the last chapter, we considered only indirectly the creation of the world, which is the main result of the activity of
God as cause. We turn our attention to this problem in the present chapter. In
the Middle Ages it was very widely, if not universally, accepted in both philosophical and religious circles that the world came into being through the
activity of an ultimate power. Whether that power was called God, the First
Cause, or the Prime Mover did not affect the basic stance: there was common
agreement that the existence of the world presupposes a force that accounts
for that existence. This agreement, however, was largely verbal. Once the
discussion moved beyond the simple statement to the serious work of explaining its meaning, then deep disagreements set in.

It seems evident that what Aristotle means when he says that the existence of the world derives from a First Cause is not necessarily what the
Bible means when it reports that God created the heavens and the earth. Because the biblical creation story is not a scientific/philosophical account of
the way in which the world was generated by God, it became the task of later
thinkers in Judaism, Christianity, and Islam to explicate the biblical account
in a way that came to terms with the then regnant perspectives of metaphysics and natural science. As religious thinkers, they were confronted
with the task of interpreting the scriptural texts responsibly and faithfully,
while remaining fully cognizant of the issues and challenges raised by the
dominant philosophical and scientific doctrines of their age. This need is not
peculiar to the Middle Ages. In every period of intellectual history it is the
responsibility of intellectually honest and sophisticated religious thinkers to
subject their sacred writings and their theological doctrines to the critical
perspectives of the most advanced scientific and philosophical learning of
their own age.

The thinkers of all three medieval religious communities had to determine what constitutes a correct reading of both the scriptural and the philosophical sources. They had to decide the meaning of the cryptic statements
of Scripture about God as creator of all that exists, and similarly they had to

251

clarify the meaning and implications of the philosophical teachings concerning the origin of the world. In the inelegant terminology of contemporary philosophical discourse, they had to "unpack" the concepts of "creation" and "first cause" that they found in the literature of their traditions.

In the work of Maimonides, particularly in the *Guide of the Perplexed,* we find one of the most important contributions to the study of this subject. We discussed in chapter 9 the complex and subtle way he approached the general problem of divine causation. Among the various issues with which he deals in connection with divine causation, the most acute and urgent is the need to explicate and justify the idea of God as creator of the world. The critical point on which opinion was divided for many centuries is whether the world was created out of nothing or whether it was eternal. We shall make clear later on how Maimonides understands these terms. Our first task, however, is to understand what makes this issue of creation or eternity so important.

For Maimonides, it is clear that nothing less is at stake in the answer to this question than the truth and tenability of the most fundamental doctrines of biblical religion. According to the Aristotelian version of the doctrine that the world is eternal, there is no possibility for God to play an active role in the affairs of the world. Conceived as the First Cause, He is nothing more than an automatically operating force that keeps the spheres in motion and thereby sustains the world. Maimonides asserts that "the belief in eternity the way Aristotle sees it—that is, the belief according to which the world exists in virtue of necessity, that no nature changes at all, and that the customary course of events cannot be modified with regard to anything— destroys the law in its principle, necessarily gives the lie to every miracle, and reduces to inanity all the hopes and threats that the Law has held out" (*Guide,* II, 25, p. 328). So strong was Maimonides' conviction on this point, at least in the period of his maturity, that he regularly reaffirmed his view that the belief in creation out of nothing is a fundamental article of faith, and he treated it as a valid criterion for determining whether an individual should be considered a member of the religious community of Israel or not. He made a special point of restating this doctrine explicitly, and with great force, in a number of works that appeared after the *Guide of the Perplexed.* He may well have been concerned that his discussion in the *Guide* was so intricate that its true point might be missed by all but the most sophisticated readers. To make certain that there would be no error or confusion about his actual teaching, he stressed repeatedly in his later writings that creation is a fundamental article of faith.

It is important to provide the evidence for this point, since some interpreters of Maimonides choose to ignore it or play down its significance. In

Maimonides' original formulation of the thirteen articles of faith, long before he had written the *Guide*, the fourth article states that we must believe that God alone is eternal and that nothing else existed before Him. Implicit in this statement is also the doctrine that nothing coexisted with God, but the doctrine of creation *ex nihilo* is not stated in unambiguous language. In a later revision of this article of faith he added the explicit instruction, "Know that the great principle of the Torah of our teacher, Moses [*ha-yesod ha-gadol shel Torat Moshe Rabbenu*], is that the world is a new creation [i.e., it is not eternal]. It was formed and created by God out of absolute non-being."[1] We should remember that Maimonides made all thirteen of the articles of faith, including this one, fixed elements of Jewish belief, mandatory for all who would be true members of the community of Israel. We should also note that he gave special emphasis to this article in his reformulated version by calling the belief in creation out of nothing *ha-yesod ha-gadol*, the great principle, of the Torah. He does not use this formulation in the case of any other article of faith. We can conclude that he felt a special need to underscore the importance of the belief in creation. It is clear from the remainder of his comment that he was particularly concerned to prevent any confusion about his views due to a failure to understand the more subtle and complex approaches to this problem in the *Guide*.

Concerning the question of creation versus eternity Maimonides writes in his "Letter on Astrology" that "the great controversy is over this point, and this is the very point that Abraham our Father discerned. . . . It is the root of the Torah that the Deity alone is primordial and that He has created the whole out of nothing; whoever does not acknowledge this is guilty of radical unbelief and of heresy."[2] Finally, in his *Essay on Resurrection*, Maimonides again states that "one who affirms the eternity of the world cannot possibly be a member of the community of Moses and Abraham, as I established in the *Guide*."[3] It would seem from these sources that his views

1. *Commentary to the Mishnah*, ed. Y. Kafih (Jerusalem, 1964), Introduction to *Sanhedrin*, chap. 10, *Nezikin*, 212. This added comment is contained in Maimonides' own hand. It certainly was written after the *Guide* had appeared, since it goes on to make a direct reference to the *Guide*. It seems that, in his advanced years, Maimonides considered it a matter of great importance to state explicitly what was implicit in the earlier version of this article of faith.

2. "Letter on Astrology," trans. Ralph Lerner, in Ralph Lerner and Muhsin Mahdi, *Medieval Political Philosophy* (Ithaca, 1972), 231. The Hebrew text is edited by Alexander Marx in *Hebrew Union College Annual*, 3 (1926). It is evident from direct statements of Maimonides that this letter was written after the *Guide*.

3. Joshua Finkel, *Maimonides' Treatise on Resurrection* (New York, 1939), 30 (Arabic/Hebrew text). For a more recent edition and Hebrew translation, see *"Maʿamar Teḥiyyat he-Metim"* in *'Iggerot Ha-Rambam*, ed. Y. Kafih (Jerusalem, 1972), 95. For the English version

on this matter were unequivocally fixed. Some people may argue that he protests too much—that this is only a way of trying to veil his own Aristotelian views, which are actually hidden in the esoteric dimensions of the *Guide*. They may claim to find support for their position in the fact that he felt constrained to stress the point in the more popular works that he wrote after the appearance of the *Guide,* which could be construed to suggest that he wanted to protect the masses of his readers from the dangers of views that might become for them a doorway to heresy. In the discussion that follows I shall attempt to show that there is no foundation to this criticism and that his views about creation in the *Guide* are consistent with these later formulations.

Let us begin by clarifying exactly what is at stake in the consideration of this topic, and how it has been treated in the scholarly and scientific literature. Speculation about the ultimate origin of all things has long occupied the thoughts of some of the most original and creative minds in human history. Their reflections have produced a remarkable series of myths, legends, and stories, as well as large numbers of rigorous scientific, philosophical, and theological treatises devoted to this subject. The efforts continue to this day as scientists develop new, highly sophisticated approaches to the problem of cosmogony. Whether these accounts are in the form of the various mythologies of the ancient Near East or Greek antiquity, the biblical creation story, or some version of the big bang theory currently at the center of the scientific stage, they all share a common characteristic: None of them is able to speak intelligibly about the absolute beginning. A recent scientific summary is instructive in this regard:

> In the beginning was nothing and then there was symmetry. This led to inflation and broken symmetry, so that the universe as we know it could begin to exist. Not quite Genesis but nevertheless a fine creation event. Our knowledge of the birth of the universe has increased enormously in the past decade, ever since the Big Bang theory became firmly established. . . . Thus, the precise thermonuclear conditions of the early universe—as early as one second after creation—are well established. . . . Since 1977 the field has driven closer and closer to the creation event itself. By current standards, three minutes is now relatively late in the history of the universe.[4]

see "The Essay on Resurrection" in Abraham Halkin and David Hartman, *Crisis and Leadership: Epistles of Maimonides* (Philadelphia, 1985), 228.

4. Astrophysicist David N. Schramm, in a review of Heinz R. Pagels, *Perfect Symmetry: The Search for the Beginning of Time, New York Times Book Review,* September 29, 1985.

One should note that even in this scientific account, the opening statement is, "In the beginning was nothing." The great mystery of how from nothing something was generated is unsolved. We may, as this writer claims, come closer and closer to the beginning, and it may well be, as he says, that from "one second after creation" to three minutes after that event "is now relatively late in the history of the universe." But the critical question still remains unsolved. What people who think about this subject most want to know is how the world began. Once there is a beginning, we may achieve varying levels of success in describing the processes by which things developed into the world as we know it today. The beginning, however, continues to be shrouded in mystery. In many respects the highly sophisticated contemporary scientific discussions have done no more to shed light on that mystery than the ancient and medieval attempts to penetrate to the absolute beginning of things.

Contemporary scientists who deal with these subjects often express confidence that the ultimate mystery will finally be penetrated and that we shall before long have scientific answers to our questions. Heinz R. Pagels writes: "I believe that physicists will someday soon understand the basic laws of the quantum creation of the universe (*most probably out of nothing whatsoever*) as well as astrophysicists now understand the interiors of the stars."[5] It may well be that, as research continues, the barrier will be pushed back further and further. Writers on this subject speak confidently of our knowledge of what took place in "the first three minutes," and as research pushes back in time they concentrate on the first one-hundredth of a second, on the first millisecond, and even on the first nanosecond (one-billionth of a second).[6] It makes no difference, however, how far back we can go in our account of the processes by which the universe came to be as we know it today. The logical/metaphysical problem of moving from one state of existence to another is of a totally different order from that of moving from nonexistence to existence. On this latter issue, the twentieth century seems to have made no conceptual advance over the twelfth century. We may choose to ignore the question of absolute origins, but if we decide to address it, there is no evident reason for thinking that Maimonides is less able to illuminate the problem than modern scientists.

5. Ibid., 17; emphasis added.

6. See such books as Steven Weinberg, *The First Three Minutes* (New York, 1977), and James S. Trefil, *The Moment of Creation* (New York, 1983), in addition to the Pagels book referred to in note 4. These are works written for a nonspecialized audience by scientists of recognized standing who represent not only the state of research, but also the style of thinking that motivates contemporary work in cosmology and cosmogony.

Like many other medieval philosophers, Maimonides was intensely concerned with this question of the absolute beginning. He believed that what is at stake is the very possibility of religion as taught in the Bible and the traditions that derive from biblical teaching. If the world is the result of an inexorable chain of causal necessity, generated by impersonal forces that have neither will nor purpose, then the entire biblical picture has been categorically refuted. In that case there is no role for God in the world. There can be no divine commandments and prohibitions, no reward, and no punishment—which is to say, no God who works in history and, for that matter, no God who is the Lord of nature in more than the most attenuated sense of the term. If He is Aristotle's First Cause, but nothing more, He is restricted to being the eternal necessary force that causes the eternal necessary motion of the eternally existing outer sphere (to use the language of Aristotelian astronomy), and thereby guarantees that the world process continues. It is easy to understand why Maimonides should have been so concerned with the question of how the world came into existence. He believed that the truth of Judaism, and the other biblically based religions, hung in the balance. He returned to this topic repeatedly in his various writings, but it is in the *Guide of the Perplexed* that he dealt with it in greatest detail and most extensively.

The attempt to determine Maimonides' actual views on the question of whether the world is eternal or was created in time has occupied scholars for generations. In the *Guide* Maimonides sets forth three positions with respect to creation/eternity, which we shall discuss later in this chapter. Although it would appear that he has stated his own view explicitly, the matter is not easy to settle. In light of the acknowledged fact that his book is written with an esoteric dimension, it is always reasonable for a student of Maimonides to ask the question, "What did he really mean, and what is truly his own view?" Even his apparently explicit statements are not necessarily to be taken at face value. In recent decades we have seen the flowering of a very considerable body of literature on the subject, where we find, as might be expected, proponents of a variety of answers to our question. They range from the confident assertion that the "real" view of Maimonides is the seemingly "heretical" doctrine that the world is eternal, as Aristotle taught, to the equally confident assurance that Maimonides accepted the "orthodox" teaching that God created the world out of absolute nothing. Proponents of the former position argue that they are representing the esoteric teaching of the *Guide* correctly, and explain that Maimonides would understandably have hidden this view so as to protect the philosophically naive reader from the dangers of such a seemingly unorthodox doctrine. Proponents of the latter view appeal to what seems to them open and apparent in the *Guide,* and to the powerful arguments Maimonides offers in defense of this position. A number of recent studies have argued that the textual evidence we have can lead only to the conclusion that Maimonides remained agnostic with respect to this question, since he could find no decisive evidence to determine his views.[7]

Scholars of the earlier part of this century tended to accept at face value Maimonides' affirmation of creation out of nothing. But they then went on to criticize him bitterly for having given up the battle for intellectual and scientific integrity. Julius Guttmann affirms that Maimonides believed in creation, but that he held this belief at the price of giving up the highly sophisticated concept of God he had developed earlier.[8] Isaac Husik feels let down by the Maimonides whom he admires, and he attacks him vehemently for having given in to the pressures of religion. Speaking of Maimonides' abandonment of the Aristotelian position in favor of creation by a God who acted freely and with purpose and intelligence, he complains:

> It is as if one said the coward is a better man than the brave warrior, because the latter is open to the danger of being captured, wounded or killed, whereas the former is not so liable. The answer would obviously be that the only way the coward escapes the dangers mentioned is by running away, by refusing to fight. Maimonides's substitution is tantamount to a refusal to fight, it is equivalent to flight from the field of battle.[9]

---

7. I list here some of the more important recent works on this subject. In the process of setting forth their own views, most of these authors tend to summarize and address the scholarship that has preceded them. More complete bibliographic guides to the literature can be found in these works. The most extensive studies have been done by Sara Klein-Braslavy. See her book, *Perush ha-Rambam le-Sippur Beri'at ha-'Olam* (Jerusalem, 1978), and her articles, "Perush ha-Rambam le-Po'al Bara' u-She'elat Ḥiddush ha-'Olam," *Da'at*, 16 (1986); "The Creation of the World and Maimonides' Interpretation of Gen. I–V," in *Maimonides and Philosophy*, ed. Shlomo Pines and Yirmiyahu Yovel, Dordrecht, 1986).

Other important works include: Alexander Altmann, "Maimonides on the Intellect and the Scope of Metaphysics," in *Von der mittelalterlichen zur modernen Aufklärung* (Tübingen, 1987); Herbert Davidson, "Maimonides' Secret Position on Creation," in *Studies in Medieval Jewish History and Literature*, ed. Isadore Twersky (Cambridge, Mass., 1979); Alfred L. Ivry, "Maimonides on Possibility," in *Mystics, Philosophers and Politicians: Essays in Jewish Intellectual History in Honor of Alexander Altmann*, ed. Jehuda Reinharz and Daniel Swetschinski (Durham, 1982); Shlomo Pines, "The Limitations of Human Knowledge according to Al-Farabi, ibn Bajja, and Maimonides," in *Studies in Medieval Jewish History and Literature*, ed. Isadore Twersky (Cambridge, Mass., 1979); Harry Austryn Wolfson, "The Platonic, Aristotelian and Stoic Theories of Creation in Hallevi and Maimonides," in *Studies in the History of Philosophy and Religion*, vol. 1 (Cambridge, Mass., 1973).

8. Julius Guttmann, *Philosophies of Judaism* (Philadelphia, 1964), 165–70.

9. Isaac Husik, *A History of Mediaeval Jewish Philosophy* (Philadelphia, 1944), 275.

Although most contemporary scholars are somewhat more temperate in their language, the feelings still run high because the issue is of urgent importance for any thoughtful person. This makes it particularly difficult to approach the discussion with the detachment and objectivity that scholarship demands.

Our discussion of Maimonides' views begins from what we have already established about his method in general and his treatment of divine causality in particular. We begin by asking whether the search for Maimonides' true view may not be itself the source of much of the problem, since it rests on the questionable supposition that he must have held one, and only one, view about creation/eternity. I have tried to establish in earlier chapters that on many fundamental matters his typical stance is the conscious and deliberate maintenance of a dialectical tension between diverse positions, each of which has its own merit. In such a situation it is obviously misleading to ask which is Maimonides' true position. In the case of divine causality, we saw that there are three positions which he advocates. Each has its own appropriate context in which it is the preferred and the most illuminating position, but no one has exclusive claim over the others. I shall try to show that something similar occurs with respect to the issue of creation vs. eternity. Maimonides fully grasps the merits as well as the limitations of each of the three positions that he expounds. He establishes that no one of them can be supported with decisive evidence based on demonstrative arguments, but also that none may be fully rejected as lacking all merit and thus having no claim at all on the human intellect. In the exposition that follows I shall attempt to trace out his arguments and see how he goes about the process of affirming both the claims and the limitations of each position. In my judgment, he ends up delicately balancing these positions, while assigning to each its proper sphere.

To those who are doubtful about the respectability of this dialectical style in the thought of Maimonides, it may be useful to note that Maimonides is not alone among Jewish thinkers in developing and using this method of simultaneously affirming multiple positions. It may be that, when we are dealing with ultimate questions, this is the only prudent and judicious way open to us, since we have no intellectual resources with which we can arrive at absolutely fixed and reliable solutions. Astrophysicists and cosmologists may debate fiercely about what took place in the cosmogonic process after the first fraction of a second, but they have types of evidence that can be subjected to some sort of empirical verification. However, when they attempt to move back from that fraction of a second to the act of creation itself, they are unable to provide us with the kind of evidence that forces our assent in one direction or another. It would seem that when a faithful Jew allows himself to talk openly about Creation, despite the rabbinic ruling that it is one of the secrets of the Torah not to be discussed publicly, he is bound to be unusually cautious in expression and particularly sensitive to the settings and contexts in which the discussion takes place.[10]

It is instructive to see how Naḥmanides, a successor of Maimonides with a rather different intellectual orientation, dealt with this problem. At the opening of his commentary on the Torah, Naḥmanides also employs a pattern of multiple explanations. Here we have a thinker who, according to some generally held views, is far more rigorously "orthodox" than Maimonides. Yet if we study carefully his comments on the opening verse of Genesis, we find that he says and does a number of things that seem to be in conflict with each other. On the one hand, he explicitly labels the creation episode as *sod ʿamok,* a profound mystery, which can in no way be understood from the text of Scripture itself. Furthermore, he makes a special point of stressing that this esoteric account of the creation of the world cannot be grasped from anything that he says or hints at in his commentary. Intellect alone is unable to penetrate these secrets or to work them out independently. They can be known only by one who has directly received the esoteric explanation from a teacher, who in turn, has received it from another teacher in a direct chain of tradition going back to Moses.

Despite these admonitions, Naḥmanides does present a brief account of the creation process in accordance with the kabbalistic tradition. In this account he introduces the idea that the word *ber'eshit* teaches us that the world was created through the ten *sefirot*. Earlier, he had already referred to another kabbalistic teaching, namely, that the entire Torah consists of divine names which we can uncover and understand only if we know how to penetrate to the hidden text underlying the publicly available surface text. Having said this much and expounded it briefly, he then pulls back and notes that it would be improper to expatiate on this subject, and that even brief hints are fraught with danger. After all this, he begins anew with the statement, "Now hear the explanation of Scripture [with regard to creation] according to its external meaning [*ʿal peshuto*] in a correct and clear account." What follows is what we might call a straightforward physical/mechanical account of the process of creation. He begins with the flat and uninterpreted statement that God created everything that exists from absolute nothingness (*me'afisah muhletet*). He then goes on to explain that, from this absolute nothingness, God brought into being a highly rarified element that was totally impalpable. This element contained the power to generate the *hyle*, the primary matter, from which ultimately everything else was formed.

Naḥmanides, not unlike contemporary scientists, proceeds to discuss some of the details of this process at length. We have here at least two accounts, one relating to the ultimate act of creation itself, which is expressed in esoteric language, and the other relating to the physical process of the production of the world of our experience, which is expressed in the fairly straightforward scientific language of his time. A study of the entire Torah commentary of Naḥmanides shows that he followed a similar pattern repeatedly. It is not a matter of one doctrine that is true but hidden, and another that is false but public. It is rather two accounts, both of which he held to be true, each of them stressing a different dimension of creation and addressed to a different context of discussion. It seems that Maimonides was not without followers who, however much they differed with him on certain points of doctrine, seem to have grasped the subtlety and the utility of his dialectical method.[11]

To appreciate fully the significance of Maimonides' views on creation, we need to become even more aware of the special importance he placed on this doctrinal issue. This strong emphasis is evident not only in some of his direct comments on the subject, which were cited earlier, but also in certain subtler indications. It is most important to understand his indirect treatment of this subject. This is reflected above all in the special place that Maimonides assigns to the statement about Abraham in Gen. 21:33, which asserts that he called upon "the name of the Lord, the Eternal God."[12] This verse seems to have an unusual attraction for Maimonides, which we can understand only if we focus on the role he assigns to Abraham in the development of the Jewish faith. Maimonides largely follows the aggadic sources for his interpretation of

11. I do not claim that Naḥmanides actually learned this method from his study of Maimonides and used it in conscious imitation of Maimonides. This is a matter about which we have no information. My intention is only to point out that Maimonides was not alone in making use of the dialectical method.

12. For the most extended discussion of the significance of Maimonides' treatment of this verse, see the study by Sara Klein-Braslavy in *Da'at*, 16 (1986), 54. Although I admire the care with which Klein-Braslavy has read the relevant texts, I cannot agree with the thrust of her reading, for reasons that will become clear in the discussion that follows. She ignores the fact that this verse is the superscript to each of the three parts of the *Guide*, although this may well be the most important clue to Maimonides' use of this verse and thus to its significance in his thought.

It should also be noted that, wherever it occurs in the *Guide*, Pines regularly translates the last phrase of this verse, "God of the World," rather than "eternal God" or "God of Eternity." In his notes he comments on this point and argues that the former translation is required by the context. Although there is much to be said in favor of Pines' rendering, I believe, as I shall try to show, that there is merit in also retaining the latter translation, since the ambiguity of the term *'olam* is itself significant.

Abraham's activity, but he also introduces some subtle emphases of his own. He records, in his own style, the standard Jewish reading of early religious history that teaches that the world had lost its knowledge of God and turned to idolatrous worship, although a few isolated individuals still knew of the existence of the true God and continued to worship Him. In this regard Abraham was unique in his generation. He lived in a home and a society committed to the worship of idols, yet in his early childhood he had already begun to engage spontaneously in intense reflection on basic scientific/metaphysical questions. As a result of these reflections, Maimonides tells us, Abraham arrived at an intellectual apprehension of the existence of the one God "who causes the rotation of the spheres and who is the creator of all, so that in the whole of being He is the only God."[13] Abraham then made it his life's mission to teach this truth to everyone he could. Not only did he proclaim this truth everywhere, but he also carried on arguments and debates to establish his claim. He even composed books on the subject. That Abraham went to such lengths to spread the doctrine that he had come to know is deduced from the verse, "He called upon the name of the Lord, the Eternal God."[14]

I believe this verse is an important key to understanding Maimonides' views on the question of creation. He cites this verse three times in the body of the *Guide*, twice directly in connection with Abraham's proclamation of the existence of God and the creation of the world. Thus he tells us:

> When the "pillar of the world" [i.e., Abraham] grew up and it became clear to him that there is a separate deity that is neither a body nor a force in a body and that all the stars and the spheres were made by Him, and he understood that the fables upon which he was brought up were absurd, he began to refute their doctrine and to show up their opinions as false; he publicly manifested his disagreement with them and called "in the name of the Lord, God of the world"—both the existence of the deity and the creation of the world in time by that deity being comprised in that call (*Guide*, III, 29, p. 516).[15]

13. *H. 'Avodah Zarah*, 1:3.

14. Ibid. Maimonides bases his account on well-known talmudic and midrashic sources, although it seems to me that he makes the intellectual dimension of Abraham's search and preaching even stronger than they do. For Abraham's having composed books on the subject, see the talmudic comment in 'Avodah Zarah, 14b, where the statement is made that Abraham's treatise on idolatry contained 400 chapters.

15. I have followed Pines' translation as it is, including his rendering of the biblical verse. The other two sources in the *Guide* are II, 13, p. 282, and II, 30, p. 358.

What I believe to be more important than these citations and the direct comments on them is the fact that Maimonides opens each of the three parts of the *Guide* with this verse, "In the name of the Lord, God of the World" (as Pines prefers to translate it). He also uses this same verse as the opening for most of his other works.[16] Given what we know about Maimonides and his method of writing, this should hardly be taken as accidental or as a mere rhetorical flourish. It is true that a similar convention was common among Arabic writers, who follow the Koran in heading their works with the superscript, "In the name of Allah, the Compassionate, the Merciful." Yet it is difficult to believe that Maimonides was doing nothing more than imitating the Arabic convention. To begin with, he obviously could not simply imitate. He therefore had to choose a biblical verse that would serve his purposes. This means that the verse itself was not selected arbitrarily, but was chosen to convey a certain idea and message to his readers. This is particularly important in the case of the *Guide,* since he assures us that he has included nothing in that book by chance. He could easily have chosen some other verse, or even done without a superscript altogether. I would contend that, although we still need to study his use of this verse in his other works, its appearance as the superscript for the three parts of the *Guide* should be viewed as deliberate and significant. It seems clear that Maimonides intended to communicate an important message to his readers and that, as is frequently the case, he was testing them in the process to see if they would discover the message on their own.

Although he cites the verse beginning only from the words "in the name of the Lord," he undoubtedly took for granted that even minimally qualified readers would know what went before and would know the context in which the verse occurs. Some commentators have correctly pointed out that this verse affirms two principles of faith, the existence of God and the creation of the world.[17] It is more than likely that Maimonides was conscious of the ambiguity in the last phrase, *'El 'olam,* which can mean either "Eternal God," or (in later usage) "God of the world." It follows then that

16. Maimonides used this verse as the superscript over almost all his works. Kafih points out that this is the case in the *Commentary on the Mishnah,* the *Mishneh Torah,* the *Sefer ha-Mitzvot,* and the *Essay on Resurrection.* He notes that the best manuscripts of these works contain this verse, although it was eliminated from many of the printed editions. See Moses Maimonides, *Guide,* ed. Y. Kafih, vol. I (Jerusalem, 1972), I n. I, and *'Iggerot ha-Rambam,* ed. Kafih, 69 n. 2. See also on this point the comments by S. Lieberman in his edition of *Hilkhot ha-Yerushalmi le-Rabbenu Moshe ben Maimon Z.L.* (New York, 1948), 5 n.7.

17. See, for example, the observations of Yehuda Even-Shmuel Kaufmann in his edition and commentary on the *Guide* (*Sefer Moreh ha-Nevukhim [Guide of the Perplexed],* vol. I [Jerusalem, 1959], 5).

he is reading this expression to mean that God, who is alone eternal, is the only possible creator of the world, which is temporal. Even if we were to stop here, we would already be aware of the deep significance of his choice of this verse as the heading for each section of the *Guide*.

It would be a mistake to stop at this point. We saw earlier that Maimonides expects his readers to have sufficient knowledge of rabbinic literature so that they react to his citations with the appropriate set of associations. Even ordinary students of this literature would be expected to know the familiar talmudic statement on this verse. The Talmud comments on the word *vayikra'*, "and he called" [on the name of the Lord] with the following observation:

> Resh Lakish said: Read not 'and he called' but 'and he made to call' [*vayakri'*], thereby teaching that our father Abraham caused the name of the Holy One, blessed be He, to be uttered by the mouth of every passer-by. How was this? After [travelers] had eaten and drunk, they stood up to bless him; but, said he to them, 'Did you eat of mine? You ate of that which belongs to the God of the Universe. *Thank, praise and bless Him who spake and the world came into being.*[18]

This familiar passage should come to mind immediately for any Jewishly educated reader of Maimonides. Let us take account of two features of the passage. First, it stresses the role of Abraham as proclaiming the truth about God to a world in which the knowledge of that truth had been lost. According to this portrayal, Abraham considered this truth to be the most important thing that he could teach to anyone who enjoyed the warmth and hospitality of his home. The food he shared with his guests was more than the extension of kindness to travelers. Its value was vastly enhanced when it served as the occasion for bringing them a far greater good, namely, the knowledge of God, which was spiritual food that would matter to them more than any material gift. In the Jewish tradition, Abraham is associated above all with *ḥesed*, acts of love and graciousness toward his fellow men. Certainly, his greatest act of *ḥesed* was to teach them the truths that were essential both to the quality of their earthly lives and to their ultimate salvation.[19] When

---

18. *Sotah*, 10b; emphasis added.

19. It has been noted in various sources that Abraham differed from Noah because, unlike Noah, he refused to accept passively the destruction of those who might be saved. The Bible records various episodes in which Abraham took up the cause of those who were in trouble, even if, as in the case of Sodom and Gomorrah, it meant that he had to challenge God Himself. The gracious concern for his fellow men shown in his determination to teach them the truth

Maimonides chose to head all three parts of the *Guide,* as well as his other works, with this scriptural verse that defines the way of Abraham, he was telling his readers that the purpose of his work is to teach the most important truths to those who have come to share the hospitality of his literary home. He is casting himself as the Abraham of his generation (and perhaps of future generations by virtue of the permanence of his book) whose mission it is to save the Jewish people from their confusions and errors with respect to the highest of all concerns, the knowledge of the existence of God and His relationship to the world. The threefold repetition of the verse, over each of the three parts of the *Guide,* serves to emphasize the point. This is Maimonides' definition of his mission, the identification of the *ḥesed* which he is extending to his contemporaries and to future generations of readers. He expects his readers to become aware of this through a process of reflection similar to what we have just now followed. Otherwise, they will fail to understand the deepest aims of his writing.

A second point also requires our attention. According to the talmudic tale, Abraham uses the occasion of hospitality to weary travelers not only to teach gratitude to God and thus to transmit the truth of His existence, but also to instruct his guests that God is the creator of the world. "Thank, praise and bless Him who spoke and the world came into being." Maimonides, by relying on our knowledge of this talmudic comment, is telling us that the two most important truths he is setting forth in his book are that God exists and that He created the world by an act of His will.[20] In this way he has made Creation an overarching theme that must be seen as occupying the center of his concern. Moreover, it should be noted that, like Abraham, he is in this superscript simply proclaiming these truths, rather than arguing them.

The implied self-comparison with Abraham carries two implications for readers of the *Guide.* Like Abraham, Maimonides is committed to argue in favor of these doctrines as fully and effectively as he can, and even to compose books about them. Also like Abraham, he is compelled to proclaim these doctrines, even without argument, whenever appropriate. For those

---

about God is one more aspect of the quality of *ḥesed* that was central to his character. For the explicit association of Abraham with *ḥesed,* see Mic. 7:20.

20. Abraham urges his guests to give thanks *le-mi she-'amar ve-hayah ha-'olam.* In *Guide,* I, 67, p. 161, Maimonides states explicitly that "the term 'to say' ['*amirah*] is figuratively used for the will in regard to everything that has been created in the 'six days of the beginning'—with reference to which it is said: 'He said, He said.' " Thus we see that Abraham should be understood from this perspective as teaching his guests that God created the world as an act of His will. We shall discuss later the problem of whether it is possible to speak of will as a separate attribute of the divine being. It is premature to take it up here.

who cannot readily follow a philosophical argument, passionate proclamation may well be the only effective mode of teaching. Even for those who can follow an argument and understand when a conclusion has been demonstrated, seeking commitment through the force of proclamation is important because it may well be that neither of these doctrines will turn out to be demonstrated or demonstrable. We saw earlier that even the claim to know the existence of God by a demonstrative argument may turn out to be problematic. Although Maimonides presents a number of proofs for the existence of God in the course of his book, he may feel that, despite the force and vigor of his arguments, none of them is absolutely definitive. Let us remember the remarkable statement, quoted earlier, in which he casts doubt on the possibility of proving the existence of God (*Guide*, II, 24, p. 327). Perhaps in the last analysis these arguments only bring us to see the high probability of the existence of God, but fall short of actual demonstration. In that case, it would be necessary to proclaim, even to the philosophically sophisticated, that although we may lack the capacity to produce an absolute demonstration, the best and most persuasive account that we can offer of the intelligible order of reality rests on the premise that God exists.

In the case of creation versus eternity, the record is especially clear. Maimonides never claims to offer a demonstration of creation, although he does present a series of considerations that he believes should incline a thoughtful person in the direction of belief in creation.[21] Despite the force of these considerations, he shows us that neither side in the debate has achieved a sound demonstration of its position, so that we can only appeal to probabilities and/or to the teachings of the religious tradition. Yet belief in creation is so fundamental both to Jewish faith and to a proper ordering of the world that, lacking demonstrative certainty, it must be proclaimed as the doctrine on which we rest. Other matters of deep concern, such as God's unity and incorporeality, can be demonstrated, because Maimonides believes that they follow necessarily from a correct understanding of the concept of God. These doctrines do not need to be proclaimed in the same

---

21. We shall discuss Maimonides' treatment of the intellectual evidence in favor of creation later in this chapter. It should be noted here that he attributes to Abraham also a method in which he exhausted the guidance that could come from the intellect in regard to creation. He tells us that "Abraham taught the people and explained to them by means of speculative proofs that the world has but one deity, that He has created all the things that are other than Himself" (*Guide*, II, 39, p. 379). The term that Pines translates "speculative proofs" (*'adilla nazariya*) means something considerably less than actual demonstration. It refers to the presentation of a set of considerations which should incline the intellect in one direction rather than another, that is, considerations which a thoughtful person should see as generating a high probability in favor of one view against another.

way as God's existence and His creation of the world. They should be demonstrated to all who are capable of following the line of argument. Maimonides does insist, however, that those who cannot follow the force of the arguments should be persuaded to accept these teachings as well on the authority of those who know (see *Guide*, I, 35, p. 81). Yet the situation with respect to these doctrines is eased by his confidence that he has demonstrations on which to rest his case, while he has far less philosophical certainty to offer in regard to God's existence and His creation of the world. These latter are nevertheless so fundamental that, demonstrated or not, Maimonides proclaims them as the foundation and framework of the entire structure that he proposes to build in the *Guide of the Perplexed*. This proclamation of Maimonides, contained and repeated in the superscript to each part of the *Guide*, must be clearly before us as we study his extended treatment of the question of whether the world is eternal or was created in time.

It is important to keep in mind that the traditions that Maimonides inherited were by no means clear and unequivocal on the subject of creation. We cannot say for certain exactly what the opening words of Genesis mean, nor do we have a universally accepted translation. The major medieval Bible commentators differ in their understanding, running from ibn Ezra who veils only slightly his belief that the divine creation was an act of forming preexistent matter, to Rashi who does not address the issue directly and can be read to yield a number of meanings, to Naḥmanides who states categorically that God created the world from absolute nothing. It has been shown that Maimonides himself offers several different interpretations of the verb *bara'*.[22] Above all, he himself said explicitly that if there were a demonstration of the eternity of the world according to the Aristotelian doctrine, he would have no problem in reconciling this view with the verses in Genesis. What greater admission could there be of his conviction that the language of Scripture is inherently ambiguous on this point?

The rabbinic literature is even more openly ambiguous. On the one hand, we have the apparently unequivocal statement of Rabban Gamliel in response to the challenge posed by an unnamed philosopher. The latter provoked him with the statement that while the God of Scripture is to be praised as a superb artisan, it should not be forgotten that He found ready at hand the raw materials from which He made the world. Rabban Gamliel re-

---

22. For an extended discussion, see Klein-Braslavy, *Perush ha-Rambam le-Sippur Beri'at ha-'Olam*, 81–90. She shows that despite the confident assertions of a number of commentators that Maimonides consistently understood *bara'* to mean creation out of nothing, the textual evidence in the *Guide* suggests that there is considerable ambiguity in his understanding of this term.

sponds with a strong curse on the heretical philosopher, and then counters his argument with what he claims is definitive scriptural evidence that the world was created out of nothing.[23] Similarly, there is an attack on those who dishonor the name of God by suggesting that he created the world out of *tohu* and *bohu,* which, according to this reading of Scripture, are thought to be the preexisting primary materials of creation. Yet, that passage ends with the statement that this is what the scriptural text appears to say and that "if it were not so written, it would be impossible for us to use such language about creation."[24] Even if we understand this last statement to convey the idea that, standing by themselves, the terms used in Scripture can be dangerous and misleading, it is nonetheless an admission that there is a lack of clarity in the opening verses of the Bible. One of the most striking statements that points to creation out of preexisting materials is that of R. Yohanan, who is quoted as saying, "How did the Holy One, blessed be He, create His world? He took two balls, one of fire and one of snow, and intermingled them, and the world was created from them."[25]

It should be noted that the Jewish philosophical tradition is equally ambiguous. We have already cited ibn Ezra in favor of creation out of preexisting matter. On the other hand, from an earlier period we have the extended argument of Saadia Gaon in defense of the doctrine of creation out of nothing as not only correct Jewish doctrine, but also philosophically correct and demonstrable.[26] (As we shall see, Maimonides argues vigorously against such Kalām claims of philosophical demonstration for the *ex nihilo* doctrine.) In between is the view of Judah Halevi, who affirms creation out of nothing, but still recognizes the so-called Platonic view of creation out of preexistent unformed matter as acceptable.

> The question of eternity and creation is obscure, whilst the arguments are evenly balanced. The theory of creation derives greater

23. *Genesis Rabbah,* I, 9, p. 8, Theodor-Albeck edition (Jerusalem, 1965). All citations from *Gen. Rab.* will be from this edition.

24. Ibid., I, 5, pp. 2–3.

25. Ibid., X, 2, p. 75. For a similar statement see IV, 7, p. 31. There are extended discussions of these and similar passages in E. E. Urbach, *Ḥazal: Pirkei'Emunot ve-De'ot* (Jerusalem, 1969), 161–89, translated into English as *The Sages,* vol. 1 (Jerusalem, 1975), 184–213. Urbach tends to dismiss any reading of these midrashic passages that construes them as referring to creation out of pre-existent matter. For a study of the evidence for the emanation theory of creation in this early literature, see Alexander Altmann, "A Note on the Rabbinic Doctrine of Creation," in *Studies in Religious Philosophy and Mysticism* (London, 1969), 128–39.

26. Rav Saadia Gaon, *Sefer'Emunot ve-De'ot,* Treatise I. In English, *The Book of Beliefs and Opinions,* trans. S. Rosenblatt (New Haven, 1948), 38–86.

weight from the prophetic tradition of Adam, Noah, and Moses, which is more deserving of credence than mere speculation. If, after all, a believer in the Law finds himself compelled to admit an eternal matter and the existence of many worlds prior to this one, this would not impair his belief that *this* world was created at a certain epoch, and that Adam and Noah were the first human beings.[27]

As we shall see, this is a view that Maimonides himself echoes at more than one point.

The most open and direct evidence that Maimonides was consciously aware of the fact that the Jewish tradition did not speak with a single voice on the subject of creation is in *Guide,* II, 26. He begins that chapter with an expression of apparent bewilderment at a statement about creation that is attributed to R. Eliezer the Great. We need to keep in mind that this sage is R. Eliezer ben Hyrcanus, one of the most revered of the tannaitic teachers. He won most extravagant praise from his teacher, R. Yohanan ben Zakkai, and was, in turn, the master of so outstanding a disciple as R. Akiba. It was out of reverence for him, and as a mark of his distinction, that the tradition attached to his name the appellation *ha-gadol,* the great. Maimonides cites the following passage from *Pirkei de-Rabbi Eliezer:*

> Wherefrom were the heavens created? From the light of His garment. He took some of it, stretched it like a cloth, and thus they were extending continually, as it is said: Who coverest Thyself with light as with a garment. Who stretchest out the heavens like a curtain. (Ps. 104:2) Wherefrom was the earth created? From the snow under the throne of His glory. He took some of it and threw it, as it is said: For He saith to the snow, Be thou earth. (Job 37:6)

Maimonides then makes this comment: "Would that I knew what that Sage believed. Did he believe that it is impossible that something should come into being out of nothing and that there must necessarily be matter out of which that which is generated is produced? . . . For he would have admitted thereby the eternity of the world, if only as it is conceived according to Plato's opinion."[28] However we explain Maimonides' professed astonishment

27. Judah Halevi, *Kuzari,* I, 67. In English, *The Kuzari,* trans. H. Hirschfeld (New York, 1964), 54.

28. We know today that *Pirkei de-Rabbi Eliezer* is a later work that was certainly not composed by R. Eliezer b. Hyrcanus, but Maimonides seems to have accepted it as authentic and as representing the actual teaching of the great sage. In any case, it had entered into the canonical works of rabbinic literature and was thus to be treated seriously, whoever its author might be.

at this statement of R. Eliezer, it is clear that he knew that the rabbinic sources open up a variety of options with regard to our understanding of creation. He may have paid little attention to the Jewish philosophers who preceded him, but he certainly tried to give full weight to the whole of the rabbinic literature.[29] We can readily conclude that there was no internal Jewish pressure on Maimonides to reach a single, fixed conclusion with respect to the problem of creation, nor was there a fixed scientific or philosophic tradition, Jewish or non-Jewish, so persuasive that he felt intellectually bound to uphold it. With this background we can now turn to our explication of Maimonides' position.

To orient ourselves properly, let us first consider how he approaches the solution of problems of such complexity and importance as the origin of the world. His first rule is that one must be guided by complete and unwavering intellectual honesty. His deepest criticism of the Kalām thinkers is not only that they are wrong on particular points, but also that they start their investigation committed to the answer they want and then adjust the evidence and the arguments so as to produce the predetermined desired result. "All the first Mutakallimūn from among the Greeks who had adopted Christianity and from among the Moslems did not conform in their premises to the appearance of that which exists, but considered how being ought to be in order that it should furnish a proof for the correctness of a particular opinion, or at least should not refute it" (*Guide*, I, 71, p. 178). This method may sometimes be effective for purposes of apologetics or propaganda, but it undermines all true intellectual inquiry. For Maimonides, the proper way is that taught by Themistius, whose rule is, "That which exists does not conform to the various opinions, but rather the correct opinions conform to that which exists" (I, 71, p. 179). Because he is committed to this principle of honest inquiry, no matter where it may lead, Maimonides is able to say, as we have already noted, that if anyone would present him with a sound demonstration of the eternity of the world, he would accept it without hesitation (II, 25, p. 327).

Now with respect to creation, Maimonides finds himself in a difficult situation. He reviews carefully all the evidence available in favor of both the creation thesis and the eternity thesis, but finds that none of it is decisive. (We shall shortly review the nature of this evidence, but we first need to consider his own account of his method.) What should he do when he confronts

---

Parallel passages occur in *Gen. Rab.* I, 6, p. 4; *Tanḥuma B.*, Gen., I, 11, p. 8; *p. Ḥagigah*, 2:1, among others.

29. See S. Pines, "The Philosophic Sources of *The Guide of the Perplexed*," the translator's introduction to his edition of the *Guide*, cxxxii–cxxxiv.

a fundamental question that is of inordinate interest for philosophy, science, and religion, but does not lend itself to resolution by the recognized methods of those disciplines? Some writers have argued that Maimonides simply chose to remain agnostic, that is, to take no stand at all, because he could not produce decisive evidence for any one of the options.[30] This seems to be patently wrong. We have the counterevidence in those of his works where he is explicit about his views. Moreover, we are dealing with a question that cannot be left unsettled, because life itself forces us to take a stand. We may claim to be agnostic, but if we behave as if there were no Creator-God, no role for Him in history, no miracles, no reward, and punishment, we have taken a stand *de facto,* if not *de jure.* Here the behavioral criterion serves to reveal our actual beliefs, no matter how strongly we affirm our agnosticism. Although we could, according to this criterion, infer Maimonides' views from his behavior as a religiously observant Jew, he does not leave us to this alone. He gives us clear indications of his views as he develops the subject in the *Guide of the Perplexed.*

Maimonides' first concern is to make sure that he will not be caught in the trap of the Kalām which manipulates the evidence to provide the desired answer. This danger exists, in particular, when we are dealing with a subject that is of great importance but does not yield demonstrated certainties. Special caution is required for such a subject. Honest and objective study is assured only if the investigator has the appropriate intellectual and moral training. "Whoever prefers one of the two opinions because of his upbringing or for some advantage, is blind to the truth. While one who entertains an unfounded predilection cannot make himself oppose a matter susceptible of demonstration, in matters like those under discussion such an opposition is often possible" (II, 23, p. 321). How can anyone be certain that he is not yielding to his own prejudices and preferences as he decides between premises not susceptible to absolute proof? Maimonides' answer is that one must have a good mind and excellent training in logic, mathematics, natural science, and philosophy. In addition, one must have a moral character of very high order. If you have these qualities, "you can rid yourself of an unfounded predilection, free yourself of what is habitual, rely solely on speculation, and prefer the opinion that you ought to prefer" (II, 23, p. 321). Clearly we have here a capsule self-description of Maimonides, assuring his readers that he can be trusted, if anyone can, to review the evidence honestly and objectively so as to arrive at the soundest possible conclusion.

30. This is argued most forcefully in the works of Klein-Braslavy cited in note 7. Using phenomenological terminology, she states that Maimonides engaged in *epoché,* the suspension of all judgment, with respect to creation or eternity.

Just what is the evidence offered by the Kalām and by Aristotle and what is wrong with it? I shall summarize here the main points and concerns that emerge from the critical examination to which Maimonides subjects the two sides of the argument. To begin with, the Kalām arguments for creation are criticized by him for a variety of logical errors. Individual premises are shown to be poorly founded, and various claims that they make are shown to be unsound. However, one crucial defect in their position seems to weigh more heavily in Maimonides' judgment than any mistake they make with respect to particular points or arguments. We learn from Maimonides that the most damaging effect of their position is to undermine our convictions about the fixity of the order of nature in the sublunar world.

We noted earlier that Maimonides repeatedly asserts that what Aristotle teaches in regard to the natural order in the sublunar world is correct and reliable. He reaches this conclusion on the basis of what he considers to be incontrovertible evidence, not simply as a matter of his personal preference or loyalty to a philosophic school. In taking this position, Maimonides is supported by the best and most advanced scientific opinion of his time; this opinion considers the order of nature to be fixed due to an inexorable chain of causal necessity. Together with most of his contemporaries, he holds that no physical science would be possible without this chain of necessary causal connections, and without such causal necessity our world would be totally unreliable and unintelligible. Such a situation is unacceptable to Maimonides, not because he find it unpleasant or offensive, but because it runs counter to what he is convinced has been firmly established by demonstration.

The Mutakallimūn arrive at their position because of their doctrine of possibility or, as it is sometimes called, doctrine of admissibility. Maimonides tells us, "This is the main proposition of the science of kalām. . . . They are of the opinion that everything that may be imagined is an admissible notion for the intellect," or put even more exactly, "that which can be imagined is, according to them, something possible, whether something existent corresponds to it or not. On the other hand, everything that cannot be imagined is impossible" (I, 73, pp. 206–7). For them "the foundation of everything is that no consideration is due to how that which exists is, for it is merely a custom; and from the point of view of the intellect, it could well be different. Furthermore, in many places they follow the imagination and call it intellect" (I, 71, p. 179). The consequence of this view is that there is no necessary order in the world. It happens that things are as they are and as we are accustomed to experiencing them, but this is not due to any inherent causal necessity. They consider the criterion of possibility to be whether something is imaginable, that is to say, whether it is possible for the human mind to conceive or to picture it. The only thing that we can neither imagine nor conceive is that which is logically impossible, that is, the self-contradictory. Thus, for the Kalām, as Maimonides represents its teachings, the only kind of impossibility is logical impossibility. Everything else is possible, even though it runs counter to the order of nature as we know and experience it. The underlying reason for this is that the Kalām assigns all causal activity directly to God, and in so doing denies that there are any fixities in the world. To cite the well-worn example, when one pours black ink on a white sheet, the sheet turns black only because at that moment God chooses to make it black. There is no independently operating causal ground for this event. Were God to choose instead to turn it into some other color or to leave its whiteness unaffected, then that would happen. At each instant of time whatever takes place happens because God wills it so. There is no other causal force operating in the world.

> They assert that when a man moves a pen, it is not the man who moves it; for the motion occurring in the pen is an accident created by God in the pen. Similarly the motion of the hand, which we think of as moving the pen, is an accident created by God in the moving hand. Only, God has instituted the habit that the motion of the hand is concomitant with the motion of the pen, without the hand exercising in any respect an influence on, or being causative in regard to, the motion of the pen (I, 73, p. 202).

The net effect of this doctrine is to destroy our scientific notions concerning the order of nature. It makes groundless all claims concerning how things must be in the world, except for claims based on the purely logical denial that contradictory properties can exist simultaneously.[31] Other than this, everything is dependent on the direct action of God at each instant. This, in turn, is purely dependent on His will. It happens that He has chosen thus far to sustain the order of the world as we know it, but this provides no assurance whatsoever about the future, not even about the next moment.

Maimonides argues that there is nothing absolutely decisive about this argument and that its premises may be viewed as no more than assumptions. He is strongly moved to resist these premises because they run counter to what he believes has been soundly established in the Aristotelian natural philosophy. Moreover, he sees clearly the price we would pay if we were to

---

31. In chapter 2, I made the point that even the claims about logical impossibility can be questioned and shown to rest on unverifiable assumptions about the nature of the world. We also saw that the consequence of such a view is to destroy all intelligibility. The Kalām apparently was not prepared to go that far, but stopped just short of that extreme.

accept the Kalām position. It might serve the interests of biblical religion in one way, by making everything dependent on God not only ultimately, but immediately and proximately. It would then be easier to establish the religious teaching about God as the creator of all, and it would not only make possible those miracles that run counter to the order of nature, but would also construe every moment of the history of the world as a miracle, so to speak. Each moment of existence would be one created and sustained by God's direct and deliberate action. Tempting as such a view might be for a religious thinker, Maimonides resists it mightily. To accept it would mean to give up the entire world-picture that had been built up by the best and most careful scientific investigation and philosophical reflection. If the views of the Kalām were demonstrated, he would have no choice but to accept them. Since he believes he has shown definitively that they neither have been nor could be demonstrated, there is no *a priori* reason why he need feel compelled to accept them. Before he can responsibly make a clear decision, it is imperative for Maimonides to consider the alternatives.

The main alternative to the teachings of the Mutakallimūn is the Aristotelian view that the world is eternal, that it is moved by a First Cause acting out of its own necessity, and that as a result of the activity of this cause, the universe has been generated and continues to exist and to move. As the highest and most perfect being, the First Cause may be thought of as possessing all perfections. The world is as it is because it follows necessarily from the nature of the First Mover and the potentialities of the eternally existing matter that is given form by that mover's action. Whether we understand this generative activity as emanation, or as in some way mechanical, is irrelevant to our problem. All that matters is that, from the point of view of Aristotle, all being, from the highest to the lowest, is generated by the inner necessity of the First Cause and operates under the continuing rule of necessity imposed by the force of that cause. From the permanent, immaterial forms of the separate intellects, to the permanent spheres that consist of form impressed on a specially elevated matter, to all the furniture of our sublunar world, which is subject to generation and corruption—all exist and move by virtue of the fixed necessity imposed by the chain of causal connections that goes back to the First Cause. The order of the world is fixed, and no intervention is possible or even conceivable on the part of the cause of all. In the very nature of the case there can be no break in the fixity of the natural order, no intervention by the highest being into the affairs of lower beings in the universe.

This view holds an obvious attraction for Maimonides. It preserves the order of nature, and for him this is of the highest intellectual and practical importance. He has told us repeatedly that all that Aristotle teaches concerning the order of the sublunar world is absolutely sound and reliable. This has been established through the combined force of what we know through demonstration and through empirical observation. Maimonides believes that this conception of a fixed natural order in the sublunar world is also the opinion of the Sages of Israel. As Maimonides reads them, they generally express the view that, except for reliably attested miracles, the world follows a fixed order without continuing miraculous interventions from above. Even the attested miracles are held by some sages to have been built into the order of the world at creation, and this too serves to reduce the effect of the breaks in the natural order resulting from active divine intervention (II, 29, pp. 345–46).[32]

The stable world order of the Aristotelian cosmology has its decided attractions, but there is of course a negative side as well. As we saw earlier, Maimonides affirms that the acceptance of the entire cosmology of Aristotle destroys the fundamental teachings of the Torah and undermines the foundations of Jewish religious faith. Now it is clear to us that for Maimonides, the Aristotelian theory, like any other theory, must be judged on its own merits and not simply by whether it is attractive or repellent to us. The critical question is whether Aristotle has established his claims by sound demonstrations. If he has, then we must accept his teachings whether we like them or not. If he has not, then we have to ask whether there is any decisive reason for accepting or rejecting them.

Just as Maimonides devotes much space to an analysis and exposition of the teachings of the Kalām, so does he devote similar effort to the analysis and exposition of Aristotle. And just as he is forced to conclude that the Mutakallimūn have not demonstrated their doctrines concerning the creation of the world, so is he forced to conclude that the Aristotelians have not demonstrated their doctrine concerning the eternity of the world. As in our discussion of his strictures against the Kalām, we shall not attempt to reproduce or summarize the extensive detail of Maimonides' argument against Aristotle. We shall rather concentrate on its central feature. What is wrong with the Aristotelian position can be stated briefly. It supposes that from the state of affairs that we know in the world after it has come into being, we can find sound and reliable evidence about the way it came into being. Maimonides argues that this is a basic error leading to unfounded conclusions. We

32. Maimonides emphasizes here that miracles do not introduce any permanent changes in the fixed order of nature. The Sages hold the view "that miracles too are something that is, in a certain respect, in nature. They say that when God created that which exists and stamped upon it the existing natures, He put it into these natures that all the miracles that occurred would be produced in them at the time when they occurred" (II, 29, p. 345).

cannot legitimately make any inferences from the created world to what may have been the case before its creation, nor can we determine anything definite about the process of its creation. Once we go beyond the limits of actual and possible experience we also go beyond the limits of what can be established by inference from that experience. Transcend experience, and you have transcended the limits of knowledge and intelligibility.[33]

> In the case of everything produced in time, which is generated after not having existed—even in those cases in which the matter of the thing was already existent and in the course of the production of the thing had merely put off one and put on another form—the nature of that particular thing after it has been produced in time, has attained its final state, and achieved stability, is different from its nature when it is being generated and is beginning to pass from potentiality to actuality. It is also different from the nature the thing had before it had moved so as to pass from potentiality to actuality. . . . No inference can be drawn in any respect from the nature of a thing after it has been generated, has attained its final state, and has achieved stability in its most perfect state, to the state of that thing while it moved toward being generated. Nor can an inference be drawn from the state of the thing when it moves toward being generated to its state before it begins to move thus (II, 17, pp. 294–95).

This is a summary statement of the point which Maimonides makes in far more elaborate form in the course of his argument against Aristotle.

The conclusion he draws is that Aristotle and the Aristotelian tradition are not able to provide us with a demonstration in support of their theory of the eternity of the world. His detailed arguments against the various methods used by the Aristotelians to demonstrate their thesis all seem to me to rest finally on this one premise—that it is not possible to argue from the created world to the state of affairs prior to what is now known to us. As we noted earlier, this argument is strongly anticipatory of the position taken by Kant in the eighteenth century. It is exactly on this ground that Kant establishes the impossibility of human knowledge about the ultimate state of things, a state that transcends all actual and all possible human experience.

Maimonides strengthens his argument by showing the critical difference between the account we are able to give of the observed facts of the sublunar world and those of the supralunar world. In the case of the sublunar world, Aristotelian doctrine is able to explain why things are as they are and why they could not be otherwise. Once the causal chain has begun, we can

33. This subject was discussed briefly in chapter 9.

enter it at any point and work out an explanation of why things occur in a particular way. Maimonides shows that, in contrast, when we are talking about the world of the spheres, no such explanations are available to us. This is what Maimonides calls the problem of particularization, that is, the effort to make intelligible each particular state of affairs that we observe in the world. He has already hinted that the issue of particularization might well be the undoing of the Aristotelian theory of the eternity of the world. In the midst of his sharp critique of the methods by which the Kalām tries to establish that the world was created in time, Maimonides takes note of the "method of particularization . . . a method to which they accord very great preference." He concludes his discussion of it with the observation that "this is to my mind a most excellent method. I have, with regard to it, an opinion which you shall hear" (I, 74, pp. 218–19). In this side remark, tucked away in the middle of a long critical discussion of the Kalām methodology, Maimonides informs us that we must pay close attention to how he himself will use this method later in his book.

He does, in fact, use it extensively to expose the flaws in the Aristotelian theory. He brings before his readers a set of empirical observations concerning the nature and motions of the heavenly bodies. These observations were generally accepted in his time as factually correct, and they present a somewhat chaotic picture of the state of supralunar astronomy. Aristotle was already aware of the problem that faced him when he tried to give an account of the causal necessities that determined the state of affairs in the world of the spheres. It is important for us to see how Maimonides expresses the problem.

> [Aristotle] wished to bring order for our benefit into the being of the spheres, as he has brought order for us into the existence of that which is beneath the sphere. He wished to do this in order that the whole should exist in virtue of natural necessity and not in virtue of the purpose of one who purposes according to his will whatever it be and the particularization of one who particularizes in whatever way he likes. *Now this task has not been accomplished by him, nor will it ever be accomplished.* For he wished to give a cause for the fact that the sphere moves from the East and not from the West; and he wished to give a cause for the fact that some of them are swift of motion and others slow. . . . *He wished to assign causes for all this so that these things would be ordered for us in a natural order that is due to necessity. However, he has accomplished none of these undertakings.* As a matter of fact, all that he has explained to us regarding what is beneath the sphere of the moon follows an order conforming to that which exists, an order whose causes are clear.

276

One can say of it that it derives of necessity from the motion and the powers of the sphere. On the other hand, one can say of all that he has stated with regard to matters pertaining to the sphere, that he has assigned no clear cause with regard to this, and that the matter, as he sets it out, does not follow an order for which necessity can be claimed (II, 19, pp. 306–7; emphasis added).

This theme is repeated a number of times by Maimonides, usually following a strong statement of support of Aristotelian physics as applied to the sublunar world. He summarizes his position with the assertion that any one who rejects Aristotle's teaching concerning the sublunar world does so either because "he does not understand it or unless he has preconceived notions that he wants to defend or that lead him to a denial of a thing that is manifest." Yet with all this regard for Aristotle, Maimonides goes on to say that what he teaches concerning "the sphere of the moon and that which is above it is, except for certain things, something analogous to guessing and conjecturing. All the more does this apply to what he says about the order of the intellects and to some of the opinions regarding the divine that he believes" (II, 22, p. 320).

Maimonides is saying that, given the order of the sublunar world that we know in our direct experience, we can work out a system of natural causation that will account for it fully. Furthermore, this system of causation, being fixed, makes it possible for us not only to understand any present state of affairs in the world, but also to predict future states with confidence. We are incapable, however, of using our own intellectual resources to arrive at a similar understanding of how things operate in the supralunar world.

Even in contemporary physics and astronomy we face similar problems. Every one recognizes that we today have far more detailed and, one presumes, far more reliable descriptions of the physical universe than were available in antiquity or the Middle Ages. Yet there are two points of crucial interest to our present discussion with respect to which contemporary scientists are no more able to give satisfactory answers than were their counterparts of earlier times. The first is the question of how it all got started. Even moving back to the first nanosecond of the process provides no explanation for the absolute beginning, for the emergence of something out of nothing. The second is the question of why things are as they are rather than otherwise, that is, what Maimonides calls the problem of particularization. If we ask why the planets in our solar system rotate in the direction that they do, rather than in the opposite direction, no answer can be given. Once the process has begun, it is relatively easy to explain why things continue as they do. But we have no explanation for why our universe is as it is rather than being a mirror image of itself.[34] Maimonides seeks a convincing explanation which will save us from having to believe that there is sheer arbitrariness in the structure and processes of the supralunar world. In his view such arbitrariness is an offense to reason, and it should be avoided if there is an intellectually honest and legitmate way to do so. Since Aristotle has not provided a satisfactory account, Maimonides must seek elsewhere

Before we consider his treatment of this question, however, we need to clear up one more matter, namely, what Maimonides thought Aristotle's true position was with respect to this issue. He is convinced that Aristotle was too good a philosopher to have made the elementary mistake of supposing that he had a demonstration for that which is both undemonstrated and undemonstrable. It is true that "the latter-day followers of Aristotle believe that Aristotle has demonstrated the eternity of the world," but Maimonides is convinced that Aristotle himself surely knew better. That is why he assures us that Aristotle "is not mistaken with regard to this. I mean to say that he himself knows that he possesses no demonstration with regard to this point." Since we know Aristotle's dazzling eminence as a philosopher, Maimonides asks, "Can Aristotle have been ignorant of the difference between mere arguments and demonstrations, as well as between opinions, which when thought about may be accepted to a greater or lesser extent, and things of demonstration?" (II, 15, pp. 289–91).

Maimonides presents what he considers to be decisive evidence that Aristotle knew very well that he had no demonstration for the eternity of the world or for the order and system of the spheres which should follow necessarily from the eternity thesis. According to Maimonides, he was fully aware that in this case he was presenting arguments from probability, but not demonstrations. This leaves Maimonides with the methodological question of how to proceed from this point. If neither the creation nor the eternity thesis has been demonstrated, and if, as Maimonides thinks he has shown, they are in principle incapable of being demonstrated, how shall we decide between them? If we are dealing only with probabilities, how do we go about determining which thesis, if any, should command our assent?

The methodological principle, as Maimonides states it, seems simple and clear. First, we should consider the doubts that can be raised against each thesis. We should then favor the opinion with the least number of doubts attached to it. He adds immediately, however, that it is not and should

34. I am grateful to my friend and colleague at Brandeis University, astrophysicist Jack S. Goldstein, for discussing these matters with me and helping me to understand the contemporary scientific setting. He informs me that there are certain special exceptions to the principle that I have stated, but that on the whole it is correct.

not be a matter simply of numbers. Of even greater importance is the gravity of the doubts that are raised. There are cases where a single counterinstance is sufficient to undermine an otherwise persuasive hypothesis. To use the familiar classroom example, the statement that all swans are white is falsified by observing a single black swan. The matter is more complicated in the case of probabilities, because we do not have absolutely decisive counterinstances. If we had such decisive counterinstances we would be able to establish certainties rather than mere probabilities. To determine how much weight to attach to a doubt and how heavily it should count against a particular hypothesis is by no means simple. Nevertheless, Maimonides is confident that, despite the difficulty of determining the degree of gravity of any given doubt, he has developed a workable rule of procedure.[35]

To be able to apply this rule, we first need to state clearly the alternate theses. In *Guide,* II, 13, Maimonides sets forth three theories concerning the origin of the world. The first is "that the world as a whole—I mean to say, every existent other than God, may He be exalted—was brought into existence by God after having been purely and absolutely nonexistent." Originally, nothing whatsoever existed but God. "Afterward, through His will and volition, He brought into existence out of nothing all the beings as they are, time itself being one of the created things" (II, 13, p. 281). Maimonides identifies this as the opinion of the Jewish religious community. It is one of the basic principles of the Torah and is the teaching proclaimed by Abraham. It should be noted that while the creation thesis is explicitly affirmed in this formulation, it says nothing whatsoever about the necessity or contingency of either the sublunar or the supralunar worlds.

"The second opinion is that of all the philosophers of whom we have heard reports and whose discourses we have seen." This opinion starts from the premise that creation out of nothing is utterly unintelligible. It is, in fact, a logical contradiction, just as it would be to assert that God can create something that has simultaneously contradictory properties. It goes on to assert that both God and prime matter exist eternally, and He forms out of this prime matter whatever He chooses. Maimonides identifies this as the view taught by Plato in the *Timaeus,* and he adds that, contrary to those who have an imprecise view of such matters, this is not "what we believe." The Jewish religious community believes that everything, including the heavens, was created by God out of "a state of absolute nonexistence," while Plato believed that all generation is from matter that had prior existence (II, 13, pp. 282–84).

The third view is that of Aristotle and the Aristotelian tradition. As we

35. The main discussion of these methodological principles is in *Guide,* II, 22–23.

already know from our earlier summary of this opinion, it affirms the eternity of matter and denies the possibility of creation out of nothing. However, unlike the Platonic view, which ascribes to God the activity that forms the entire world from prime matter, including the generation of the heavens, Aristotle holds that the heavens are eternal and not brought into being. He also holds that "time and motion are perpetual and everlasting and not subject to generation and passing-away. . . . He thinks furthermore that this whole higher and lower order cannot be corrupted and abolished, that no innovation can take place in it that is not according to its nature." He can speak of God's will only in a purely figurative way, since he allows for no possibility of any change in that will. It is fixed permanently, just as the rest of the world order is fixed permanently. "Accordingly it follows that this being as a whole has never ceased to be as it is at present and will be as it is in the future eternity" (II, 13, p. 284).

Maimonides now introduces certain restrictions into the discussion. He limits himself to these three opinions, since the demonstration for the existence of God is established according to any one of them. There is no point then in considering the views of Epicurus and others who deny the existence of God and attribute all existence and process in the world to chance. He also excludes the Platonic theory from the present discussion, because once we grant the eternity thesis, we ought to deal with it in its most complete and purest Aristotelian form.

At first glance it would appear that we already have an answer to the question about Maimonides' own view, since he tells us explicitly that the doctrine of creation out of nothing is the view of the Jewish religious community, of which we know him to be a loyal member. Before we hastily accept this seemingly obvious conclusion, however, we need to see how he deals with the matter in his elaborate discussions. He has already shown us earlier how grave are the doubts he raises against the contentions of the Mutakallimūn in their attempt to demonstrate creation. The price they exact for this conclusion is the denial of any natural order in the world and thus the denial of all intelligibility in the world. This runs so strongly counter to our intuitive sense of how things are and to our convictions about what has been demonstrated that we are forced to reject it as wildly improbable. Against Aristotle, Maimonides considers his argument from particularization to be equally decisive in its gravity. Once we have lost all those controls that reason and experience provide for our knowledge of the sublunar world, we can neither demonstrate nor conjecture responsibly about the supralunar world. It is a serious mistake to suppose that there is any satisfactory support for probability claims about the nature of the supralunar world, since it completely transcends our capacity to know.

To grasp the full force of Maimonides' argument against Aristotle, we must keep in mind that all probability arguments are based on analogy. We begin with a state of affairs that is directly known to us. We then note that another state of affairs resembles the first in a variety of ways that we have been able to observe, and we conclude that it is probable that it will also resemble the first state in some other way that we have not yet been able to observe. It is impossible to justify in advance any claim of absolute certainty about what will happen when a particular person is injected with smallpox vaccine. No logical necessity forces us to conclude that he or she will become immune to the disease, since it is logically possible that what has happened millions of time in the past will not happen in this case. Our confidence rests completely on the force of an analogical argument. We note that this case resembles millions of others in a large number of respects that we can identify, and we conclude that, given the analogy, it is highly probable that it will resemble them in the one respect not yet known, namely, the final result of the injection. It is not necessary to consider what we might learn about these questions from the highly sophisticated methods of statistical analysis which are used in contemporary probability theory. These were not known to Maimonides, but they are, in any case, irrelevant since they do not affect the basic conceptual structure of probability arguments. Maimonides is saying that the Aristotelian claims about the eternity of the universe and the order of the supralunar world cannot be validly determined by probability arguments no matter how advanced their methodology. The reason is immediately evident. No sound analogy is possible between the postcreation world that we know directly, and the precreation world that transcends our actual and possible knowledge. It follows that no valid probability arguments can be made by Aristotle for his claims about the order of the spheres or about the origins of all existence.[36]

It seems to me that this is the substance of Maimonides' argument against Aristotle, and it is obvious that we have here a "doubt" of the greatest gravity and force. If the doubts that have been raised against both the Kalām and the Aristotelian views are so devastating, he must find some other way to proceed in determining what position to take concerning the origin of the world. Maimonides will not accept weak or shoddy arguments. He will not grant the claim of presumed evidence which he can show is unsound and poorly founded. He follows rigorously his own rule that one should decide such an issue only on the basis of the strongest possible intel-

36. Indirect confirmation for the correctness of this interpretation may be seen in the fact that in his *Treatise on Logic,* Maimonides uses "the creation of the heavens" as a paradigm case of analogical or inductive argument. See Israel Efros' edition (New York, 1938), 46.

lectual foundations. Even if the decision is necessarily short of demonstrative force, it does not follow that it should be taken arbitrarily, or that every view is as good as every other.

His striking statement about his procedure is, I believe, critical to an understanding of how he attacks this problem and reaches his conclusions. In opposition to Aristotle, Maimonides affirms his opinion "that all things exist in virtue of a purpose and not of necessity, and that He who purposed them may change them and conceive another purpose, though not absolutely any purpose whatever. For the nature of impossibility is stable and cannot be abolished, as we shall make clear" (II, 19, p. 303).

In this formulation Maimonides has clearly stated his position against the Aristotelians. The world exists neither through chance, nor through inexorable necessity, but as the result of the purposive activity of an intelligent Creator. He now sets forth his own program:

> My purpose in this chapter is to explain to you, *by means of arguments that come close to being a demonstration,* that what exists indicates to us of necessity that it exists in virtue of the purpose of One who purposed; and to do this without having to take upon myself what the Mutakallimūn have undertaken—to abolish the nature of that which exists and to adopt atomism, the opinion according to which accidents are perpetually being created, and all their principles, which I have explained to you and which they only wished to use as an introduction in order to establish the method of particularization. Do not think that they have also said what I shall say. On the other hand, there is no doubt that they wished what I wish (II, 19, p. 303; emphasis added).

It is clear that Maimonides is trying to preserve what he perceives as the best of two worlds. He is not willing to yield to the extreme results of either the Kalām or the Aristotelians. Like the Kalām he wants to preserve the doctrine of creation in time, and like Aristotle he wants to preserve the fixed order of nature in the sublunar world. Against the Kalām, he rejects their atomism and its concomitant denial of the order of nature, and against Aristotle, he rejects the extension of sublunar natural necessity to the supralunar world and its concomitant denial of a purposive creator.[37] He has positioned himself carefully on a narrow ridge between these two extremes.

37. In the discussion of Maimonides' attack on the Kalām earlier in this chapter I presented evidence of his intense commitment to maintaining the fixed order of nature in the sublunar world. It is revealing that even in so late a work as his *Essay on Resurrection* he continues to emphasize this point. In the process of assuring his readers that he believes in the resurrection of

We should pay careful attention to the exact terminology Maimonides employs here. He says that in support of his position he intends to present "arguments that come close to being a demonstration."[38] He is fully aware that he is no more able to demonstrate the soundness of his views than his predecessors were able to demonstrate the soundness of theirs. Yet he believes that he can present a set of arguments—admittedly short of having the force of demonstration—that will nevertheless have sufficient power to persuade his readers that the view that he defends is the best available option. An intelligent and honest thinker should commit himself to nothing less than the strongest and best-defended position that he can formulate, and it is this that Maimonides claims to offer. He makes no pretense of being able to demonstrate his conclusions, but he believes that his evidence is so strong that it should convince us that his is the position most to be preferred among the options.

We have already seen part of the pattern of the argument he develops. The Aristotelian theory of the eternity of the world and the consequent necessity of the structure of the supralunar system of the heavens has been shown, he believes, to be untenable. Its theoretical foundations are unsound, and it is unsupported by any observable empirical evidence. According to Maimonides, Aristotle makes the mistake of supposing that the way to protect the order of the heavens from the dangers of arbitrariness is to fit it forcibly into the structure that accounts for the sublunar world. Maimonides believes he has shown that this simply doesn't work, because we can given no satisfactory account of the particularization of the supralunar world. There is no apparent inherent reason why the number, order, distribution, and motions of the spheres must be as they are. To say that they follow necessarily from the fixed order of necessary natural causation is not an acceptable answer, because we are unable to discern anything remotely resembling natural necessity in the supralunar world.

Maimonides' alternative is to view the world as the creation of a purposive Creator. In explaining the results of that Creator's activity, we can say

---

the dead, he takes great pains to make clear that this does not mean that he finds it acceptable to undermine the order of nature. Unlike the unreflective masses, says Maimonides, "I try to reconcile the Law and reason, and wherever possible consider all things as of the natural order. Only when something is explicitly identified as a miracle, and reinterpretation of it cannot be accommodated, only then I feel forced to grant that this is a miracle." See Halkin and Hartmann, *Crisis and Leadership,* 225; *'Iggerot Ha-Rambam,* ed. Kafih, 87–88; Finkel, *Maimonides' Treatise,* 22.

38. The key terms are *dalīl* and *burhān.* The former, as we have already seen, denotes an argument that is persuasive, but does not carry the force of demonstrative certainty. The latter term means "demonstration."

only that He willed it so. Why is the supralunar world as it is and no other way? Just because that is how God chose to make it. There is, however, an unspoken, but critically important, premise here which must be made explicit—namely, that God, the absolutely perfect being, never acts arbitrarily. We may not always be able to give an account of why He has chosen to make things one way rather than another, but that reflects the finite limits of our intellect. Knowing that the world derives from God is, nevertheless, the strongest possible guarantee that it must be constructed and ordered in accordance with a plan and purpose that derive from the highest intelligence. To say that God created the world as an act of His will is in no way equivalent to saying that He acted willfully, that is, arbitrarily or capriciously. Such a notion is only possible if we take the idea of divine will with excessive literalness and fail to understand the limits which Maimonides imposed on discourse about God's attributes. Since we cannot speak correctly about individual and separate attributes in God, it follows that to single out His will as the operative explanation for the particular details of Creation can only be a concession to the limitations on our capacity of expression. The nature of the absolute unity of God requires that there be no multiplicity in Him, and thus means that there can be in Him no separate attributes. "There does not exist in Him anything other than His essence in virtue of which object He might act, know or will" (I, 46, p. 102). "This essence has created everything that it has created and knows it, but absolutely not by virtue of a superadded notion" (I, 53, pp. 122–23). His will is identical with His wisdom and with all other positive perfections that are His essence.

We speak of God's decisions concerning the particularization of the heavens as an act of His will because we have no other intelligible language with which to express the idea that the created world derives from God, not by inexorable necessity, but by what we must perceive as free and purposeful choice. An earlier discussion gave us occasion to cite the passage in which Maimonides gives full expression to his sense of the limits of our intellect and our language. He says, "Glory then to Him who is such that when the intellects contemplate His essence, their apprehension turns into incapacity; and when they contemplate the proceeding of His actions from His will, their knowledge turns into ignorance; and when the tongues aspire to magnify Him by means of attributive qualifications, all eloquence turns into weariness and incapacity" (I, 58, p. 137).

Although we cannot speak literally and accurately about God's will, it is clear that for Maimonides it is never permissible to identify any aspect of divine behavior with the arbitrary or the capricious. This point is illuminated in a later discussion, where he is setting the background for his exposition of the reasons for the commandments. Maimonides confronts there an analogous problem. Does God command us to follow a certain pattern of behavior arbitrarily or for good reasons? He comments acerbically on those "who consider it a grievous thing that causes should be given for any law; what would please them most is that the intellect would not find a meaning for the commandments and prohibitions" (III, 31, p. 523).

Maimonides shows that this is one of the most serious of all possible misunderstandings of the nature of God. He approaches the problem by first delineating four types of actions: futile, frivolous, vain, or good and excellent. He goes on to show that, in the nature of the case, we cannot conceive of God as performing any action that is futile, frivolous, or vain. All His actions must be good and excellent; otherwise He would not be God. "Consequently everything that He, may He be exalted, has done for the sake of a thing is necessary for the existence of the thing aimed at or is very useful" (III, 25, p. 503). This principle applies to all divine action, not only to the divine commandments. It follows that when Maimonides attributes the creation and ordering of the heavens to God, he is asserting that they must have been made with an intelligent and desirable purpose. There can then be nothing arbitrary about their structure and movements, although we are unable to penetrate the divine intellect and will in order to give an account of why God chose to make the heavens precisely as they are. Ascribing creation to God provides us with an explanation that eliminates the possibility that there may be any element of arbitrariness or caprice in the highest reaches of the created universe. The heavenly realm, like the earthly one, is governed by an intelligent and purposive plan. Scientific study can reveal to us the plan of the earthly realm, but that of the heavenly realm remains hidden from us. So long as we believe the universe to have been created by God, it follows with certainty that a plan and purpose are present even in those dimensions of reality where we are unable to find clear evidence of them.

It is certainly appropriate to ask at this point whether the creation hypothesis may not be just some wild imagining. What reason is there for us to accept it as a serious doctrine worthy of commanding our assent? True, it solves the problem of the order of the heavens, and this makes it attractive. Maimonides, however, has repeatedly warned us not to accept an opinion only because we approve of its consequences or because it tells us what we would like to hear. Even if, in the nature of the case, we cannot simply suspend judgment, we still need to justify our acceptance of one particular view over all its competitors.

Maimonides addresses this question in the following way. First, he shows that the creation hypothesis is possible, that the truth of its contradictory has not been demonstrated. "What I myself desire to make clear is that the world's being created in time . . . is not impossible and that all those

285

philosophic proofs from which it seems that the matter is different from what we have stated, all those arguments have a certain point through which they may be invalidated and the inference drawn from them against us shown to be incorrect" (II, 16, pp. 293–94; cf. II, 17, p. 298). So long as the creation hypothesis is not ruled out *a priori* as a logical impossibility, and so long as there is no decisive scientific evidence against it, we are free to consider it as a serious option. The field is open among the contending opinions concerning the origin of the world. One needs to examine the arguments and other evidence that can be offered in favor of the doctrine of creation out of nothing.

We have so far considered one argument that Maimonides offers, namely, that the creation hypothesis answers questions that cannot be answered by the Aristotelian eternity/necessity thesis. He now adds a second argument that is, I believe, decisive for him. The creation of the world by God out of nothing is supported by the consistent testimony of prophecy, and this testimony must be taken with the highest seriousness.

When Maimonides invokes the testimony of prophecy, he is not engaging simply in an act of piety. In his view a true prophet has attained the highest level of moral and intellectual development. Such a person can achieve conjunction with the Active Intellect, and, ultimately, with the divine intellect—that is to say, he can become a true prophet. The prophet has insight and receives illumination beyond what is open even to the most gifted of ordinary men. Maimonides asserts that the reality of the phenomenon of prophecy is recognized not only by the religious communities, but by the philosophers as well. If we have the teachings of authentic prophecy available to us, we certainly must give them a decisive voice in our speculations. "Inasmuch as this question—I mean to say that of the eternity of the world or its creation in time—becomes an open question, it should in my opinion be accepted without proof because of prophecy, which explains things to which it is not in the power of speculation to accede. For as we shall make clear, prophecy is not set at nought even in the opinion of those who believe in the eternity of the world" (II, 16, p. 294).[39]

---

39. It is not possible within the framework of the present study to provide a full account of Maimonides' theory of prophecy. This is a subject of immense complexity that would carry us far beyond the limits of this book. It will be sufficient for our purposes to set forth in the body of the text only those points which are required for our discussion of Maimonides' position on creation. The most extensive continuous discussion of prophecy is contained in *Guide*, II, 32–48, although important references are strewn throughout the *Guide*. In addition, there is an important discussion of prophecy in *H. Yesodei ha-Torah*, chaps. 7–10. There are relevant passages also in his other works. For a specific statement on the power of prophecy to know more than is available to the unaided intellect, see *Guide*, II, 38, p. 377.

There are three points to note here. First is Maimonides' assertion that when we have an open question that cannot be solved by purely philosophic/scientific means, it is appropriate and even desirable that we accept the testimony of prophecy. Second, the true prophet has the power to acquire knowledge about matters that transcend the capacity of the nonprophetic intellect. Third, this latter point is affirmed by the Aristotelian philosophers as well as by the religious communities. There is, in addition, a question not expressed here but which we must address, namely, how we determine the actual message of prophecy.

The appropriateness of turning to prophecy for guidance when philosophy and science have reached their limits is affirmed repeatedly by Maimonides. In the context of his critique of the Kalām he says that if someone is persuaded to accept the doctrine of creation because he considers the Kalām arguments to be sound, then so be it. Such a person is not a good philosopher, but he is, nevertheless, affirming a sound doctrine. Alternately, if one rejects the Kalām arguments but accepts creation in time on the authority of the prophets, Maimonides says that "there is no harm in that" (I, 71, p. 181). Some recent commentators have argued that this expression is a grudging concession to those who do not have the intellectual resources to face the issues correctly on their own. They conclude that Maimonides is not really supporting the reliance on prophecy but saying, in effect, that if you can do no better, there is no harm in accepting the prophetic testimony. This seems to me to be a serious misreading of Maimonides. All he is saying is that, for someone who is properly trained in philosophic inquiry, there are some intermediate steps to take before deciding to rely above all on the testimony of prophecy. A person perceptive enough to reject the claims of the Mutakallimūn that they have demonstrated creation should properly consider all the other philosophic options which are available before coming to a final decision. However, if instead he goes from the rejection of the Kalām to the acceptance of prophecy with no intermediate steps, Maimonides says there is no serious injury to him. He has, in any case, ended up with the correct view of the matter, and this is where philosophic inquiry will, in fact, finally lead. In the chapters containing the heart of the discussion of creation, we find that Maimonides regularly invokes the testimony of prophecy as decisive, once we have reached the point where the intellect alone can no longer help us.[40] In II, 25 he states explicitly that, in the absence of any

40. See II, 22–24. The great Greek model for this method is Plato. In the major dialogues we regularly find that rational discourse is pushed to its outer limit, but when it reaches that limit Plato resorts to a myth to give expression to the insight that he is trying to communicate. Whether Platonic myths are a form of pagan prophecy is a subject that needs to be investigated.

decisive reasons to accept the eternity hypothesis, the teachings of the texts that have been revealed to us through prophecy should determine our opinion.

The power of the prophet to penetrate to a level of insight that is beyond the capacity of the ordinary intellects is well established by Maimonides in his extensive discussions of the nature of prophecy. It is, as a matter of fact, part of the actual definition of prophecy (see II, 36, p. 369, and II, 38, p. 377). Leo Strauss expressed the point with admirable clarity:

> Since in the case of prophecy, not only the intellect (as in the case of philosophical knowledge) but also the power of imagination is influenced by the Active Intellect, prophecy is, as directly following his definition of prophecy Maimonides explains: "the highest stage of man and the most extreme perfection that can be found in the human race." Even on this ground, the prophet is unconditionally *superior* to the philosopher, and all the more to all other men. He is, however, also superior to the philosopher in his own realm, as a knower. He can know *directly*, without "premises and conclusions," what all other men can only know indirectly. Accordingly, he has command over insights that the man who only knows philosophically is not capable of reaching. Thus it becomes understandable that, in respect of the central question whose scientific answer man is incapable of giving (the question of whether the world is eternal or created), Maimonides can instruct the philosopher to follow the prophet. In his philosophizing, the philosopher can orient himself according to the prophet because the prophet has command over insights that are not accessible to mere philosophical knowledge.[41]

The prophecy of Moses in particular is understood as having special status and reaching a level of illumination that is unique. Maimonides can establish very easily that Moses had a level of knowledge that was beyond the capacities of ordinary human beings to achieve on their own through the functioning of the unaided human intellect. At Sinai, says Maimonides, "not everything that reached Moses also reached all Israel" (II, 33, p. 363). A prophet acquires knowledge and insight that are not given to others and which he alone can teach to others. That is why Maimonides goes to so much trouble to distinguish between what can be known by demonstration and what is known only through prophecy. "Now with regard to everything that can be

---

What is beyond doubt is that the myth serves to transmit insights that are beyond the grasp of discursive reason.

41. Leo Strauss, *Philosophy and Law* (Philadelphia, 1987), 85.

known by demonstration, the status of the prophet and that of everyone else who knows it are equal; there is no superiority of one over the other" (II, 33, p. 364). So long as they are relying on their own rational powers, all human beings have the same potential for acquiring knowledge. It does not require any special powers that transcend ordinary human capacity. For that reason Maimonides argues that prophets have no superior knowledge of such demonstrable truths as the existence and unity of God. On the other hand, Moses alone knows and teaches the divinely given rules for human behavior, since they are apprehended only through the powers of prophecy. Similarly, the prophets, and Moses in particular, apprehend certain metaphysical truths through their prophetic powers that the nonprophetic intellect could not grasp on its own. Just as we are dependent on the prophets to instruct us concerning the rules of virtuous behavior, so are we dependent on them to instruct us concerning such ultimate questions as the origin of the world.

As to the third point, the recognition of prophecy by the philosophers is fully discussed by Maimonides. In his classification of three opinions concerning prophecy, the second opinion "is that of the philosophers." They fully accept the reality of prophecy, differing with the official Jewish opinion only on the point of whether prophecy is a natural state or is dependent on God's will (II, 32, p. 361). Throughout the long discussion that follows there seems never to be any question about the recognition, even by the pagan philosophers, that prophecy is an authentic phenomenon. Hence it is fully appropriate for Maimonides to invoke with confidence the testimony of prophecy as an intellectually legitimate source of instruction.

This leaves us with the question as to what actually is the teaching of prophecy concerning the creation of the world. We noted earlier that the scriptural texts are laden with ambiguity, and that the rabbinic interpretations of those texts also leave room for different opinions. If reason had been able to give us independent guidance, it would have been possible to proceed as we did with respect to God's corporeality. In that case we saw that Maimonides determined the meaning of Scripture by first finding out what reason teaches. With respect to creation, however, we are in the position of having to determine the meaning of the prophetic message without the assured guidance of reason, since reason has shown itself to be unable to resolve this question. Our only option is to see what we can learn from the biblical text itself that will give us reliable insight into its teaching.

It is immediately evident that Scripture cannot accommodate the Aristotelian doctrine that the world is eternal and necessary. It may be objected that Maimonides says that if there were a demonstration of eternity, he would accept it and would then be able, with no special difficulty, to read the verses concerning creation figuratively so that they would harmonize with that doctrine. This may seem to refute the statement that Scripture cannot accommodate the Aristotelian theory, but this is not the case. So far as I can determine, Maimonides never says that he would be able to make the eternity thesis harmonize with all of scriptural teaching and not just with the opening verses of Genesis. On the contrary, he states repeatedly that some of the fundamental teachings of the Bible would be undermined by that thesis. Remember his key statement on the subject, which was quoted earlier: "The belief in eternity the way Aristotle sees it . . . destroys the Law in its principle, necessarily gives the lie to every miracle, and reduces to inanity all the hopes and threats that the Law has held out" (II, 25, p. 328). We can begin then with the certainty that, for Maimonides, Scripture cannot and does not approve the Aristotelian position. This is established not by the explication of individual terms or even isolated verses in the Bible, but by understanding the central thrust of biblical teaching. Even the most casual reading makes it clear that the active role of God in the events of nature and history is perhaps the most all-pervasive single doctrine in the Bible. To interpret the Bible as teaching the Aristotelian doctrine of the eternity of the world is to turn the scriptural text on its head and to tear it away forcibly from its clear meaning. This is why we can say with confidence that Maimonides was completely serious and straightforward in his various statements about the absolute contradiction between the Bible and the Aristotelian eternity/necessity thesis. As he puts it, the biblical teachings on this point are so numerous and so clear that "no intelligent man has any doubt that they are to be taken in their external meanings" (II, 25, pp. 329–30).

We are left then with only two possibilities. The Bible must be understood either as teaching creation out of nothing, or else as teaching its own version of the Platonic doctrine that prime matter is eternal but that God alone creates the world by giving form and structure to that hylic material. In either case, the independent activity of God in the world is asserted; His intervention, at His will, is made possible, and miracles and divine reward and punishment are provided for. We know that, for the most part, Maimonides seems to affirm the theory of creation out of nothing, yet his seeming ambivalences with respect to the Platonic theory require our attention.[42] When he sets forth the three positions on creation, Maimonides states explicitly that Plato "does not believe what we believe, as is thought by him who does not examine opinions and is not precise in speculation" (II, 13, pp. 283–84). On the following page he makes the remarkable statement that there is no

42. For an extensive discussion of some of these ambivalences, see Davidson, "Maimonides' Secret Position on Creation," in *Studies in Medieval Jewish History and Literature,* ed. Twersky.

important philosophical difference between the Aristotelian and the Platonic theories, since both affirm the eternity of matter. It is important to note that he makes these statements without explaining or defending them, simply laying them down dogmatically. This means that it is left to readers to work out on their own what Maimonides is saying in his apparent rejection of the Platonic theory.

What shall we make now of the fact that, only a few chapters later, after having rejected the Aristotelian view in the strong language that we just quoted, he goes on to affirm the acceptability of the Platonic view? It is remarkable that he does so in language that is the direct negation of what he has just said about Aristotle. Of the Platonic opinion he asserts that "this opinion would *not* destroy the foundations of the Law and would be followed *not* by the lie being given to miracles, but by their becoming admissible. It would also be possible to interpret figuratively the texts in accordance with this opinion. And many obscure passages can be found in the texts of the Torah and others with which this opinion could be connected" (II, 25, pp. 328–29; emphasis added). On the very next page he adds the observation concerning the Aristotelian thesis that "if creation in time were demonstrated—if only as Plato understands creation—all the overhasty claims made to us on this point by the philosophers would become void."

In the next chapter Maimonides takes up, with expressions of professed astonishment, the midrash of R. Eliezer the Great, which we discussed earlier, and identifies it as seeming to follow the Platonic opinion concerning creation. As we saw earlier, this is by no means the only midrash supporting this doctrine, and we can be certain that Maimonides knew the texts in *Genesis Rabbah* and the other midrashim very well indeed. He seems to want to avoid making it easy for people to accept the Platonic view, and we shall shortly offer an explanation for his reluctance. Yet it seems evident that, even though he does not consider the Platonic view to be the preferred or the exclusively correct view, Maimonides does admit it, alongside the theory of creation out of nothing, as a legitimate and acceptable opinion on both philosophical and religious grounds. It can be shown to accord with one acceptable reading of Scripture and with the teachings of numerous canonical midrashim. From this evidence, we seemingly must conclude that Maimonides accepts the Platonic position as consistent with prophetic teaching, although it does not follow that he considers it to be the best interpretation of that teaching. It should be added that this acceptance of the Platonic position should not be viewed as an esoteric position; it is perfectly open and direct. I shall try to explain shortly Maimonides' shift from apparent rejection to apparent acceptance of this theory.

We return finally to our key question: Which of the three theories about

291

the creation or eternity of the world did Maimonides himself really believe? We noted earlier that we can find in the scholarly literature almost every imaginable view. There is one line that stretches from such early medieval commentators as Narbonne and Caspi down to such contemporaries as Pines, Strauss, and their disciples who seem convinced that Maimonides believed in the Aristotelian doctrine of eternity, although he hid this belief so that only readers with special powers of penetration would discover it. Another line includes such figures as Isaac Abravanel and a whole series of others who read Maimonides more straightforwardly and are equally firm in their certainty that Maimonides believed exclusively in the theory of creation out of nothing. Among our contemporaries, Herbert Davidson holds that there is evidence for the view that Maimonides definitely rejected the eternity theory and held either the theory of *ex nihilo* creation or the Platonic theory. Davidson considers it impossible to decide with certainty in favor of one over the other. Sara Klein-Braslavy, as we have noted, argues vigorously that Maimonides took no personal stand at all on this subject, but chose to remain agnostic. She holds that he followed the phenomenological method of *epoché,* the deliberate suspension of all judgment.

None of these positions seems to me to be correct, and I believe that the evidence presented in this chapter offers a powerful argument against these approaches to the problem. The fundamental error lies in the way in which the question is formulated. Once we ask, "Which *one* of the three theories did Maimonides himself really believe?" we already presuppose that the answer must be in favor of one, and only one, of the positions that he has discussed. Alternately, we may entertain the Klein-Braslavy option that he believed none of them because he could find no decisive evidence forcing him to give preference to one over the others. Our study of this question leads us in a different direction. To say that Maimonides chose to remain detached from any judgment runs against the whole tenor of the *Guide* and his other writings. However clever and intriguing this hypothesis is, it is simply unconvincing.[43] We would be forced to conclude that absolutely nothing that Maimonides said or did may be taken at face value. This violates our sense of the man and his work. Nothing in his entire body of writings supports the contention that he was fearful or incapable of making hard decisions or difficult choices. He knew the full meaning of intellectual

---

43. Klein-Braslavy has done an admirable piece of work in her effort to expound and defend the view that Maimonides took no position. I believe that she has made as strong a case as it is possible to make for this view, but it still falls short of the mark. There is something inherently unconvincing in the notion that Maimonides invested so much energy, passion, and intellect in dealing with this question, only to arrive at no conclusion.

responsibility, and he made it quite clear that, even when we do not have demonstrative certainty, we still have to choose a position and justify it.

I want to argue, however, that in the case of creation vs. eternity Maimonides did not feel forced to make an either/or decision. We should note first that Maimonides distinguishes five, not just three, positions on the question of creation vs. eternity. In addition to the Aristotelian, Platonic, and Jewish (*ex nihilo*) positions he records in *Guide,* II, 13, there is the position of the Kalām which he discussed at great length earlier and the position of the Epicureans. He dismisses the latter in two sentences. Since the existence of God has been demonstrated and they start from the contrary premise, they have no useful place in this discussion. I did try to show earlier, however, that the Kalām position must be taken seriously as part of the entire structure that Maimonides builds for us. Despite the fact that he does not include it among the views he sets forth in II, 13, it is undeniably a variant of the *ex nihilo* position, just as the Platonic theory of the eternity of matter is a variant of the Aristotelian position. My contention is that Maimonides did not simply choose one of these positions and reject the others absolutely. Instead he found a measure of merit in each of them that makes it worthy of playing a role in our understanding of the origin of the world. One could say either that Maimonides' position is a syncretistic unification of elements of each of the four positions or, alternately, that he affirms the truth of each up to a point and in a restricted context.

Certain elements in his doctrine rest heavily on Aristotle, who taught us how to counter the Epicurean picture of a totally anarchic world with no governing power in control and with all events occurring through pure chance. We need the clarity of the Aristotelian arguments in order to stand firm on the contrary principle that the world is an ordered and intelligible structure. The eternity hypothesis gives strong grounding to this way of understanding the order of all existence. Moreover, even if we start from the eternity hypothesis, as Maimonides deliberately chose to do for tactical reasons, we can establish the existence of God. Therefrom emerges a world that, contra Epicurus, has an ultimate cause, an ultimate governing power, and a stable, fixed natural order. Maimonides accepts these features of the Aristotelian theory fully and enthusiastically, but at the same time he sees clearly the limitations of the theory when it is used to explain the supralunary world as well as the sublunary world.

To help solve this problem, Maimonides sees a useful counterweight to the Aristotelian theory in the Kalām affirmation of creation out of nothing and the absolute power of the Creator-God. This conception of God as the sole causal power and as a causal power that acts out of volition rather than necessity is an important alternative to Aristotle's God who can only act out

293

of the absolute necessity of His own being. Such a God can account for the supralunary world in a way that Aristotle fails to do. On the negative side, however, the Kalām knows how to achieve that end only by denying all necessity, and thus all stability, even in the sublunar world. The Kalām God, as pictured by Maimonides, seems to generate a world as unstructured and anarchic, in its own way, as the world of Epicurus. It is important for Maimonides to retain the desirable features of the Kalām teaching while rejecting its undesirable elements.

His version of the scriptural doctrine of creation out of nothing retains the positive features of the Kalām and of Aristotle, while avoiding the negative features. It does so by developing a delicate balance between these views. Following the Kalām, Maimonides affirms creation *ex nihilo* by an all-powerful, self-motivated God. This makes it possible for him to give an account of the otherwise unintelligible order and structure of the supralunar realm, something that Aristotle's theory cannot do. At the same time, he affirms the reliability of Aristotle's teachings with respect to the sublunar world. In this way he protects the stable order of nature in the sublunar world, viewing it as deriving from causal necessity rather than as being purely volitional. It depends on God's will, but He has made it clear that having created the world, He also guarantees the permanent stability of the natural order.

We see that Maimonides accepted and assimilated significant parts of both the Kalām and the Aristotelian teaching. These constitute the main elements of what he now calls "the opinion of all who believe in the Law of Moses our Master" (II, 13, p. 281). As he expounds that view in various places in the *Guide,* it is evident that he has built on elements of the teachings of both Aristotle and the Kalām. Creation out of nothing guarantees that the world will be permanently dependent on God's power, will, and wisdom, that is to say, on His essence. Thus it accounts for miracles, divine commandments, and reward and punishment. At the same time, by rejecting the Kalām account of the sublunar world and accepting the account that follows from Aristotle's theory, this view saves us from the anarchic chaos that is a constant threat of the Kalām theory. Simply to say that God creates the world out of nothing is not enough. We need to know the consequences of either affirming or denying that view. Maimonides neither fully accepts nor fully rejects the extremes represented by Aristotle and the Kalām. Instead he brings them together in a new doctrine that accepts part of each while rejecting another part. At times Maimonides finds it most important to stress the claims of the creation aspect of his theory, while at other times it serves his purpose to stress the fixed order of nature which follows from his theory. Effectively, he has formulated a third theory that mediates between Aristotle and the Kalām. When his subject is primarily philosophic/scientific in character, he gives greatest prominence to the Aristotelian dimension of his theory, with its emphasis on the necessary order of nature. When his concerns are primarily religious, he gives greatest prominence to the idea of a freely acting Creator-God. When he needs an intelligible account of the otherwise inexplicable structure of the supralunary realm, his stress is on the will and purposiveness of the Creator, which transcend our understanding. When he needs to guarantee the stability of nature in the sublunar world, his emphasis is on the discernible order that the Creator has built into the realm of human experience. His own position should be understood as one in which the strongest elements of Aristotle and of the Kalām are affirmed and are brought together in a new synthesis.

What place does the Platonic theory have in Maimonides' system? He admits openly that both the religious and the philosophical/scientific concerns can be served as well by this theory as by creation out of nothing. For this reason he can have no objection to it in principle. If someone finds it persuasive, there is no reason to object, since it does not contradict any principle of the Torah or of philosophy. There is nevertheless good reason for refusing to accept it wholeheartedly or make it the first choice. Granted that it is substantively acceptable and can legitimately achieve the same objectives that are gained by the synthesis of doctrines in Maimonides' version of the creation theory, the Platonic theory suffers from a serious methodological defect.

A careful study of the way Maimonides formulates his account of this theory reveals that defect clearly. We are told that what forces the proponents of this theory to affirm the eternity of matter is that "they say that it is absurd that God would bring a thing into existence out of nothing. . . . To predicate of God that He is able to do this is, according to them, like predicating of Him that He is able to bring together two contraries in one instant of time" (II, 13, pp. 282–83). Two things are wrong with this argument. First, it applies to the act of creation the same standards of judgment that we use for the world after it has been created. Maimonides criticized Aristotle severely for this error, and it is clear that he would have to consider the Platonic theory as suffering from the same defect. Just because we can give no account of creation out of nothing in the world of our experience, it does not follow that this is impossible in the original Creation, which transcends our experience. Such an event is not logically impossible, although we cannot explain its mechanism or process. The second error is closely connected to the first. The problem is caused by people who hold this view thinking about metaphysical abstractions in pictorial images, a practice that has been shown by Maimonides to be the enemy of sound philosophy. It is true that we are un-

295

able to imagine—that is, to picture to ourselves—the process by which something is created out of nothing. It is a classic philosophic mistake to identify the limits of the possible with the limits of our imagination. We saw earlier that this mistake was made by the Mutakallimūn, and we see now that it is an error built into the Platonic theory of creation as well. Maimonides has no objection to the content of the Platonic theory. In fact, he admits openly that it can serve both philosophy and religion effectively. What he rejects is the intellectual muddle out of which that theory is formed. Hence he concludes that it is acceptable, if someone finds it persuasive, and that there is no reason to do battle against it. He sees no reason, however, to choose or to recommend a theory that rests on unsound philosophical premises.

Maimonides' theory of creation should be understood as a conscious bridge between the world-view of the Kalām and that of Aristotle. He grasps fully the ways in which these views are opposed, but he also grasps the powerful arguments with which key elements in each view can be supported. In affirming the partial soundness of each theory he creates a synthesis between them, a synthesis that maintains a delicate balance in the ongoing tension between Aristotle and the Kalām. The nuances, the shadings of expression, the differing emphases are his subtle accommodation of his writing to diverse contexts and purposes. Here, as in other cases, his deep and comprehensive insight leads him to embrace dialectically what he perceives as the closest approach to the truth of which he is capable. This is not an exercise in some sort of intellectual sleight of hand, nor is it a program of intellectual deception. It is rather the honest position of a profound thinker—a position won with great struggle and with subtle understanding of the complexity of the issues. Maimonides had the courage to reject the relatively easy answers that were available to him. For the comfort of a monochromatic account of the origins of the world, he substituted a polychrome, an account made up of diverse elements that generated strain when he joined them together, but which helped him to apprehend and to express the truth as he honestly saw it.

11

Prayer and the Religious Life

Maimonides' theory of creation, which we have just discussed, leads directly to a related question. If we believe that God is the creator of the world, that He maintains an ongoing connection with the world, and that He can intervene in both nature and history when He chooses, it is then reasonable to ask what role human prayer plays in this drama. In this chapter I propose to examine Maimonides' views concerning prayer, as set forth in the *Guide* and in his earlier writings. I shall attempt to explicate his doctrine and to give an account of the way in which he brings together differing, and even opposed, views with respect to the nature of prayer and its philosophical and theological foundations. Here too, as in his treatment of some of the other topics that we have discussed, Maimonides has developed a position that takes account of diverse intellectual and spiritual contexts. His final position, as I shall try to show, is again a balanced dialectical unification and tension of opposed elements.

An initial reading of the relevant sources in the corpus of Maimonides leads to the conclusion that he advances two different and apparently inconsistent views about prayer. One seems to be conventional, simple, and in accord with popular, uncritical religious sentiment. In this account God is seen as master of the world. He is at one and the same time a stern judge and loving father. His majesty merits and evokes our praise. His kindness and compassion merit and evoke our thanks. And in our awareness of our total dependence on Him, we turn to Him in plea and supplication for our needs. He hears (or knows, if we want to avoid the anthropomorphism) our prayers and responds to them favorably or not as our merit warrants and His judgment determines. Moreover, even though we lack merit, He may choose nevertheless to respond to our supplications. As a loving and compassionate father, He knows our faults, yet He may choose to change His stern decree in response to our prayers.

The opposed view emerges from Maimonides' philosophical understanding of the nature of God and His relationship to man and the world. From his philosophical perspective all conventional notions of prayer seem deeply problematic. From within the philosophical understanding it may still be possible to provide for expressions of thanks to God, but there is little place left for either praise of God or supplication for His help. Praise seems to be impossible, since according to the philosophical doctrine, there is nothing we can say about God that does not detract from His glory. This is a reflection of the limits of human language, and as such is also a reflection of the limits of our intellectual capacity. Maimonides has established through an elaborate set of arguments that we can have no knowledge of God that can properly be expressed in the language of positive attributes. To think or speak of God using positive predicates and intending them literally is a major philosophical error. Insofar as we can think or speak about Him correctly at all, it can only be through negative attributes.[1] From this perspective, every positive statement about God turns out to be false or meaningless. Having set forth the elements of the theory of negative attributes, Maimonides urges us:

> Desire then wholeheartedly that you should know by demonstration some additional thing to be negated, but do not desire to negate merely in words. For on every occasion on which it becomes clear to you by means of a demonstration that a thing whose existence is thought to pertain to Him, may He be exalted, should rather be negated with reference to Him, you undoubtedly come nearer to Him by one degree. . . . On the other hand, the predication of affirmative attributes of Him, may He be exalted, is very dangerous (I, 60, p. 144).

It seems then that it is not possible for us truly to praise God in prayer. Whatever we might say in our paeans of praise that is phrased in the language of affirmative attributes will certainly be wrong, if not downright insulting, as we shall soon see.

The problem is even more aggravated with respect to prayers of supplication. It would appear that the presuppositions of all petitionary prayer are not only unsound but, in Maimonides' view, border on the heretical. Petitionary prayer presupposes that there is some meaningful sense in which it can be affirmed that God hears us when we address Him, and that He takes account of our petition. If our prayer is successful, God is affected by our

---

1. This doctrine is developed by Maimonides at great length in Part I of the *Guide*, especially in chaps. 52–60, although like most other subjects in his book, the problem of attributes is also dealt with in many other places. To get some sense of the tenor of the discussion it is useful to note that Maimonides begins I, 57 with the words: "On the attributes; more obscure than what preceded." And I, 58 begins, "More obscure than what preceded."

petitions in such a way that He changes His intentions with respect to us. If we fail to move Him, then He rejects our petition. The classical model for such prayer may be found in the supplications of Moses, some of which are answered and some denied. When he pleads for a change in the divine decree that prevents him from entering the land of Israel, Moses employs every device to play on God's sympathy. Yet he fails to move Him, and his petition is denied. In fact it is denied with a show of irritation. "But the Lord was wrathful with me on your account and would not listen to me. The Lord said to me, 'Enough! Never speak to Me of this matter again! . . . for you shall not go across yonder Jordan' "[2] On the other hand, when he pleads for the people of Israel after the golden calf episode, he succeeds. God condemns the people for their faithlessness and says, "Now, let Me be, that My anger may blaze forth against them and that I may destroy them."[3] God announces His fixed intention, yet the Midrash sees in His words, *hanihah li,* let Me be, an invitation to Moses to plead for the people.[4] He implores God with a variety of petitionary arguments and pleas, and his prayer is accepted. "And the Lord renounced the punishment, He had planned to bring upon His people."[5]

The Talmud goes so far as to suggest not only that the prayers of the righteous have the power of changing original divine intentions, but that God so desires the prayers of human beings that He deliberately casts people into circumstances that will force them to turn to Him for help. In an especially striking formulation, one of the Sages asks, "Why were our ancestors childless?" They answer that it is "because the Holy One, blessed be He, longs for the prayer of the righteous." The passage continues with the following observation. "Why is the prayer of the righteous compared to a pitchfork? Just as a pitchfork turns the grain from one position to another, so does the prayer of the righteous turn the disposition of the Holy One, blessed be He, from the attribute of anger to the attribute of mercy."[6]

These rabbinic texts are typical of the genre. They are in no way un-

---

2. Deut. 3:26–27.

3. Exod. 32:10.

4. *Ex. Rab.,* 42:10.

5. Exod. 32:14.

6. *Yevamot,* 64a. This talmudic passage should not be understood as teaching that God is so taken up with His own desires that He uses devices that may seem crude and even cruel in order to have men worship Him. The statement that He "longs for the prayers of the righteous" is a way of expressing God's love for us and His desire that we, in turn, be close to Him and draw ever nearer to Him. It is one of the sad facts of common experience that we tend to think of God and turn to Him most when we are in need.

usual or exceptional. Although they express ideas that recur throughout rabbinic literature, we must recognize that if we construe them more or less literally, they affirm ideas about God that Maimonides rejected vigorously. First, this conception of prayer postulates the kind of relationship between God and man that Maimonides explicitly denied. We discussed earlier his denial of such relations between God and anything outside Himself. We saw that Maimonides takes the position that predicating any relations of God is a fundamental error that misrepresents His nature. Yet conventional prayer, as represented in these samples of the traditional literature, appears to depend on the affirmation of relations between God and man. Second, and even more troubling, this notion of prayer leads to the conclusion that God is subject to change, and this is a direct contradiction of a fundamental principle of Maimonidean theology. Third, following from what has already been said, change in God implies that He is corporeal, and this is, in turn, a denial of His absolute ontological unity. Finally, this conception views God as subject to affections because He is moved by man's efforts to change His ways. This last doctrine is very nearly an ultimate heresy in Maimonides' opinion. These points will be clarified in our later discussion of Maimonides' philosophical views.

In the light of what has been said, we might expect Maimonides to reject outright every form of petitionary prayer or prayers of praise. They seem, prima facie, to be contrary to his most deeply held views, so that it is difficult to imagine that he would be able to include a place for prayers of this type in his system of thought. Yet, despite these difficulties, numerous texts in the corpus of Maimonides treat petitionary prayer straightforwardly, expressing no hesitation and seeming to see no difficulty in the notion that God hears and responds to human prayers. On the other hand, there are also passages (especially in the *Guide of the Perplexed*, but not only there) that make such a conception of prayer seriously suspect, if not untenable.

To arrive at some clear idea of what Maimonides had to say about this subject we must begin by confronting and considering the meaning of a sample selection of texts which reflect these diverse positions. In his halakhic writings conventional notions of prayer prevail with few exceptions. Here, where Maimonides is functioning above all as rabbinic teacher and jurist, his task is to codify and explicate the Law. It is certainly not his task to reject the Law, or even to remodel it extensively, because it may seem to him to be philosophically unsound. The jurist is, after all, not an independent legislator, but one charged with formulating and systematizing the received Law and addressing new situations from the perspective of and in accordance with the methods and principles on which the legal system is built. It is beyond all question that the Law includes statutory forms and occasions of

300

prayer among its fixed duties, as well as other acts of worship connected with prayer. Consequently, the jurist has no choice but to acknowledge the obligation and to set forth its rules and patterns in detail. In so doing, Maimonides usually adopts a purely conventional traditional tone, in which he advises his readers to seek God's help for the fulfillment of their needs. It is remarkable that he does not limit such petitions to ordinary human desires for health and sustenance, but even extends them to the exalted region of the ultimate religious quest. In speaking of man's aspiration to penetrate the deepest hidden mysteries of the Torah in order to be capable of true intellectual apprehension of God, Maimonides urges that we seek divine help and turn to God in prayer. In the introductory essay to his *Commentary on the Mishnah* he explains that an understanding of the deep and hidden meanings of rabbinic aggadah will lead one to grasp "the absolute good, than which there is none greater, and there will then be revealed those truly divine matters" which the philosophers have struggled all their lives to come to know. To achieve an apprehension of this precious esoteric truth, it is not enough to devote ourselves to the task with the most intense intellectual effort of which we are capable. We must also seek divine assistance.

> For this end [i.e., the knowledge of esoteric doctrine] it is not sufficient for a man to devote himself with all his effort to the study of the Torah, but he must also direct his heart to God and pray to Him and plead with Him to grant him this special knowledge and to help him by revealing to him the secrets which are hidden in sacred Scripture. Just as we find that David did, when he prayed: Open my eyes, that I may perceive the wonders of your teaching.[7]

Thus we have a case in which Maimonides even makes prayer an important condition for the success of man's highest intellectual/spiritual quest.

Let us, however, first review the teachings of Maimonides about more usual subjects of prayer as they are reflected in his legal writings. In his Mishnah commentary he teaches that the primary meaning of *tefillah* is "petition" (*bakkashah*). The Law requires that one recite a prayer preceding and following the study of Torah. Maimonides explains that these prayers are called *tefillah* "in accordance with the root meaning of the word, namely, that all petition is called *tefillah*."[8] For the most part *tefillah* is identified with ordinary petitionary prayer in which we ask for our basic human needs. It is significant that, as we have seen, this common conception of prayer as

7. Introduction to *Commentary on the Mishnah*, ed. Y. Kafih (Jerusalem, 1964), 35–36.
8. Commentary to *M. Berakhot*, 4:2; see also 9:4.

petition is extended to include petitions for knowledge of God's secret lore. In the *Commentary on the Mishnah,* however, Maimonides simply records the usual obligations for petitionary prayer as they emerge from his explication of the relevant mishnaic texts. So far as I can determine, at no point in his commentary does he raise theological or philosophical problems that would call into question the possibility of petitionary prayer. He also affirms the propriety of prayers of praise and thanks and records our duty to offer such prayers. The unquestioned assumption appears to be that God hears our supplications and that, when we merit it in His eyes, He accepts our petitions and grants our requests. Furthermore, our hymns of praise are pleasing to Him as expressions of our devotion and reverence.[9]

I can identify only three discussions in the *Commentary on the Mishnah* that might possibly be construed as reflecting some philosophical/theological reservations about the conventional idea of prayer that I have set forth. In my opinion not one of them is a serious or decisive objection to the propriety of conventional prayer. Commenting on the principle that we are obligated to praise God for the evil things that happen to us just as we praise Him for the good,[10] Maimonides explains it as follows: Because of the limits of our perspective we never know the full significance or consequences of any event; therefore we should always assume that whatever happens is ultimately for our good, although at the moment it may appear to be disastrous. Confident that God does only what is good, we can praise Him in faith and trust, assured that in the end we shall come to see that today's apparent catastrophe is tomorrow's blessing. If this is the case, it might seem to follow that all petitionary prayer is improper, because one is asking God to change present circumstances. If we trust Him and are certain that whatever He causes to happen must be for the good, then why is it ever right to question His judgment through prayers for improved circumstances?

In response we must note that there is nothing original in Maimonides' interpretation of this Mishnah. It is simply a summary paraphrase of what is offered in the Gemara.[11] There the various modes of explaining this principle are captured in the single aphorism, "All that God does is only for the good." Just as the Sages saw no inherent contradiction between this confident trust in God under all circumstances and the requirements of petitionary prayer, so does Maimonides seem to find no difficulty here. It is right that he

9. For some typical instances in the *Commentary on the Mishnah* of such conventional views concerning the nature and effectiveness of prayer, see Maimonides' comments to *M. Berakhot,* 4:2; 4:4; 5, passim; 9:3; 9, 4; *M. Sotah,* 7:5.

10. *M. Berakhot,* 9:5.

11. *Berakhot,* 60b.

should not, since it is clear enough that accepting in good faith whatever God causes to happen need not preclude the hope and prayer that He might help us achieve our ends in less painful ways.

Elsewhere, Maimonides presents us with a second occasion that might be construed as opposed to petitionary prayer.[12] We are told there that among the deeds for which Hezekiah was praised was *ganaz sefer refu'ot,* that he removed from public use certain books containing formulas for healing diseases. In his comment Maimonides refers to an interpretation he has heard which commends Hezekiah because if people rely on medical knowledge rather than prayer to heal themselves, they show their lack of faith in God. In language of unmitigated ferocity, Maimonides attacks the idiocy of such a view. Prayer, he says, is not intended to be a substitute for human effort. We not only *may,* but *must,* use all available knowledge for human benefit. There is here no defect of faith at all. On the contrary, we show our faith by thanking God for having made known to us the ways of healing. Again, this is no rejection of petitionary prayer, but only an attack on what he takes to be wholly unsound and dangerous views. There is no inconsistency whatever between making the maximum effort to help ourselves, and seeking divine blessing on our efforts and divine aid for that which lies beyond our own capacities. To those who think otherwise, Maimonides suggests that we should reply, "Just as I thank God when I eat for providing me with a substance that removes my hunger, thus giving me life and sustaining me, so should we thank Him for having provided us with the medicine which heals us when we are ill."[13]

The third instance in the *Commentary on the Mishnah* which might be construed as a possible rejection of conventional prayer is in the text of the fifth of Maimonides' thirteen principles of faith.[14] He stresses here that God alone must be worshiped and exalted, but that it is not permitted to worship any lower being. In the development of this principle he speaks only of praise and worship, but says nothing about petition. It seems to me that one would have to strain hard and tendentiously to conclude from the omission of any reference to petitionary prayer here that Maimonides is subtly indicating his rejection of it. Remote as the issue seems, I raise it here only because the contemporary mode of reading Maimonides lays so much stress on the esoteric character of his writing that it is easy to imagine that some inter-

---

12. Commentary to *M. Pesaḥim,* 4:10. Maimonides points out that this section is actually a Tosefta passage and not part of the Mishnah, but he says that he chooses to comment on it, in any case, because there are important and valuable points to be made.

13. Ibid.

14. See Introduction to *M. Sanhedrin,* chap. 10.

preter might read this as a subtle clue to a hidden doctrine. Although I clearly accept the general view that Maimonides was anything but a straightforward writer of ordinary expository prose, I see no ground for seeking anything hidden in this text. It is openly labeled as an attack on idolatry, and it is reasonable that he should make his point without feeling constrained to spell out every type of prayer or every form of divine service.

When we turn to the *Mishneh Torah* we find an essentially similar situation. To the extent that it is a law code, it reflects standard talmudic teaching and does not differ significantly in its treatment of prayer from what we found in the *Commentary on the Mishnah*. Here, too, Maimonides sets forth and codifies the accepted laws of prayer and reflects the accepted attitudes with regard to the nature of prayer and its effectiveness. As one might expect, there are numerous passages in which he specifies the obligation to pray regularly and explicates the rabbinic teachings concerning the three varieties of prayer: praise, petition, and thanks. The rules for the statutory times for prayer and the required forms are all set forth in detail, and the special occasions for worship are also codified. With respect to praise, he follows the official teaching limiting praise to the specific forms and language that were instituted and approved by the Sages. A typical example is his formulation and treatment of a familiar mishnaic prohibition. As Maimonides expresses it, "We should silence one who expresses a petition saying, 'May he who had mercy on a bird's nest, commanding us not to take the young in the presence of the mother bird, also have mercy on us.' " He reproduces the tenor of the talmudic discussion and concludes, as does the Talmud, that praise of God should be limited to the specific language used by Moses. Anything more is improper and becomes denigration rather than praise.[15] Given his philosophic conviction that all praise of God expressing itself in terms of positive attributes is necessarily in error, it is only reasonable that Maimonides should simply follow this rabbinic ruling in his code.[16]

In his discussions of supplication and petitionary prayer Maimonides again codifies the law and expresses no doubt whatsoever about the principle that God hears and responds to our prayers. In fact, there are cases where His

15. *H. Tefillah,* 9:7.

16. His statement in *H. Berakhot,* 10:26, that the more one praises God the better, should not be construed as going counter to his general position. This statement comes near the end of his discussion of the laws of *berakhot* and should be seen in its context. By virtue of the fact that the precise text of the *berakhot* was established by the Sages, these liturgical forms have a privileged status similar to that accorded to the form of praise that Moses instituted. The point is made in *H. Berakhot,* 1:3: "Our Sages instituted many *berakhot* as forms of praise, thanks, and supplication so that we might constantly be mindful of our Creator."

favorable response seems to be assured. Thus, following explicit talmudic sources, Maimonides teaches that "with respect to a community [in contrast with an individual], whenever its members repent and offer supplications with sincere hearts, they are answered, as it is said, 'For what great nation is there that hath God so nigh unto them, as the Lord our God, whensoever we call to Him.' "[17] This is not an isolated instance but reflects a doctrine that occurs repeatedly and in a variety of contexts in the *Mishneh Torah*. Not only is the supplication of a righteous community heard and answered directly, but such is also the case with respect to the petitions of certain individuals. For example, "Whoever feeds the poor and the orphaned at his table—if he calls out to God, He answers him, for it is written, 'Then shalt thou call, and the Lord will answer.' "[18] It appears that this kind of prayer is understood as affecting God's judgments and His actions with respect to given individuals or communities. Whatever may have been God's original intention, He sometimes changes His plan in response to these prayers. This is explicitly stated by Maimonides when he sets forth the conditions for judging the authenticity of a supposed prophet. We expect his predictions to come true, but not necessarily. For if they are predictions of punishment, calamity, or doom, it may be that the intended victims repented and prayed, which caused God to regret His earlier intention and to change it.[19]

Such a conventional treatment of prayer seems to run directly contrary to the philosophical principles with which Maimonides opened his code. Early in the first book, where he sets out the basic elements of a sound understanding of God, Maimonides states forcefully that God does not change because there is nothing either in the world or in Him that can cause change in Him. There is in Him neither "passion nor frivolity; neither joy nor melancholy; . . . it is said, 'I am the Lord, I change not.' If God was sometimes angry and sometimes rejoiced, He would be changing."[20] We can interpret nonliterally all the prophetic statements about God's feelings and His active responses to the ways in which those feelings are caused by human beings. In fact, Maimonides insists that we must read them in this way only. What then happens to the literal significance of petitionary prayer? Whatever possible purpose it might serve, it can hardly continue to be understood literally as a way in which human beings affect God by arousing His sympathy or

17. *H. Teshuvah*, 2:6.

18. *H. Mattenot 'Aniyyim*, 10:16. For similar assurances that God hears and answers human prayers, see *H. Teshuvah*, 7:7; *H. Tefillah*, 8:1, 15:7; *H.Ta'anit*, 1:1–4; *H. Mattenot 'Aniyyim*, 10:3; *H. Mekhirah*, 14:18.

19. *H. Yesodei ha-Torah*, 10:4.

20. Ibid., 1:11–12.

compassion. The model of the merciful father is helpful only so long as we can take seriously the analogy between the heavenly and the earthly father. Once we are forced to admit that they do not resemble each other in any regard, and that God is absolutely unchangeable and subject to no affections, the analogy breaks down completely. At this point it seems impossible to bring together conventional popular notions concerning the nature of prayer and the sophisticated philosophical notion of the nature of God that Maimonides holds to be a foundation of the Jewish religion. Provisionally we can perhaps do little more to resolve what appears to be an unresolvable tension in his thought, other than to suggest that he talks on one level as jurist and on another as philosopher-theologian. As we shall see, this does not seem to be a satisfactory solution.

The problems, as well as some direction toward a solution, emerge most fully when we turn to a study of the treatment of prayer in *The Guide of the Perplexed*. The major philosophic themes essential for an understanding of Maimonides' theory of prayer include in particular his views concerning the nature of God, our knowledge of God, providence, true worship, and the proper end of man. These doctrinal areas are at best adumbrated in the *Mishneh Torah*, but are given full, if obscure, treatment in the *Guide*. To the extent that any solution of the problems in the *Mishneh Torah* is possible, it will depend on a grasp of the way in which Maimonides deals with these same issues in the *Guide*. For this purpose we are best served by turning our attention to the problem of prayer in the *Guide*. In the *Guide* we confront the full ambiguity of Maimonides' treatment of the problem of prayer; here he cannot ignore or treat lightly the difficult philosophical questions. Given the admittedly esoteric character of the *Guide*, it becomes extremely difficult to determine precisely (and with complete confidence) what Maimonides' views are. Yet, the lines emerge with sufficient clarity to allow us to make reasonably sound judgments.

Considered from the perspective of the philosophical doctrines of the *Guide*, conventional prayer would seem to be a meaningless and even improper activity. Praise of God is impossible, because we have neither the language nor the knowledge to speak about Him in any meaningful way. Petition becomes equally impossible, since God is a being so utterly unlike anything that is created that there is no way to conceive intelligibly a relation between Him and us. Yet petitionary prayer presupposes just such a relation. Among the many statements that Maimonides makes on this subject, the following is typical: "In view of the fact that the relation between us and Him, may He be exalted, is considered as non-existent—I mean the relation between Him and that which is other than He—it follows necessarily that likeness between Him and us should also be considered non-existent" (I, 56, p. 130). How, given such a view of God, can He either be praised or petitioned? What do we know of Him that would make such praise in any sense possible or such petition in any way sensible? Maimonides goes on to argue that all terms that are used to speak of God are used in a way that is completely equivocal, that is to say that we use the words in ways that are semantically empty. As Maimonides expresses it, "the term 'existent' is predicated of Him, may He be exalted, and of everything that is other than He, in a purely equivocal sense. Similarly the terms 'knowledge,' 'power,' 'will,' and 'life,' as applied to Him, may He be exalted, and to all those possessing knowledge, power, will, and life, are purely equivocal, so that their meaning when they are predicated of Him is in no way like their meaning in other applications" (I, 56, p. 131). What can it possibly mean then to address praise and petition to a being who is remote and absolutely inaccessible to our intellect and whose nature is inexpressible in our language?

The problem grows even more severe when we consider that Maimonides denies all motion to God. In his insistence on an absolutely pure conception of the divine unity, he is driven to eliminate any suggestion of corporeality. He holds that "it has already been demonstrated that everything that is capable of motion is endowed with a magnitude that, without any doubt, can be divided" (I, 26, pp. 56–57). Thus it follows that God cannot be understood as having motion among His predicates. Though Maimonides does argue subsequently that God may be understood as acting purely through His will despite the denial of motion to God, this does not help us very much. His position is that will cannot be understood as a separate faculty in God, since that would compromise the divine unity. In that case, what can we make of petitionary prayers addressed to a being who is unlike us in every way and whose mode of causation is utterly unintelligible to us?

These difficulties reach a climax when we see the intensity with which Maimonides defends God against any suggestion that He is subject to external causes that can in any way affect Him. So severe are his strictures against any such views that he classes them as worse than idolatry. Speaking of a man who "does not believe that He exists; or believes that there are two Gods, or that He is a body, *or that He is subject to affections*," he goes on to say that "such a man is indubitably more blameworthy than a worshipper of idols" (I, 36, p. 84; emphasis added). It would appear that prayer cannot have any meaningful petitionary function if God is utterly beyond being affected by any force outside Himself. Human prayers would seem in that case to have no proper object to whom they are directed, and supplications would emerge as utterly pointless. Yet even in the *Guide,* Maimonides also speaks

307

positively about prayer and about divine providence. To come to terms with this apparent internal contradiction, we need to examine systematically the ways in which he treats this topic in the *Guide*.

In a key statement Maimonides expresses what some might well consider to be his true view of prayer. He has just explained the commandments concerning animal sacrifices as a concession to the needs of a people accustomed to think of such sacrifice as the only proper mode of worship. It would have been impossible for them, he argues, to accept a commandment forbidding them to offer such sacrifices to God. Consequently they were instructed to sacrifice, but under carefully specified and restricted conditions. In this way they were turned away from idolatry to the worship of the true God, but with sufficient sensitivity to their general level of development so as not to demand of them what would seem impossible. Maimonides explains the need for concessions to that early Israelite generation by a comparison with his own. For anyone to have tried to eliminate animal sacrifice at that time "would have been similar to the appearance of a prophet in these times who, calling upon the people to worship God, would say: 'God has given you a Law forbidding you to pray to Him, to fast, to call upon Him for help in misfortune. Your worship should consist solely in meditation without any works at all' " (III, 32, p. 326).

Maimonides is here treating the laws of prayer as a concession to our present state of religious and intellectual development, comparable to the concessions required in an earlier age when worship without animal sacrifices was unthinkable. Prayer is our way of religious expression, just as sacrifice was theirs. Neither is ideally desirable, nor is either consistent with a proper metaphysical understanding of God, His nature, and His relationship to the world. However, since people today would almost surely construe a prohibition against prayer as an attack on the very possibility of the religious life, we concede this point and permit them to pray in controlled ways so that we can lead them eventually to right opinion in matters of religion. It should be noted, however, that this is not a concession only to those who are intellectually undeveloped or philosophically naive. Prayer is, after all, a divine commandment obligatory for all Jews, whatever the level of their knowledge. Maimonides, and even Moses himself, are bound by the statutory duty to pray in exactly the same way as the simplest and most ordinary member of the religious community. If the permission—to say nothing of the obligation—to pray is a concession, it is not a concession to a temporary state of human backwardness or lack of development. Rather it recognizes ultimate human intellectual limitations and spiritual needs. No one ever fully achieves a true intellectual apprehension of God, and no one is ever without the deep inner need to express gratitude for God's beneficence, to praise and glorify Him, and to turn to Him for help. Yet the intellectual problems are real.

Unlike what we saw in our brief survey of Maimonides' halakhic works, the *Guide* has hardly any statements concerning prayer that can be viewed as purely conventional. Those few are quickly qualified. To begin with, Maimonides stresses the inherent limitations of all human language so that true praise of God seems to be impossible. What matters most is not simply saying the correct words—for in truth there are no correct words— but having a sound intellectual apprehension of God. Maimonides stresses the principle that we cannot correctly predicate any positive attributes of God. Once we grasp this, we are prepared to deal appropriately with the prayers we are required to offer. This applies even to the case of *keri'at shema'* (the proclamation of God's unity), for which the exact words are very carefully specified.

> When you shall have cast off desires and habits, shall have been en- dowed with understanding, and shall reflect on what I shall say in the following chapters, which shall treat of the negation of at- tributes, you shall necessarily achieve certain knowledge of it. Then you shall be one of those who represent to themselves "the unity of the Name" and not one of those who merely proclaim it with their mouth without representing to themselves that it has a meaning. With regard to men of this category, it is said: Thou art near in their mouth, and far from their reins. (Jer. 12:2). *But men ought rather belong to the category of those who represent the truth to themselves and apprehend it, even if they do not utter it, as the virtuous are commanded to do*—for they are told: Commune with your own heart upon your bed, and be still. Selah. (Ps. 4:5) (*Guide*, I, 50, pp. I I I–12; emphasis added).

Despite his own (and the Talmud's) explicit ruling that one is required to speak the words of the *shema'* so that they are audible at least to oneself, Maimonides permits himself to say that for those who must make the choice, it is better to understand the truth, "even if they do not utter it," than to speak the prescribed words without a correct grasp of their philo- sophical meaning.

In the *locus classicus* for his attack on the language of prayer, and in particular on prayers of praise, Maimonides argues that because God can only be spoken of properly in the language of negative attributes, it follows that all positive praise of Him must in the nature of the case be erroneous.

His slogan is the verse of the Psalmist, "Silence is praise to Thee," which he interprets as follows:

> The most apt phrase concerning this subject is the dictum occurring in the Psalms, "Silence is praise to Thee" (Ps. 65:2), which interpreted signifies: silence with regard to You is praise. This is a most perfectly put phrase regarding this matter. For of whatever we say intending to magnify and exalt, on the one hand we find that it can have some application to Him, may He be exalted, and on the other we perceive in it some deficiency. Accordingly, silence and limiting oneself to the apprehensions of the intellects are more appropriate (I, 59, pp. 139–40).

Maimonides believes that this is why the rabbis themselves put such severe limitations on praise of God. He cites with strong approval the well-known talmudic passage in which R. Haninah attacks a Jew who praises God with a series of extravagant adjectives. All that is permitted is the exact language of praise that Moses instituted, and even that limited form is permissible to us only because it was formally enjoined by the men of the Great Synagogue. To go beyond their formulations is not to add to God's praise, but to detract from Him.

The best model we can have for the praise of God is that provided by the heavenly spheres. These are intellects far superior to our own, who constantly pay homage to God, but their praise is wordless silence. "There is no speech, there are no words, neither is their voice heard." Their true praise of God is in their sound intellectual apprehension of Him, and this should be our true praise as well (II, 5, pp. 259–60). It would appear then that, according to Maimonides, the commandment to praise God in prayer is a grudging accommodation to the limits of both our intellect and our language. Given that despite these limitations we are moved to sing out our homage to the Most High, the Law permits us, as a concession, a restricted mode of expressing divine praise. The ideal, however, is to come to the point where we render Him the true praise of sound intellectual apprehension, rather than the false praise that is contained in the formulations of human language.[21]

If even praise is so severely limited, how shall we understand the supplications and petitions included in the standard liturgy? What shall we make

21. We should, however, always keep in mind that the ideal is unattainable for human beings in this life. The intellectual perfection of the spheres is their praise of God or is, at least, a necessary condition for that wordless praise. In contrast, the imperfect human intellect can never free itself completely of its dependence on language and therefore of the limitations of human language.

of the many recommendations and even injunctions in the halakhah to turn to God and plead with Him for our needs? What of the biblical passages in which God is petitioned and responds? We must first consider how Maimonides deals with the notion of God's response to prayer. Given his severe strictures against the doctrine that God is subject to any affections, together with his view of God as utterly unlike man and utterly without relations to anything outside Himself, it is obvious that petitionary prayer can hardly be interpreted by Maimonides in accordance with the common religious view. In fact, he takes a position that is, to say the least, daring. This position, according to some, may well be open to charges of destroying the foundations of religious faith. Maimonides' theory is that the Torah at times adopts certain metaphysically unsound teachings, because they are useful means for leading men to desirable ends that cannot be achieved otherwise. As he expresses it:

> The Law also makes a call to adopt certain beliefs, belief in which is necessary for the sake of political welfare. Such, for instance, is our belief that He, may He be exalted, is violently angry with those who disobey Him and that it is therefore necessary to fear Him and to dread Him and to take care not to disobey. . . . In some cases a commandment communicates a correct belief, which is the one and only thing aimed at—as, for instance, the belief in the unity and eternity of the deity and in His not being a body. In other cases, the belief is necessary for the abolition of reciprocal wrongdoing or for the acquisition of a noble moral quality—as, for instance, the belief that he, may He be exalted, has a violent anger against those who do injustice, according to what is said: 'And my wrath shall wax hot, and I will kill, and so on,' and as the belief that He, may He be exalted, responds instantaneously to the prayer of someone that is wronged or deceived: "And it shall come to pass, when he crieth unto Me, that I will hear; for I am gracious" (III, 28, pp. 513–14).

The suggestion is clear enough here that the conventional picture of a God who hears the cry of the oppressed and hastens to their succor is not to be taken literally. It is a doctrine that the Torah, if read literally, teaches, together with the practice of petitionary prayer that it implies, in order to reinforce a belief that is essential for the welfare of the individual and society.

Prayer is for Maimonides one of a number of sets of commandments whose main concern is to implant in us a deep commitment to sound doctrine. He explains that petitionary prayer

> is an action through which the correct opinion is firmly established that He, may He be exalted, apprehends our situations and that it

depends upon Him to improve them, if we obey, and to make them ruinous, if we disobey; we should not believe that such things are fortuitous and happen by chance. . . . For their belief that this is chance contributes to necessitating their persistence in their corrupt and unrighteous actions, so that they do not turn away from them. . . . For this reason we have been commanded to invoke Him, may He be exalted, and to turn rapidly toward Him and call out to Him in every misfortune (III, 36, pp. 539–40).

The act of petitionary prayer already serves to establish the sound belief that we are dependent on God for all that happens to us in our world. Such prayer combats belief that the world is governed by chance, and roots in us the awareness of the presence of God as a force in nature and history. Prayer does not give us an explanation of how God works as the Lord of history, but that is in any case beyond our capacity to know.

It is the mature view of Maimonides that we have, in fact, no literal understanding at all about the way in which God governs the world. At the one extreme, his views come very close to a theory of fixed natural causation, in which all things are held to depend on God as First Cause, but in which the order of the natural world is adhered to rigorously. When he opts for the theory that the world is created in time out of nothing, he does so for the explicit reason that only in this way can one protect the Jewish faith against the onslaught of fixed natural causation. As he sees it, the belief in the eternity of the world "destroys the Law in its principle, necessarily gives the lie to every miracle, and reduces to inanity all the hopes and threats that the Law has held out" (II, 25, p. 328).[22] Yet even when he adopts the theory of *creatio ex nihilo,* he never claims to be able to offer a coherent explanation of God's governance of the world except that all that happens is due to His will. We have already seen that this explanation poses problems even when viewed as a statement of faith, and that it generates problems of a different sort when offered as a philosophical explanation of God's creative action. When he confronts these topics as purely philosophical issues, Maimonides is forced to conclude that they are matters about which we can claim no proper understanding. "The character of His governance of the world, the 'how' of His providence with respect to what is other than He, the notion of His will . . . it should be considered that these are obscure matters. In fact, they are truly the mysteries of the Torah and the secrets constantly mentioned in the books of the prophets and in the dicta of the Sages" (I, 35, p. 80).

22. I have had more than one occasion earlier to cite this passage and to consider its force. In chapter 10 I discussed in detail the tension between the creation and eternity theses in Maimonides' thought.

We have no capacity to understand how the God whom we seek to apprehend in His metaphysical purity also functions as a power directly concerned with the world and human affairs. It is nevertheless of the highest practical importance to inculcate in people the belief that He does direct their affairs. What we must do, Maimonides urges, is to treat all events in such a way that we talk about them as flowing from a being of supreme power whom we conceive on the model of a man. Therefore we explain events as deriving from God's anger or compassion in the same way as we would if such events had been caused by men. Great catastrophes that occur to individuals or communities, had men caused them, "would proceed from one of us in reference to another only because of a violent anger or a great hatred or a desire for vengeance. With reference to these actions He is called 'jealous and avenging and keeping anger and wrathful' " (I, 54, p. 126). This is only a way of speaking for the instruction of the masses, not a sound literal representation of God's way in the world. Though Maimonides is almost always careful to add, when he discusses this question, that the people affected by God's action merit the treatment they receive, there is no way in which he can make this intelligible in the light of his general principles.[23] It is easy to trace out consistently in the *Guide* the doctrine that political and social necessity made it mandatory for the Torah to impose such beliefs on the people, as a whole, although we cannot claim any systematic understanding of these doctrines.

Within the framework of these literalized conventional beliefs, prayer makes very good sense indeed. If God is viewed as subject to passion, even in a manner of speaking, then it is appropriate to try to influence Him by our petitions and supplications. Even if we grant that these prayers must not be merely in words, but must be accompanied by repentance and efforts to become virtuous, this conventional religious notion of prayer still poses for us massive metaphysical problems. Although this manner of speaking about God's actions is also adopted by the Sages, Maimonides holds that they never intended it to be understood literally by sophisticated men, although they did recognize that one must speak this way for the masses.[24] The Torah itself also teaches a doctrine of prayer that aims to protect ordinary men from falling into the errors of idolatry, as well as to maintain sound social order. As

23. See, e.g., *Guide*, III, 17, where Maimonides is dealing with divine providence. When he sets forth the first version of his own view, he states that the events affecting people are "not due to chance, but to divine will in accordance with the deserts of those people as determined in His judgments." He hastens to add, however, that these are judgments "the rule of which cannot be attained by our intellects."

24. See *Guide*, I, 46 for an extended discussion of this point.

Maimonides understands the matter, to take just one case, the idolatrous cults all held that only through appropriate worship of their particular gods could people bring about rain, fertile fields, and all that is needed for human sustenance. To save us from the danger of idolatry the Torah teaches explicitly that if we worship idols, precisely the opposite will happen. No rain will fall, the fields will be barren, and people will suffer grave calamities.

> You will find that this intention is reiterated in the whole of the Torah: I mean that it is a necessary consequence of the worship of the stars that rains will cease to fall, that the land will be devastated, that circumstances will become bad, and that the bodies will suffer from diseases, and that lives will be short: whereas, a necessary consequence of the worship of God will be rainfall, the fertility of the land, good circumstances, health of body, and length of life. This is the contrary of what was preached by the idolators to the people in order that they worship idols. For the foundation of the Law consists in putting an end to this opinion and effacing its traces, as we have explained (III, 30, p. 523).

Now, even in this case, where the reference is to one of the three paragraphs of the *shema'*, (Deut. 11:13–21), Maimonides still hesitates to accept it as literally correct from any philosophic point of view. It is rather a mode of worship that is enjoined as a way of combating the dangers of false gods. Just as we were allowed to continue to offer sacrifices so that we could be weaned away from *'avodah zarah* (idol worship), so are we enjoined to pray in certain ways in order to be brought to the belief in the one true God. It seems that while no sophisticated man believes literally that rainfall is a "necessary consequence" of a particular kind of worship, it is thought to be good that unsophisticated men should think so. Furthermore, even the sophisticated must recognize their total dependence on God. As members of a common religious community, the intellectually advanced join with their simpler brothers in common rites and patterns of worship in order to build a community of faith that reinforces movement away from idolatrous practices and toward a sound apprehension of God.

This is not the place to discuss thoroughly Maimonides' theory of divine providence. However, we must make some brief reference to it, since it is in the context of that theory that he offers his most carefully crafted explanation of the way in which the truly meritorious are protected by God. He is anxious to give a philosophically acceptable account of God's connection with man, but it turns out to be an account that could hardly justify any conventional notions of prayer. God, in this view, is related to man ex-

314

clusively by way of the intellect. The higher the level of an individual's intellectual development, the closer the connection with God. This is because the human intellect is activated by way of the divine overflow, which is mediated through the Active Intellect and activates the rational faculty of man. "Accordingly everyone with whom something of this overflow is united, will be reached by providence to the extent to which he is reached by the intellect" (III, 17, p. 474).[25] "When any human individual has obtained, because of the disposition of his matter and his training, a greater portion of this overflow than others, providence will of necessity watch more carefully over him than over others. . . . Accordingly divine providence does not watch in an equal manner over all the individuals of the human species, but providence is graded as their human perfection is graded" (III, 18, p. 475).

This theory of providence seems to have the effect of making all petitionary prayer superfluous and useless. Prayer cannot be legitimately understood as having a direct causal connection with the way in which God governs us and determines our destiny. For as Maimonides insists, given a certain level of intellectual development (which is to say a certain level of intellectual apprehension of God and concern with the knowledge of God), a given decree of providential care follows "of necessity." In that case, it would appear that prayer has no more direct function than that of guiding man toward an intellectually sound apprehension of God and a morally sound social order.

In his discussion of the true form of divine worship at the end of the *Guide,* Maimonides introduces a brief excursus on providence. There too he stresses that being with God is the highest achievement of the intellect, and he argues that this is the only way in which man is protected from the evils that might befall him. The divine overflow elevates man in such a way that

> the providence of God is constantly watching over those who have obtained this overflow, which is permitted to everyone who makes efforts with a view to obtaining it. If a man's thought is free from distraction, if he apprehends Him, may He be exalted, in the right way and rejoices in what he apprehends, that individual can never be afflicted with evil of any kind. For he is with God and God is with him. When, however, he abandons Him, may He be exalted, and is thus separated from God and God separated from him, he becomes in consequence of this a target for every evil that may happen to befall him. For the thing that necessarily brings about providence and

25. It is significant that he adds the comment, "This is the opinion that to my mind corresponds to the intelligible and to the texts of the Law."

315

deliverance from the sea of chance consists in that intellectual overflow (III, 51, p. 625).[26]

Not prayer, not petition or supplication, but the intellectual apprehension of
God is the way in which man is protected from evil and is granted the highest
rewards. Without making any attempt to explicate further the theory of providence which has been summarized here, we can still see clearly what a
devastating effect it could easily have on literalist notions of petitionary
prayer. With all his desire to protect the intellectually innocent from the dangers of discovering truths they are not able to grasp or handle, Maimonides
still makes his intentions concerning prayer sufficiently clear so that no attentive reader can fail to understand the force and the threat of his doctrine.

The treatment of prayer reaches its climax in the final chapters of the
Guide, where true worship is specifically characterized as a kind of *amor dei
intellectualis.* In his parable of those who seek to enter the chamber of the
king, Maimonides concludes that only those who achieve sound intellectual
apprehension of God can be said to worship Him truly. Those who merely
observe the commandments without any kind of intellectual reflection on
theological questions have no access to God at all. In his language they are
"ignoramuses who observe the commandments." This group includes the
"multitude of the adherents of the Law" who, because of their lack of philosophical interest and development, are remote from God and unprotected by
His providence. Traditional *talmidei ḥakhamim* who do engage in serious
intellectual activity, but do not devote themselves to philosophical/theologi-
cal studies, are only slightly better off. They are at least moving in the right
direction, but they are still far from God.

Only those who are fully devoted to philosophic speculation at the highest level and have achieved demonstrative knowledge concerning God are
truly with Him. The intellectual activity in which they engage is the mode of
worship of these highest of men, and that mode of worship is alone sound; it
alone is the ideal toward which all should aspire. What Maimonides explicitly seeks to achieve as the climax of his great book is "to confirm men in
the intention to set their thought to work on God alone after they have

26. I am inclined to think that Maimonides' point here is not that God actively intervenes
in the natural order so as to protect the deserving from every misfortune, but rather that when
one has achieved this very high level of intellectual fellowship with God no earthly misfortune
is of any consequence. From a mature perspective the troubles of a child are childish and have
little true importance. Men of true knowledge have a similar view of what ordinary men consider to be great misfortunes, and are thus protected from them. It is not that nothing happens to
them that is from an ordinary perspective painful or injurious, but that such events are of little
consequence in their scheme of values.

achieved knowledge of Him. . . . This is the worship peculiar to those who have apprehended the true realities; the more they think of Him and of being with Him, the more their worship increases" (III, 51, p. 620). This worship, the intellectual apprehension and contemplation of God, constitutes the true love of God. This is what is intended in the commandment to love Him with all our capacity. For "love is proportionate to apprehension" (III, 51, p. 621).

Maimonides sees this as the ultimately true and perfect mode of worship; compared with this, every other form is defective. This is the worship that is meant when we speak of 'avodah shebelev (worship of the heart). Yet he knows full well, and indicates so in his code, that the normal meaning of this term is tefillah, and that this refers to the set liturgical forms. When he appropriates this term for intellectual worship, which consists of knowledge and contemplation, he is deliberately telling us that the rabbinic tradition will be understood in new ways by those who are at the highest level of intellectual and philosophic sophistication. This is why he can go on to affirm that such true worship is best achieved in solitude, in direct contrast with the ideal for tefillah, which is best achieved betzibbur, in a communal setting.

Those who reach this high level of intellectual apprehension, and thus of intellectual love and worship of God, might now be considered to have transcended the Law and its norms, because presumably they have achieved the highest ends that the Law is intended to foster. Ordinary prayer and fulfillment of mitzvot serve as a propaedeutic, a discipline that guides and prepares us for the life of true worship. "Know that all the practices of the worship, such as reading the Torah, prayer, and the performance of the other commandments, have only the end of training you to occupy yourself with His commandments, may He be exalted, rather than with matters pertaining to this world" (III, 51, p. 622). Out of this discipline grows the state of mind and soul in which one is fully preoccupied with God, seeking that demonstrative knowledge and philosophic contemplation that are the highest fulfillment of the human intellect. Ideally then we must move from ordinary prayer and ordinary fulfillment of commandments to the only life in which man is finally redeemed, the life in which he elevates himself to God and is connected with Him permanently by way of the intellect. Even in the Mishneh Torah, the redemptive power of the intellectual apprehension of God is elevated to the level of being the ultimate goal of man's striving. Messianic fulfillment is characterized by Maimonides as the time when, as the prophet Isaiah puts it, "the earth shall be full of the knowledge of the Lord, as the waters cover the sea." It is not without significance that he chooses these words with which to conclude the Mishneh Torah.

From our discussion it is clear that we can discern two different theories of prayer in the teachings of Maimonides. What is far less clear is how we should understand the relationship between these different teachings. One standard line of Maimonides scholarship, discussed earlier, stresses the presence of contradictory teachings and resolves the contradictions by arguing that Maimonides truly affirms the philosophical view and sets forth the popular views for political purposes. Whatever merit this approach may have, it is in no sense a resolution of contradictions. It is rather the affirmation of one of the contradictories at the expense of the other. We remember the elementary rule of logic that contradictories cannot both be true, nor can they both be false. It follows that, if we are in fact dealing with genuine contradictories, then we have no choice but to conclude that Maimonides must be affirming one and denying the other. Our extended discussion of the method of contradictions should have alerted the reader to beware of such facile conclusions. It is evident that the statements about God and prayer that we have examined generate a problem for us requiring careful study and reflection. We should by now recognize that scholarly responsibility requires far more care by us than the simple offhand announcement that we have found a contradiction and that one of the two propositions is necessarily false while the other is true. We may have here a "divergence" of the type we discussed earlier at great length, a divergence that is made more complicated by the fact that its subject is God. As in the case of some of the other divergences we examined, it may well be that the correct approach is not to seek a resolution that affirms one pole against the other, but indeed to see whether Maimonides did not somehow unite them into a single body of teaching.

Despite what some contemporary scholars might say, it is by no means obvious that Maimonides intends the conventional theory of prayer only for the masses and the philosophical theory only for the intellectually sophisticated. Such a solution is neat and easy, but it simply does not take account of all the facts. The Maimonides whose personal life and practice are well known to us was a man of great piety. He was not only a man of the highest intellectual sophistication and subtlety, but also a man of deep religious feelings and impulses. Not only was he meticulous in his concern for the Law and in his own religious observance, but he often went far beyond what the Law required. As a decisor he was required to codify the Law and to render decisions in accordance with the rules and methods of the Jewish legal system, but this does not explain those acts of personal piety that go beyond ordinary legalism.

Let us consider a case that is directly relevant to prayer and worship. On the sea voyage that led Maimonides from Fez to Palestine, his ship was beset by violent and threatening storms. When the storm had ended and the ship was able to sail without further danger, Maimonides declared the day on which the storm began and the day on which it ended (six days later) as permanent fast days for himself and all his descendants. He himself tells us, "It was my vow that I would spend the tenth day of Iyyar [the day of the storm's end] in solitude, that I would see no man but would for that entire day devote myself to private prayer and study. Just as on that day I found in the stormy sea no one but the Holy One, blessed be He, so would I on the annual day of commemoration see no one unless circumstance forced me to do so."[27] This is hardly the thinking or the practice of a man who holds that prayer is intended only for the protection of the masses from heresy, while the truly educated should serve God exclusively through the activity of the intellect.

Our effort to understand Maimonides' doctrine of prayer must take account of the implications of relevant aspects of his personal life. In this case we have a striking instance of his assuming a stance of personal piety that seems on the face of it to be far more appropriate for a man of the people than for a philosopher. Should the objection be raised that this is an event that occurred in the early part of his life when he may not yet have reached his full intellectual sophistication, we may reply that the many expressions and acts of prayerful piety recorded in all his writings bear witness to the fact that, to the end of his life, he engaged in prayer in ways that go far beyond the fixed statutory requirements.

I suggest that the key to understanding the way in which Maimonides keeps both the popular and the philosophic ideas of worship in a single system lies in his notion of "necessary beliefs." It is my contention that, if we interpret this notion correctly, we shall be able to see that Maimonides has no choice but to maintain simultaneously conventional and philosophical ideas of prayer. These ideas, and practices, are not, as many suppose, intended to be mutually exclusive. They are intended to exist side by side within a single system of thought, maintaining a delicate and difficult balance. They are conceptions that live together in severe dialectical tension. At times the tension may indeed be so strong as to threaten the balance. Nevertheless Maimonides is saying that our human condition leaves us no option but to live in the precarious situation in which we affirm and pursue in practice both a philosophically sophisticated conception of divine worship and a popular conventional pattern of prayer.

Speaking of the commandments codified and explicated in the second book of the *Mishneh Torah,* specifically those which concern prayer and all that is connected with it, Maimonides says, "The end of these actions pertaining to divine service is the constant commemoration of God, the love of

27. Cited in J. L. Maimon, *Rabbi Moshe ben Maimon* (Jerusalem, 1960), 55, from *Sefer Ḥaredim* of R. Eleazar Azikri.

Him and the fear of Him, the obligatory observance of the commandments in general, and the bringing-about of such belief concerning Him, may He be exalted, as is necessary for every one professing the Law" (*Guide*, III, 44, p. 574). This idea of necessary belief is introduced earlier also with respect to the view that God hears and answers prayers (III, 28). It is widely held that by "necessary beliefs" Maimonides means doctrines which are contrary to the truth, but which have great social utility. One recent writer speaks of the necessary beliefs as *hashlayah,* that is "deliberate deception," and goes on to say of them that they are "directly contrary to the true knowledge of God."[28] This seems to me to miss the point completely and to set up a false interpretation of Maimonides. In the passage from the *Guide* just quoted, Maimonides explicitly states that these beliefs are "necessary for everyone professing the Law." The key term here is *everyone,* and we must give it its due weight. "Everyone professing the Law" includes the philosophers who are faithful members of the Jewish religious community, even Maimonides himself.

In my opinion there is here not a simple opposition between what the philosophers believe and what the masses should be taught to believe, but rather between two kinds of belief both of which are necessary. The philosophic beliefs are necessary for any reflective individual, because they are demonstrated and thus command our assent. These philosophic beliefs, however, are incomplete—as is the case, for example, with respect to the problem of creation. Our own limitations are such that we can never have total and complete philosophic knowledge. We can never avoid the profession of some beliefs that are undemonstrated and, perhaps, undemonstrable. This is the case not only because our intellect is limited. If this were the sole problem, then we might simply suspend belief and profess agnosticism with respect to such matters. This might, in fact, be the soundest and most defensible intellectual stance. We are, however, not only philosophers. We are human beings. We live in societies that must be ordered. We have a higher nature that must be served. We have hopes, aspirations, fears, and anxieties, and all demand attention. Our hearts long for fellowship with God, and our minds struggle to find evidence of His presence in our world.

Prayer is a basic and irrepressible expression of the human spirit. Perhaps the pure intellect that has advanced to the true intellectual apprehension of God no longer needs ordinary prayer. For such an intellect, knowledge of God is, in the fullest sense, both its worship and its fulfillment. But human beings, even philosophic ones, are not perfect disembodied intellects. The ideal praise of God may well be, as Maimonides suggests, the wordless

28. Ya'akov Becker, *Mishnato ha-Pilusufit shel ha-Rambam* (Tel-Aviv, 1955), 74–75.

praise of the spheres, but how can this ideal ever be realized in actual human lives? Our apprehension is imperfect at best, and our dependence on language is deep. We cannot conceptualize without language, although we are fully aware that our conceptions are defective and our language inaccurate with respect to God. The spheres have no such problems, but then they are spheres and not human beings. If the human heart overflows with gratitude and awe before God, we have no way to express these sentiments except in the language of prayer. Our human condition makes it necessary for us not only to pray, but to believe sincerely in the significance and meaningfulness of prayer. These are necessary beliefs, not in the unpleasant and morally shoddy sense that they are encouraged for the masses by superior intellects who know them to be false, but in the significant and admirable sense that no religious person can do without them, however sophisticated he or she may be. If God cannot be praised, if He cannot be thanked, if He cannot be petitioned honestly, then for the religious person He is not God.

Maimonides is thoroughly aware of the dilemma in which religious man finds himself. While aspiring to that intellectual perfection which is pure *amor dei intellectualis,* he never fully achieves that ideal in this life. Not even Moses can claim to have achieved the goal fully or to have freed himself completely from his human limitations. Moses does not only teach others to pray, but also prays himself, praises God, thanks Him, and petitions Him. Maimonides understands full well the complexity of the problem confronting man as he seeks to develop his relationship with God within the framework of the human condition. On the one hand, Maimonides wants to make certain that we know what the ultimate ideal is and that we not only aspire toward it, but use all our powers to move ourselves ever closer to it. At the same time, he wants to be certain that no man will so misunderstand his situation that he rejects the Torah and its commandments. These are not only necessary instruments for moving us toward the ideal; they are also the intrinsically precious ways by which we achieve religious fulfillment within those finite limitations of our nature that make the ideal ever beyond our grasp.

12

Epilogue

The Significance of Maimonides
for Contemporary Judaism

The study of Maimonides is a rewarding experience for anyone who seeks to benefit from a confrontation with one of the greatest minds of the ages and one of the profoundest of all interpreters of Judaism. We have seen that he provides us with penetrating original insights into the classical Jewish sources and builds an all-encompassing system that provides an unparalleled account of Jewish law and Jewish faith. He is for us a figure of intrinsic interest, and at the same time the best example of the heights reached by Jewish thinkers in the Middle Ages. This alone would make the study of his thought irresistibly attractive. Yet Maimonides also has much to say that is of the greatest importance for contemporary Judaism. In this final chapter I reflect on some of the specific lessons that can be learned from Maimonides and that can and should be applied to an understanding of Judaism in our age.

Every traditional religion faces the problem of how to remain loyal to its received principles while living in a changing world. If we think of this as the confrontation of religion with modernity, we should remember that every era is modern in its own time. Human culture is continually changing, even while some of its fundamental elements remain fixed. Every age is a new age and brings with it new challenges to the established ways of acting, thinking and believing. For a religion to continue to be relevant to its own era, it is not enough simply to affirm vigorously that it stands for eternal truth. Appealing to the eternal and condemning current fashions of thought and practice is a style that may satisfy and reinforce the loyalties of a limited proportion of the religious community, but it does so at the risk of alienating a great many others. Maimonides chose to confront and address the challenges of the modernity of his own day, and we can benefit from his example.

The challenge of modernity may be met in a number of ways. One style is to reject the contemporary world completely and withdraw into a closed circle of life and thought. This is likely to result in a stance of obscurantism and parochialism for which we pay a heavy price. First, because we cannot really attain a total withdrawal from the world in which we live, it means that we shall continue to be influenced by it without being conscious of those influences and controlling our responses to them. Second, it means that we deny ourselves the positive contributions we might gain from the contemporary world. For example, even those Jews of our era who have chosen to be completely isolated from modernity still use the best that modern medicine has to offer when they are ill. However great their piety, they do not seek healing in the medical wisdom of the Talmud or, for that matter, of Maimonides. In this regard the twentieth century has taken precedence for them over the fifth or the twelfth centuries. This is a typical example of choosing to benefit from the advances of modern science while claiming to reject, in principle, the achievements of modern science. The third result of such a stance is that it makes Judaism appear so far removed from current reality that it may well be viewed by most people as irrelevant to contemporary concerns and problems.

An alternate way is simply to reject the tradition and, above all, its religion in favor of a total commitment to modernity. One may object to this stance, first of all, on purely intellectual grounds. Every age is in some respects the product of what has gone before, and it is a distortion of reality to claim that we must cut ourselves off from our past in order to live fully in the contemporary world. Our language, our ideas, our religion, our philosophy, and even our science are unintelligible without the traditions of thought from which they have emerged. In this sense, no one can be exclusively and completely contemporary. When we try consciously to reject all tradition in favor of the modern, we are not only intellectually confused, but we also risk the loss of our roots and the loss of the wisdom of a great heritage. Without the perspective and stability that these confer, we are the unprotected victims of every passing fad. We have lost the criteria for judging and evaluating the newest directions of our society.

The third way, which is the way of Maimonides, is to keep the old and the new in balance. It is characterized by deep and abiding loyalty to the received tradition while maintaining full interest in and regard for the achievements and the problems, the certainties and the doubts, of contemporary society. It is uncompromising in its adherence to the teachings of the classical Jewish tradition while being fully open to whatever is good and true in contemporary thought. It preserves the long established verities of the past, but seeks to illuminate them through the perspective of the best of the world in which we ourselves live. This way does not sacrifice the past to the present or the present to the past. As we have seen, Maimonides' way is not the method of superficial synthesis that tends to be merely cosmetic rather than substantive. Rather it is the way of dialectical tension, the conscious achievement of a delicate balance between the old and the new, the traditional and the contemporary.

The world that Maimonides confronted was in many respects strikingly similar to our own. Internally, Judaism was beset by deep and acrimonious schisms. The Karaites were a strong force that threatened the integrity of the rabbanite Judaism of the established tradition. There were serious efforts on both sides to win the loyalty of the people, with each side claiming to be the authentic representative of the true teachings of the Torah. Within the rabbanite community there were struggles for power and supremacy. The Gaonate was beset by conflict, and scholars who were beyond the immediate orbit of the effective authority of the Geonim were ever ready to challenge their supremacy. In relation to their neighbors, the Jews lived as a minority people in the superbly developed culture of Islam, and the flourishing majority religion and culture were a constant challenge. Islam was a highly sophisticated religious community that claimed for itself exclusive truth. The Muslims believed that while their faith was related to that of the Hebrew Bible, their prophet had superseded all the earlier prophets of Israel, and their religion was the only true religion. In a culture where it represented the overwhelming majority of the people, Islam stood as a constant challenge and threat to Judaism and the Jews.

Not only did Jews have to come to terms with the religious claims of Islam, but they also had to confront and deal with the highly sophisticated science and philosophy that constituted the intellectual framework of the contemporary Islamic culture. For Maimonides and his generation it would have been self-defeating simply to ignore the challenges posed by science and philosophy. If they were to be intellectually honest, they had to face the claims of the most advanced contemporary knowledge and modes of thought. This knowledge and thinking could easily be construed as incompatible with the teachings of Jewish religious faith. It might have been tempting for a figure such as Maimonides simply to turn his back on this world of advanced thought so as to avoid any danger that it might pose to traditional religion. Yet it was his deliberate policy to face the truth as he learned it from whatever source and to treat it with the fullest measure of intellectual integrity. It is hardly necessary to spell out the similarities between the internal and external circumstances that confronted the Jews living under Islam in the twelfth century and those faced by Jews living in the Western world in the late twentieth century.

In describing Maimonides' response to his culture and determining what lessons he has for us today, we begin with certain external manifestations. In the light of a growing tendency in certain Jewish circles in the

English-speaking world so to isolate themselves from contemporary culture that they even reject the use of the vernacular language, it is instructive to remember that Maimonides mastered and adopted the language and the literary forms of the dominant culture. He wrote a large part of his work in Arabic, including even works intended for the purely internal use of the Jewish community. One might want to argue that he wrote his *Treatise on Logic* in Arabic because it was aimed at a general readership that did not know Hebrew. No one can say this, however, of his *Commentary on the Mishnah, Book of the Commandments,* or *Guide of the Perplexed.* These works, which are internal Jewish works, were also all written in Arabic. We should not suppose for one moment that Maimonides chose Arabic as the language in which he wrote because his Hebrew was not up to the task. We know that he was, in fact, one of the greatest masters of this language. The *Mishneh Torah,* for example, is generally considered to have introduced a new era in the development of the Hebrew language because of the purity, beauty, and originality of its style. Maimonides wrote in Arabic because that was the language in which he was able to communicate most effectively with the Jews whom he wanted most to reach. He understood that what matters is not the outer form, but the inner substance. It may well be that if his works had not been translated into Hebrew they would not have survived as a permanent part of Jewish literature. No one can take issue with the claim that a work is most likely to enter permanently into the canon of recognized and authoritative Jewish teaching if it is in Hebrew, the one language common to Jews everywhere. It is also true that in his advanced years Maimonides expressed regret that he had not written more of his works in Hebrew. This in no way changes the fact that he considered it a major responsibility to teach Torah to all Jews using the most effective tools that were available to him. The most obvious demand that modernity imposes on us is the challenge to teach the truth of Torah in whatever language will be most effective. Like many of his Jewish predecessors from the Arabic-speaking world, Maimonides has taught us that use of the vernacular is not only legitimate and effective, but in certain circumstances even becomes obligatory.

There are, however, elements far more important than the outer dress of language in Maimonides' response to his world. He not only mastered its language, but also grasped the highest intellectual achievements of the Islamic culture in which he lived. He knew thoroughly and profoundly the science, philosophy, and religion of his society. He did not study this material grudgingly or only to be able to polemicize effectively against an alien challenge to Judaism. Maimonides shared the view of many of his predecessors and of a diminishing number of his successors that truth has no fixed national or ethnic boundaries. We must be prepared to learn the truth from whatever source it may come even if it is external to our own community of faith. The greatest minds and the deepest thinkers of all ages and places must always be taken seriously. We can always learn from them and find illumination in their insights, even if we do not always find them persuasive. People who are intellectually responsible and prudent do not simply accept whatever comes to them from the past or from the high culture of their own time. They approach every philosophic and scientific argument critically, and use their own learning and intelligence to sift out the true from the doubtful or the patently false. For Maimonides, knowledge of the truth has to be won with deep thought and intense intellectual effort. It is not given to us as a gift. The search for truth, however, must be open. We must close no doors arbitrarily and make no *a priori* determination that non-Jewish sources could not possibly have anything to teach the community of Jewish faith.

One of Maimonides' most striking statements on this subject occurs in the context of a purely halakhic discussion. In the *Mishneh Torah* he lays out in elaborate detail the rules for determining the time of the new moon. This is a matter of critical importance on which the entire Jewish religious calendar depends. The method used in Jewish antiquity had to be abandoned when there was no longer an authoritative high court to proclaim the new moon. For many centuries we have had to depend on accurate astronomic calculations for this purpose, and Maimonides frankly admits that such astronomic knowledge comes to us from outside the Jewish tradition.

> With respect to the principle which governs all these calculations, why we have to add or deduct certain figures, how all these matters became known and the proof for each of them—this is the science of astronomy and mathematics about which the Greek philosophers composed many books which are still today in the possession of contemporary philosophers/scientists. . . . Since all these matters have been established by clear demonstrations in which there are no fallacies, demonstrations which no one can refute, we have no concern with who the author of them was, or whether he was a prophet [of Israel] or a gentile. For in the case of any claim whose principles have been exposed [to our scrutiny] and whose truth has been established by sound proofs in which there is no fallacy, we rely on the person who has set it forth or taught it only to the extent that his claim has been unequivocally demonstrated and its principles stand up to our scrutiny.[1]

1. *H. Kiddush ha-Hodesh*, 17:24. This numbering of the paragraphs is standard in most printed editions today. However, in what is probably the first printed edition (Rome, 1480), this is 17:25. This numbering is also followed in the translation in the Yale Judaica Series.

Even in this internal Jewish legal context, Maimonides had no hesitation about looking to Greek science for what it could teach us about the correct way to make the requisite astronomic calculations. The only relevant consideration is whether we are convinced by sound proofs that these astronomical principles are true, not who formulated them or from whom we received them.

Maimonides' general approach to this matter is well stated in a passage to which I called attention in an earlier discussion.[2] In the introductory essay to his commentary on *Pirke 'Avot,* which is a purely internal Jewish work, Maimonides says:

> Know, however, that the ideas presented in these chapters and in the following commentary are not of my own invention; neither did I think out the explanations contained therein, but I have gleaned them from the words of the wise occurring in the *Midrashim,* in the *Talmud,* and in other of their works, as well as from the words of the philosophers, ancient and recent, and also from the works of various authors, *as one should accept the truth from whatever source it proceeds.*[3]

This was a guiding principle for Maimonides. Torah has nothing to fear from truth, whatever its source may be. We should, therefore, seek the truth wherever it may be found. This is essential to our correct understanding of the teachings of the Torah no less than for our knowledge of those subjects not dealt with directly in the Jewish sources. This conviction enabled Maimonides to expand in a bold and striking way the requirements for membership in the Sanhedrin set forth in the Talmud. Both the Great Sanhedrin and the Small Sanhedrins carried weighty judicial and legislative responsibilities. The members of these bodies had to be men of great Torah learning and, according to the requirements set forth in the Talmud, also of some substantial secular knowledge. This included specifically knowing "the seventy languages of mankind."[4]

In Maimonides' codification of this law, he expands the requirements for secular learning beyond knowledge of languages. In his version the members of the Sanhedrin are also required to know the sciences, including medicine, mathematics, astronomy, and others.[5] Interestingly enough he

2. See chapter 5.

3. *The Eight Chapters of Maimonides on Ethics,* trans. and ed. Joseph I. Gorfinkle (New York, 1966; rpt. of 1912 edition), 35–36; emphasis added.

4. See *Sanhedrin,* 17a and the parallel passage in *Menaḥot,* 65a.

5. *H. Sanhedrin,* 2:1.

softens the talmudic demand for a knowledge of seventy languages to the more reasonable requirement that they should know many languages.[6] To function as a sound and responsible teacher of Torah, in the view of Maimonides, one must have control of a substantial body of outside learning needed to illuminate the Torah itself. This openness to all sources of truth is not, in Maimonides' view, a radical departure from traditional attitudes. Because truth is universal, all scientific and philosophic truth is necessarily already a part of Torah.

In commenting on a passage of the *Guide* in which Maimonides speaks in behalf of the legitimacy of non-Jewish sources of knowledge, Isadore Twersky observes, "Awareness of the universality of true philosophic views and the conceptual-methodological parallelism between Jewish and non-Jewish sources puts Maimonides' seemingly bold statement about the use of 'foreign' materials into perspective. These are not really 'foreign' sources, just as certain philosophic views are not really 'foreign' to the Torah. These views are displaced; the sources are complementary."[7] This lesson could be learned with profit by those among our contemporaries who reject out of hand every non-Jewish source of knowledge and truth. Against this kind of self-defeating intellectual obscurantism Maimonides stands out as a beacon of light, showing us that Judaism has nothing to fear from the best and most advanced sources of knowledge in any given age. In fact, it has much more to fear from an attitude that deliberately builds a protective wall around us, denies the legitimacy of independent thought and inquiry, and shuts out the world in order to protect Judaism from the seemingly dangerous ideas that abound in contemporary science, philosophy, and theology. Maimonides teaches us to approach all ideas with critical intelligence, to sift the wheat from the chaff, and to determine what is certainly true, what is at best conjectural, and what is patently false. The false we must reject; the true we must accept; that which is merely probable has to be judged on its own merit and against competing probability claims.

In the earlier chapters of this book we saw how Maimonides used reason as a criterion for the meaning of Scripture. He established, for example, that all statements that ascribe corporeal qualities to God must be read non-

---

6. Ibid., 2:6. There is no doubt that Maimonides perceived these adjustments of the law not as his independent personal decision, but as the correct understanding of the passage in the Talmud.

7. Isadore Twersky, *Introduction to the Code of Maimonides (Mishneh Torah)* (New Haven, 1980) 498–99. Twersky has dealt with this subject extensively in various places throughout his book. See, e.g., 59–60, 219, 367, 495, and all the additional passages listed in the Index, s.v. *Ḥokhmah*.

literally because we know by way of rational demonstration that God is necessarily incorporeal. We saw some cases in which he explicitly gave preference to contemporary astronomy over the astronomy of the talmudic Sages (and, for that matter, over Aristotle). He argued there that in these matters the Sages did not speak with direct or even derivative prophetic authority, but simply as men of learning who relied on the best knowledge of natural phenomena then available. As astronomical knowledge grew, their views became obsolete, and it was not only permissible, but obligatory, to replace those teachings with what was in Maimonides' day thought to be demonstrated scientific truth.

Perhaps the most striking case is his rejection of astrology against the views of almost all his predecessors and contemporaries and against what seems clearly to be the view of a number of talmudic Sages. The belief in astrology was very deep among the Jews, persisting in even the most distinguished scholarly circles long after Maimonides had condemned it. Despite the popularity of astrology and the fact that it is endorsed by certain authorities in the Talmud, Maimonides ruled in his code that astrology is absolutely forbidden. He goes so far as to include it among prohibited idolatrous practices. On this point he states explicitly that it is "forbidden to engage in astrology, even if one did not perform any overt act, but only spoke the lies which fools imagine are words of truth." He adds that one who engages in astrology is subject to the penalty of flogging.[8] When a group of rabbis in Provence, who apparently had not seen this section of the *Mishneh Torah,* wrote to Maimonides to seek his opinion about astrology, he responded with a long letter. He set forth his grounds for rejecting astrology as both false and contrary to Jewish religious doctrine. He realized that his correspondents would certainly be familiar with the passages in the Talmud that support astrology and addressed this concern directly.

> What we have said about this from the beginning is that the entire position of those who predict the future from the stars is regarded as false by all masters of science. I know that you may search and find sayings of some individual sages in the Talmud and the Midrashim whose words affirm that at the moment of a man's birth the stars will cause such and such to happen to him. Do not regard this as a problem. It is not proper for one to reject an established rule of law and raise once again the counterarguments and replies [that preceded its enactment]. Similarly, it is not proper to abandon matters of established knowledge that have been verified by proofs, shake loose of them, and depend instead on teachings of individual sages who may

8. *H. 'Avodah Zarah,* 11:8–9. See also his commentary to *M. 'Avodah Zarah,* 4:6.

have possibly overlooked what was essential to these matters. It may be the case that these sages did not intend their words to be taken literally, but were hinting at some other point. Or else they may have said these words in order to deal with an immediate, but passing, situation that was before them for action. You surely know that many verses of the holy Torah are not to be understood according to their simple external meaning. That is why when it was known by sound demonstration that the literal external meaning [of certain biblical verses] could not be the case, the Translator [i.e., Onkelos] translated them in a way that accorded with the requirements of reason. A man should never cast his reason behind him, for the eyes are set in front, not in back.[9]

Here we see the full force of Maimonides' commitment to truth from whatever source. Once he is convinced on solid scientific grounds that astrology is unfounded and false, he rejects it without hesitation. Even if the talmudic Sages seem to say otherwise, we cannot follow them when we are dealing with a question of fact as distinct from questions determined by faith or tradition. Maimonides gives the Sages the best reading possible and suggests that perhaps we should not take literally the passages in the Talmud that seem to support astrology. In any case, he rules as a matter of law that astrology is false and constitutes a prohibited form of idolatrous activity, and he tells his learned and pious correspondents that this is a case in which scientific truth must prevail. It is hardly necessary to spell out the implications of his method and his position for Jewish thought today.

This openness to all sources of truth is balanced by a deep conviction that no study of philosophical or scientific matters is appropriate until one has mastered the classical disciplines of Torah study. Philosophical speculation is intended to expand and deepen our understanding of Torah. It is never intended by Maimonides as a substitute for the study of Torah. One can only assimilate outer sources of truth into the world of Torah if one is deeply rooted in the knowledge and understanding of the teachings of Torah. Without this anchor we constantly run the danger of misconstruing the Torah itself and of grafting onto it foreign branches that are misplaced and cannot grow in its soil. The *Guide of the Perplexed* is addressed specifically to readers

9. For the Hebrew text of the "Letter on Astrology" see the edition by Alexander Marx in *Hebrew Union College Annual*, 3 (1926), 311–58. This passage is on p. 356, lines 10–19. For an English translation of part of the letter, see the version by Ralph Lerner in *Medieval Political Philosophy*, ed. Ralph Lerner and Muhsin Mahdi (Ithaca, 1972), 227–36. This passage is on pp. 234–35. I have followed Lerner's translation in considerable degree, but have made a number of changes and adjustments.

who have deep mastery of Torah knowledge, a sound knowledge of the sciences and philosophy, and are puzzled by certain problems that arise from this combination of learning. "For the purpose of this Treatise and of all those like it is the science of the Law in its true sense. Or rather its purpose is to give indications to a religious man for whom the validity of our Law has become established in his soul and has become actual in his belief—such a man being perfect in his religion and character, and having studied the sciences of the philosophers and come to know what they signify" (I, Introduction, p. 5).

Even if Maimonides had not stated this explicitly, I have shown earlier the extent to which the *Guide* presupposes a readership that is thoroughly at home in classical Torah learning, a readership that knows Bible, Talmud, Midrash, and the other relevant literatures. Maimonides begins the *Mishneh Torah* with four chapters that he himself identifies as dealing with basic issues in physics and metaphysics. These are for him the foundations of the Torah. Yet he concludes this discussion with the observation that "it is not proper for one to stroll in the Pardes [i.e., the orchard of scientific and metaphysical speculation] until he has first filled his belly with bread and meat. Bread and meat refers to knowing what is forbidden and what is permitted and similar knowledge of all other types of precepts."[10] He has just gone to great lengths to establish that without the scientific/metaphysicial knowledge about God and the world expounded in the opening chapters of the *Mishneh Torah* we cannot properly fulfill certain basic commandments. Yet he feels constrained to add that one should not engage in the kind of philosophic reflection that these commandments require until he has first mastered the standard disciplines of Torah learning and become expert in the details of the law. It is true that many students of this passage are troubled by the next statement, which, relying on a talmudic source, judges philosophical reflection to be the highest level of Torah learning, even higher than standard talmudic studies. It should be clear, however, that Maimonides is saying that only one who is already a master of Torah in the more common sense of the term can ascend to the activity of true philosophical reflection that is religiously motivated and religiously valid.

In a letter written late in his life to R. Jonathan ha-Kohen of Lunel, the recognized rabbinic leader of the Jewry of Provence, Maimonides expresses his commitment to the primacy of Torah learning, and even evinces some regret that he had to turn to other disciplines in order to complete his knowledge of the Torah. Yet these disciplines are described by him as purely

10. *H. Yesodei ha-Torah*, 4:13.

ancillary to the main task, which is the deepest possible mastery of the Torah. Speaking of the Torah, Maimonides says:

> She is my loving hind, the bride of my youth, whose love has rav- ished me (enraptured me continuously) since I was a young man (Prov. 5:19). Many strange and foreign women have nevertheless become rival wives to her: Moabites, Edomites, Sidonites, Hittites. The Lord, may He be blessed, knows that I took these other women in the first instance only in order to serve as perfumers, cooks, and bakers for her (my true bride), and to show the peoples and the prin- ces her beauty for she is exceedingly fair to behold (Esther 1:11). Still, her conjugal rights were diminished (i.e., the attention paid to her suffered) because my heart was divided into many parts through its concern for all the other branches of wisdom. And yet, how hard I have worked, day and night, for these past ten years, in order to compile this composition [i.e., the *Mishneh Torah*].[11]

Commenting on this passage, Twersky wisely observes: "The emphasis upon the ancillary role of philosophy, its teleological and axiological subser- vience to Torah, is particularly significant, for there was no apparent need for apologetics in this context—the Provençal scholars were enthusiastic about Maimonides' philosophical activities and were requesting the last part of the *Moreh* and negotiating for its Hebrew translation."[12] Maimonides is stating clearly his principle that the other disciplines assume their true im- portance only in relationship to Torah learning. They add an indispensable dimension to that learning, but only when they are brought into the context of the teachings of the Torah.

This provides a needed perspective on Maimonides' actual views. It has been widely held that Maimonides believed that the highest realization of man's human/divine potential is achieved when man apprehends the ulti- mate metaphysical truths and devotes himself to the contemplation of those truths. The usual corollary of this claim is that Maimonides considers all Torah study inferior to metaphysical speculation, and that he relegates those who engage in such study to a much lower rank than that held by the true philosophers. Now there is a measure of truth to this description of the value scheme that Maimonides propounds, and it is supported by many things that he says. I noted one such instance in my comments on his statement that

11. J. Blau, *Teshuvot ha-Rambam*, vol. 3 (Jerusalem, 1961), 55–57. The passage cited here is on p. 57. I have followed the translation given in Twersky, *Introduction to the Code*, 40.

12. Twersky, *Introduction to the Code*, 38.

standard Talmud study is "a small thing" compared to reflection on the chariot vision, that is, metaphysical speculation, which is "a great thing." I tried
to explain this in its context, which does not treat this metaphysical speculation as an independent intellectual activity but establishes that it is the
climactic height of true Torah study. Similarly, if one studies carefully the
famous palace parable, we see that Maimonides clearly gives the highest
place to those whose metaphysical speculations have finally led them to demonstrative knowledge of the highest matters. A person "who has achieved
demonstration, to the extent that that is possible, of everything that may be
demonstrated; and who has ascertained in divine matters, to the extent that
that is possible, everything that may be ascertained; and who has come close
to certainty in those matters in which one can only come close to it—has
come to be with the ruler in the inner part of the habitation" (*Guide*, III, 51,
p. 619). We should not ignore the fact that the achievement of this ultimate
human perfection presupposes all that has gone before. What is wrong with
the standard Torah scholars, as Maimonides describes them in this same passage, is not at all that they devote great intellectual energy to the study of the
Law. This activity is not only desirable; it is absolutely essential for the proper development of the Jewish religious consciousness. Their defect is that
they do not then take the critical next step, that they "do not engage in speculation concerning the fundamental principles of religion and make no
inquiry whatever regarding the rectification of belief." Maimonides' letter
to R. Jonathan ha-Kohen of Lunel serves as an important corrective for those
who have misunderstood his earlier statements on the subject of the relationship between Torah study and philosophy. The latter serves its proper
purpose only when it emerges from and is integrally related to the classical
modes of Torah learning.

The lesson for our own situation is clear enough. Without the deepest
roots in the Torah, and without the profoundest understanding of its teachings, no one can provide a responsible account of Jewish religious and
philosophical thought. The idea that one can be a philosopher of Judaism, as
Maimonides was in the highest degree, without first achieving mastery of
Bible, Talmud, Midrash, codes, the whole of the primary literature of Judaism, is one of the greatest misperceptions of our own age. We have the
widespread phenomenon of people who presume to tell us what the Bible
means although they are unable to read a word of Hebrew. We have people
who pontificate with seeming authority about the nature and the processes of
Jewish law although they are unable to make their way through even one
page of the Talmud. And we have people who formulate seemingly high-
level accounts of Jewish religious doctrine, often in elegant philosophical or
theological language, but who are at the same time without any intellectual

or spiritual roots in the literature of Judaism. What we have learned from Maimonides should reveal the inherent absurdity in this situation. To presume to speak in the name of Judaism and to teach its doctrine without a mastery of its sources is irresponsible, if not fraudulent.

Maimonides has taught us that openness to every source of truth, non-Jewish as well as Jewish, is essential. But he has also taught us that such truth can only be understood in ways that are Jewishly legitimate and relevant by those who are already masters of all classical Jewish learning. He himself serves as the model. No one surpassed him in Jewish learning or in creative contributions to that learning. It is precisely for this reason that he could legitimately use his vast and deep philosophic and scientific knowledge to clarify fundamental issues of Jewish faith and to set forth as a Jewish ideal the ultimate perfection of man through his efforts to achieve knowledge of God and of His world. It seems to me instructive and decisive that, with the possible exception of his youthful *Treatise on Logic,* Maimonides wrote no purely philosophic works. Apart from his medical writings, every one of his works, however informed and engaged philosophically, is a Jewish book in the full sense of the term. Leo Strauss is right in his contention that the *Guide* is a Jewish book. In my view, he is wrong only in concluding that because it is a Jewish book, it follows that it cannot also be a work of philosophy.

Another important lesson for contemporary Jewish thought is to be found in Maimonides' intense concern with defining the fundamentals of Jewish faith. It has long been fashionable to repeat Moses Mendelssohn's statement that Judaism has no dogmas. The implication, at least for those who have said this in our century, is that adherence to the Jewish religious community does not involve the affirmation of any particular doctrine. There are even Orthodox Jewish circles in which it is asserted that so long as one observes the Law, it doesn't matter what one believes. This view has come to be known by such awkward terms as *orthopraxy* or *halakhic behaviorism.* This way of understanding what the Torah requires of us is inherently unintelligible. It may make perfectly good sense to choose to adhere to certain traditional Jewish practices because they are attractive folkways that give one a sense of ethnic identity. Even this involves some ideology, although it does not require a statement of religious faith. However, the moment one conceives and understands these practices as *mitzvot,* as divine commandments, one has committed oneself implicitly to an entire theology.

Maimonides considered it one of his major duties to clarify and state explicitly the fundamental principles of Jewish faith. He did this in a highly structured way in his formulation of the thirteen articles of faith in the introduction to his commentary on chapter 10 of *M. Sanhedrin.* He pursued this same goal, although in a less formulaic fashion, in each of his later works. In the *Mishneh Torah* and the *Guide,* for example, this concern with the fundamentals of faith is a pervasive and even passionate driving force. It may be correct, as some contemporary scholars claim, that he was motivated by political concerns in putting such strong emphasis on principles of faith. What I deny is that this political motivation was the only reason for his propounding and explicating articles of faith.

Maimonides understood that it was not possible to make sense out of Judaism as a religion without formulating the beliefs on which it is based. The opening sentences of Scripture rest on a belief in the existence of God and in Him alone as creator of the world. The commandments are explicitly identified in Scripture as deriving from God as He who commanded. Scripture and the rabbinic literature do not formulate these articles of faith in explicit language nor do they give them systematic form. Yet without such a theological foundation these literatures are unintelligible. Jewish religion is not concerned only with our doing or not doing certain things, and it is not simply a mode of ethnic belonging. It is a system of faith that entails certain modes of behavior, loyalty, and identification. To treat it as anything less is to convert it into a house without a foundation, a house suspended in mid-air.

It is precisely to prevent this misconception of Judaism that Maimonides opens his code with the "Laws of the Foundation of the Torah." It is not only a question of intellectual clarity, but also one of being able to fulfil certain specific *mitzvot* properly. The first five commandments explicated in this opening section of the *Mishneh Torah* are: to know that God exists; to deny categorically the existence of any other gods; to know and affirm His absolute unity; to love Him; to fear Him. No one can fulfill these commandments without certain clear doctrinal commitments and a basic understanding of those doctrinal commitments. Maimonides considers it essential to all Jewish religious practice that we know and accept the foundations of faith on which it rests. This is evident throughout the *Guide* where he is repeatedly concerned with establishing principles of sound doctrine and eliminating what he considers to be basic doctrinal errors, such as ascribing corporeal properties to God.

Perhaps the most revealing instance is his codification of the procedures for accepting converts to the Jewish faith. The Talmud puts the emphasis on teaching basic Jewish practices to the potential convert but is silent about doctrinal instruction. Maimonides expands the well-known talmudic source to include a strong emphasis on doctrinal points. Before we teach the convert the details of the commandments, Maimonides requires that we first "teach him the fundamentals of our religion, specifically the unity of God and the prohibition against idolatry [i.e., the worship of other gods]. We are required to teach these matters to him at great length."[13] Maimonides takes for granted that this kind of doctrinal instruction was presupposed by the Sages of the Talmud and that they were probably silent about it because it seemed self-evident. He chose to spell it out in order to make clear again what he repeatedly emphasized about the critical place of sound doctrinal understanding and commitment in Judaism.

Contemporary interpreters of Judaism may not be convinced that the articles of faith in Maimonides' specific formulation are necessarily binding. They are aware that this topic has a long history and that over the centuries various other formulations have been offered. It is not my intention here to defend the Maimonidean formulation against all others; this is not the point of the discussion. What is important is to learn from Maimonides that Judaism without a body of doctrine on which it rests is an anomaly. Modern Judaism in all its forms needs to confront this issue. We need to come to terms with the fact that Judaism as a religion demands affirmations of faith and that it is the responsibility of the teachers of Jewish lore to formulate and define those affirmations. We should learn from Maimonides that these affirmations need not necessarily take a fixed creedal form, if that should prove inimical to contemporary style. The principles of faith are no less present in the *Mishneh Torah* and in the *Guide,* where they are not confined to a single creedal statement, than they are in the *Commentary on the Mishnah,* where they are set forth in a compact statement of thirteen articles. What matters for us is that we confront the need for principles of faith, and we need not be concerned with whether a formal creedal statement results from our theological reflections. Maimonides continued to be preoccupied with these questions till the end of his life. They are the basic questions from which serious religious thought can never be free.

We need also to learn an important lesson from Maimonides concerning our orientation toward the Law and commandments. The great philosopher whose mind was constantly devoted to the highest and most abstract metaphysical speculation was also preoccupied with even the smallest details of the Law. This was true with respect to his personal pattern of observance, concerning which we have ample evidence. He was meticulously scrupulous in following in practice every provision of the Law. He was also a lifetime student of the Law in all its complexity and subtlety. Not only did he compose great halakhic works, but he also served to the end of his life as a respondent to questions concerning Jewish law and practice that came to him from many parts of the Jewish world. This aspect of the life and work of Maimonides may not speak effectively to large segments of contemporary

13. *H. Issurei Bi'ah,* 14:2.

Jewry. What should be considered by all, however, is the way in which Maimonides dealt with the complicated question of the reasons for the commandments.

In the classical Jewish tradition there are two opposed trends. One holds that we cannot and should not seek to know the reasons that underlie God's commandments; we should simply treat them all as divine edicts which bind us for that reason alone. It is not our business to understand these edicts, nor do we have the capacity to penetrate into the divine mind so as to understand its motivations. From this perspective true piety is construed as unquestioning submission to God's will without claim or effort to know His reasons.

The second trend considers it not only legitimate, but even obligatory, to try to grasp to the best of our ability the reasons for the commandments. To the extent to which we can penetrate the world of divine thought and understand why God commanded us to behave in certain ways, we deepen our own religious life and in so doing glorify God. Maimonides took his stand uncompromisingly with this second group. He devoted a very long section of the *Guide* to setting forth his own account of the reasons for the commandments.

Maimonides' basic premise in his treatment of this subject is that God does not command us arbitrarily or capriciously. It would be contrary to His nature to command without reason or purpose. We must therefore assume that every commandment has a good reason and serves a useful purpose, even where we are unable to explain the reason or to give an account of the purpose.[14] Maimonides devotes great effort and much thought to classifying and categorizing the commandments so as to be able to account for them, initially in large blocks and then in more individual detail. Great emphasis is put on the idea that many of the commandments have obvious social utility, many others are important for the ordering of society, and still others are needed to teach us correct doctrine and protect us from pagan beliefs and practices. "Thus all [the commandments] are bound up with three things: opinions, moral qualities, and political civic actions" (III, 31, p. 524). Maimonides derides those who refuse on principle to accept the idea that there are reasons for the commandments and that we do right in seeking to know them. As he describes them, "There is a group of human beings who consider it a grievous thing that causes should be given for any law; what would please them most is that the intellect would not find a meaning for the commandments and prohibitions. What compels them to feel thus is a sick-

14. For the extended discussion of this subject see *Guide*, III, 25–34. For the exposition of the reasons for the commandments, see *Guide*, III, 35–50.

ness that they find in their souls, a sickness to which they are unable to give utterance and of which they cannot furnish a satisfactory account" (III, 31, pp. 523–24).

Maimonides does not claim to be able to give a definitive account of the reason for every single commandment, but he is determined to try. He is fully conscious, however, of the inherent limit to our capacity to explain and justify every commandment. We are limited by our finite intellects and by the particular personal and historical perspective from which we consider the matter. Such limits make it unreasonable to suppose that we can ever fully penetrate the infinite divine wisdom which stands behind each commandment.

> Marvel exceedingly at the wisdom of His commandments, may He be exalted, just as you should marvel at the wisdom manifested in the things He has made. It says: The Rock, His work is perfect; for all His ways are judgment (Deut. 32:4). It says that just as the things made by Him are consummately perfect, so are His commandments comsummately just. However, our intellects are incapable of apprehending the perfection of everything that He has made and the justice of everything He has commanded. We only apprehend the justice of some of His commandments just as we only apprehend some of the marvels in the things He has made, in the parts of the body of animals and in the motions of the spheres. What is hidden from us in both these classes of things is much more considerable than what is manifest (III, 49, pp. 605–6).[15]

Maimonides is telling us that we have limitations we cannot overcome when we try to give a full account of any action, thought, or commandment of God. This should also be taken as a caution against accepting any particular explanation of specific commandments as final and definitive. Even Maimonides' own explanations must, by his instructions to us, be viewed as tentative rather than absolute. That is why what seemed to him sound and persuasive explanations are, in many cases, not persuasive for us today. From the viewpoint of contemporary knowledge we are unable any longer to accept many of his reasons for the commandments because they are based on historical claims that are not supported by the best contemporary scholarship. The point is not that we consider any given explanation of the reasons

15. For a similar statement, see *Guide*, III, 26, p. 507, where Maimonides states explicitly that if any commandment seems to us unjustified and serving no useful purpose, the problem is not with God's commandment but with our incapacity to understand: "the deficiency lies in your apprehension."

for the commandments to be absolutely correct, but only that it is the best we can offer at a given time. Our accounts may change from one age to the next. What Maimonides demands of us is that we shall always continue the effort to know and understand the commandments and their reasons.

In modern times this activity has been pursued by many people. They have given explanations of the commandments that are historical, psychological, anthropological, medical, and more. In many cases there is an assumption that, once we can explain the supposed original purpose of a commandment, we are in a position to judge whether it is still binding upon us or not. If, for example, we accept the view of those who claim the purpose of the dietary laws is to protect and advance good health, then it would seem to follow that, given the advances of modern medicine and hygiene, the old dietary rules are no longer relevant to us and may be discarded. There are some who would like to draw similar conclusions from Maimonides' account of the reason of the commandments. In doing so they misunderstand and distort his teachings. According to Maimonides, we seek to understand the reasons for the commandments in order to avoid the danger of turning God into a capricious ruler who commands with tyrannical disdain for the welfare of His subjects. He never suggests for a moment, however, that knowing or not knowing the reasons has anything to do with acknowledging that they come from God and obligate us absolutely. He does not abolish any commandment on the ground that the reason he has discovered for it has made it obsolete.

The classic case is that of the biblical and rabbinic rules concerning animal sacrifices. It is well known that Maimonides explained the entire sacrificial order on historical grounds. According to his account, animal sacrifices were the universal norm of worship in the world in which ancient Israel emerged. No one could imagine a mode of worship that did not include such sacrifices and all the rituals surrounding them. To have prohibited such sacrifices would have subjected the people to a religious/cultural shock they could not have sustained. "For a sudden transition from one opposite to another is impossible. And therefore man, according to his nature, is not capable of abandoning suddenly all to which he was accustomed" (III, 32, p. 526). In this light the sacrificial system of ancient Judaism is perceived as a concession to the state in which the people of Israel found themselves when they received the Torah. Had they been denied worship through sacrifices, they would have been unable to accept the Torah. What God did, according to Maimonides, is to permit sacrifices, but to impose a variety of rules and restrictions that removed from the practice every last vestige of idolatry. There are those who suppose, therefore, that Maimonides was opposed to the practice of animal sacrifice and that, having explained its presence in early Judaism on historical grounds that are no longer operative, he intended to bring about the abolition of this form of divine worship. The same logic would apply to every other case in which the reasons offered in explanation of a particular commandment seem to make it obsolete and therefore inoperative.

Yet there is every evidence that nothing could have been further from Maimonides' mind. In the case of sacrifices we have the most concrete evidence possible. Two of the fourteen books of the *Mishneh Torah* are fully occupied with the Temple, Temple ritual, and sacrifices. Unlike other codifiers, Maimonides did not restrict his code to those laws which were currently operative. He included all the detailed legislation concerning sacrifices and the Temple, making clear that this is a permanent part of Jewish law. He does not suggest by even a hint that since he understands the sacrificial order to be rooted in a no longer existing historical situation, therefore it is no longer a binding part of Torah legislation. We have decisive evidence for Maimonides' views in his description of the Messianic age and in his setting forth of the criteria for determining the validity of any claimant to be the Messiah.

> The King Messiah, who is destined to appear in the future, will restore the royal house of David to its pristine glory and to its original rulership. He will build the Holy Temple and gather in all the dispersed exiles of Israel. In his day all the laws will be reinstituted as they were originally. Sacrifices will again be offered and the Sabbatical and Jubilee years will again be observed in accordance with all the commandments set forth in the Torah. . . . The essential point is as follows. This Torah, with all its statutes and ordinances is for ever and ever. We may not add to it, nor may we subtract from it.[16]

There could be no greater error than to suppose that Maimonides made the observance of the Law, now or in the future, contingent on our finding reasons that make the individual commandments clearly relevant to our time or to our perception of our needs. From his perspective, the Torah has no obsolete laws. Some laws are inoperative in our present historical circumstances, but they will be restored to their full force when we move into another era of history.

Those who occupy themselves today with trying to understand the reasons for the commandments are to be commended for engaging in an activity that aims at helping us to understand the glory of the divine plan. They

16. *H. Melakhim*, 11:1,3.

should, however, take to heart Maimonides' explicit and carefully formulated caution. Man is encouraged, even obligated, by him to understand to his fullest ability the commandments of the Torah. He adds, however, that "a law for which he finds no reason and for which he knows no cause should not be viewed as trivial by him." On the contrary, one should take special care "not to kick aside [i.e., reject arrogantly] a commandment which was decreed for us by the Holy One, blessed be He, just because he does not understand its reasons." That this is a special concern with respect to the integrity and binding force of the laws of the sacrifices is evident in the conclusion of this section. Maimonides follows the classical sources in identifying *ḥukkim* as "commandments whose reason is not known to us." He then adds that "all the sacrifices are in the category of *ḥukkim*. Our sages have taught us that the world continues to stand because of divine service through the offering of sacrifices."[17] Maimonides is no ally to anyone who supposes that we can dispense with the hope for the restoration of the Temple and the sacrificial order just because we can no longer fit it into our current conception of how to worship God. The lesson he teaches us is clear. For those who believe that the Law is divine in origin, who have faith in the truth of the revelation at Sinai, there can be no self-justified dismissal of any law of the Torah. We are charged by Maimonides to study and understand the commandments as fully and deeply as we are able, but we are also charged by him never to substitute our limited human understanding for the infinite and benevolent divine wisdom.

My purpose in this closing chapter has been to consider some of the lessons we can learn from Maimonides as we pursue our own reflections on the nature and meaning of Judaism today. In addition to the grand design of his system and the light that comes to us from his specific teachings, we should also learn from his style and his method. We can discover in Maimonides not only the unexcelled figure of medieval Judaism, but no less one of the greatest of all teachers, whose voice speaks effectively to our own age. With all the differences between our circumstances and his, we share a common world with him in many respects. Maimonides' learning and his wisdom have as much to teach us today as they did his contemporaries.

17. All the passages cited are from *H. Me'ilah*, 8:8.

Index